版权和相关权
国际法律文件集

International Instruments on Copyright and Related Rights

裘安曼　译

图书在版编目（CIP）数据

版权和相关权国际法律文件集 / 裘安曼译 . —北京：中国书籍出版社，2015.12
ISBN 978-7-5068-5302-6

Ⅰ . ①版… Ⅱ . ①裘… Ⅲ . ①版权—著作权法—汇编—世界 Ⅳ . ① D913.09

中国版本图书馆 CIP 数据核字（2015）第 283294 号

版权和相关权国际法律文件集

裘安曼　译

责任编辑　牛　超　宋　然
责任印制　孙马飞　马　芝
封面设计　亦琳
出版发行　中国书籍出版社
地　　址　北京市丰台区三路居路 97 号（邮编：100073）
电　　话　(010) 52257143（总编室）　　(010) 52257140（发行部）
电子邮箱　eo@chinabp.com.cn
经　　销　全国新华书店
印　　刷　三河市顺兴印务有限公司
开　　本　787 毫米 ×1092 毫米　1/16
字　　数　710 千字
印　　张　32.25
版　　次　2016 年 5 月第 1 版　2016 年 5 月第 1 次印刷
书　　号　ISBN 978-7-5068-5302-6
定　　价　95.00 元

目 录

序

版权和相关权国际法律文件，即是我们常说的各种版权国际公约，版权国际条约，版权国际协定等。

从 1886 年签署的《保护文学和艺术作品伯尔尼公约》，到 2013 年签署的《便利失明、视力障碍或阅读失能者利用已出版作品的马拉喀什条约》，在 120 多年期间，一共签署了 14 部国际法律文件。这 14 部国际版权公约、条约、协定文本的中英文，都包括在本书之中，应该是很全面的。需要说明的是，其中《字体保护及其国际交存维也纳协定》和《视听作品国际注册条约》两部法律文件是上世纪七、八十年代签署的，但签署以后一直没有生效。1989 年签署的《与集成电路有关知识产权条约》后来也未生效。其间原因究竟是什么，也是值得探究的。《视听表演北京条约》和《便利失明、视力障碍或阅读失能者利用已出版作品的马拉喀什条约》分别于 2012 年和 2013 年签署。这两部国际条约的签署是世界知识产权组织工作的重大突破：前者曾因为欧洲与美国存在分歧而一直难以达成，而后者则是体现限制版权、利用版权、关注弱势群体，体现人文关怀的最好范例。两条约的签署展现了世界知识产权组织卓越的协调能力。现在，它们仍在批准加入和生效过程中。

国际上第一部关于版权的法律文件是《保护文学和艺术作品伯尔尼公约》。该公约于 1886 年在瑞士伯尔尼签署并生效，到现在已经 129 年了；伯尔尼这个欧洲不起眼的小城市，也因此而闻名于世。

伯尔尼公约出台的背景，是欧洲雨果、狄更斯等一些作家发现，他们创作的脍炙人口的作品大量流入美国等其他一些国家，欧洲作家的作品被大量盗版，而这些问题在欧洲本国是解决不了的，因此，催生了版权国际条约来实现跨国的对等保护。与伯尔尼公约一样，其他每一个国际版权公约的出台，都有其当时的客观背景。我们仔细观察一下就会发现，这些客观的背景，最重要的是由于技术进步带来的。例如磁光电的发明使版权作品的载体和介质发生了很重要的变化，因此催生出关于唱片的版权保护，关于视听作品的版权保护，关于软件的版权保护等等。互联网的出现使版权的保护面临前所未有的挑战，带来了许多严峻的现实问题。面对这些问题和挑战，世界知识产权组织出台了《世界知识产权组织版权条约》（WCT）和《世界知识产权组织表演和录音制品条约》（WPPT）。

中国加入了上述国际版权条约中的大多数条约。特别值得一提的是，2012 年 6 月世界知识产权组织由中国承办在北京举行国际外交会议。这次外交会议，主旨是签署一项视听表演条约，即北京条约。这是新中国成立之后在中国境内缔结的第一个国际条约，也是中国参与并在国际版权事务中发挥了重要作用的一个国际条约。这个条约签署以后，很多专家学者以及各界人士给予了很高的评价，普遍认为，旧中国，特别是清王朝在一百多年前，我们签署过很多条约，而那些都是丧权辱国的条约。视听表演北京条约的签署，表明了中国在国际知识产权领域的国际地位和国际影响力。时任国务院副总理王岐山亲自担任这次世界知识产权组织外交会议组委会的主任；王岐山副总理和刘延东副总理以及时任北京市市委书记刘淇和北京市市长郭金龙多次主持参与有关的工作，并对这次会议给予了高度的评价。

这个条约在北京缔结，对北京建设国际一流大都市必将产生深远影响，同时也表明中国现在已经不再是被动地参与国际活动和参与国际条约的制定，而是已经能够积极主动地进入国际社会，并且发挥自己应有的作用。

在中国迈向世界知识产权强国的进程中，需要全方位提升包括版权在内的知识产权制度建设能力。在这样的背景下，应当深入细致研究各种国际版权条约的内涵及其与我们国家著作权法律制度的关联，深入分析这些国际版权条约产生的时代背景和发展现状，准确评价这些国际版权条约现实意义和综合作用，并就有关领域下一步的走向进行分析思考，这对于研究如何推进我国的版权制度建设，具有十分重要的意义。

还需说明，编译这部文件集是国家版权局确定的一个重要研究项目。这是一个基础性的工作。目前，在世界知识产权组织框架下，正在讨论制定与传统文化表达、图书档案馆使用和广播组织新权利等有关的国际文件。将来缔结了新的文件，就可以在这部文集的基础上进行增补。另外，本书请裘安曼先生担任译者，他是非常恰当、非常合适的人选。裘安曼先生曾在上世纪 80 年代就职于国家版权局，其后又在世界知识产权组织工作近十五年。他不仅有语言和版权专业方面的双重优势，而且他缜密的思维和严谨的工作态度，也给我留下了非常深刻的印象。读者可在本书的译者说明中以及在条约的中英文对比中印证这一点。

阎晓宏

2016 年元月

保护文学和艺术作品伯尔尼公约

1886年9月9日签订，1896年5月4日在巴黎完备，1908年11月13日在柏林修订，1914年3月20日在伯尔尼完备，1928年6月2日在罗马、1948年6月26日在布鲁塞尔、1967年7月14日在斯德哥尔摩、1971年7月24日在巴黎修订，1979年9月28日更改。

目录*

* 目录为读者方便而增加，不出现在原始文本中。

附件
与发展中国家有关的特别条款

本联盟国家，同等受以尽可能有效和一致的方式保护文学和艺术作品中作者权利之愿望的鼓舞，

承认 1967 年斯德哥尔摩修订会议工作的重要性，决定修订斯德哥尔摩会议通过的公约文本，同时原样保留该文本第 1 条至第 20 条和第 22 条至第 26 条。

由此，经递交形式妥当的全权委托书，签字的全权代表达成一致如下：

第 1 条
[成立联盟][①]

本公约适用的国家，为保护文学和艺术作品中作者权利组成一个联盟。

第 2 条
[受保护的作品]

（1）“文学和艺术作品”包括文学、科学和艺术领域内的所有成果，无论其表现方式或形式如何，诸如书籍、小册子和其他文字作品；演说、讲话、布道和其他同样性质的作品；戏剧或音乐剧作品；舞蹈作品和哑剧；带词或不带词的音乐作品；电影作品和以类似摄制电影的方法表现的作品；线条画、色彩画、建筑、

① 条款和附件标题为读者方便而增加，不出现在原始文本中。

雕塑、雕版和平版作品；摄影作品和以类似摄影的方法表现的作品亦同；实用艺术作品；与地理、地形、建筑或科学有关的示意图、地图、设计图、草图和三维作品。

（2）但是，联盟国家的法律可以规定，除非以某种物质形式固定，作品或任何特定类别的作品不受保护。

（3）翻译本、改编本、音乐编配和文学或艺术作品的其他改变形式，作为原创作品保护，原作中的版权不受损害。

（4）对立法、行政和法律性质的官方文件以及此种文件的官方译本的保护，由联盟国家的法律确定。

（5）文学或艺术作品的汇编，诸如百科全书和文集，由于内容的选取和编排而构成智力创作的，本身受保护，构成此种汇编的每个作品中的版权不受损害。

（6）本条中提到的作品应在所有联盟国家受到保护。此种保护应有益于作者和其合法继承人。

（7）以本公约第 7 条第（4）款的规定为条件，由联盟国家的立法确定其法律对实用艺术作品及工业设计和模型的适用程度，以及保护此种作品、设计和模型的条件。在起源国仅作为设计和模型保护的作品，在其他联盟国家只受该国给予设计和模型的专门保护；但是，如果该国不给予此种专门保护，此种作品应被作为艺术作品保护。

（8）本公约的保护不适用于日常新闻或纯属报刊消息性质的各种事实。

第 2 条之二

[可以限制对某些作品的保护]

（1）联盟国家的法律可以将政治宣讲和法律程序中作出的宣讲全部或部分地排除于前条规定的保护。

（2）联盟国家的法律亦可以确定，在何种条件下，公开发表的演说、讲话和其他同样性质的作品，可以在符合提供消息的目的时被报刊转载、广播、以有线方式向公众传播，或用于本公约第 11 条之二第（1）款中预设的公共传播。

（3）尽管如此，作者享有对其在前款中提到的作品进行汇编的专有权利。

第 3 条

[保护资格标准]

（1）本公约的保护适用于：

（a）联盟国家之一国民的作者，无论其作品是否已经出版的；

（b）不是联盟国家之一国民的作者，因其首先在联盟国家之一出版的作品，或同时在一个联盟外国家和一个联盟国家出版的作品；

（2）不是联盟国家之一国民的作者，但在联盟国家之一有常住居所的，为本公约的目的，视同该国的国民。

（3）“已出版的作品”指经作者同意出版的作品，无论复本的制作方式，

只要复本的提供就作品性质而言已满足公众的合理需求。戏剧、音乐剧、电影作品或音乐作品的上演，文学作品的公开朗诵，文学或艺术作品的有线传播或广播，美术作品的展出和建筑作品的建造，不构成出版。

（4）一部作品如果于首次出版后三十天内在两个或更多国家出版，视为同时在数个国家出版。

第4条

[电影作品、建筑作品和某些艺术作品保护资格的标准]

本公约的保护适用于以下，即使未满足第3条的条件：

（a）制片人总部或常住居所在联盟国家之一的电影作品的作者；

（b）建于一个联盟国家内的建筑作品或位于一个联盟国家内的建筑物或其他结构中包含的其他艺术作品的作者。

第5条

[保障的权利]

（1）作者就其受本公约保护的作品，在起源国之外的联盟国家中享有各国法律现在或今后可能赋予其国民的权利以及本公约特别赋予的权利。

（2）享有和行使这些权利，不以任何手续为条件；此种享有和行使，不依赖于作品起源国是否存在保护。因此，除本公约的规定外，保护的程度以及为保护作者权利向其提供的补救手段，完全由主张保护所在国家的法律规制。

（3）在起源国的保护由国内法规制。但是，作者不是其受本公约保护的作品的起源国的国民，在该国享有与国民作者相同的权利。

（4）起源国应被认为是：

（a）对于首先在一个联盟国家出版的作品，该国家；对于同时在数个提供不同保护期的联盟国家出版的作品，其法律给予最短保护期的国家；

（b）对于同时在一个联盟外国家和一个联盟国家出版的作品，后一国家；

（c）对于未出版的作品或首次在一个联盟外国家出版而未同时在一个联盟国家出版的作品，作者为其国民的联盟国家，条件是：

（i）这些作品是制片人总部或常住居所在一个联盟国家的电影作品的，起源国为该国家。

（ii）这些作品是建于一个联盟国家内的建筑作品或位于一个联盟国家内的建筑物或其他结构中包含的其他艺术作品的，起源国为该国家。

第6条

[可以限制对某些联盟外国家国民某些作品的保护]

（1）任何联盟外国家未能充分保护联盟国家之一的国民作者的作品，后一国家可以对作者在首次出版之日是该其他国家国民并且不是联盟国家之一常住居民的作品的保护作出限制。如果首次出版国利用此项权利，其他联盟国家无须给由此受特别待遇的作品以比首次出版国给予的更宽的保护。

（2）任何凭借前款采取的限制，不影响作者在此种限制生效前已就在联盟国家出版的作品获得的权利。

（3）根据本条对赋予版权进行限制的联盟国家，应以书面声明通知世界知识产权组织总干事（以下称“总干事”），具体说明限制保护涉及的国家和那些国家的国民作者的权利所受的限制。总干事应立即将此声明通报所有联盟国家。

第6条之二

[精神权利]

（1）不依赖于作者的经济权利，即使在该权利转让之后，作者有权主张作品作者的身份和反对与作品有关的、可损害其尊严或名誉的任何歪曲、篡改或其他更动，或其他损毁行为。

（2）根据前款赋予作者的权利，在他去世后至少保留到经济权利终止，并由主张保护所在国家的法律授权的人或机构行使。但是，批准或加入本公约文本时法律未规定在作者去世后保护前款陈述的所有权利的国家，可以规定这些权利中的一些在他去世后不再保留。

（3）保障本条赋予的权利的救济手段，由主张保护所在国家的法律规制。

第7条

[保护期]

（1）本公约给予的保护期为作者有生之年加去世后五十年。

（2）但是，对于电影作品，联盟国家可以规定，保护期在作品经作者同意向公众提供后五十年终止，或者，自作品制作起五十年内无此事件发生的，在制作后五十年终止。

（3）对于匿名作品或假名作品，本公约给予的保护期在作品合法向公众提供后五十年终止。但是，作者采用的假名于其身份没有疑问的，保护期为第（1）款规定的。匿名作品或假名作品的作者在上述时段中披露身份的，适用的保护期为第（1）款规定的。不得要求联盟国家保护有理由推定作者已去世五十年的匿名或假名作品。

（4）摄影作品和作为艺术作品保护的实用艺术作品的保护期，由联盟国家的法律确定；但是，此期限至少持续到自此一作品制作起一个二十五年的时段结束。

（5）作者去世后的保护期和第（2）款、第（3）款和第（4）款规定的期限，从那几款中提到的去世或事件之日开始，但此种期限应始终被视为于去世或此种事件翌年的一月一日开始。

（6）联盟国家可以给予超出前述各款规定的保护期。

（7）受本公约罗马文本约束的联盟国家，在本文本签署时有效的国内法律中规定短于前述各款规定的保护期的，有权在批准或加入本文本时保留此种期限。

（8）无论如何，期限由主张保护所在国家的法律规制；但是，除非该国法律另有规定，期限不超过作品起源国确定的。

第7条之二

[合作作品的保护期]

前条的规定亦适用于合作作品，条件是自作者去世起算的期限自最后在世的作者去世起算。

第8条

[翻译权]

受本公约保护的文学和艺术作品的作者，在对原作所享权利的整个保护期中，享有翻译和授权翻译其作品的专有权利。

第9条

[复制权]

（1）受本公约保护的文学和艺术作品的作者，享有授权以任何方式或形式复制这些作品的专有权利。

（2）联盟国家的法律可以允许在某些特殊情况下复制此种作品，只要此种复制不与作品的正常利用相冲突并且不过度损害作者的合法利益。

（3）为本公约的目的，任何录音或录像被视为复制。

第10条

[对作品的某些自由使用]

（1）可以允许引用已经合法向公众提供的作品，只要引用符合正当惯例，并且不超出与目的相符的程度，包括以新闻提要的形式引用报纸文章和期刊。

（2）联盟国家的法律和它们之间现有或将要达成的专门协议，可以允许在与目的相符的程度上为了教学在出版物、广播节目或录音或录像中以说明的方式使用文学或艺术作品，条件是此种使用符合正当惯例。

（3）如果根据前述各款使用作品，应提及出处和出现在出处上的作者姓名。

第10条之二

[可以另有对作品的自由使用]

（1）联盟国家的法律可以允许报刊转载、广播或以有线方式向公众传播报纸或期刊上发表的关于当前经济、政治或宗教题目的文章或广播中具有同样性质的作品，如果其转载、广播或此种传播未被明确保留。尽管如此，必须始终清楚指明出处；违反此项义务的法律后果，由主张保护所在国家的法律确定。

（2）联盟国家的法律还可以确定，在什么条件下，为通过摄影、摄制电影、广播或有线方式向公众传播的手段报导当前事件的目的，可以在与提供消息的目的相符的程度上复制和向公众展示在事件过程中看到或听到的文学或艺术作品。

第11条

[戏剧和音乐作品中的某些权利]

（1）戏剧、音乐剧和音乐作品的作者享有授权以下的专有权利：

（i）公开表演其作品，包括任何手段或方法的公开表演；

(ii)将其作品的表演向公众进行任何传播。

(2)戏剧作品或音乐剧作品的作者，在对原作所享权利的整个期限中，对其翻译本享有同样的权利。

第11条之二

[广播和有关的权利]

(1)文学和艺术作品的作者享有授权以下的专有权利：

(i)广播其作品，或以任何其他无线发送信号、声音或图像的手段向公众传播其作品；

(ii)以有线方式或转播将作品的广播向公众进行任何传播，如果此种传播由原广播组织以外的组织进行；

(iii)为公共传播通过扩音器或任何其他类似工具以信号、声音或图像传送作品的广播。

(2)行使前款中提到的权利的条件，由联盟国家的法律确定，但这些条件仅在规定它们的国家适用。它们在任何情况下不得损害作者的精神权利，也不得损害其获得公平报酬的权利，没有协议的，报酬由主管当局确定。

(3)如无任何相反规定，根据本条第(1)款给予的许可，不意味着允许以录音或录像工具录制作品的广播。但是，联盟国家的法律可以为广播组织利用自己的设施和为自己播放之用进行临时录制订立法规。由于这些录制品的特殊文献性质，法律可以准许将其保存在官方档案中。

第11条之三

[文学作品中的某些权利]

(1)文学作品的作者享有授权以下的专有权利：

(i)其作品的公开朗诵，包括以任何手段或方法的公开朗诵；

(ii)将其作品的朗诵向公众进行任何传播。

(2)文学作品的作者，在对原作所享权利的整个期限中，对其翻译本享有同样的权利。

第12条

[改编、编配和其他改动的权利]

文学或艺术作品的作者享有授权对其作品进行改编、编配和其他改动的专有权利。

第 13 条

[可以限制音乐作品和任何有关语词的录制权]

（1）音乐作品的作者和已授权与音乐作品一同录制的任何歌词的作者，有授权对音乐作品连同如有的歌词进行录音的专有权利，联盟各国可以为自己对此权利规定保留和条件；但所有保留和条件仅在有此规定的国家适用，并且任何情况下不得损害作者获得公平报酬的权利，没有协议的，报酬由主管当局确定。

（2）根据 1928 年 6 月 2 日在罗马和 1948 年 6 月 26 日在布鲁塞尔签署的公约的第 13 条第（3）款在一个联盟国家制作的音乐作品的录音，可以在该国不经音乐作品的作者许可进行复制，直至该国开始受本文本约束后两年之日。

（3）根据本条第（1）款和第（2）款制作的录音制品，未经有关方许可进口到视其为侵权录音制品的国家，应受到扣押。

第 14 条

[电影和有关的权利]

（1）文学或艺术作品的作者享有授权以下的专有权利：

（i）对这些作品进行电影改编和复制，以及发行如此改编或复制的作品；

（ii）公开上演和以有线方式向公众传播如此改编的作品。

（2）将由文学或艺术作品派生的电影作品改编成任何其他艺术形式，仍以原作作者的授权为条件，电影作品作者的授权不受影响。

（3）第 13 条第（1）款的规定不适用。

第 14 条之二

[有关电影作品的特别条款]

（1）电影作品作为原创作品保护，任何可能已被改编或复制的作品的版权不受损害。电影作品版权的所有者享有与原作作者相同的权利，包括前条提到的权利。

（2）（a）电影作品版权的归属，由主张保护所在国家的法律规定。

（b）但是，在通过法律将为制作电影作品做出贡献的作者包括在版权所有者当中的联盟国家，这些作者如果已经承诺做出此种贡献，在没有任何相反或特别规定的情况下，不可以反对对该作品进行复制、发行、公开上演、以有线方式向公众传播、广播或向公众的任何其他传播，或给原文配字幕或配音。

（c）上面提到的承诺，为适用前述（b）项是否应当以书面协议或相同效力书面文件的形式，由电影作品制作者总部或常住居所处在的联盟国家的法律确定。但是，主张保护所在联盟国家的法律可以规定该承诺以书面协议或相同效力书面文件的形式。法律有此规定的国家，应以书面声明的方式通知总干事，声明将立即由总干事通报所有其他联盟国家。

（d）“相反或特别规定”指与前述承诺有关的任何限制性条件。

（3）除非国内法律有相反规定，以上第（2）款（b）项的规定不适用于为制作电影作品创作的剧本、台词和音乐作品的作者或电影作品的主要导演。但是，法律中没有条文规定将第（2）款（b）项适用于电影导演的联盟国家，应以书面声明的方式通知总干事，声明将立即由总干事通报所有其他联盟国家。

第14条之三

［艺术作品和手稿的“追续权”］

（1）对于艺术作品的原件以及作者和作曲者的原始手稿，作者或他去世后由国内法律授权的人或机构应在作品首次被作者转让后的任何出售中享有不可剥夺的收益权。

（2）可以在一联盟国家主张前款规定的保护，但只有作者所属国家的法律允许，并在主张这一保护所在国家允许的程度上。

（3）收取的程序和数额由国家法律确定。

第15条

［有权行使受保护的权利］

（1）为使受本公约保护的文学或艺术作品的作者在没有相反证明的情况下被视为作者并因此有权在联盟国家提起侵权诉讼，其姓名以通常方式出现在作品上即应足够。即使此姓名为假名，如果作者采用的假名于其身份没有疑问，本款可以适用。

（2）如无相反证明，以通常方式在电影作品上署名的人或法人团体被推定为该作品的制作人。

（3）对于上述第（1）款中提到以外的匿名作品和假名作品，如无相反证明，名称出现在作品上的出版者被视为代表作者并有权以此身份保护和行使作者的权利。当作者披露身份并主张作品作者的身份，本款规定停止适用。

（4）（a）对于未出版的作品，如果作者身份不明，但有充分理由推定其为一个联盟国家的国民，该国法律可以指定主管当局，代表作者并有权保护和行使作者在各联盟国家的权利。

（b）在本规定之下作出此种指定的联盟国家，应以书面声明的方式通知总干事，就指定的当局提供完整信息。总干事应立即将此声明通报所有其他联盟国家。

第16条

[侵权复本]

（1）作品的侵权复本应在作品受法律保护的任何联盟国家被扣押。

（2）前款规定亦适用于来自不保护或停止保护该作品的国家的复制品。

（3）扣押根据每个国家的法律进行。

第17条

[可以管控作品的流通、上演和展览]

本公约的规定无论如何不能影响每个联盟国家的政府有权在主管当局认为必要时通过法律或法规允许、限制或禁止任何作品或制品的流通、演出或展览。

第18条

[公约生效时存在的作品]

（1）本公约适用于在其生效时尚未由于保护期终止而在起源国进入公有领域的所有作品。

（2）一部作品如果由于先前规定的保护期终止而在主张保护所在的国家进入公有领域，不得重新受保护。

（3）此原则的适用，以联盟国家之间现有或将要缔结的相同意思的特别公约中包含的任何规定为条件。没有此种规定的，各个国家在各自相关的范围内确定适用此原则的条件。

（4）前述各款的规定亦适用于新加入联盟和因适用第7条或放弃保留而延长保护的情况。

第19条

[比公约所予更多的保护]

本公约的规定不得阻止主张享有一个联盟国家法律可能给予的任何更多的保护。

第20条

[联盟国家之间的特别协议]

联盟国家的政府保留在它们自己之间达成特别协议的权利，只要此种协议给予作者比本公约给予的更多的权利，或包含不与本公约抵触的其他规定。现有协议的规定，符合这些条件的，得继续适用。

第21条

[有关发展中国家的特别条款]

（1）有关发展中国家的特别条款包括在附件中。

（2）以第28条第（1）款（b）项为条件，附件构成本文本的组成部分。

第22条

[大会]

（1）（a）联盟设有由受第22条至第26条约束的联盟国家组成的大会。

（b）各国政府由一名会议代表作为代表，会议代表可有替补代表、顾问和专家协助。

（c）各代表团的费用由委派它的政府负担。

（2）（a）大会应：

（i）处理与联盟的维持和发展以及本公约的实施有关的所有事项；

（ii）就修订会议的筹备对《成立世界知识产权组织（以下称“产权组织”）公约》中提到的知识产权国际局（以下称“国际局”）作出指示，其中适当考虑不受第22条至第26条约束的联盟国家的任何意见；

（iii）审议和批准产权组织总干事与联盟有关的报告和活动，并就联盟职权范围内的事项对他作出所有必要指示；

（iv）选举大会执行委员会成员；

（v）审议和批准执行委员会的报告和活动，并对此委员会作出指示；

（vi）决定联盟的计划和通过联盟的双年度预算，并批准其决算；

（vii）通过联盟的财务规章；

（viii）成立可能为联盟工作所必要的专家委员会和工作组；

（ix）决定接受哪些非联盟成员国家以及哪些政府间和国际非政府间组织作为观察员参加其会议；

（x）通过对第 22 条至第 26 条的更改；

（xi）采取旨在推进联盟目标的任何其他适当行动；

（xii）履行在本公约之下为适当的其他职能；

（xiii）以大会接受为条件，行使《成立产权组织公约》中赋予它的权力。

（b）对于亦与产权组织管理的其他联盟有关的事项，大会应在听取产权组织协调委员会的意见后做出决议。

（3）（a）大会每个国家成员拥有一票。

（b）大会国家成员的半数构成法定人数。

（c）尽管有（b）项的规定，如果在任何会议中出席的国家不足半数但相当或多于大会国家成员的三分之一，大会可以做出决议，但与其自身程序有关的决议除外，所有此种决议只有满足以下条件才生效。国际局应将所述决议通报未出席的国家成员，请它们在通报之日起三个月的时段内以书面表示投票或弃权。在此时段届满时，如果表示投票或弃权的国家的数目达到会议自身法定人数所欠缺的国家数目，只要同时仍然获得所需要的多数，此种决议应生效。

（d）以第 26 条第（2）款为条件，大会决议需要投票的三分之二。

（e）弃权不视为投票。

（f）一名会议代表只可以代表一个国家和以一个国家的名义投票。

（g）不是大会成员的联盟国家应被接受作为观察员参加会议。

（4）（a）大会每两个历年举行一次例会，由总干事召集，如无特殊情况，与产权组织全体大会在同一时段和同一地点举行。

（b）应执行委员会或大会四分之一国家成员的要求，大会由总干事召集举行非常会议。

（5）大会应通过自己的程序规则。

第 23 条

[执行委员会]

（1）大会设有一个执行委员会。

（2）（a）执行委会由大会从国家成员中选出的国家组成。此外，产权组织总部在其领土上的国家，以第 25 条第（7）款（b）项为条件，凭借地位在该委员会中拥有一个席位。

（b）执行委会每个国家成员的政府由一名会议代表作为代表，会议代表可有替补代表、顾问和专家协助。

（c）各代表团的费用由委派它的政府负担。

（3）执行委员会国家成员的数目应相当于大会国家成员数目的四分之一。在确定填补的席位的数目时，以四相除之后的余数忽略不计。

（4）选举执行委员会成员时，大会应适当考虑合理的地区分配和可能就联盟签订特别协议的国家成为执行委员会组成国的需要。

（5）（a）执行委员会每个成员，应从选举它的大会会议结束起担任至大会下一次例会结束。

（b）执行委员会的成员可以重新当选，但不超过其中三分之二。

（c）大会应就执行委员会成员的当选和可能的连任制定规则细节。

（6）（a）执行委员会应：

（i）准备大会议程草案；

（ii）就总干事准备的计划和双年度预算草案向大会提出建议；

（iii）[取消]；

（iv）向大会提交总干事的阶段报告和年度账目审计报告，并提出适当意见；

（v）根据大会决议并考虑大会两次例会之间出现的情况，采取所有必要措施以保证总干事对联盟计划的执行；

（vi）履行在本公约之下分派给它的其他职能。

（b）对于亦与产权组织管理的其他联盟有关的事项，执行委员会应在听取产权

组织协调委员会的意见后做出决议。

（7）（a）执行委员会每年举行一次例会，由总干事召集，以与产权组织协调委员会在同一时段和同一地点举行为宜。

（b）由总干事主动或应其主席或其四分之一成员要求，执行委员会应在总干事召集下举行非常会议。

（8）（a）执行委员会每个国家成员拥有一票。

（b）执行委员会成员的半数构成法定人数。

（c）决议应通过投票的简单多数做出。

（d）弃权不视为投票。

（e）一名会议代表只能代表一个国家，并只能以一个国家的名义投票。

（9）不是执行委员会成员的联盟国家应被接受作为观察员参加其会议。

（10）执行委员会应通过自己的程序规则。

第24条

[国际局]

(1)(a)与联盟有关的行政任务，由作为与《保护工业产权国际公约》设立的联盟局合并的联盟局之延续的国际局执行。

(b)尤其是，国际局供作联盟各机构的秘书处。

(c)产权组织总干事是联盟的首席执行官并代表联盟。

(2)国际局应汇集并出版与版权保护有关的信息。联盟各国应及时将所有与版权保护有关的新法律和官方文件通报国际局。

(3)国际局出版一个月刊。

(4)遇有请求，国际局应就与版权保护有关的事项向任何联盟国家提供信息。

(5)国际局应开展研究并应提供旨在促进版权保护的服务。

(6)总干事和由他指定的任何工作人员，应参加大会、执行委员会和任何其他专家委员会或工作组的所有会议，但无表决权。总干事或由他指定的一名工作人员凭借职权是这些机构的秘书。

(7)(a)国际局根据大会的指示并与执行委员会合作，为修订公约第22条至第26条以外条款的会议进行筹备。

(b)国际局可以就修订会议的筹备与政府间组织和国际非政府组织磋商。

(c)总干事和由他指定的人应参加这些会议的讨论，但无表决权。

(8)国际局应承担委派给它的任何其他任务。

第25条

[财务]

(1)(a)联盟应有一部预算。

(b)联盟的预算包括属于联盟的收入和开支、它对各联盟共同开支预算的贡献和适用情况下向产权组织会议预算提供的款项。

(c)不专属于联盟而亦属于产权组织管理的其他一个或更多联盟的开支，应被视为各联盟的共同开支。联盟在此种共同开支中的份额，应与联盟在其中的利益相称。

(2)确定联盟的预算，应适当考虑与产权组织管理的其他联盟的预算相协调的要求。

(3)联盟预算从以下来源获得经费：

（i）联盟国家的会费；

（ii）国际局与联盟有关的服务的计费和收费；

（iii）国际局与联盟有关出版物的销售或版税；

（iv）捐赠、遗赠和资助；

（v）租金、利息和其他杂项收入。

（4）（a）为确定其对预算的贡献，每个联盟国家应属于一个级别，并根据以下确定的单位缴纳年度会费：

第 I 级 ………………… 25

第 II 级 ………………… 20

第 III 级 ………………… 15

第 IV 级 ………………… 10

第 V 级 ………………… 5

第 VI 级 ………………… 3

第 VII 级 ………………… 1

（b）除非已经这样做，每个国家应在交存批准或加入书的同时表明希望所属的级别。任何国家可以更换级别。如果选择一个更低的级别，必须在其一次例会上向大会声明。任何此种更换应在该次会议后历年的开始生效。

（c）每个国家年度会费的数额，在所有国家向联盟预算缴纳的总额中占的比例，应与其单位数在所有缴费国家的单位总数中占的比例相同。

（d）会费于每年 1 月 1 日到应付期。

（e）拖欠缴纳会费的国家，如果拖欠的数额相当或超过为此前两个整年应缴纳的数额，在它作为成员的任何联盟机构中不得有表决权。但是，任何联盟机构可以允许此国家继续在该机构中行使表决权，如果并只有拖欠缴纳被认为是由于非常和无法避免的情况。

（f）如果预算未在新的财务时段开始前通过，根据财务规章，应与前一年预算的水平相同。

（5）为国际局与联盟相关提供的服务应支付的计费和收费的数额，由总干事确定并向大会和执行委员会报告。

（6）（a）联盟应有一项由每个联盟国家的单笔缴纳构成的工作基金。如果基金出现不足，由大会决定增加。

（b）每个国家首次向所述基金缴纳的数额或在增加中的分担，应是该国为成立基金之年或决定增加之年的会费的一定比例。

(c) 缴纳的比例和期限，由大会根据总干事的建议并在听取产权组织协调委员会的意见后确定。

(7)(a) 与产权组织总部所在地国家签订的总部协议中应规定，一旦工作基金不足，此国家应提供预付金。预付金的数额和提供条件，应每一次由此国家和产权组织之间的另外协议规定。只要仍有义务提供预付金，此国家凭借地位在执行委员会中拥有一个席位。

(b)(a) 项中提到的国家和产权组织各自有权以书面通知声明提供预付金的义务无效。声明无效应在通知之年结束后满三年生效。

(8) 账目审计应如财务规章中规定的由一个或更多联盟国家或外部审计人进行。他们应经自身同意由大会指定。

第 26 条

[更改]

(1) 更改第 22 条、第 23 条、第 24 条、第 25 条和本条的建议，可以由大会任何成员国、执行委员会或总干事提出。此种建议应由总干事在大会对其作出考虑之前至少六个月通报大会成员国。

(2) 更改第(1) 款中提到的条款，应经大会通过。通过需要投票的四分之三，条件是对第 22 条和本条的任何更改需要投票的五分之四。

(3) 对第(1) 款中提到的条款的任何更改，应在总干事从通过更改时大会成员国的四分之三收到根据其各自宪法程序进行的书面承认通知一个月后生效。如此承认的对所述条款的任何更改，应约束更改生效时为大会成员的所有国家，或在随后一个日期成为其成员的国家，条件是任何增加联盟国家财政义务的更改只约束已通知承认此种更改的国家。

第 27 条

[修订]

(1) 本公约可以修订以引入旨在完善联盟体系的更改。

(2) 为此目的，应依次在联盟国家之一举行联盟国家会议代表的会议。

(3) 以适用于第 22 条至第 26 条的更改的第 26 条为条件，本文本包括附件的任何修订，要求投票一致同意。

第28条

[承认和本文本对联盟国家的生效]

(1)(a)已签署本文本的任何联盟国家，可以批准它，如果尚未签署，可以加入它。批准书或加入书应交存于总干事。

(b)任何联盟国家可以在批准书或加入书中声明，其批准或加入不适用于第1条至第21条和附件，条件是，如果此国家先前在附件第VI条第(1)款之下作出过声明，可以仅在文书中声明其批准或加入不适用于第1条至第20条。

(c)任何联盟国家根据(b)项将其中提到的条款排除于批准或加入的效力，可以在任何较晚时间声明将批准或加入的效力延伸至那些条款。此种声明应交存于总干事。

(2)(a)第1条至第20条和附件在以下两个条件均得到满足后三个月生效：

(i)至少五个联盟国家已经批准或加入本文本而未在第(1)款(b)项之下作出声明；

(ii)法国、西班牙、大不列颠及北爱尔兰联合王国和美利坚合众国已开始受1971年7月24日在巴黎修订的《世界版权公约》的约束。

(b)(a)项中提到的生效，适用于在生效至少三个月之前已交存不包含第(1)款(b)项之下声明的批准书或加入书的联盟国家。

(c)对于不在(b)项范围的和批准或加入本文本而未作出第(1)款(b)项之下声明的任何联盟国家，第1条至第21条和附件在总干事通知批准书或加入书的交存之日后三个月生效，除非交存的文书中指明一个后续日期。在后一情况下，第1条至第21条和附件在指明的日期对该国生效。

(d)(a)至(c)项的规定不影响附件第VI条的适用。

(3)对于批准或加入本文本而作出或未作出第(1)款(b)项之下声明的任何联盟国家，第22条至第38条在总干事通知批准书或加入书的交存之日后三个月生效，除非交存的文书中指明一个后续日期。在后一情况下，第22条至第38条在指明的日期对该国生效。

第29条

[承认和对联盟外国家的生效]

(1)任何联盟外国家可以加入本文本并由此成为本公约缔约方和本联盟成员。加入书应交存于总干事。

（2）（a）以（b）项为条件，本公约在总干事通知任何联盟外国家加入书的交存之日后三个月对其生效，除非交存的文书中指明一个后续日期。在后一情况下，本公约在指明的日期对该国生效。

（b）如果根据（a）项生效先于第1条至第21条和附件根据第28条第（2）款（a）项生效，该国在此期间应受本公约布鲁塞尔文本第1条至第20条而不是第1条至第21条和附件的约束。

第29条之二

[承认文本为WIPO公约第14条第（2）款的目的具有的效力]

任何不受本公约斯德哥尔摩文本第22条至第38条约束的国家批准或加入本文本，仅为《成立产权组织公约》第14条第（2）款的目的，等于批准或加入斯德哥尔摩文本，以其第28条第（1）款（b）（i）项中的规定为限。

第30条

[保留]

（1）以本条第（2）款、第28条第（1）款（b）项、第33条第（2）款和附件允许的例外为条件，批准或加入自动要求接受本公约的所有条款和得到本公约的所有利益。

（2）（a）任何批准或加入本文本的联盟国家，以附件第V条第（2）款为条件，可以维持先前提出的保留，条件是在交存批准或加入书时作出表示该意思的声明。

（b）任何联盟外国家，加入本公约时和以第V条第（2）款为条件，可以声明它意图至少暂时以1896年在巴黎完备的1886年联盟公约的第5条代替有关翻译权的本文本第8条，明确条件是所述条款只适用于以在该国通用的一种语文进行的翻译。以附件第I条第（6）款（b）项为条件，任何国家，对于起源国为利用此种保留的国家的作品的翻译权，有权适用与后一国给予的同等的保护。

（c）任何国家可以在任何时间以给总干事的通知撤回此种保留。

第31条

[对某些领土的适用]

（1）任何国家可以在批准或加入书中声明，或在之后任何时间以书面通知告知总干事，本公约可适用于在声明或通知中指明的、由它负责其对外关系的那些领土的全部或部分。

（2）任何作出此种声明或发出此种通知的国家，可以在任何时间通知总干事本公约不再适用于此种领土的全部或部分。

（3）（a）在第（1）款之下作出的任何声明，与包含该声明的批准或加入同日生效，在该款之下发出的任何通知，在总干事对其进行通报后三个月生效。

（b）在第（2）款之下发出的任何通知在总干事收到后十二个月生效。

（4）本条无论如何不得被理解为意味着一个联盟国家承认或默认另一个联盟国家凭借第（1）款之下的声明使本公约对之适用的任何领土的实际状况。

第32条

[本文本和早先文本的适用]

（1）涉及联盟国家之间的关系，本文本在其适用程度内取代1886年9月9日的《伯尔尼公约》和后续修订文本。在与未批准或加入本文本的国家的关系中，先前生效的文本可以全部或在本文本不凭借前一句取代它们的程度内继续适用。

（2）参加本文本的联盟外国家，以第（3）款为条件，应对不受本文本约束的国家或虽受本文本约束但根据第28条第（1）款（b）项作出声明的任何联盟国家适用本文本。此种国家承认，该联盟国家在与它们的关系中：

（i）可以适用其受约束的最近文本的条款；

（ii）以本附件第I条第（6）款为条件，有权使保护与本文本规定的水平相适应。

（3）利用附件中规定的任何权利的任何国家，可以适用附件中与其在与不受本文本约束的任何其他联盟国家的关系中已经利用的一项或数项权利有关的条款，条件是后者国家同意适用所述条款。

第33条

[争议]

（1）两个或更多联盟国家之间与本公约的解释或适用有关的争议，谈判解决不成的，可以由任何有关国家之一依照国际法院章程申请提交该法院，除非有关国家就其他某种解决办法达成一致。将争议提交国际法院的国家应通知国际局；国际局应将此事提请联盟其他国家注意。

（2）每个国家在签署本文本或交存批准或加入书时，可以声明不认为自己受第（1）款规定的约束。对于此种国家和任何其他联盟国家之间的任何争议，第（1）款的规定不适用。

（3）任何根据第（2）款的规定作出声明的国家，可以在任何时间以给总干事的通知撤回其声明。

第 34 条

[某些早先条款的关闭]

（1）以第 29 条之二为条件，第 1 条至第 21 条和附件一经生效，任何国家不可以批准或加入本公约的早先文本。

（2）第 1 条至第 21 条和附件一经生效，任何国家不可以在斯德哥尔摩文本附加的《有关发展中国家的议定书》的第 5 条之下作出声明。

第 35 条

[公约的有效期]

（1）本公约持续有效，没有时间限制。

（2）任何国家可以通过给总干事的通知声明本文本无效。声明无效亦构成声明所有早先文本无效，并只影响作出声明的国家，对于联盟其他国家，公约仍然具有完全效力。

（3）声明无效自总干事收到通知之日后一年生效。

（4）任何国家在成为联盟成员之日起满五年之前不得行使本条规定的声明无效权。

第 36 条

[公约的适用]

（1）参加本公约的任何国家承诺根据其宪法采取必要措施保证本公约的适用。

（2）不言而喻，一国开始受本公约约束，应具备条件在其国内法律之下实施本公约的条款。

第 37 条

[最后条款]

（1）（a）本文本以英文和法文的独一份签署，并且，以第（2）款为条件，应交存于总干事。

（b）经与利益相关政府磋商，总干事应以阿拉伯文、德文、意大利文、葡萄牙文和西班牙文以及大会可能指定的其他语文制定正式文本。

（c）如果就各种文本的解释有不同意见，以法文本为准。

（2）本文本持续开放供签署，直至1972年1月31日。在该日期之前，第（1）款（a）项中提到的一份应交存于法兰西共和国政府。

（3）总干事应将本文本签字本的两份经确认的复本送交所有联盟国家的政府，并根据请求送交任何其他国家的政府。

（4）总干事应将本文本向联合国秘书处登记。

（5）总干事应将签署情况，批准书或加入书的交存和此种文件中包含的或根据第28条第（1）款（c）项、第30条第（2）款（a）和（b）项和第33条第（2）款作出的任何声明，本文本任何条款的生效，声明无效的通知，根据第30条第（2）款（c）项、第31条第（1）款和第（2）款、第33条第（3）款和第38条第（1）款以及附件所作的通知，通报所有联盟国家的政府。

第38条

[过渡条款]

（1）未批准或加入本文本和不受本公约斯德哥尔摩文本第22条至第26条约束的联盟国家，如果有此意愿，截至1975年4月26日，可以行使所述条款之下规定的权利，如同它们受其约束。任何希望行使此种权利的国家应将有此意思的书面通知送交总干事；此通知于收到之日生效。截至该日期，这些国家应被视为大会成员。

（2）只要联盟国家尚未全部成为产权组织的成员，产权组织国际局亦行使联盟局的职能，并且，总干事行使该局局长的职能。

（3）一俟所有联盟国家成为产权组织的成员，联盟局的权利、义务和财产应移交产权组织国际局。

附件　[有关发展中国家的特别条款]

第Ⅰ条

[对发展中国家开放的权利]

（1）任何依照联合国大会既定惯例被视为发展中国家的国家，批准或加入本附件为其组成部分的本文本的，并鉴于其经济状况和社会或文化需求不认为自己具备条件为保护本文本规定的所有权利做出安排的，可以通过在交存批准书或加入书时交存于总干事的一项通知，或以附件第V条第（1）款（c）项为条件在之后任何时间，声明它将利用附件第II条中规定的权利或第III条中规定的权利，或那些权利皆利用。它可以不利用第II条中规定的权利，而是根据第V条第（1）款（a）项作出声明。

（2）（a）第（1）款之下的任何声明，在第1条至第21条和本附件根据第28条第（2）款生效起十年时段终止之前通知的，有效至所述时段终止。任何此种声明可以整体或部分地以每个为十年的时段续展，方式为在当时进行中的十年时段终止前不超过十五个月和不少于三个月向总干事交存通知。

（b）第（1）款之下的任何声明，在第1条至第21条和本附件根据第28条第（2）款生效起十年时段终止之后通知的，有效至当时进行中的十年时段终止。任何此种声明可以依照（a）项第二句中的规定续展。

（3）任何联盟国家，停止被认为是第（1）款中提到的发展中国家的，不得再有资格依照第（2）款中的规定续展其声明，并且，无论是否正式撤回其声明，此国家自当时进行中的十年时段终止或自停止被视为发展中国家后一个三年时段终止，以较晚终止的时段为准，不得利用第（1）款中提到的权利。

（4）在第（1）款或第（2）款之下作出的声明停止有效时，如果库存中有凭借本附件发放的许可证制作的复本，此种复本可以继续发行直至库存用尽。

（5）任何国家，受本文本条款约束并根据第31条第（1）款就本文本对一可被认为与第（1）款中提到国家情况类似的特定领土适用交存声明或通知的，可以就此领土作出第（1）款中提到的声明和第（2）款中提到的续展通知。只要此种声明或通知持续有效，本附件的规定应适用于就其作出声明或通知的领土。

（6）（a）一个国家利用第（1）款中提到的任何一项权利，并不使另一个国家可以给起源国为前者国家的作品以低于它在第1条至第20条之下有义务给予的保护。

（b）适用第30条第（2）款（b）项第二句中规定的对等待遇的权利，不得对起源国是根据第V条第（1）款（a）项作出声明的国家的作品行使，直至在第I条第（3）款之下适用的时段终止之日。

第II条

[翻译权的限制]

（1）任何已声明将利用本条中规定的权利的国家，对于以印刷或类似形式的复制品出版的作品，有权由主管当局根据下述条件并以第IV条为条件发放非专有和不可转让的许可证，以此制度取代第8条中规定的专有翻译权。

（2）（a）以第（3）款为条件，在自作品首次出版之日开始的一个三年时段或该国国内法律确定的任何更长时段终止之后，如果未由翻译权所有者或经其授权以该国通用的语文出版此作品的翻译本，此国家的任何国民可以取得一项许可证，以所述语文制作该作品的翻译本并以印刷或其他类似形式的复制品出版该翻译本。

（b）如果以有关语文出版的翻译本的所有版本停印，亦可以发放本条中规定条件之下的许可证。

（3）（a）翻译本的语言不是联盟成员中一个或更多发达国家通用的语文的，以一年的时段取代第（2）款（a）项中提到的三年时段。

（b）任何第（1）款中提到的国家，经通用同一种语文的发达国家联盟成员一致协议，可以在以该种语文进行翻译的情况下，以由此种协议确定的更短但不少于一年的时段取代第（2）款（a）项中提到的三年时段。但是，如果所涉语文为英文、法文或西班牙文，前段的规定不得适用。任何此种协议应由达成同意的政府通知总干事。

（4）（a）不得在本条之下发放三年后才能取得的许可证，直至自下述起再过去一个六个月的时段，并且，不得在本条之下发放一年后才能取得的许可证，直至自下述起再过去一个九个月的时段：

（i）申请人遵守第 IV 条第（1）款中提到的要求之日；

（ii）如果翻译权所有者的身份或地址不详，申请人按第 IV 条第（2）款中的规定将提交发放许可证的主管当局的申请的复本寄出之日。

（b）在所述六个月或九个月的时段期间，如果由翻译权所有者或经其授权以申请所涉的语文出版了翻译本，不得发放本条之下的许可证。

（5）本条之下的任何许可证，应仅为教学、学术或研究的目的发放。

（6）如果一部作品的翻译本由翻译权所有者或经其授权以与国内类似作品的正常定价合理联系的价格出版，在本条之下发放的任何许可证应终止，如果此翻译本与在许可证之下出版的翻译本使用同种语文并且内容基本相同。在许可证终止之前已经制作的复本，可以继续发行直至库存用尽。

（7）对于主要由插图组成的作品，只有亦满足第 III 条的条件，才可以发放制作和出版文字的翻译本以及复制和出版插图的许可证。

（8）当作者从流通中收回其作品的所有复本，不得在本条之下发放许可证。

（9）（a）制作已经以印刷或其他类似形式复制品出版的作品的翻译本的许可证，经总部位于一个第（1）款中提到的国家的任何广播组织向该国主管当局提出申请，亦可以发给该组织，只要符合以下所有条件：

（i）翻译本根据依照所述国家法律制作和得到的复本制作；

（ii）翻译本仅供在完全为教学或为向特定职业的专家传播专门技术或科学研究成果的广播中使用；

（iii）翻译本通过合法制作并提供所述国家领土上接收者的广播，包括以合法和完全为此种广播的目的制作的录音或录像为媒介制作的广播，完全用于条件（ii）中提到的目的；

（iv）对翻译本的所有使用没有任何商业目的。

（b）一个广播组织在凭借本款发放的许可证之下制作的翻译本的录音或录像，为（a）项中提到的目的并取决于该项中提到的条件，并经该广播组织同意，亦可以被总部在主管当局发放有关许可证的国家内的任何其他广播组织使用。

（c）只要符合（a）项中陈述的所有标准和条件，亦可以向一个广播组织发放许可证，以翻译音像固定物中的文字，如果此种固定物本身是为系统教学活动相关使用的唯一目的制作和出版。

（d）以（a）项至（c）项为条件，前述各款适用于本款之下发放的任何许可证的发放和行使。

第 III 条

[复制权的限制]

（1）任何已声明将利用本条中规定的权利的国家，有权由主管当局根据以下条件并以第 IV 条为条件发放非专有和不可转让的许可证，以此制度取代第 9 条中规定的专有复制权。

（2）（a）对于本条凭借第（7）款对之适用的一部作品。

（i）第（3）款中规定的、在该作品一个特定版本首次出版之日开始的有关时段；

（ii）由第（1）款中提到的国家的国内法律确定的、在相同日期开始的任何更长时段终止后，此种版本的复本尚未由复制权所有者或经其授权在该国以与国内类似作品的正常定价合理联系的价格向一般公众或与系统教学活动相关发行，此国家的任何国民可以取得一项许可证，以该价格或更低价格复制和出版此种版本，供与系统教学活动相关的使用。

（b）复制和出版已经如（a）项中所述发行的版本的许可证，亦可以在本条规定的条件下发放，如果在可适用的时段终止后，没有该版本的经授权复本在有关国家以与国内类似作品正常定价合理联系的价格向一般公众或与系统教学活动相关销售达六个月。

（3）第（2）款（a）（i）项中提到的时段为五年，例外是：

（i）对于包括数学的自然和物理科学以及技术作品，时段为三年；

（ii）对于小说、诗歌、戏剧和音乐作品以及美术书籍，时段为七年。

（4）（a）三年后才能取得的许可证，不得在本条之下发放，直至自以下起过去六个月的时段。

（i）申请人遵守第 IV 条第（1）款提到的要求之日；

（ii）如果复制权所有者的身份或地址不详，申请人依照第 IV 条第（2）款中的规定将向发放许可证的主管当局提交的申请的复本寄出之日。

（b）如果可以在其他时段之后取得许可证并且可以适用第 IV 条第（2）款，不得发放许可证，直至自寄出申请的复本之日起一个三个月的时段过去。

（c）如果在（a）和（b）项中提到的六个月或三个月时段中发生第（2）款（a）项中所述的发行，不得在本条之下发放许可证。

（d）如果作者从流通中收回为其申请过复制和出版许可证的版本的所有复本，不得发放许可证。

（5）不得在以下情况下根据本条发放复制和出版一部作品的翻译本的许可证：

（i）如果翻译本非由翻译权所有者或经其授权出版；

（ii）如果翻译本不使用申请许可证所在国家通用的语文。

（6）如果一部作品的一个版本的复制品，由复制权所有者或经其授权，在第（1）款中提到的国家里以与该国内类似作品正常定价合理联系的价格向一般公众或与系统教学活动相关发行，在本条之下发放的任何许可证应终止，如果此种版本与在所述许可证之下出版的版本使用相同语文并且内容基本相同。许可证终止前制作的所有复本，可以继续发行直至库存用尽。

（7）（a）以（b）项为条件，本条适用的作品限于以印刷或其他类似形式的复制品出版的作品。

（b）本条亦适用于以音像形式复制合法制作的音像固定物，包括其中包含的任何受保护作品，并适用于将包含的任何文字翻译成申请许可证所在国家通用的语文，条件始终是，所涉音像固定物是为与系统教学活动相关使用的唯一目的制作和出版。

第IV条

[第II条和第III条之下许可证共用的规定]

（1）第II条或第III条之下的许可证，只有申请人根据有关国家的程序证明，他或者已经请求或者已被权利所有者拒绝授权制作和出版翻译本或复制和出版该版本，或者经过努力无法找到权利所有者，才可以发放。在提出请求的同时，申请人应通知第（2）款中提到的任何国家或国际信息中心。

（2）如果无法找到权利所有者，许可证申请人应通过航空挂号信，将向发放许可证的主管当局提交的申请的复本寄给名称出现在作品上的出版者，并寄给据信出版者主要业务地所在国家的政府在交存于总干事的通知中可能指定的任何国家或国际信息中心。

（3）根据在第II条和第III条之下发放的许可证出版的翻译本或复制品的所有复本，应指明作者的姓名。在翻译本的情况下，作品的原始标题应无论如何出现在所有复本上。

（4）（a）在第II条或第III条之下发放的许可证不得延及复本的出口，并且，任何此种许可证仅对在申请许可证所在国家领土内出版翻译本或许是复制本有效。

（b）为（a）项的目的，出口的概念包括从任何领土向在第I条第（5）款之下就该领土作出声明的国家发送复本。

（c）在第II条之下为制作使用英文、法文或西班牙文以外语文的翻译本发放许可证的国家的政府或其他公共机构，将在此种许可证之下出版的翻译本的复本发送另一个国家，为（a）项的目的，不得被认为构成出口，如果符合以下所有条件：

（i）接收者是主管当局发放许可证的国家的国民个人，或集合此种个人的组织；

（ii）复本仅用于教学、学术或研究的目的；

（iii）发送复本和随后向接收者发行没有任何商业目的；

（iv）复本已被发往的国家与主管当局发放许可证的国家达成协议，允许接收或发行或两者皆允许，并且发放许可证所在国家的政府已将协议通知总干事。

（5）在凭借第II条或第III条发放许的许可证之下出版的所有复本，应以适当的语文载有一条标记，申明复本仅供在所述许可证适用的国家或领土内发行。

（6）（a）应在国家层次作出适当规定以保证：

（i）许可证为翻译权或复制权所有者规定与两个有关国家中人员之间自由谈判

的许可证通常实行的版税标准一致的公正补偿；

（ii）补偿的支付和转交；如果国家外汇管制进行干预，主管当局应尽一切努力利用国际机制保证以可国际兑换的货币或其同等物转交。

（b）国家法律应作出适当规定保证作品的正确翻译或许是特定版本的严格复制。

第V条

[限制翻译权的其他可能性]

（1）（a）任何有权宣布利用第II条中规定的权利的国家，在批准或加入本文本时，可以改为：

（i）如果是第30条第（2）款（a）项适用的国家，在涉及翻译权的情况下，在该条之下作出声明；

（ii）如果是第30条第（2）款（a）项不适用的国家，即使它不是联盟之外的国家，依照第30条第（2）款（b）项第一句作出声明。

（b）对于停止被认为是第I条第（1）款中提到的发展中国家的国家，根据本款作出的声明应有效至在第I条第（3）款之下适用的时段终止。

（c）任何已根据本款作出声明的国家，即使撤回该声明，不可以随后利用第II条中规定的权利。

（2）以第（3）款为条件，任何已利用第II条中规定的权利的国家，不可以随后根据第（1）款作出声明。

（3）任何停止被认为是第I条第（1）款中提到的发展中国家的国家，尽管不是一个联盟之外的国家，可以不晚于在第I条第（3）款之下适用的时段终止前两年作出第30条第（2）款（b）项第一句中规定意思的声明。此种声明应于在第I条第（3）款之下适用的时段终止之日生效。

第VI条

[受附件约束之前可以适用或同意适用其某些条款]

（1）任何联盟国家可以自本文本之日起并在开始受第1条至第21条和本附件约束之前在任何时间声明：

（i）如果它是倘若受第1条至第21条和本附件约束便有权利用第I条第（1）款提到的权利的国家，它将适用第II条或第III条或两者的规定，于起源国是根据以下第（ii）项同意对其适用那些条款的或受第1条至第21条和本附件约束的国家的作品；此种声明可以援引第V条而不是第II条；

（ii）它同意已在上述第（i）项之下作出声明或在第I条之下作出通知的国家将本附件适用于以它为起源国的作品。

（2）在第（1）款之下作出的任何声明，应以书面形式并交存于总干事。声明自交存之日起生效。

世界版权公约

（1971年7月24日在巴黎修订）

目录*

* 为编者所加，原文中无目录，条款无标题。

第 XIX 条：与其他多边公约和双边协定的关系

第 XX 条：保留

第 XXI 条：复本和通知

有关第 XVII 条的附加声明

有关第 XI 条的决议

1971 年 7 月 24 日在巴黎修订的《世界版权公约》的关于将该公约适用于无国籍人士和难民的作品的附加议定书一。

1971 年 7 月 24 日在巴黎修订的《世界版权公约》的关于将该公约适用于某些国际组织的作品的附加议定书二。

缔约国，

受在所有国家确保文学、科学和艺术作品版权保护之愿望的驱动，

深信已生效的国际体系之外且于之无损的一个适合世界所有国家并由一个普遍适用的公约体现的版权保护体系，将确保个人权利得到尊重并鼓励文学、科学和艺术的发展；

相信一个普遍适用的版权体系将促进人类智力成果的更广泛传播和增进国际了解，决定修订 1952 年 9 月 6 日在日内瓦签署的《世界版权公约》（以下称“1952 年公约”），

并由此达成一致如下：

第 I 条

[受保护的作品]

各缔约国承诺，充分和有效地保护作者和其他版权所有者对文学、科学和艺术作品，包括著作，音乐、戏剧和电影作品以及绘画、雕版和雕塑，所享有的权利。

第Ⅱ条

[国民待遇]

1. 任何缔约国国民已出版的作品和首先在该国出版的作品，在其他各缔约国中，享有与其他国家给予其国民首先在自己领土内出版的作品相同的保护，以及本公约特别给予的保护。

2. 各缔约国国民未出版的作品，在其他各缔约国中，享有与其他国家给予自己国民未出版的作品相同的保护，以及本公约特别给予的保护。

3. 为本公约的目的，任何缔约国可以通过国内法律将居住在该国的任何人视同自己的国民。

第Ⅲ条

[无须手续]

1. 任何缔约国，在国内法律之下要求履行手续作为版权的条件，诸如交存、登记、标注、公证证明、付费或在该国制作或出版，对于所有依照本公约保护的和首先在其领土以外出版而作者不是其国民之一的作品，如果自首先出版之时，经作者或其他版权所有者授权出版的作品的所有复本载有以合理提示版权主张的方式和部位置放的、伴有版权所有者名称和首次出版年份的符号 ©，应认为这些要求已得到满足。

2. 第 1 款的规定不得阻止任何缔约国就首先在其领土内出版的作品或其国民的无论在何地出版的作品为取得和享有版权规定手续或其他条件。

3. 第 1 款的规定不得阻止任何缔约国规定，寻求司法救助的人提起诉讼时必须遵守程序要求，诸如起诉人必须通过国内律师到庭，或起诉人必须将诉讼所涉作品的复本交存法院和行政机关之一或两者；条件是，未遵守此种要求不得影响版权的有效性，如果此种要求未施加给主张保护所在国家的国民，任何此种要求亦不得施加给另一缔约国的国民。

4. 在各缔约国，应有法律手段在无须手续的情况下保护其他缔约国国民未出版的作品。

5. 如果一缔约国给予一个以上版权期限且第一个期限比第Ⅳ条规定的最短时段之一更长，此国家无须就第二个或任何后续的版权期限遵守本条第 1 款的规定。

第IV条

[保护期；同时出版]

1. 作品的保护期限应根据第II条和本条的规定由主张保护所在缔约国的法律规制。

2.（a）本公约之下保护的作品的保护期，不得短于作者有生之年并去世后二十五年。但是，任何缔约国在本公约对该国生效之日已就某些种类的作品将此期限定为自作品首次出版起算的一个时段，应有权保留这些例外并将其延伸至其他种类的作品。对所有这些种类的作品，保护期不得短于自首次出版之日起二十五年。

（b）任何缔约国，在本公约在该国生效之日不根据作者有生之年计算保护期的，应有权自作品首次出版之日起或许是出版前的登记起计算保护期，条件是，保护期不得短于自首次出版之日起或许是出版前的登记起二十五年。

（c）如果一缔约国的法律给予两个或更多连续的保护期，第一个期限的长度不得短于（a）项和（b）项中规定的最短时段之一。

3. 第2款的规定不适用于摄影作品或实用艺术作品；但条件是，在将摄影作品或实用艺术作品作为艺术作品保护的缔约国，对每一所述种类的作品，保护期不得短于十年。

4.（a）缔约国均没有义务，在未出版作品的情况下通过作者为其国民的缔约国的法律，和在已出版作品的情况下通过作品首次出版所在缔约国的法律，为一部作品提供比为其所属类别的作品确定的更长时段的保护。

（b）为适用（a）项的目的，如果任何缔约国的法律给予两个或更多连续的保护期，该国的保护时段应被视为那些期限的总和。但是，如果一特定作品因任何理由在第二个或在任何后续期限中不受此国家保护，其他缔约国不应有义务在第二个或在任何后续期限中保护它。

5. 为实施第4款的目的，一缔约国国民的作品，首先在一个非缔约国出版的，应以首先在作者为其国民的缔约国出版对待。

6. 为实施第4款的目的，在同时在两个或更多缔约国出版的情况下，作品应以首先在提供最短保护期的缔约国出版对待；任何作品，首次出版三十日内在两个或更多缔约国出版的，应被视为同时在所述缔约国出版。

第Ⅳ条之二

[受保护的权利]

1. 第Ⅰ条中提到的权利，应包括保障作者经济利益的基本权利，包括授权以任何手段复制、公开表演和广播的专有权利。本条的规定应延及以原始形式或以任何显见从原始作品派生的形式在本公约之下受保护的作品。

2. 但是，任何缔约国可以通过国内法律对本条第1款中提到的权利规定不与本公约精神和条款冲突的例外。尽管如此，法律有此规定的任何国家，应给每一项被规定例外的权利以合理程度的有效保护。

第Ⅴ条

[翻译权和翻译权的限制]

1. 第Ⅰ条中提到的权利，应包括作者制作、出版以及授权制作和出版受本公约保护作品的翻译本的专有权利。

2. 但是，任何缔约国可以通过国内法律限制文字作品的翻译权，但只有在遵守以下规定的情况下：

（a）如果在一部文字作品首次出版之日起七年时段终止后，未由翻译权所有者或经其授权以缔约国通用的语文出版此种文字作品的翻译本，此种缔约国的任何国民可以从主管当局取得一项非专有许可证，将作品翻译成该语文并出版如此翻译的作品。

（b）此国民应根据有关国家的程序证明，他已经请求权利所有者授权制作和出版翻译本而被拒绝，或者经过在他一方的适当努未能找到权利所有者。如果使用缔约国通用语文的翻译本的所有先前版本均停印，亦可以根据相同条件发放许可证。

（c）如果无法找到翻译权所有者，许可证申请人应将申请的复本寄送名称出现在作品上的出版者，如果知道翻译权所有者的国籍，并寄送所有者为其国民的国家的外交或领事代表，或寄送该国政府可能指定的组织。许可证不得在申请书复本寄出之日起两个月时段终止前发放。

（d）国内法律应做出适当规定，保证翻译权所有者得到公正和符合国际标准的补偿，保证此种补偿的支付和转送，并保证作品的准确翻译。

（e）作品的原始标题和作者的姓名应印在出版的翻译本的所有复本上。许可证应仅对在申请它所在的缔约国出版翻译本有效。如此出版的复本可以进口和销售到另一缔约国，如果另一国的通用语文与作品被翻译成的语文相同，并且如果另一国的国内法律规定此种许可证并且不禁止此种进口和销售。不存在前述条件的，此种复本在一个缔约国的进口和销售应由其国内法律和协议规制。许可证不得由被许可人转让。

（f）当作者从流通中撤回作品的所有复本，不得发放许可证。

第Ⅴ条之二

[为发展中国家的例外]

1. 任何依照联合国大会既定惯例被视为发展中国家的缔约国，可以通过在批准、承认或加入公约时或随后向联合国教育、科学和文化组织总干事（以下称“总干事”）交存的通知利用第Ⅴ条之三和第Ⅴ条之四规定的任何或所有例外。

2. 任何此种通知应在本公约生效之日起十年有效，或在该十年时段于交存通知之日剩余的部分中有效，并且可以整个或部分地以每个为十年的更多时段延展，如果缔约国在相关的十年时段终止前不超过十五个月或不少于三个月向总干事交存进一步通知。在这些后来的十年时段中，也可以根据本条的规定作出初始通知。

3. 尽管有第2款的规定，被停止认为是第1款中提到的发展中国家的缔约国，不得再有权延展其在第1款或第2款之下作出的通知，并且，无论其是否正式撤回通知，此国家在进行中的十年时段结束时不得利用第Ⅴ条之三和第Ⅴ条之四规定的例外。

4. 任何已经在第Ⅴ条之三和第Ⅴ条之四规定的例外之下制作的作品复本，可以在本条之下的通知对之有效的时段终止前继续发行，直至库存用尽。

5. 任何缔约国，根据第XIII条就本公约对可被认为情况与本条第1款中提到的国家类似的一个特定国家或领土的适用交存通知的，亦可以根据本条的规定就任何此种国家或领土交存或延展通知。在此种通知有效的时段中，第Ⅴ条之三和第Ⅴ条之四的规定可以对此国家或领土适用。从该国家或领土向缔约国发送复本，应被视为第Ⅴ条之三和第Ⅴ条之四意思中的出口。

第Ⅴ条之三

[为发展中国家对翻译权的例外]

1.（a）第Ⅴ条之二第1款适用的任何缔约国，可以将第Ⅴ条第2款规定的七年时段替换为三年时段或其法律规定的任何更长时段。但是，对于译成在一个或更多是本公约或仅是1952年公约缔约国的发达国家中不通用的语文的翻译本，该时段应为一年而不是三年。

（b）第V条之二第1款适用的一个缔约国，经是本公约或仅是1952年公约缔约国的并通用同一种语文的发达国家一致协议，在以该种语文进行翻译的情况下，可以将（a）项规定的三年时段替换为由此种协议确定的另一个但不短于一年的时段。但是，如果涉及的语文为英文、法文或西班牙文，此项不得适用。任何此种协议应被通知总干事。

（c）只有申请人根据有关国家的程序证明，他已经请求并被翻译权所有者拒绝授权，或者经过在他一方的适当努力无法找到权利所有者，才可以发放许可证。在提出申请的同时，他应通知由联合国教育、科学和文化组织设立的国际版权信息中心，或者通知据信出版者主要营业地所在国家的政府向总干事交存的有此意思的通知书中可能指定的任何国家或地区信息中心。

（d）如果无法找到翻译权所有者，许可证申请人应通过航空挂号信将申请书的复本寄送名称出现在作品上的出版者或任何（c）项中提到的国家或地区信息中心。如果无此种中心被通知，他还应将一份复本寄送联合国教育、科学和文化组织设立的国际版权信息中心。

2.（a）三年后才能取得的许可证，不得在本条之下发放，直至再过一个六个月的时段，一年后才能取得的许可证，直至再过一个九个月的时段。再过的时段应或者自第1款（c）项提到的请求准许翻译的日期开始，或者，如果翻译权所有者的身份或地址不明，自第1款（d）项提到的寄送许可证申请复本的日期开始。

（b）如果在所述六个月或九个月的时段中，已由翻译权所有者或经他授权出版了翻译本，不得发放许可证。

3. 本条之下的任何许可证，应只为教学、学术或研究的目的发放。

4.（a）本条之下发放的任何许可证不得延及复本的出口，并且应只对申请许可证所在缔约国领土内的出版有效。

（b）根据在本条之下发放的许可证出版的任何复本，应载有使用适当语文的标注，说明该复本仅供在发放许可证的缔约国发行。如果作品载有第III条第1款规定的标注，复本应载有同样的标注。

（c）在本条之下发放将一部作品翻译成英文、法文或西班牙文以外语文的许可证的一国政府或其他公共机构，将在此种许可证之下制作的翻译本的复本发往另一个国家，（a）项禁止出口的规定不适用，如果：

（i）接收者是发放许可证的缔约国的国民个人，或集合此种个人的组织；

（ii）复本仅为教学、学术或研究的目的使用；

（iii）发送复本和复本随后发行给接收者没有商业目的；

（iv）复本被发往的国家与缔约国协议允许接收、发行或两者皆允许，并且，达成协议的政府任何之一已将此协议通知总干事。

5. 应在国家层次做出适当规定以保证：

（a）许可证规定与两个有关国家中人们之间自由谈判许可证情况下正常采用的版税标准一致的公正补偿；

（b）补偿的支付和转交；但是，如果国家外汇管制进行干预，主管当局应尽一切努力通过国际机制保证以可国际兑换的货币或同等形式转交。

6. 如果翻译权所有者或经其授权在一缔约国出版与发放许可证所涉版本语文相同和内容基本相同的作品翻译本，并且以与类似作品在同一国的正常定价合理相关的价格，该国在本条之下发放的任何许可证应终止。许可证终止前已经制作的任何复本，可以继续发行，直至库存用尽。

7. 对于主要由插图组成的作品，只有亦满足第Ⅴ条之四的条件，才可以发放翻译文字和复制插图的许可证。

8.（a）经总部位于第Ⅴ条之二第1款适用的缔约国的广播组织在该国基于以下条件申请，亦可以向该组织发放许可证，翻译一部在本公约之下受保护的、以印刷或类似形式的复制品出版的作品：

（i）翻译本译自依照缔约国法律制作和获得的复本；

（ii）翻译本仅供在完全为教学或为向特定职业的专家传播专业性技术或科学研究成果的广播中使用；

（iii）翻译本仅为条件（ii）中列举的目的使用，使用系通过合法制作的、提供缔约国领土上接收者的广播，包括以合法并完全为此种广播的目的制作的录音或录像为媒介制作的广播；

（iv）翻译本的录音或录像只可以在总部位于发放许可证的缔约国的广播组织之间交换；

（v）对翻译本的所有使用无任何商业目的。

（b）只要符合（a）项列举的所有标准和条件，亦可以向广播组织发许可证，翻译本身为系统教学相关使用的唯一目的制作和出版的视听固定物中包含的任何文字。

（c）以（a）项和（b）项为条件，本条其他规定应适用于许可证的发放和行使。

9. 以本条的规定为条件，在本条之下发放的任何许可证应由第Ⅴ条的规定规制，并且，即使在第Ⅴ条第2款规定的七年时段终止后，应继续由第Ⅴ条和本条的规定规制。但是，在所述时段终止后，被许可人可以请求以完全受第Ⅴ条的规定规制的新许可证取代该许可证。

第Ⅴ条之四

[为发展中国家对复制权的例外]

1. 第Ⅴ条之二第1款适用的任何缔约国可以采取以下规定：

（a）如果：

（i）第（c）项规定的自第3款提到的文学、科学或艺术作品的特定版本首次出版之日开始的有关时段；

（ii）该国国家法律确定的任何更长时段终止后，此种版本的复本尚未由复制权所有者或经他授权以与类似作品在该国正常定价合理相关的价格在该国向一般公众或与系统教学活动相关发行，此国家的任何国民可以从主管当局取得一项非专有许可证，以该价格或更低价格出版此种版本供与系统教学活动相关使用。只有此国民依照有关国家的程序证明，他已经请求权利所有者授权出版此种作品而被拒绝，或者经过在他一方的适当努力无法找到权利所有者，才可以发放许可证。在提出请求的同时，他应通知联合国教育、科学和文化组织设立的国际版权信息中心或（d）项中提到的任何国家或地区信息中心。

（b）如果没有所涉版本的经授权复本在有关国家以与类似作品在该国正常定价合理相关的价格向公众或与系统教学活动相关销售达六个月，亦可以基于同样条件发放许可证。

（c）（a）项中提到的时段应为五年，例外是：

（i）对包括数学的自然和物理科学以及技术作品，时段为三年；

（ii）对小说、诗歌、戏剧和音乐作品以及艺术书籍，时段为七年。

（d）如果无法找到复制权所有者，许可证申请人应通过航空挂号信将申请的复本寄送名称出现在作品上的出版者以及据信出版者主要营业地所在国家向总干事交存的通知中指明的任何国家或地区信息中心。没有任何此种通知的，他亦应将一份复本寄送联合国教育、科学和文化组织设立的国际版权信息中心。在申请的复本寄出之日起三个月的时段终止前，不得发放许可证。

（e）三年后才能取得的许可证，不得在本条之下发放：

（i）直至自（a）项中提到的请求批准之日起或者，如果复制权所有者的身份或地址不明，自（d）项中提到的许可证申请的复本寄出之日起，一个六个月的时段过去；

（ii）如果在该时段中发生任何（a）项中提到的版本复本的发行。

（f）作者的姓名和作品特定版本的标题应印在出版的复制品的所有复本上。许可证不得延及复本的出口，并应只对在申请许可证所在国家领土内的出版有效。被许可人不得转让许可证。

（g）国内法律应做出适当规定保证所涉特定版本的准确复制。

（h）下列情况下，不得在本条之下发放复制和出版作品翻译本的许可证：

（i）翻译本不是由翻译权所有者或经其授权出版的；

（ii）翻译本不使用在有权颁发许可证的国家中通用的语文。

2. 第1款中规定的例外取决于以下另加的条件：

（a）根据在本条之下发放的许可证出版的任何复本，应载有使用适当语文的标注，表明该复本仅供在该许可证适用的缔约国发行。如果版本载有第III条第1款规定的标注，复本应载有同样的标注。

（b）应在国家层次做出适当规定以保证：

（i）许可证规定与两个有关国家中人们之间自由谈判许可证的情况下正常采用的版税标准一致的公正补偿；

（ii）补偿的支付和转交；但是，如果国家外汇管制进行干预，主管当局应尽一切努力利用国际机制保证以可国际兑换的货币或同等形式转交。

（c）一旦作品一个版本的复本在缔约国由复制权所有者或经其授权以与类似作品在该国正常定价合理相关的价格向公众或与系统教学相关发行，在本条之下发放的任何许可证应终止，如果此种版本与许可证之下出版的版本语文相同并且内容基本相同。许可证终止之前已经制作的复本可以继续发行，直至库存用尽。

（d）当作者从流通中撤回所涉版本的所有复本，不得发放许可证。

3.（a）以（b）项为条件，本条适用的文学、科学或艺术作品应限于以印刷或类似形式复制品出版的作品。

（b）本条的规定亦适用于合法制作的视听固定物（包括其中包含的任何受保护作品）的视听形式的复制品，并适用于其中包含的任何文字的使用有权发放许可证的国家中通用语文的翻译本；条件始终是，所涉视听固定物仅为与系统教学活动相关使用的目的制作和出版。

第VI条

[出版]

本公约中使用的“出版”，指以有形形式复制并向一般公众发行作品的能够阅读或另外视觉感知的复本。

第 VII 条

[不保护公有领域的作品]

本公约不适用于公约在主张保护所在的一个缔约国生效之日在该缔约国永久处于公共领域的作品或此种作品中的权利。

第 VIII 条

[签署]

1. 本公约，所载日期为 1971 年 7 月 24 日的，应交存于总干事并应在本公约之日后一百二十天的时段中保持开放供 1952 年公约所有缔约国签署。公约应经签署国批准或承认。

2. 任何未在本公约上签字的国家可以加入公约。

3. 批准、承认或加入公约应通过向总干事交存有此意思的文件进行。

第 IX 条

[生效]

1. 本公约在交存十二份批准、承认或加人书之后三个月生效。

2. 随后，对每个国家，本公约在该国交存批准、承认或加入书之后三个月生效。

3. 不是 1952 年公约参加方的国家加入本公约，亦构成加入该公约；但是，如果其加入书在本公约生效之前交存，此国家可以在本公约生效的条件下加入 1952 年公约。本公约生效后，任何国家不可以仅加入 1952 年公约。

4. 本公约参加国与仅是 1952 年公约参加国之间的关系，应由 1952 年公约规制。但是，任何仅参加 1952 年公约的国家，可以通过向总干事交存的通知书声明，同意将 1971 年公约适用于其国民的作品或本公约所有参加国首次在其领土内出版的作品。

第 X 条

[实施的义务]

1. 各缔约国承诺根据其宪法采取必要措施保证本公约的适用。

2. 不言而喻，在本公约就任何国家生效之日，该国必须在其国内法律之下具备条件实施本公约的条款。

第 XI 条

[政府间委员会]

1. 兹设立一个具有以下职能的政府间委员会：

（a）研究与《世界版权公约》的适用和运作有关的问题；

（b）为本公约的阶段性修订进行筹备；

（c）与各有关国际组织，诸如联合国教育、科学和文化组织，保护文学和艺术作品国际联盟以及美洲国家组织，合作研究任何与国际版权保护有关的其他问题；

（d）将其活动通报《世界版权公约》参加国。

2. 委员会由参加本公约或仅参加 1952 年公约的十八个国家的代表组成。

3. 委员会的选出应基于地理位置、人口、语言和发展阶段适当考虑国家利益的合理平衡。

4. 联合国教育、科学和文化组织总干事，世界知识产权组织总干事以及美洲国家组织秘书长或他们的代表，可以顾问身份参加该委员会的会议。

第 XII 条

[修订会议]

一俟政府间委员会认为有必要或应本公约至少十个参加国的请求，应召集修订会议。

第 XIII 条

[对其他国家和领土的适用]

1. 任何缔约国，在交存批准、承认或加入书时，或在随后任何时间，可以通过给总干事的通知声明，本公约适用于由它负责其国际关系的所有或任何国家或领土，并且，本公约应随即在第 IX 条规定的三个月期限终止后适用于此种通知中提到的国家或领土。没有此种通知的，本公约不得适用于任何此种国家或领土。

2. 但是，本条任何内容不得被理解为一缔约国承认或默认另一缔约国根据本条规定使本公约对之适用的国家或领土的现实状况。

第 XIV 条

[声明公约无效]

1. 任何缔约国可以以自己的名义，或代表所有或任何在第 XIII 条之下就其给出通知的国家或领土，声明本公约无效。声明无效应通过给总干事的通知提出。此种声明无效亦构成声明 1952 年公约无效。

2. 此种声明无效仅对被代表作出声明的国家或国土或领土有效，并且不得生效直至收到通知之日后十二个月。

第 XV 条

[争议的解决]

两个或更多缔约国之间与本公约的解释或适用有关的争议，谈判解决不成的，除非有关国家就某种其他解决办法达成一致，应提交国际法院裁决。

第 XVI 条

[语文]

1. 本公约以英文、法文和西班牙文制定。三种文本应经签字并应有同等效力。

2. 总干事应在与有关政府磋商后以阿拉伯文、德文、意大利文和葡萄牙文制定本公约的官方文本。

3. 任何缔约国或一组缔约国有权通过与总干事的安排使之以其选择的语文制定其他文本。

4. 所有此种文本应为本公约签字文本的附件。

第 XVII 条

[与《伯尔尼公约》和联盟的关系]

1. 本公约无论如何不得影响《保护文学和艺术作品伯尔尼公约》的条款或该公约成立的联盟的成员资格。

2. 适用前款规定，本条已附有一项声明。对于在 1951 年 1 月 1 日受《伯尔尼公约》约束的国家或在一个较晚日期已经或可能开始受其约束的国家，此声明是本公约的一个组成部分。此种国家在本公约上签字，亦构成在该声明上签字，此种国家批准、承认或加入，应包括该声明以及本公约。

第 XVIII 条

[与美洲共和国之间公约和协定的关系]

本公约不得取消完全在两个或更多美洲共和国之间生效或可能生效的多边或双边版权公约或协定。如果此种现有公约或协定与本公约的条款之间，或本公约的条款与两个或更多美洲共和国之间在本公约生效后可能达成的任何新公约或协定的条款之间有差异，最近达成的公约或协定应在各方之间有效。本公约对之生效之日前根据现有公约或协定在任何缔约国获得的对作品的权利，不得受影响。

第 XIX 条

[与其他多边公约和双边协定的关系]

本公约不得取消在两个或更多缔约国之间有效的多边或双边公约或协定。如果此种现有公约或协定的条款与本公约的条款有差异，应以本公约的条款为准。本公约对之生效之日前根据现有公约或协定在任何缔约国获得的对作品的权利，不得受影响。本条任何内容不得影响第 XVII 条和第 XVIII 条的规定。

第 XX 条

[保留]

不允许对本公约做出保留。

第 XXI 条

[复本和通知]

1. 总干事应将本公约经正式确认的复本送交有关国家并送交联合国秘书长注册。

2. 他亦应将交存的批准、承认和加入书，本公约生效的日期，本公约之下的通知和第 XIV 条之下的声明无效，通知所有有关国家。

有关第 XVII 条的附加声明

保护文学和艺术作品国际联盟（以下称“伯尔尼联盟”）成员的和本公约签字方的国家，

希望在所述联盟的基础上加强它们的相互关系和避免可能由《伯尔尼公约》和《世界版权公约》的并存产生的任何冲突，

承认某些国家暂时需要根据它们的文化、社会和经济发展阶段调整其版权保护水平，

经一致同意，承认以下声明的要求：

（a）（b）项规定的除外，其根据《伯尔尼公约》而有的起源国在 1951 年 1 月 1 日之后退出伯尔尼联盟的作品，不得在伯尔尼联盟国家受《世界版权公约》的保护。

（b）如果一缔约国依照联合国大会既定惯例被视为发展中国家，并在退出伯尔尼联盟的同时向联合国教育、科学和文化组织总干事交存认为自己是发展中国家的通知，（a）项的规定不得适用，只要此国家可以根据第 V 条之二利用本公约规定的例外。

（c）《世界版权公约》不得适用于伯尔尼联盟国家间的关系，只要涉及有一个伯尔尼联盟国家是其《伯尔尼公约》意思中起源国的作品的保护。

有关第 XI 条的决议

《世界版权公约》修订会议，

经考虑与本决议为其附件的本公约的第 XI 条中规定的政府间委员会有关的问题，

兹决议：

1. 在其开端，委员会应包括在 1952 年公约第 XI 条和其决议附件之下设立的政府间委员会的十二个成员国的代表，并加上以下国家的代表：阿尔及利亚、澳大利亚、日本、墨西哥、塞内加尔和南斯拉夫。

2. 任何不是 1952 年公约参加方并且没有在本公约生效后委员会第一次例会之前加入本公约的国家，应由委员会在第一次例会上依照第 XI 条第 2 款和第 3 款的规定选出的其他国家取代。

3. 一俟本公约生效，第 1 款中规定的委员会应被视为依照本公约第 XI 条成立。

4. 本公约生效后一年内应举行一次委员会会议；此后，委员会应以不超过两年的间隔举行例会。

5. 委员会应选出主席和两名副主席。它应考虑以下原则制定其程序规则：

（a）参加委员会的成员任期的正常持续时间为六年，每两年退出三分之一，但是经同意，在最初任期中，三分之一应在本公约生效后的委员会第二次例会结束时退出，再三分之一应在第三次例会结束时退出，剩余三分之一应在第四次例会结束时退出。

（b）委员会填补空缺的程序规则、成员身份期限终止的顺序、再度当选的资格以及选举程序的规则，应基于成员连续性和代表轮换之需要的平衡以及第 XI 条第 3 款陈述的考虑。

表达由联合国教育、科学和文化组织提供其秘书处的愿望。

为表明对以上的诚意，经交存各自的全权委托书，下方签字人已签署本公约。

1971 年 7 月 24 日在巴黎以独一份制定。

1971 年 7 月 24 日在巴黎修订的《世界版权公约》的关于将该公约适用于无国籍人士和难民的作品的附加议定书一

本议定书的参加国，亦是 1971 年 7 月 24 日在巴黎修订的《世界版权公约》（以下称“1971 年公约”）参加方的，

承认以下规定：

1. 在参加本议定书的国家有常住居所的无国籍人士和难民，为 1971 年公约的目的，应视同该国家的国民。

2.（a）本议定书应经签署并经批准或承认，或可以加入，如同 1971 年公约第 VIII 条的规定在此适用。

（b）对每个国家，本议定书应在有关国家交存批准、承认或加入书之日或在 1971 年公约对此国家生效之日的较晚者生效。

（c）当本议定书对一个不是 1952 年公约附加议定书参加方的国家生效，后一议定书应被视为对此国家生效。

为表明对以上的诚意，经正式授权，下方签字人已签署本议定书。

1971 年 7 月 24 日在巴黎以英文、法文和西班牙文三种同等有效的文本并以应交存于联合国教育、科学和文化组织总干事的独一份签署。总干事应将经确认的复本送交各签字国，并送交联合国秘书长注册。

1971 年 7 月 24 日在巴黎修订的《世界版权公约》的关于将该公约适用于某些国际组织的作品的附加议定书二

本议定书的参加国，亦是 1971 年 7 月 24 日在巴黎修订的《世界版权公约》（以下称“1971 年公约”）参加方的，

承认以下规定：

1.（a）1971 年公约第 II 条第 1 款规定的保护，应适用于由联合国、其有关专门机构或美洲国家组织首先出版的作品。

（b）同样，1971 年公约第 II 条第 2 款应适用于所述组织或机构。

2.（a）本议定书应经签署并经批准或承认，或可以加入，如同 1971 年公约第 VIII 条的规定在此适用。

（b）对每个国家，本议定书应在有关国家交存批准、承认或加入书之日或 1971 年公约对此国家生效之日的较晚者生效。

为表明对以上的诚意，经正式授权，下方签字人已签署本议定书。

1971 年 7 月 24 日在巴黎以英文、法文和西班牙文三种有同等效力的文字并以应交存于联合国教育、科学和文化组织总干事的独一份制定。总干事应将经确认的复本送交各签字国，并送交联合国秘书长注册。

罗马公约

保护表演者、唱片制作者和广播组织国际公约

（1961年10月26日在罗马签署）

目录*

* 目录为读者方便而增加，不出现在原始文本中。

缔约国，

受保护表演者、唱片制作者和广播组织权利的愿望的驱动，达成一致如下：

第 1 条

[对版权本身的保障*]

本公约之下给予的保护不触动并无论如何不影响文学和艺术作品版权的保护。因而，本公约任何条款不可以作有损于此种保护的解释。

第 2 条

[公约给予的保护。国民待遇的定义]

1. 为本公约的目的，国民待遇指主张保护所在缔约国国内法律给予以下人的待遇：

(a) 是其国民的表演者，对于在其领土发生、广播或首先固定的表演；

* 条款标题为读者方便而增加，不出现在原始文本中。

（b）是其国民的唱片制作者，对于首先在其领土固定或出版的唱片；

（c）总部在其领土上的广播组织，对于从位于其领土的发送台发送的广播。

2. 国民待遇以本公约中明确承诺的保护和明确规定的限制为条件。

第3条

[定义]

为本公约的目的：

（a）“表演者”指演员、歌唱者、演奏者、舞蹈者和其他演出、歌唱、讲述、朗诵、演奏或以另外方式表演文学或艺术作品的人；

（b）“唱片”指表演的声音或其他声音的完全用于听的固定物；

（c）“唱片制作者”指首次将表演的声音或其他声音固定的人或法律实体；

（d）“出版”指以合理数量向公众提供唱片的复本；

（e）“复制”指制作唱片的一件或多件复本；

（f）“广播”指为公众接收以无线手段发送声音或图像和声音；

（g）“转播”指一广播组织同时播放另一广播组织的广播。

第4条

[受保护的表演。表演者的依附地]

各缔约国应给表演者以国民待遇，如果符合以下任何条件：

（a）表演发生在另一缔约国；

（b）表演被在本公约第5条之下受保护的唱片包含；

（c）未固定在唱片上的表演被受本公约第6条保护的广播承载。

第5条

[受保护的唱片]

1. 各缔约国应给唱片制作者以国民待遇，如果符合以下任何一个条件：

（a）唱片制作者是另一缔约国的国民（国民标准）；

（b）声音的首次固定在另一缔约国进行（固定标准）；

（c）唱片首先在另一缔约国出版（出版标准）。

2. 如果唱片首先在一个非缔约国出版，但首次出版后三十天内亦在一个缔约国出版（同时出版），应被视为首先在该缔约国出版。

3. 任何缔约国可以通过向联合国秘书长交存的通知声明，它将不适用出版标准或固定标准。此种通知可以在批准、承认或加入公约时交存，或在之后任何时间。在后一情况下，通知在交存后六个月生效。

第6条

[受保护的广播]

1. 各缔约国应给广播组织以国民待遇，如果符合以下任何一个条件：

（a）广播组织的总部位于另一缔约国；

（b）广播从位于另一缔约国的发送台发送。

2. 任何缔约国可以通过向联合国秘书长交存的通知声明，它只保护总部位于另一缔约国的广播组织的并且从位于同一缔约国的发送台发送的广播。此种通知可以在批准、承认或加入公约时交存，或在之后任何时间。在后一情况下，通知在交存后六个月生效。

第7条

[表演者的最低保护]

1. 本公约为表演者提供的保护包括可以防止：

（a）不经其同意广播和向公众传播他们的表演，用于广播或公共传播中的表演本身已经是广播过的表演或从固定物进行的除外；

（b）不经其同意固定他们未固定的表演；

（c）不经其同意复制他们的表演的固定物：

（i）如果原始固定物本身是未经他们同意制作的；

（ii）如果进行复制的目的与表演者同意的不同；

（iii）如果原始固定物是根据第15条的规定制作的，而复制的目的与那些规定中提到的不同。

2.（1）如果广播系经表演者同意，针对转播、为广播目的固定和为广播目的复制此种固定物的保护，由主张保护所在缔约国的国内法律规制。

（2）广播组织使用为广播目的制作的固定物的期限和条件，根据主张保护所在缔约国的国内法律确定。

（3）但是，运用第（1）项和第（2）项中提到的国内法律，不得使表演者丧失通过合同控制其与广播组织关系的能力。

第 8 条

[共同表演的表演者]

如果数名表演者参与同一表演，任何缔约国可以通过其国内法律和法规明确代表他们行使权利的方式。

第 9 条

[杂耍和马戏艺人]

任何缔约国可以根据国内法律和法规，将本公约中规定的保护延及不表演文学或艺术作品的艺人。

第 10 条

[唱片制作者的复制权]

唱片制作者享有授权或禁止直接或间接复制其唱片的权利。

第 11 条

[唱片的手续]

如果一缔约国在其国内法律之下要求履行手续，作为保护唱片制作者或表演者或两者的与唱片有关权利的条件，只要已出版的唱片的所有商业复本或其包装载有由伴随有首次出版年份的、以合理提示保护主张的方式置放的符号○ PP 构成的标记，应认为这些手续得到满足；如果复本或其包装不（通过登载他的姓名、商标或其他适当指明）指出制作者或制作者的被许可人，标记还应包括制作者权利所有者的姓名；此外，如果复本或其包装不指出主要表演者，标记还应包括在进行固定所在国家拥有此种表演者权利的人的姓名。

第 12 条

[唱片的后续使用]

如果为商业目的出版的唱片或此种唱片的复制品被直接用于广播或任何向公众的传播，使用者应向表演者或唱片制作者或向两者支付单笔的公平报酬。这些当事方之间没有协议的，国内法律可以就报酬的分享设定条件。

第13条

[广播组织的最低保护]

广播组织享有权利授权或禁止：

（a）转播其节目广播；

（b）固定其节目广播；

（c）复制：

（i）未经其同意制作的其节目广播的固定物；

（ii）根据第15条的规定制作的其节目广播的固定物，如果复制目的与那些规定中提到的不同。

（d）向公众传播其电视节目广播，如果此种传播在公众支付入场费进入的地点进行；由主张保护此权利所在国家的国内法律确定可以行使它的条件。

第14条

[最短保护期]

本公约之下给予的保护的期限，至少持续到一个从发生以下情形之年年底起算的二十年时段终止：

（a）固定物制作 — 对于唱片和其中包含的表演；

（b）表演发生 — 对于未包含在唱片中的表演；

（c）广播发生 — 对于节目广播。

第15条

[允许的例外]

1. 任何缔约国可以在其国内法律和法规中就以下情况对本公约承诺的保护作出例外规定：

（a）私人使用；

（b）与时事报道相关使用短小摘录；

（c）广播组织利用自己的设施和为自己的节目广播进行临时固定；

（d）仅为教学或科学研究目的使用。

2. 尽管有本条第1款，任何缔约国可以在其国内法律和法规中就表演者、唱片制作者和广播组织的保护，规定与它在国内法律和法规中就文学和艺术作品版权的保护规定的同类的限制。但是，只可以在符合本公约的程度上规定强制许可。

第 16 条

[保留]

1. 任何国家参加本公约，应受其所有义务的约束，并享有其所有利益。但是，一国可以随时通过向联合国秘书长交存的通知声明：

（a）对于第 12 条：

（i）它不适用该条的规定；

（ii）它不就某些使用适用该条的规定；

（iii）对于制作者不是另一缔约国国民的唱片，它不适用该条；

（iv）对于制作者是另一缔约国国民的唱片，它将该条规定的保护，限于后者国家对作出声明的国家的国民首次固定的唱片所予保护的程度和期限；但是，制作者是其国民的缔约国不与作出声明的国家保护同一个或几个受益人，不得认为是保护程度的不同。

（b）对于第 13 条，它将不适用该条（d）项；如果一缔约国作出此种声明，其他缔约国无义务将第 13 条（d）项中提到的权利赋予总部在该缔约国的广播组织。

2. 如果本条第 1 款提到的通知在批准、承认或加入书交存之日以后作出，声明在通知交存后六个月生效。

第 17 条

[某些仅适用"固定"标准的国家]

任何国家，在 1961 年 10 月 26 日仅根据固定标准为唱片制作者提供保护的，可以在批准、承认或加入公约时通过向联合国秘书长交存的通知声明，它为第 5 条的目的只适用固定标准，并为第 16 条第 1 款（a）项（iii）和（iv）的目的适用固定标准而非国民标准。

第 18 条

[保留的撤回]

任何在第 5 条第 3 款、第 6 条第 2 款、第 16 条第 1 款或第 17 条之下交存通知的国家，可以通过向联合国秘书长交存进一步通知缩小其范围或将其撤回。

第19条

[表演者在电影中的权利]

尽管有本公约中的任何内容，一俟表演者同意将其表演包含在可视或视听固定物中，第7条不再适用。

第20条

[追溯力]

1. 本公约不得损害本公约对任何缔约国生效前在该国获得的权利。

2. 任何缔约国无须有义务将本公约的条款适用于本公约对该国生效之日前发生的表演或广播或固定的唱片。

第21条

[其他保护手段]

本公约规定的保护不得妨害给予表演者、唱片制作者和广播组织的任何其他保护。

第22条

[特别协议]

缔约国保留在它们之间达成特别协议的权利，只要此种协议给表演者、唱片制作者和广播组织以比本公约给予的那些更广泛的权利或包含其他不与本公约抵触的条款。

第23条

[签署和交存]

本公约应交存于联合国秘书长。它应开放供任何被邀参加表演者、唱片制作者和广播组织国际保护外交会议的并是《世界版权公约》参加方或保护文学和艺术作品国际联盟成员的国家签署，直至1962年6月30日。

第24条

[参加公约]

1. 本公约应经签署国批准或承认。

2. 本公约应开放供任何被邀参加第 23 条中提到的会议的国家和联合国任何成员国加入，条件是在任一情况下此国家是《世界版权公约》加入方或保护文学和艺术作品国际联盟成员。

3. 批准、承认或加入公约应通过向联合国秘书长交存相同意思的文书进行。

第 25 条

[生效]

1. 本公约在第六份批准、承认或加入书交存之日后三个月生效。

2. 之后，本公约对每个国家在交存其批准、承认或加入书之日后三个月生效。

第 26 条

[通过国内法律规定实施公约]

1. 各缔约国承诺根据其宪法采取必要措施保证本公约的适用。

2. 交存批准、承认或加入书时，每个国家应在其国内法律之下具备条件实施本公约的条款。

第 27 条

[公约对某些领土的适用]

1. 任何国家在批准、承认或加入时，或在之后任何时间，可以通过给联合国秘书长的通知声明，本公约延及由它负责其国际关系的所有或任何领土，条件是《世界版权公约》或《保护文学和艺术作品国际公约》适用于有关的领土。此通知在被收到之日后三个月生效。

2. 第 5 条第 3 款、第 6 条第 2 款、第 16 条第 2 款以及第 17 条和第 18 条中提到的通知，可以延伸至包括本条第 1 款中提到的所有或任何领土。

第 28 条

[声明公约无效]

1. 任何缔约国可以代表自己或代表第 27 条中提到的所有或任何领土声明公约无效。

2. 声明无效应通过给联合国秘书长的通知进行，并在通知被收到之日后十二个月生效。

3. 一缔约国不得在自公约对该国生效之日起一个五年时段终止之前行使声明

无效的权利。

4．一缔约国从它既不是《世界版权公约》参加方也不是保护文学和艺术作品国际联盟成员之时起，不再是本公约参加方。

5．本公约从《世界版权公约》和《保护文学和艺术作品国际公约》均不适用于第 27 条中提到的领土之时起，不再适用于该领土。

第 29 条

[公约的修订]

1．本公约生效五年之后，任何缔约国可以通过给联合国秘书长的通知请求为修订公约的目的召开会议。联合国秘书长应将此请求通知所有缔约国。在联合国秘书长发出通知之日后六个月的时段内，如果不少于一半的缔约国通知同意该要求，秘书长应通知国际劳工局总干事，联合国教育、科学和文化组织总干事和保护文学和艺术作品国际联盟局局长，他们应与第 32 条中提到的政府间委员会合作召开修订会议。

2．通过本公约的任何修订，需要参加修订会议的三分之二国家的赞成票，条件是这一多数包含在修订会议时为公约参加方的国家的三分之二。

3．在通过一个对本公约作出全部或部分修订的公约的情况下，除非作出修订的公约另有规定：

（a）本公约自作出修订的公约生效之日起停止开放供批准、承认或加入；

（b）本公约对未参加作出修订的公约的缔约国之间的或与它们的关系保持有效。

第 30 条

[争议的解决]

两个或更多缔约国之间可能就本公约的解释或适用发生的任何争议，谈判解决不成的，应在争议当事方任何之一的请求下提交国际法院裁决，除非他们同意另一解决方式。

第 31 条

[对保留的限制]

不可以对本公约做出保留，第 5 条第 3 款、第 6 条第 2 款、第 16 条第 1 款和第 17 条不受损害。

第32条

[政府间委员会]

1. 兹设立一个具有以下职责的政府间委员会：

(a) 研究与本公约的适用和运作有关的问题；

(b) 为本公约可能的修订收集建议和准备文件。

2. 委员会由适当考虑公平地域分配选出的缔约国代表组成。成员的数目，如有十二个或以下缔约国应为六个，如有十三至十八个缔约国为九个，如有十八个以上缔约国为十二个。

3. 委员会在公约生效后十二个月通过由国际劳工局总干事，联合国教育、科学和文化组织总干事和保护文学和艺术作品国际联盟局局长根据所有缔约国之大多数先前批准的规则组织的由缔约国每国一票参加的选举组成。

4. 委员会应选出其主席和官员。它应制定自己的程序规则。这些规则应尤其为委员会将来的运作以及为将来以保证不同缔约国之间轮换的方式挑选成员作出规定。

5. 由国际劳工局，联合国教育、科学和文化组织和保护文学和艺术作品国际联盟局的由其总干事或局长指定的官员组成委员会的秘书处。

6. 在其大多数成员认为有必要时随时召开的委员会会议，依次在国际劳工局，联合国教育、科学和文化组织和保护文学和艺术作品国际联盟局的总部举行。

7. 委员会成员的开支由各自政府负担。

第33条

[语文]

1. 本公约以英文、法文和西班牙文制定，三种文本具有同等效力。

2. 另外，以德文、意大利文和葡萄牙文制定本公约的正式文本。

第34条

[通知]

1. 联合国秘书长应将以下事项通知第23条中提到的被邀参加会议的国家和联合国所有成员国，以及国际劳工局总干事，联合国教育、科学和文化组织总干事和保护文学艺术作品国际联盟局局长：

(a) 每件批准、承认或加入书的交存；

（b）公约生效的日期；

（c）本公约中规定的所有通知、声明或信函；

（d）如果发生第 28 条第 4 款和第 5 款提到的任何情况。

2．联合国秘书长还应将根据第 29 条送交他的请求以及就公约的修订从缔约国收到的任何信函通知国际劳工局总干事，联合国教育、科学和文化组织总干事和保护文学艺术作品国际联盟局局长。

为表明对以上的诚意，经正式授权，下方签字人已签署本公约。

1961 年 10 月 26 日在罗马以英文、法文和西班牙文的独一份签署。经确认的准确复本由联合国秘书长送发第 23 条中提到的被邀参加会议的所有国家和联合国每个成员国，以及国际劳工局总干事，联合国教育、科学和文化组织总干事和保护文学和艺术作品国际联盟局局长。

保护唱片制作者防止未经授权复制其唱片的公约

（1971年10月29日）

目录*

缔约国，

关切未经授权复制唱片的广泛存在和不断增加以及这给作者、表演者和唱片制作者利益带来的损害，

* 目录为读者方便而增加，不出现在原始文本中。

相信保护唱片制作者防止此种行为还将有益于录制在唱片上的表演和作品的表演者和作者，

承认联合国教育、科学和文化组织和世界知识产权组织在这一领域所做工作的价值，

希望无论如何不削弱已经生效的国际协定，尤其是无论如何不妨害更广泛承认保护表演者、广播组织和唱片制作者的 1961 年 10 月 26 日《罗马公约》，

达成一致如下：

第 1 条

[定义*]

为本公约的目的：

（a）“唱片”指表演的声音或其他声音的任何完全用于听的固定物；

（b）“唱片制作者”指首次固定表演的声音或其他声音的自然人或法人；

（c）“复本”指一个包含直接或间接从唱片提取的声音并收录固定在该唱片中的声音的全部或实质部分的物件；

（d）“向公众发行”指直接或间接向一般或任何部分公众提供唱片的复本的行为。

第 2 条

[缔约国的义务；必须保护谁和防止什么]

各缔约国应保护是其他缔约国国民的唱片制作者，防止不经制作者同意制作复本和防止此种复本的进口，只要任何此种制作或进口是为向公众发行的目的，并且防止向公众发行此种复本。

第 3 条

[缔约国的实施手段]

实施本公约的手段，由每个缔约国的国内法律规定，并应包括下列之一或多项：通过赋予版权或其他专项权利保护；通过有关不正当竞争的法律保护；通过刑事制裁保护。

* 条款标题为读者方便而增加，不出现在原始文本中。

第 4 条

[保护期]

给予保护的期限由每个缔约国的国内法律规定。但是，如果国内法律为保护规定一个具体期限，该期限不得短于自唱片中包含的声音被首次固定之年的年底或自唱片首次出版之年的年底起二十年。

第 5 条

[手续]

如果一缔约国在其国内法律之下要求履行手续作为保护唱片制作者的条件，只要所有向公众发行的经授权的唱片复本或其包装登载由伴随有首次出版年份的、以恰当提示保护主张的方式置放的符号 ℗ 构成的标记，应认为这些手续得到满足；并且，如果复本或其包装不（通过登载其名称、商标或其他适当指明）指出作者、其合法继承人或专有被许可人，标记还应包括制作者、其合法继承人或专有被许可人的名称。

第 6 条

[对保护的限制]

任何缔约国，通过版权或其他专项权利或通过刑事制裁保护的，可以在其国内法中就唱片制作者的保护规定与就文学和艺术作品作者的保护允许的相同种类的限制。但是，除非满足以下所有条件，不得允许任何强制许可：

（a）复本仅用于教学或科学研究的目的；

（b）许可证仅对主管当局已发放许可证的缔约国领土内的复制有效，并不得延及复本的出口；

（c）在许可证之下进行复制，由主管当局考虑复本制作数量以及其他因素确定公平报酬。

第 7 条

[法律保留]

（1）本公约无论如何不得被解释为限制或妨害在任何国内法律或国际协定之下另外给予作者、表演者、唱片制作者或广播组织的保护。

（2）固定在唱片中的表演的表演者可享有的保护，如果有的限度以及享受任何此种保护的条件，由每个缔约国的国内法律规定。

（3）任何缔约国无须将本公约的条款适用于本公约对该国生效之前固定的任何唱片。

（4）任何缔约国，在 1971 年 10 月 29 日仅根据首次固定的地点为唱片制作者提供保护的，可以通过向世界知识产权组织总干事交存的通知，声明它将适用这个标准而不是制作者国籍的标准。

第 8 条

[秘书处]

（1）世界知识产权组织国际局应汇集和出版与保护唱片有关的信息。各缔约国应将有关此主题的所有新定法律和官方文件及时传送国际局。

（2）国际局应根据请求就与本公约有关的事项向任何缔约国提供信息，并开展和提供旨在促进本公约规定的保护的研究和服务。

（3）国际局应行使上述第（1）款和第（2）款列举的职能，并与联合国教育、科学和文化组织和国际劳工组织就各自职权范围内的事项进行合作。

第 9 条

[参加公约]

（1）本公约应交存于联合国秘书长。它应开放供任何是联合国、与联合国有关任何专门机构或国际原子能机构成员或是国际法院宪章加入方的国家签署，直至 1972 年 4 月 30 日。

（2）本公约应经签署国批准或承认。它应开放供本条第（1）款中提到的任何国家加入。

（3）批准、承认或加入书应向联合国秘书长交存。

（4）不言而喻，一国开始受本公约约束，应具备条件根据其国内法律实施公约的条款。

第 10 条

[保留]

不允许对本公约做出保留。

第11条

[生效和适用]

（1）本公约在第五份批准、承认或加入书交存后三个月生效。

（2）对于在第五份批准、承认或加入书交存后批准、承认或加入的每个国家，公约在世界知识产权组织总干事根据第13条第（4）款将其文书的交存通知各国之日后三个月生效。

（3）任何国家在批准、承认或加入时或在任何较晚日期，可以通过给联合国秘书长的通知声明，本公约适用于由其负责国际关系的领土的全部或任何之一。此通知在被收到之日后三个月生效。

（4）前款无论如何不得被理解为意味着一个缔约国承认或默认另一缔约国凭借该款使本公约对之适用的领土的现状。

第12条

[声明公约无效]

（1）任何缔约国可以代表自己或代表第11条第（3）款中提到的任何领土通过给联合国秘书长的书面通知声明本公约无效。

（2）声明无效在联合国秘书长收到通之日后十二个月生效。

第13条

[语文和通知]

（1）本公约以英文、法文、俄文和西班牙文的独一份签署，四种文字具有同等效力。

（2）世界知识产权组织总干事应在与利益相关政府磋商后制定阿拉伯文、荷兰文、德文、意大利文和葡萄牙文的正式文本。

（3）联合国秘书长应向世界知识产权组织总干事，联合国教育、科学和文化组织总干事和国际劳工局秘书长通知：

（a）本公约的签署；

（b）批准、承认或加入书的交存；

（c）本公约的生效日期；

（d）根据第11条第（3）款通知的任何声明；

（e）声明无效通知的接收。

（4）世界知识产权组织总干事应将根据前款收到的通知和在第 7 条第（4）款之下作出的声明通知第 9 条第（1）款中提到的国家。他还应将此种声明通知联合国教育、科学和文化组织总干事和国际劳工局秘书长。

（5）联合国秘书长应将本公约两份经确认的复本传送第 9 条第（1）款中提到的国家。

字体保护及其国际交存维也纳协定

（1973年6月12日在维也纳签署）

目录*

* 目录为读者方便而增加，不出现在协定签署文本中。

缔约国，

希望为字体提供有效的保护以鼓励字体的创作，

意识到字体在文化传播中的作用和其保护必须满足的特殊要求，

达成一致如下：

引介条款

第1条

成立联盟

参加本协定的国家组成一个保护字体的联盟。

第2条

定义

为本协定和条例的目的，

(i)“字体”指以下各项的成套的设计：

(a) 字母以及连同诸如重音和标点等附加符号的字母系列；

(b) 数字以及惯用符号、记号和科学符号等其他象征符号；

(c) 为以任何图形技法排版文字提供手段的装饰，诸如边饰、花饰和小图案等。“字体”一词不包括形式由单纯技术要求决定的字体；

(ii)“国际注册薄”指国际字体注册薄；

(iii)“国际交存”指为在国际注册簿中登记的目的进行的交存；

(iv)“申请人”指进行国际交存的自然人或法律实体；

(v)“国际交存的所有者”指以其名义在国际注册簿中登记国际交存的自然人或法律实体；

(vi)“缔约国”指参加本协定的国家；

(vii)“联盟”指由本协定成立的联盟；

(viii)“大会”指联盟大会；

(ix)“巴黎公约”指1883年3月20日签署的保护工业产权公约，包括其任何修订；

(x)“产权组织”指世界知识产权组织；

(xi)“国际局”指产权组织国际局和只要存在的保护知识产权联合国际局(BIRPI)；

（xii）“总干事”指产权组织总干事；

（xiii）“条例”指本协定之下的条例。

第一章　国内保护

第3条

保护的原则和种类

缔约国承诺，根据本协定的条款，通过设立一个专门的国家交存，或通过调适国家工业设计法中规定的交存，或通过国家版权条款，确认对字体的保护。这些类别的保护可以是累加的。

第4条

受保护的自然人或法律实体

（1）在根据第34条声明意图通过设立专门的国家交存或通过调适国家工业设计法确认保护的缔约国中，本协定的保护应适用于是一缔约国居民或国民的自然人或法律实体。

（2）（a）在根据第34条声明意图通过国家版权条款确认保护的缔约国中，本协定的保护应适用于：

（i）是缔约国之一的国民的字体创作者；

（ii）不是缔约国之一的国民的但其字体首先在缔约国之一发表的字体创作者。

（b）任何（a）项中提到的缔约国，可以将在一个缔约国有惯常住所或居所的字体创作者视同该国国民的字体创作者。

（3）为本协定的目的，任何自然人或法律实体的协会，在它据以成立的国内法律之下可以取得权利和承担义务的，尽管不是一个法律实体，应被视同一个法律实体。但是，任何缔约国可以取代该协会而保护组成它的自然人或法律实体。

第5条

国民待遇

（1）每个缔约国应有义务，将根据该缔约国在第34条之下声明的保护给予其国民的保护，提供给所有有权主张本协定利益的自然人和法律实体。

（2）如果一个第4条第（2）款中提到的缔约国在其国内法律之下要求履行手续作为保护字体的一个条件，对于在第4条第（2）款中提到的其创作者的字体，如果经创作者或其他所有者授权出版的字体的所有复本伴有或载有由伴有受保护的所有者的名称和首次出版年份的、以恰当提示保护主张的方式置放的符号 @ 组成的标记，应认为这些手续已得到满足。

第 6 条

居所和国籍的概念

（1）（a）为第 4 条第（1）款和第 13 条的目的，任何自然人应被视为一个缔约国的居民，如果：

（i）根据该国的国家法律他是该国的居民；

（ii）他在该国拥有真实和有效的工业或商业机构。

（b）任何自然人应为第 4 条第（1）款和第 13 条的目的被视为一个缔约国的国民，如果他根据该国的国家法律是该国的国民。

（2）（a）任何法律实体应为第 4 条第（1）款和第 13 条的目的被视为一个缔约国的居民，如果它在该国拥有真实和有效的工业或商业机构。

（b）任何法律实体应为第 4 条第（1）款和第 13 条的目的被视为一个缔约国的国民，如果它根据该国的国家法律组成。

（3）如果任何诉诸本协定利益的自然人或法律实体是一个国家的居民并是另一个国家的国民，并且如果其中只有一个国家是缔约国，为本协定和条例的目的应只考虑缔约国。

第 7 条

保护的条件

（1）字体的保护应以它们是新颖的为条件，或以它们是独创的为条件，或以兼具两者为条件。

（2）字体的新颖性和独创性应联系其样式和总体外观确定，如有必要考虑有资格专业人士承认的标准。

第 8 条

保护的内容

（1）字体的保护应赋予所有者权利以禁止：

（i）不经其同意为以任何图形技法排版文字提供手段而制作任何相同或稍加改动的复制品，无论使用的技术手段或材料；

（ii）不经其同意商业发行或进口此种复制品。

（2）（a）以（b）项为条件，第（1）款中限定的权利得适用，无论受保护字体是否为复制品的制作者所知。

（b）以独创性为一个保护条件的缔约国，无须适用（a）项。

（3）第（1）款中规定的权利，亦应涵盖以任何纯技术手段将受保护字体变形得到的字体复制品，如果其基本特征仍然可以辨认。

（4）获得字体的人在通常文字排版过程中制作字体的成分，不得被认为是第（1）款（i）项意思中的复制。

（5）缔约国可以采取法律措施，在除有关受保护字体之外无其他字体可用于实现一个特定公益目标的情况下，避免可能因行使本协定之下规定的专有权利导致滥用。但是，法律措施不得损害所有者为使用其字体得到公正报酬的权利。任何情况下对字体的保护，亦不得由于使用不成或由于受保护字体复制品的进口而有任何丧失。

第 9 条

保护的期限

（1）保护的期限不可以短于十五年。

（2）保护的期限可以分为若干时段，每次延展仅在受保护字体所有者的请求下准予。

第 10 条

累加的保护

本协定的规定不得阻止对国家法律提供的更广泛保护提出主张，并且无论如何不得影响其他国际公约提供的保护。

第 11 条

优先权

为优先权的目的，如果适用，字体的国家交存应被认为是工业设计的交存。

第二章　国际交存

第12条

国际交存和登记

（1）以第（2）款的规定为条件，国际交存应直接向国际局进行，国际局应根据本协定和条例将其登记在国际注册簿中。

（2）（a）任何缔约国的国家法律可以规定，居住在各国的自然人或法律实体的国际交存可以通过该国主管机构的中介进行。

（b）如果一项国际交存如（a）项规定的通过一缔约国主管机构的中介进行，该机构应指明收到国际交存的日期，并应及时以条例中规定的方式将该交存传送国际局。

第13条

进行国际交存和拥有此种交存的权利

（1）任何是一个缔约国居民或国民的自然人或法律实体，可以进行国际交存并是其所有者。

（2）（a）任何自然人或法律实体的协会，在它据以成立的国家法律之下可以获得权利和承担义务的，尽管不是一个法律实体，应有权进行国际交存并拥有此种交存，如果它是一个缔约国的居民或国民。

（b）（a）项不得妨害任何缔约国国家法律的适用。但是，就一个（a）项中提到的协会，任何此种国家不得以它不是一个法律实体为由拒绝或取消第18条中规定的效力，如果在该国主管机构给它的正式请求之日起两个月内，该协会向该机构提交组成它的所有自然人或法律实体的名称和地址的清单，连同一项关于其成员在从事一项共同事业的声明。在此种情况下，该国家可以认为组成该协会的自然人或法律实体而非协会本身是国际交存的所有者，只要所述人或实体符合第（1）款中陈述的条件。

第14条

国际交存的内容和形式

（1）国际交存应包括：

（i）一份经签字的国际交存书，其中声明交存在本协定之下进行，并指明申请人的身份、居所、国籍和地址，以及为之寻求保护的字体的创作者的姓名或创作者放弃被以此提及；

（ii）字体的展示；

（iii）缴纳规定的费用。

（2）国际交存书可以包括：

（i）一项声明，主张在或为一个或多个《巴黎公约》参加国进行的一项或多项较早交存的优先权；

（ii）指明申请人给字体的命名；

（iii）代理人的任命；

（iv）条例中规定的另加说明。

（3）国际交存书应使用条例规定的语文之一。

第 15 条

国际交存的登记和拒绝

（1）以第（2）款为条件，国际局应及时将国际交存登记在国际注册簿中。国际交存的日期为国际局收到它的日期，或者，如果国际交存按第 12 条第（2）款规定通过一缔约国主管机构的中介进行，为该机构收到交存的日期，条件是交存在该日期后一个月时段届满前到达国际局。

（2）（a）如果国际局发现以下缺陷任何之一，应正式请求申请人在发出请求之日起三个月内改正缺陷，除非显然无法与他取得联系：

（i）国际交存书未包含它在本协定之下进行的指明；

（ii）国际交存书未包含有关申请人居所和国籍的指明以得出他有权进行国际交存的结论；

（iii）国际交存书未包含有关申请人的为识别和邮件到达他所必需的指明；

（iv）国际交存书未指明字体创作者的姓名或创作者放弃被以此提到之情况；

（v）国际交存书未签字；

（vi）国际交存书未使用条例规定的语文之一；

（vii）国际交存书未包含字体的呈现；

（viii）未缴纳规定的费用。

（b）如果适时改正缺陷，国际局应将国际交存登记在国际注册簿中，而国际交存的日期应是国际局收到缺陷改正的日期。

（c）如果未适时改正缺陷，国际局应拒绝国际交存，相应通知申请人，并按条例规定返还部分缴纳的费用。如果国际交存按第 12 条第（2）款的规定通过缔约国主管机构的中介进行，国际局还应将拒绝通知该机构。

第 16 条

避免拒绝的某些影响

（1）如果国际局拒绝国际交存．申请人可以在通知拒绝之日起两个月内，就国际交存对象的字体向任何通过设立专门国家交存或通过调适其国家工业设计法中规定的交存确认字体保护的缔约国的主管机构进行国家交存。

（2）如果该缔约国的主管机构或任何其他主管当局认为国际局错误地拒绝国际交存．只要国家交存符合该国国家法律的所有要求，该国家交存应被认为在倘若国际交存未被拒绝本来应是国际交存日的日期进行。

第 17 条

国际交存的公布和通知

登记在国际注册簿中的国际交存应由国际局公布并通知缔约国的主管机构。

第 18 条

国际交存的效力

（1）在根据第 34 条声明意图通过设立专门国家交存或通过调适其国家工业设计法规定的交存确认字体保护的缔约国，登记在国际注册簿中的国际交存应与在相同日期进行的国家交存具有相同效力。

（2）第（1）款中提到的缔约国不可以要求申请人履行任何另加的条件，其国家法律为权利的行使可能规定的手续除外。但是，实行依职权的新颖性审查或为异议程序做出规定的缔约国，可以规定此种审查或此种程序要求的手续，并收取其国家法律为此种审查、保护的准予和其延展规定的除公布费以外的费用。

第 19 条

优先权

（1）为优先权的目的，如果适用，字体的国际交存应被认为是《巴黎公约》第 4A 条意思中的工业设计交存。

（2）如果国际交存未被根据本协定第 15 条第（2）款（c）项拒绝，应是《巴黎公约》第 4A 条意思中的正常提交，并应被认为已在本协定第 15 条第（1）款或第

（2）款（b）项之下给予的日期进行。

第 20 条

国际交存所有权的变更

（1）国际交存所有权的任何变更，应经请求由国际局登记在国际注册簿中。

（2）如果根据请求登记变更的人提供的指明，国际交存的新所有者无权进行国际交存，国际交存所有权的变更不得被登记在国际注册簿中。

（3）国际交存所有权的变更可以涉及第 18 条第（1）款提到中的一个或更多缔约国。在此种情况下，国际交存的延展必须随后由国际交存的每个所有者在与其相关的范围内分别申请。

（4）国际交存所有权变更登记的请求，应以条例规定的形式并连同条例规定的费用提交。

（5）国际局应将国际交存所有权的变更登记在国际注册簿中，予以公布，并通知缔约国的主管机构。

（6）国际注册簿中国际交存所有权变更的登记，应与此种登记的请求直接向第 18 条第（1）款提到中的每个与该所有权变更有关缔约国的主管机构提出具有同样的效力。

第 21 条

国际交存的撤回和放弃

（1）申请人可以通过给国际局的声明撤回他的国际交存。

（2）国际字体所有者可以随时向国际局声明放弃他的国际字体。

（3）撤回和放弃可以涉及国际字体交存对象的字体的一部分或整体，或涉及其命名，以及涉及第 18 条第（1）款提到中的一个或更多缔约国。

（4）国际局应将放弃登记在国际注册簿中，予以公布，并通知缔约国的主管机构。

（5）在国际注册簿中登记的放弃，应与它被直接通知每个第 18 条第（1）款中提到缔约国的主管机构具有同样的效力。

第 22 条

国际交存的其他更改

（1）国际交存的所有者可以随时更改国际交存书中出现的指明。

（2）作为国际交存对象的字体不可以更改。

（3）更改应以缴纳条例规定的费用为条件。

（4）国际局应将更改登记在国际注册簿中，予以公布，并通知缔约国的主管机构。

（5）在国际注册簿中登记的更改，应具有与它们被直接通知每个第18条第（1）款中提到缔约国的主管机构同样的效力。

第23条

国际交存的期限和延展

（1）国际交存应自交存之日起在一个初始的十年期间有效。

（2）国际交存的效力可以根据国际交存所有者提出的延展请求不断以五年的期限延长。

（3）每个新期限应在前一期限终止之日的翌日开始。

（4）延展请求应以条例规定的形式并附带条例规定的费用提交。

（5）国际局应将延展登记在国际注册簿中，予以公布，并通知缔约国的主管机构。

（6）国际交存的延展应取代国家法律中可能规定的更新。但是，在任何第18条第（1）款中提到的缔约国，国际交存不可以在该国国家法律中规定的最长保护期限终止后有效。

第24条

地区条约

（1）两个或更多缔约国可以通知总干事，以一个共同的机构代替它们各自的国家机构，以及它们的领土作为一个整体为国际交存的目的应被视为一个单一国家。

（2）此种通知在总干事收到之日后三个月生效。

第25条

国际局程序中的代表

（1）国际交存的申请人和所有者可以在国际局的程序中由他们明确委托的任何人作为代表（“正式任命的代表”）。

（2）国际局发给正式任命的代表的任何正式请求、通知或其他信函，应与它被发给国际交存的申请人或所有者具有同样的效力。任何交存、请求、要求、声明或其他文件，在国际局的程序中要求由申请人或所有者签字的，任命代表或撤销其任命的文件除外，可以由正式任命的代表签字，并且，正式任命的代表发给国际局的任何信函，应与它由申请人或所有者发给具有同样的效力。

（3）（a）有若干申请人的，应任命一名共同代表。没有此种任命的，国际交存书中首先被提到的申请人应被认为是所有申请人的正式任命的代表。

（b）一项国际交存有若干所有者的，应任命一名共同代表。没有此种任命的，国际交存书中所述所有者当中首先被提到的自然人或法律实体，应被认为是该国际交存的全体所有者的正式任命的共同代表。

（c）（b）项不得在所有者就不同缔约国拥有国际交存的情况下适用。

第三章　行政条款

第 26 条

大会

（1）（a）大会由缔约国组成。

（b）每个缔约国的政府由一名会议代表作为代表，会议代表可有候补代表、顾问和专家协助。

（2）（a）大会应：

（i）处理与联盟的维持和发展以及本协定的实施有关的所有事项；

（ii）行使和执行本协定之下赋予的权力和任务；

（iii）就修订会议的筹备给总干事以指示；

（iv）审查和批准总干事与联盟有关的报告和活动，并就联盟职权内的所有事项给他以必要的指示；

（v）确定项目，通过联盟的三年度预算，批准其决算；

（vi）通过联盟的财务规章；

（vii）成立它认为于便利联盟及其机构工作适宜的委员会和工作组；

（viii）确定哪些缔约国以外国家以及哪些政府间组织和国际非政府间组织应被接受作为观察员参加会议；

（ix）采取任何其他行动促进联盟目标并履行其他在本协定之下恰当的职能。

（b）对于亦与产权组织管理的其他联盟有关的事项，大会应在听取产权组织协调委员会的意见后做出决议。

（3）一名会议代表只可以代表一个缔约国和以一个缔约国的名义投票。

（4）每个缔约国拥有一票。

（5）（a）半数缔约国构成法定人数。

（b）不够法定人数的，大会可以做出决议，但是，所有此种决议，与其自身程序有关的除外，应仅在按条例规定通过信函投票取得法定人数和要求多数的情况下生效。

（6）（a）以第29条第（3）款和第32条第（2）款（b）项为条件，大会决议需要投票的多数。

（b）弃权不视为投票。

（7）（a）大会应在总干事召集下每三个历年以例会开会一次，以与产权组织大会在同一时段和同一地点为宜。

（b）大会应由总干事自己主动或应四分之一缔约国的请求召集非常会议。

（8）大会应通过自己的程序规则。

第27条

国际局

（1）国际局应：

（i）执行与联盟有关的行政任务，尤其应执行本协定之下或由大会分派的任务；

（ii）担任修订会议、大会、大会成立的委员会和工作组以及任何其他由总干事召集和处理与联盟有关事项的会议的秘书处。

（2）总干事是联盟的首席执行官并代表联盟。

（3）总干事应召集大会成立的任何委员会和工作组的以及所有其他处理与联盟有关事项的会议。

（4）（a）总干事或由他指定的任何工作人员，应参加大会、大会成立的委员会和工作组的会议以及由总干事召集的任何其他处理与联盟有关事项的会议，但无表决权。

（b）总干事或由他指定的一名工作人员凭借职权应是大会、委员会和工作组以及（a）项中提到的其他会议的秘书。

（5）（a）总干事应根据大会的指示为修订会议进行筹备。

（b）总干事可以就修订会议的筹备与政府间和国际非政府间组织磋商。

（c）总干事和由他指定的人应参加修订会议的讨论，但无表决权。

（d）总干事和由他指定的一名工作人员凭借职权应是任何修订会议的秘书。

第28条

财务

（1）（a）联盟应有一部预算。

（b）联盟的预算应包括联盟本身的收入和开支，它对产权组织管理的其他联盟的开支预算的贡献，以及向产权组织会议预算提供的任何款项。

（c）不完全属于联盟而亦属于产权组织管理的其他一个或更多联盟的开支，应被认为是各联盟的共同开支。联盟在此种共同开支中的份额，应与联盟在其中的利益相称。

（2）制定联盟的预算，应适当考虑与产权组织管理的其他联盟的预算相协调的要求。

（3）（a）联盟的预算应从以下来源获得资金：

（i）国际局与联盟有关服务的计费和收费；

（ii）国际局与联盟有关出版物的销售或版税；

（iii）捐赠、遗赠和资助；

（iv）租金、利息和其他杂项收入；

（v）缔约国的会费，只要由（i）至（iv）之下提到来源产生的收入不足以弥补联盟的开支。

（b）在（a）项（i）之下应付给国际局的计费和收费的数额以及其出版物的价格，应以在正常情况下足以弥补国际局与本协定管理有关的开支确定。

（c）如果收入超过开支，差额应被转入储备基金。

（d）如果预算未在新的财务时段开始前通过，根据财务规章的规定，应与前一年预算的水平相同。

（4）（a）为确定其在第（3）款（a）项（v）中规定的会费，每个缔约国应属于一个级别，并应根据以下确定的单位缴纳其会费：

第一级…… 25

第二级…… 20

第三级…… 15

第四级…… 10

第五级…… 5

第六级…… 3

第七级…… 1

（b）除非已经这样做，每个国家应在交存批准或加入书的同时表明希望所属的级别。任何国家可以更换级别。如果选择一个更低的级别，必须在其一次例会上向大会声明。任何此种更换应在该次会议后一个历年的开始生效。

（c）每个缔约国会费的数额在缴纳会费总额中所占的比例，应与其单位数在所有缔约国单位总数中所占的比例相同。

（d）会费应在缴费年度的1月1日缴纳。

（5）（a）联盟应有一项由每个缔约国的单笔缴纳构成的工作基金。如果基金出现不足，大会应安排增加。如果部分基金不再需要，应予返还。

（b）每个缔约国向所述基金的最初缴纳或它在其增加中分担的数额，应是该缔约国可以在第（3）款（a）项（v）之下须缴纳的会费的一定比例。

（c）缴纳的比例和期限应由大会根据总干事的建议和在听取产权组织协调委员会的意见后决定。

（d）任何（a）项之下的返还，应与每个缔约国缴纳的数额相称，其中考虑缴纳日期。

（e）如果能够通过向储备基金借款形成足够的工作基金，大会可以中止（a）至（b）项的适用。

（6）（a）与产权组织总部所在地国家签订的总部协议中应当规定，一旦工作基金不足，此国家应提供预付金。预付金的数额和提供条件，应每一次由此国家和产权组织之间的另外协议规定。如果不是一个缔约国，只要继续有义务提供预付金，此国家凭借此地位应在大会中拥有一个席位。

（b）（a）项中提到的国家和产权组织应各自有权以书面通知声明提供预付金的义务无效。声明无效应在通知之年的年底之后三年生效。

（7）账目审计应依照财务规章中的规定由一个或更多缔约国或由外部审计者进行。它们应经自身同意由大会指定。

第29条

条例

（1）条例规定与以下有关的规则：

（i）本协定就其明确提到条例或明确规定对其有或应有规定的事项；

（ii）任何行政要求、事宜或程序；

（iii）任何于实施本协定有用的细节。

（2）与本协定同时通过的条例为本协定的附件。

（3）大会可以更改条例，此种更改需要投票的三分之二。

（4）本协定的条款与条例的条款有冲突的，本协定的条款应优先。

第四章　争议

第 30 条

争议

（1）两个或更多缔约国之间与本协定的解释或适用有关的任何争议，谈判解决不成的，可以由有关缔约国任何之一根据国际法院章程通过申请提交国际法院裁决，除非有关缔约国同意某个其他解决方法。将争议提交国际法院的缔约国应通知国际局；国际局应将此事项提请其他缔约国注意。

（2）每一缔约国可以在签署本协定或交存批准或加入书时，声明不认为自己受第（1）款的约束。对于任何作出此种声明的缔约国和任何其他缔约国之间的任何争议，第（1）款的规定不适用。

（3）任何根据第（2）款的规定作出声明的缔约国，可以随时以给总干事的通知撤回其声明。

第五章　修订和更改

第 31 条

协定的修订

（1）本协定可以不时通过缔约国会议修订。

（2）任何修订会议的召集由大会决定。

（3）第 26 条、第 27 条、第 28 条和第 32 条可以通过修订会议或根据第 32 条的规定更改。

第 32 条

协定某些条款的更改

（1）（a）建议更改第 26 条、第 27 条、第 28 条和本条，可以由任何缔约国或由总干事提出。

（b）此种建议应由总干事在大会考虑它们之前至少六个月通知缔约国。

（2）（a）对第（1）款中提到条款的更改应由大会通过。

（b）通过需要投票的四分之三，条件是通过对第26条和对本条的任何更改需要投票的五分之四。

（3）（a）对第（1）款中提到条款的任何更改，应在总干事从大会通过更改时大会缔约国成员的四分之三收到根据其各自宪法程序进行的书面承认通知后一个月生效。

（b）如此承认的对所述条款的任何更改，应约束所有在大会通过更改时为缔约国的缔约国，条件是任何增加所述缔约国财政义务的更改应只约束通知接受此种更改的国家。

（c）任何已被承认和已根据（a）项的规定生效的更改，应约束所有在大会通过更改后成为缔约国的国家。

第六章　最后条款

第33条

参加协定

（1）（a）以（b）项为条件，任何是保护工业产权国际联盟或保护文学和艺术作品国际联盟的成员或是《世界版权公约》或后者公约修订本的参加方的国家，可以通过以下参加本协定：

（i）签署后交存批准书；

（ii）交存加入书。

（b）意图通过设立专门的国家交存或通过调适国家工业设计法中规定的交存确认字体保护的国家，只有是保护工业产权国际联盟的成员，才可以参加本协定。意图通过国家版权条款确认字体保护的国家，只有是保护文学和艺术作品国际联盟的成员或是《世界版权公约》或后者公约修订本的参加方，才可以参加本协定。

（2）批准或加入书应向总干事交存。

（3）《保护工业产权巴黎公约》斯德哥尔摩文本第24条应适用于本协定。

（4）第（3）款无论如何不得被理解为意味着一个缔约国承认或默认另一缔约国凭借该款使本公约对之适用的领土的现状。

第34条

与国内保护有关的声明

（1）在交存批准或加入书时，每个国家应通过给总干事的通知，声明它意图通过设立专门的国家交存，或者通过调适国家工业设计法中规定的交存，或者通过国家版权条款，或者通过这些种类保护的一个以上确认字体的保护。任何意图通过其国家版权条款确认字体保护的国家，应同时声明它是否意图将在一个缔约国有惯常居所的字体创作者视同该国国民的字体创作者。

（2）对根据第（1）款作出的声明的任何随后修改，应通过给总干事的进一步通知指明。

第 35 条

协定的生效

（1）本协定在五个国家交存批准或加入书后三个月生效。

（2）任何不在第（1）款提到的那些当中的国家，应在交存批准或加入书之日后三个月开始受本协定约束，除非在批准或加入书中指明一个较晚的日期。在后一情况下，本协定应在如此指明的日期对该国生效。

（3）但是，本协定第二章的条款，只有在本协定依第（1）款对其生效的国家中至少三个通过设立专门的国家交存或调适国家工业设计法中规定的交存为字体提供保护之日，才可以适用。为本款的目的，在第 24 条之下作出通知的参加同一地区条约的国家，应只计为一个国家。

第 36 条

保留

不允许对本协定做出第 30 条第（2）款之下的保留以外的保留。

第 37 条

协定参加方地位的丧失

任何缔约国，当不再符合第 33 条第（1）款（b）项陈述的条件，应停止作为本协定的参加方。

第 38 条

声明协定无效

（1）任何缔约国可以通过给总干事的通知声明本协定无效。

（2）声明无效应在总干事收到通知之日后一年生效。

（3）第（1）款中规定的无效声明的权利，不得由任何缔约国在参加本协定之日起满五年之前行使。

（4）（a）对于在任何缔约国的声明无效生效之日前一日享有第 12 条至第 25 条的利益的字体，本协定应在该国继续有效，直至以第 23 条第（6）款为条件根据第 23 条在该日正在持续中的保护期终止。

（b）同样的规定，在声明无效的国家以外的缔约国中，对于声明无效的国家的居民或国民拥有的国际交存，应当适用。

第 39 条

协定的签署和语文

（1）（a）协议以英文和法文的独一份原始件签署，两种文本具有同等效力。

（b）正式文本应由总干事在与利益相关政府磋商后以德文、意大利文、日文、葡萄牙文、俄文和西班牙文以及大会可以指定的其他语文制定。

（2）本协定在维也纳持续开放供签署，直至 1973 年 12 月 31 日。

第 40 条

保管事宜

（1）协定的原始件，当不再开放供签署，应由总干事保管。

（2）总干事应将本协定和所附条例的两份经他确认的复本传送所有第 33 条第（1）款（a）项中提到的国家的政府，并根据请求传送任何其他国家的政府。

（3）总干事应将本协定向联合国秘书处注册。

（4）总干事应将对本协定和条例的任何修改的两份经他确认的复本传送缔约国政府，并根据请求传送任何其他国家的政府。

第 41 条

通知

总干事应将以下事项通知第 33 条第（1）款（a）项中提到的国家的政府：

（i）在第 39 条之下的签署；

（ii）在第 33 条第（2）款之下批准或加入书的交存；

（iii）本协定在第 35 条第（1）款之下生效的日期和自它起第二章根据第 35 条第（3）款可以适用的日期；

（iv）在第 34 条之下通知的与国家保护有关的声明；

（v）第 24 条之下的与地区条约有关的通知；

（vi）在第 30 条第（2）款之下作出的声明；

（vii）在第 30 条第（3）款之下通知的对任何声明的撤回；

（viii）根据第 33 条第（3）款作出的声明和通知；

（ix）对本协定在第 32 条第（3）款之下的更改的承认；

（x）此种更改的生效日期；

（xi）在第 38 条之下收到的无效声明。

字体保护及其国际交存维也纳协定细则条例

目录*

* 为读者方便而增加，不出现在原始文本中。

与条例有关的细则

细则 1

简略语

1.1 “协定”

在条例中，“协定”一词指《字体保护及其国际交存维也纳协定》。

1.2 “条款”

在条例中，“条款”一词指协定的具体条款。

1.3 “公报”

在条例中，“公报”一词指字体国际公报。

1.4 “费用表”

在条例中，“费用表”一词指条例所附的费用表。

与协定第二章有关的细则

细则 2

国际局程序中的代表

2.1 正式任命的代表的数目

（a）申请人和国际交存的所有者只可以任命一名代表。

（b）如果申请人或国际交存的所有者指明若干自然人或法律实体为代表，在指明他们的文件中首先提到的自然人或法律实体应被认为是唯一的正式任命的代表。

（c）代表是由律师或专利或商标代理人组成的合伙或公司的，应被认为是一个代表。

2.2 任命的形式

（a）代表应被认为是“正式任命的代表”，如果其任命符合（b）至（e）项的规定。

（b）对任何代表的任命应要求：

（i）其名字在国际交存书中作为代表的名字出现，并且此文件载有申请人的签字；

（ii）或者向国际局另外递交一份经申请人或国际交存的所有者签字的委托书

（即任命代表的文件）。

（c）如果有若干申请人或国际交存的所有者，包含或构成对其共同代表之任命的文件应经所有人签字。

（d）任何包含或构成对代表之任命的文件应指明他的名字和地址。如果代表是自然人，名字以姓和名指明，姓在名的前面。如果代表是法律实体或律师或专利或商标代理人的合伙或公司，"名字"指法律实体或合伙或公司的全称。代表的地址应以与细则 5.2（c）项中就申请人规定的相同的方式指明。

（e）包含或构成任命的文件，不得包含有悖于第 25 条第（2）款将代表的权利限于某些事项或将某些事项排除于代表权力或从时间上限制此种权力的措词。

（f）如果任命不符合（b）至（e）项的要求，应被国际局认为如同没有作出，此情况应由国际局通知国际交存的申请人或所有者以及看来是任命中被指明为代表的自然人、法律实体、合伙或公司。

（g）行政指令应当为任命提供建议的措词。

2.3 任命的撤销或放弃

（a）对任何代表的任命可以随时由任命该代表的自然人或法律实体撤销。即使任命代表的自然人或法律实体中只有一个撤销任命，撤销应有效。

（b）撤销应有经（a）项中提到的自然人或法律实体签字的书面文件。

（c）细则 2.2 中规定的对代表的任命，应被认为是撤销任何早先对任何其他代表的任命。该任命以指明其他更早任命的代表的名字为宜。

（d）任何代表可以通过经他签字并送交国际局的通知放弃对他的任命。

2.4 总委托书

以另外的委托书（即任命代表的文件）对代表的任命，可以是总的任命，即涉及一个以上国际交存书和同一有关自然人或法律实体的一个以上的国际交存。此种国际交存书和此种国际交存的识别，以及与此种总委托书和它的撤销或放弃有关的细节，应在行政指令中规定。行政指令可以规定提交总委托书应缴纳的相关费用。

2.5 替补代表

（a）细则 2.2（b）项中提到的对代表的任命，亦可以指明一个或更多自然人作为替补代表。

（b）为第 25 条第（2）款第二段的目的，替补代表应被认为是代表。

（c）对任何替补代表的任命，可以随时由任命代表的自然人或法律实体或由代表撤销。撤销需要经该自然人、法律实体或代表签字的书面文件。就国际局而言，它应从该局收到所述文件之日起有效。

2.6 登记、通知和公布

代表或替补代表的每项任命、撤销和放弃，应被登记、通知申请人或国际交存的所有者、公布和通知缔约国的主管机构。

细则 3

国际注册簿

3.1 国际注册簿的内容；国际注册簿的维持

（a）就登记在其中的每项国际交存，国际注册簿应包含：

（i）所有在协定或条例之下必须或可以提交的和已实际提交国际局的指明以及，如果相关，国际局收到此种说明的日期；

（ii）交存的字体的展示；

（iii）国际交存的编号和日期，以及与该交存有关的所有登记的日期和如有的编号；

（iv）所有收到付费的数额以及被国际局收到的日期；

（v）协定或条例规定登记的任何其他指明。

（b）行政指令应规制国际注册簿的建立，并且，以协定和条例为条件，应明确它藉以维持的形式，以及国际局为在其中进行登记和为保护其免遭丢失或其他损坏应遵循的程序。

细则 4

申请人；国际交存的所有者

4.1 若干申请人；国际交存的若干所有者

（a）如果有若干申请人，只有所有的人是缔约国的居民或国民，才有进行国际交存的权利。

（b）如果一项国际交存有若干所有者，只有所有的人是缔约国的居民或国民，才有拥有此交存的权利。

细则 5

国际交存书的规定内容

5.1 在协定之下进行国际交存的声明

（a）第 14 条第（1）款（i）项中提到的声明，应措词如下：

“下方签字人请求，所附展示中的字体的交存，被登记在《字体保护及其国际交存维也纳协定》之下设立的国际注册簿中。”

（b）但是，如果意思相同，声明可以有不同的措词。

5.2 与申请人有关的指明

（a）申请人的身份应以其名字指明。如果申请人是自然人，名字应以姓和名指明，姓在名的前面。如果申请人是法律实体，名称应以该实体的正式全称指明。

（b）申请人的居所和国籍应以它是其居民和是其国民的国家的名称指明。

（c）申请人地址的指明，应满足向指明的地址及时递送邮件的通常要求，并无论如何应包含所有行政单元，直至并包括如果有的房屋号码。申请人可能有的电报和电传打字电报地址以及电话号码，应以指明为宜。对每个申请人，只应指明一个地址；如果指明若干申请人，应只考虑国际交存书中最先提到的一个。

（d）如果申请人以在一个缔约国有真实和有效的工业或商业机构为根据有权进行国际交存，应提到该情况并具体说明涉及的国家。

5.3 字体创作者的名字

字体创作者应以其名字指明。其名字应包含姓和名，姓在名前面指明。

5.4 与字体有关的指明

国际交存书应指明载有交存对象字体之展示的纸页的数目。

5.5 与费用有关的指明

国际交存书应指明已缴纳的数额并包含细则 22.5 规定的其他指明。

5.6 通过缔约国主管机构的中介进行的国际交存

第 12 条第（2）款（b）项中提到的指明应措词如下：

“……（1）证明本国际交存于…（2）由它收到。”

（1）指明主管机构的名称。（2）指明日期。

细则 6

国际交存的选择内容

6.1 代表的提名

国际交存书可以指明一名代表。

6.2 主张优先权

（a）第 14 条第（2）款（i）项中提到的声明，应包含意思为主张一项早先交存的优先权的陈述，并应指明：

（i）如果早先交存不是一项国际交存，进行早先交存所在的国家；

（ii）如果早先交存不是一项国际交存，该交存的性质（字体交存或工业设计交存）；

（iii）早先交存的日期；

（iv）早先交存的编号。

（b）如果声明未包含（a）项（i）至（iii）中提到的指明，国际局应视该声明没有作出。

（c）如果声明中未指明（a）项（iv）中提到的早先交存的编号，但由申请人或国际交存的所有者在早先交存之日起满十个月之前提交，应被认为已经包含在声明中并应由国际局公布。

（d）如果声明中指明的早先交存的日期在国际交存的日期之前超过六个月，国际局应视该声明没有作出。

（e）如果第14条第（2）款（i）项中提到的声明主张一项以上早先交存的优先权，（a）至（d）项的规定应适用于其中每一项。

6.3 字体的命名

如果一个命名只涉及字体的一部分，国际交存书应明确指出它涉及的那些。指明一个以上命名的，适用同样规定。

细则 7

国际交存书、登记、通知和函件的语文

7.1 国际交存书的语文

（a）国际交存书应使用英语或法语。

（b）行政指令可以规定，细则8.1中提到的示范格式的标题还应使用英语和法语以外的语文。

7.2 登记、通知和信函的语文

（a）国际局的登记和通知应使用与国际交存书相同的语文。

（b）国际局与申请人或国际交存的所有者之间的信函，应使用与国际交存书相同的语文。

（c）缔约国主管机构给国际局的信件或其他函件应使用英语或法语。

（d）国际局给任何缔约国主管机构的信件，应根据该机构的意愿使用英语或法语；此种信件中任何引自国际注册簿的事项，应使用此事项出现在该注册簿中使用的语文。

（e）如果国际局有义务将任何（c）项中提到的函件转交申请人或国际交存的

所有者，应以收到它们的语文转交。

细则 8

国际交存书的格式

8.1 示范表格

（a）国际交存书应根据国际局颁布的示范表格制定。国际局应根据请求免费提供示范表格的印制复本。

（b）表格应以打字填写为宜并应可以容易地辨读。

8.2 份数；签字

（a）国际交存书应以一份提交。

（b）国际交存书应经申请人签字。

8.3 不得有另加事项

（a）国际交存书不得包含并不得伴随有本协定和条例规定或允许以外的任何事项和任何文件。

（b）如果国际交存书包含规定或允许以外的事项，国际局应依职权将其删除；如果伴随有规定或允许以外的任何文件，国际局应视其没有被送交给它并应将该文件退还申请人。

细则 9

字体的展示

9.1 展示的形式

（a）国际交存对象的字体，应在与国际交存书分开的一张或更多张 A4 尺寸（29.7 厘米 ×21 厘米）纸的单面上展示。每张纸自所有四边应至少留有 1.5 厘米的空白。

（b）展示字母和符号，一套内最高的字母或符号应不低于 10 毫米，并且，它们应以通常的字母间空隙相互分开。

（c）字体的展示还应包括不短于三行的由国际交存对象的字母排印的文字。该文字无需一定使用英语或法语，或以（b）项之下要求的最低尺寸。

（d）字体的展示，应具有可以通过影印和印刷方法直接复制的质量。

9.2 其他指明

展示字体的纸页还应载有申请人的名字和签字。如果有若干纸页，每张应包含同样的指明并且每张应标有页码。

细则 10

国际交存应缴纳的费用

10.1 费用的种类和数额

（a）国际交存应缴纳的费用是：

（i）交存费；

（ii）公布费。

（b）这些费用每项的数额在费用表中指明。

细则 11

国际交存中的缺陷

11.1 拒绝国际交存的通知和公布费的返还

如果国际局在第 15 条第（2）款（c）项之下拒绝国际交存，应通知申请人，陈述拒绝的理由，并应向其返还已经缴纳的公布费。

11.2 通过缔约国主管机构的中介进行的国际交存特有的缺陷

如果在第 12 条第（2）款之下通过缔约国主管机构的中介提交的国际交存书：

（i）未指明申请人是通过其主管机构的中介进行国际交存的国家的居民；

（ii）或者未包含该机构指明收到所述交存之日期的陈述；

（iii）或者包含该陈述，指明一个在国际局收到国际交存的日期之前超过一个月的日期，国际交存应被视为已经在到达国际局之日直接向它进行。国际局应就此通知通过其中介进行国际交存的机构。

细则 12

寻求避免拒绝的某些影响的程序

12.1 向缔约国主管机构提供的信息

根据申请人或有关主管机构的请求，国际局应将被拒绝的国际交存的案卷的复本，连同一份陈述拒绝该申请的理由和达至拒绝的各个步骤的备忘录，送交该机构。

细则 13

国际交存证书

13.1 国际交存证书

一俟国际局登记国际交存，应向其所有者颁发一份国际交存证书，证书的内容在行政指令中规定。

细则 14

国际交存的公布

14.1 国际交存的公布的内容

任何国际交存的公布应包含：

（i）申请人的名字和地址以及，如果基于是其地址所在以外一个国家的居民或国民或在该国家有真实和有效的工业或商业机构而有权进行国际交存，他是其居民或国民或他在其中有真实和有效的工业或商业机构的国家的名称；

（ii）字体创作者的名字或指明创作者放弃被以此提及；

（iii）字体的呈现，包括细则 9.1（c）项中提到的文字，其展示和尺寸与交存时相同的；

（iv）国际交存的日期；

（v）国际交存的编号；

（vi）如果主张优先权，细则 6.2（a）项中列举的指明；

（vii）如果任命代表，代表的名字和地址；

（viii）如果为字体指明命名，该命名。

细则 15

国际交存的通知

15.1 通知的形式

第 17 条中提到的通知应对每个主管机构分别进行，并应包含国际局每项国际交存公布本的另外重印本。

15.2 通知的时间

通知应在公布国际交存的一期公报之日的同日进行。

细则 16

所有权的变更

16.1 所有权变更登记的请求

（a）请求进行第 20 条第（1）款中提到的登记，应指明其目的并包含：

（i）在国际注册簿中以所有者出现的国际交存的所有者（以下称“原先所有者”）的名字；

（ii）国际交存的新所有者（以下称“新所有者”）的名字、居所、国籍和地址，以细则 5.2 之下为提供与申请人有关的指明规定的方式；

（iii）国际交存的编号；

（iv）如果所有权变更涉及的少于所有第 18 条第（1）款中提到的缔约国，对所涉及的那些国家的指明。

（b）请求书应经原先所有者签字或者，如果无法得到他的签字，经新所有者签字，条件是，如果由新所有者签字，请求书应附带早先所有者在所有权变更时是其国民的缔约国的主管机构或者，如果原先所有者在该时间不是一个缔约国的国民，他在该时间是其居民的缔约国的主管机构的证明书。主管机构应证明，根据向其出具的证据，新所有者在请求书中讲述的程度上看来是原先所有者的合法继承人，并且前句中规定的条件得到满足。证明书应注有日期并应带有主管机构的图章或封印以及其官员的签字。提供证明书应仅为使所有权变更登记到国际注册簿中的目的。

（c）第 20 条第（40）款中提到的费用在费用表中指明。

16.2 登记、通知和公布；登记请求的拒绝

（a）如果根据所有权变更请求书中提供的指明，新所有者是有权拥有国际交存的人，并且请求符合其他规定的要求，国际局应就所有或请求书中指明的那些缔约国登记所有权的变更。此种登记应包含细则 16.1（a）项（ii）和（iv）中提到的指明，并应提及进行登记的日期。

（b）国际局应将所有权变更的登记通知原先和新的所有者。

（c）第 20 条第（5）款中提到的公布和通知，应包含细则 16.1（a）项中提到的指明和登记的日期。

（d）如果根据所有权变更请求书中提供的指明，新所有者是无权拥有国际交存的人，或如果请求书不符合其他规定的要求，国际局应予拒绝，通知在请求书上签字的人并陈述拒绝的理由。

细则 17

国际交存的撤回和放弃

17.1 国际交存的撤回

国际交存的任何撤回应被国际局作为撤回处理，如果撤回声明在公布准备完成之前到达国际局。如果声明后来到达国际局，应被作为放弃国际交存处理。

17.2 程序

（a）撤回和放弃应通过发给国际局并经申请人或国际交存的所有者签字的书面声明进行。

（b）如果仅为部分撤回或放弃，应明确指明所涉及的国家或字体，否则将不被考虑。

（c）国际局应告知收到撤回声明。如果为全部撤回，国际局应向申请人返还已经缴纳的公布费。

（d）国际局应对放弃进行登记，将登记通知国际交存的所有者，将放弃进行公布并通知缔约国的主管机构。

细则 18

对国际交存的其他更改

18.1 允许的更改

国际交存的所有者可以根据细则 5.2、细则 5.3、细则 6.1 和细则 6.3 更改国际交存书中出现的规定和选择性的指明。

18.2 程序

（a）任何细则 18.1 中提到的更改，应通过发给国际局并经国际交存的所有者签字的书面信函进行。

（b）第 22 条第（3）款中提到的费用在费用表中指明。

（c）国际局应对更改进行登记，将登记通知国际交存的所有者，将更改进行公布并通知缔约国的主管机构。

细则 19

国际交存的续展

19.1 国际局的提醒函

国际局应在有效中初始或续展的期限届满之前致函国际交存的所有者，通知它此期限将届满。与提醒函内容有关的更多细节应在行政指令中规定。提醒函应在届满之日至少六个月前发出。未发送或收到提醒函，或在所述时段之外发送或收到，或提醒函中的任何错误，不影响届满日期。

19.2 续展请求

请求第 23 条第（4）款中提到的续展，宜用国际局免费提供的印制表格连同细则 19.1 中提到的提醒函提出。请求应无论如何指明目的并包含：

（i）国际交存的所有者的名字和地址；

（ii）国际交存的编号。

19.3 时限；费用

（a）以（b）项为条件，续展请求和第 23 条第（4）款中提到的费用应不晚于保护期届满后六个月到达国际局。

（b）如果续展请求或应付的费用在保护期届满后到达国际局，续展应以缴纳必须在（a）项中确定的时限内缴纳的附加费为条件。

（c）如果国际局在（a）项中确定的时限内收到：

（i）不符合细则 19.2 要求的续展请求；

（ii）或者续展请求但无缴费或不足以弥补应缴费用的缴费；

（iii）或者似乎用于弥补与续展有关费用的钱款，但没有续展请求，应及时正式请求国际交存的所有者提交正确的请求并缴纳或补齐应缴纳的费用，或提交一项请求。正式请求应指明适用的时限。

（d）未发送或收到（c）项中提到的正式请求，或发送或接收正式请求有任何延迟，或正式请求中有任何错误，不得延长（a）和（b）项中确定的时限。

（e）本细则之下规定的费用的数额在费用表中指明。

19.4 续展的登记、通知和公布

国际局应对续展进行登记，将登记通知国际交存的所有者，公布细则 19.2 中提到的指明，连同续展终止日期的指明，并将该指明和日期通知缔约国的主管机构。

19.5 续展请求的拒绝

（a）如果未遵守细则 19.2（a）项中确定的时限，或者续展请求不符合细则 19.2 的要求，或者未按规定缴纳应缴纳的费用，国际局应拒绝请求，通知国际交存的所有者并陈述拒绝请求的理由。

（b）国际局不得在续展期开始之日后满六个月之前拒绝任何续展请求。

19.6 无续展请求的登记、通知和公布

如果至续展期开始之日后满六个月没有向国际局提交续展请求，国际局应将此情况登记，通知国际交存的所有者，予以公布并通知缔约国的主管机构。

细则 20

向国际局传送文件

20.1 传往地点和方式

国际交存书及其附件、请求书、通知书和任何其他用于向国际局提交、通知或另外传送的文件，应在行政指令中规定的工作时间向国际局主管部门交存或邮寄给该局。

20.2 收到文件的日期

国际局通过交存或邮寄收到的任何文件，应被视为在国际局实际收到的日期收到，条件是，当它实际在工作时间后或者在国际局关闭业务之日被收到，应被视为在国际局下一个业务开放日收到。

20.3 法律实体；合伙和公司

（a）如果任何提交国际局的文件要求经一个法律实体签字，法律实体的名称应在用于签字的地方指明，并伴随有根据法律实体依其法律成立之国家的国家法律有权为此种法律实体签字的一名或数名自然人的签字。

（b）（a）项的规定经必要修改适用于由律师或专利或商标代理人组成的但不是法律实体的合伙或公司。

20.4 确认的免除

对在协定或条例之下提交国际局的文件，不得要求签字的鉴定、法律认可或其他确认。

细则 21

历法；时限的计算

21.1 历法

为协定和条例的目的，国际局、缔约国主管机构、申请人和国际交存的所有者应以公元纪年和格雷戈里历法表示任何日期。

21.2 以年、月或日表示的时段

（a）当一个时段以一年或某一数量的年表示，计算应从相关事件发生之日的翌日开始，并且，该时段应在相关的下接年份在与该事件发生的月份和日期有相同名称和相同数字的月份和日期终止，条件是，如果相关的下接月份没有相同数字的日期，该时段应在该月份的最后一天终止。

（b）当一个时段以一个月或某一数量的月表示，计算应从相关事件发生之日的翌日开始，并且，该时段应在相关的下接月份在与该事件发生的日期有相同数字的日期终止，条件是，如果相关的下接月份没有相同数字的日期，该时段应在该月份的最后一天终止。

（c）当一个时段以某一数量的天表示，计算应从相关事件发生之日的翌日开始，并且，该时段应在计数到达最后之日的一天终止。

21.3 当地日期

（a）被考虑作为任何时段起算日的日期，应是在相关事件发生时的地点通行的日期。

（b）任何时段终止的日期，应是在提交要求的文件或缴纳要求的费用所在的地点通行的日期。

21.4 在非工作日终止

任何时段，任何文件或费用必须在其中到达国际局的，如果在该局不办公或在日内瓦不投递普通邮件的一天终止，应在下一个两种所述情况均不存在的日期终止。

细则 22

费用

22.1 应缴纳的费用

（a）在协定和条例之下应缴纳的费用在费用表和在行政指令中确定。

（b）应缴纳的费用是：

（i）如果涉及国际交存，在国际交存收到之日有效的费用或者，如果交存通过缔约国主管机构的中介提交，在该机构收到费用之日有效的费用；

（ii）如果涉及续展请求，在续展期限开始之日前六个月的日期有效的费用。

22.2 向国际局缴纳

所有应缴纳的费用应向国际局缴纳。

22.3 货币

所有应缴纳的费用应以瑞士法郎缴纳。

22.4 预存账户

（a）任何自然人或法律实体可以在国际局开设一个预存账户。

（b）与预存账户有关的细节应在行政指令中规定。

22.5 缴纳方式的指明

（a）除非以现金向国际局的出纳缴纳，国际交存、请求以及联系任何国际交存向国际局提交的任何其他要求或其他文件，以缴纳任何费用为条件的，应指明：

（i）进行缴纳的自然人或法律实体的名字和地址，如细则 5.2（a）项中规定的，除非缴纳以附于文件的支票进行；

（ii）缴纳的方式，可以是授权将费用数额记入此人的预存账户，或是通过向国际局的银行账户或邮政支票账户转账，或是以支票。行政指令应规定细节，尤其是规制缴纳中应被接受的支票的种类的。

（b）如果缴纳根据将费用数额记入预存账户的授权进行，该授权应明确指出所涉及的事项，除非有将涉及某申请人、国际交存的所有者或正式任命的代表的任何费用记入具体预存账户的总授权。

（c）如果缴纳通过向国际局的银行账户或邮政支票账户转账，或以未附于国际交存书、续展请求或任何其他要求或其他文件的支票进行，转账或支票（或伴随它的票据）应以行政指令中规定的方式指明缴纳涉及的事项。

22.6 进行缴纳的日期

任何缴纳应被国际局认为在以下指明的日期收到：

（i）如果以现金向国际局的出纳缴纳，在进行此种缴纳的日期；

（ii）如果缴纳根据记账的总授权通过记入在国际局的预存账户进行，在国际局收到必然涉及缴纳费用义务的国际交存书、续展请求或任何其他要求或其他文件的日期，或者，在特定记账授权的情况下，在国际局收到特定授权的日期；

（iii）如果缴纳通过向国际局的银行账户或邮政支票账户转账进行，在款项被记入此种账户的日期；

（iv）如果缴纳以支票进行，在国际局收到支票的日期，条件是在提交支票开具的银行时被承兑。

细则 23

公报

23.1 内容

（a）国际局根据协定或条例有义务公布的所有事项应在公报中公布。

（b）行政指令可以规定将其他事项收入公报中。

23.2 频率

公报应根据需求发布，从而任何要求公布的交存或信函得以在三个月内公布。

23.3 语文

（a）公报应以双语（英语和法语）版发布。

（b）行政指令应指出要求翻译的部分和不要求翻译的部分。

（c）如果事项以两种语文公布，公报应指明哪个是原始语文。译文应由国际局准备。原始本和译文之间有任何差异的，所有法律效力应由原始本规制。

23.4 销售

公报的销售价格应在行政指令中确定。

23.5 给缔约国主管机构的公报复本

（a）每年7月1日之前，各缔约国的主管机构应将它希望在下接年份收到的公报复本的数目通知国际局。

（b）国际局向各主管机构提供所要求数目的复本：

（i）应免收费用，数目直至与主管机构所属缔约国在第28条第（4）款之下选择的级别相应的单位数相同；

（ii）对超过所述数目的复本应收销售价格的一半。

（c）免费供给的或在（b）项之下销售的复本，应供索取它们的主管机构内部使用。

细则 24

复本、摘录和信息；国际局颁发的文件的确认

24.1 复本、摘录和与国际交存有关的信息

（a）任何人可以通过缴纳行政指令中确定的费用从国际局获得任何国际交存的经确认或未经确认的复本，或国际注册簿中登记事项的摘录或案卷中的任何文件。每件复本或摘录应反映国际交存在一具体日期的状况；此日期应在该复本或摘录中指明。

（b）根据请求并通过缴纳行政指令中确定数额的费用，任何人可以从国际局获得与国际注册簿中和任何国际交存案卷内任何文件中出现的任何事实有关的口头或书面信息或通过电传复印装置的信息。

（c）尽管有（a）项和（b）项的规定，如果与提供复本、摘录或信息有关的工作或花费微不足道，行政指令可以不要求缴纳任何费用的义务。

24.2 国际局颁发的文件的确认

如果国际局颁发的任何文件载有该局的封印和总干事或代表他行事的人的签字，任何缔约国的当局不得要求由任何其他人或机构鉴定、法律认可或确认此文件或签字。

与协定第三章有关的细则

细则 25

代表团的开支

25.1 由政府负担的开支

每个参加大会和任何委员会、工作组或其他处理与联盟有关事项的机构的会议的代表团，其开支由委派它的政府负担。

细则 26

大会不够法定人数

26.1 通过信函投票

（a）在第 26 条第（5）款（b）项规定的情况下，国际局应将大会的与大会自己程序有关以外的任何决议传送做出决议时未参加的缔约国，并应正式请求它们在传送之日起三个月的时段内以书面表示投票或弃权。

（b）如果在所述时段终止时表示投票或弃权的缔约国的数目达到做出决议时取得法定人数所缺欠的缔约国的数目，该决议应有效，条件是同时仍然达到所要求的多数。

细则 27

行政指令

27.1 行政指令的制定；由其规制的事项

（a）总干事应制定行政指令。他可以修改指令。他应与在建议的行政指令或建议的修改中有直接利益关系的缔约国的主管机构磋商。

（b）行政指令应涉及条例明确诉诸此种指令的事项和与条例的实施有关的细节。

（c）所有与申请人和国际交存的所有者有关的表格应被包括在行政指令中。

27.2 由大会掌控

大会可以正式请求总干事修改行政指令的任何条款，总干事应照此进行。

27.3 公布和生效日期

（a）行政指令和其任何修改应在公报中公布。

（b）每次公布应具体说明公布的条款生效的日期。该日期无需对所有条款相同，条件是任何条款不可以在公布它的一期公报出版后一个月时段届满之前被宣布有效。

27.4 与协定和条例的冲突

行政指令的任何条款与协定或条例的任何条款有冲突的，应以后者为准。

最后条款

细则 28

生效

28.1 条例的生效

条例应与协定第二章在同一时间生效，细则 25 和细则 26 除外，它们应与协定本身在同一时间生效。

条例附件费用表

国际局应收取以下费用：

	瑞郎
I. 交存	
1.（a）交存费，上至 75 个字母或符号	500
（b）为每个另加的 10 个字母或符号的底版的补充费	100
2. 作为最低出版费的为每个用到的标准篇幅单元（26.7 厘米 × 18 厘米）的出版费	200
II 续展	
1. 续展费	600
2. 附加费（细则 19.3（b））	300
III. 其他费用	
1. 完全或部分变更所有权的登记费	100
2. 变更国际交存所有者名字或地址或与所有者有关其他指明的登记费：每次交存	100
3. 代表的任命、代表的变更或其名字或地址变更的登记费：每次交存	50
4. 任何其他更改的登记费	50

《字体保护及其国际交存维也纳协定》与保护期有关的议定书

参加《字体保护及其国际交存维也纳协定》（以下称“协定”）和参加本议定书的国家，就以下规定达成一致：

1. 保护期应为最短二十年而不是协定第 9 条第（1）款中提到的十五年。

2.（a）本议定书应开放供签署协定的国家签署。

（b）本议定书可以由签署议定书和批准协定的国家批准。

（c）本议定书应开放供尚未签署议定书但已经批准或加入协定的国家加入。

（d）本议定书应在三个国家交存本议定书的批准或加入书后三个月生效，但不得在协定本身生效之前。

（e）本议定书可以由议定书参加方国家的会议修订，该会议由总干事根据那些国家至少一半的请求召开。属于任何不与修订协定的会议在同一时段和同一地点举行的修订本议定书的会议的开支，应由参加本议定书的国家负担。

（f）协定第 30 条、第 33 条、第 35 条第（2）款、第 36 条、第 37 条、第 38 条、第 39 条、第 40 条以及第 41 条第（i）款、第（ii）款、第（iii）款、第（vi）款、第（vii）款、第（viii）款和第（xi）款经必要修改应适用。

与分播人造卫星传送的载有节目的信号有关的公约

（1974年5月21日在布鲁塞尔签署）

目录*

缔约国，

了解到利用人造卫星分播载有节目的信号在数量和地域覆盖上都在快速增长；

关切没有一个世界性的制度防止分播者分播非为其提供的由人造卫星传送的载有节目的信号，且这一缺失可能妨碍卫星通信的使用；

承认在此方面作者、表演者、唱片制作者和广播组织利益的重要性；

---

* 为编者所加，原文中无目录。

相信应建立一个国际体系，以在其之下规定措施，防止分播者分播非为其提供的由人造卫星传送的载有节目的信号；

意识到需要无论如何不损害已经生效的国际协议，包括《国际电信公约》和该公约附加的《无线电广播条例》，尤其是无论如何不妨碍保护表演者、唱片制作者和广播组织的 1961 年 10 月 26 日《罗马公约》得到更广泛承认，

达成一致如下：

第 1 条

[定义*]

为本公约的目的：

(i)“信号”是一种电子生成的能够传送节目的载波；

(ii)“节目”是以分播为最终目的发射的信号中包含的由图像、声音或两者组成的一套实况或录制的资料；

(iii)“人造卫星”是地球外层空间中任何能够传送信号的装置；

(iv)“发射的信号”或“被发射的信号”是去往或经由人造卫星的任何载有节目的信号；

(v)“衍生的信号”是通过改变发射的信号的技术特点获得的信号，无论是否有过一个或更多中间固定物；

(vi)“首播组织”是决定发射的信号承载何种节目的人或法律实体；

(vii)“分播者”是决定进行将衍生的信号传送给一般或任何一部分公众的人或法律实体；

(viii)“分播”是分播者进行操作将衍生的信号传送给一般或任何一部分公众。

第 2 条

[缔约国的义务]

（1）各缔约国承诺采取适当措施，防止任何分播者在或从其领土分播任何非为其提供的发射至或经由人造卫星的载有节目的信号。如果首播组织是另一缔约国的国民，且如果分播的信号是衍生的信号，此义务应适用。

（2）任何缔约国，对适用第（1）款中提到的措施有时间限制的，期限应由其国内法律确定。此种期限应在批准、承认或加入时，或如果国内法律在其后生效或更改，在法律生效或更改六个月内，书面通知联合国秘书长。

* 为编者所加，原文中条款无标题。

（3）第（1）款中规定的义务，不适用于分播从被提供发射信号的分播者已经分播的信号提取的衍生信号。

第3条

[对某些信号不适用]

如果由或代表首播组织发射的信号是为一般公众直接从人造卫星接收，本公约不得适用。

第4条

[限制和例外]

任何缔约国无须适用第2条第（1）款中提到的措施，如果所发射信号非为其提供的分播者在其领土上分播的信号：

(i) 载有由发射的信号载有的由时事报导组成的节目的短小摘录，但仅在与此种片断的提供消息的目的相符的程度上；

(ii) 或者作为引用载有由发射的信号载有的节目的短小摘录，条件是此种引用符合公平做法并与此种引用的提供消息的目的相符；

(iii) 或者在该领土属于一个按照联合国大会既定惯例被认为是发展中国家的缔约国的情况下，载有由发射的信号载有的节目，条件是分播仅为教学，包括成人教育范围的教学，或科学研究的目的。

第5条

[无追溯力]

任何缔约国无须对本公约在该国生效前发射的任何信号适用本公约。

第6条

[其他规定权利的保障]

本公约无论如何不得被解释为限制或损害在任何国内法律或国际协定之下给予作者、表演者、唱片制作者或广播组织的保护。

第7条

[防止滥用垄断的权利]

本公约无论如何不得被解释为限制任何缔约国为防止滥用垄断而适用其国内

法律的权利。

第8条

[保留]

（1）以第（2）款和第（3）款为条件，不允许对本公约做出保留。

（2）任何缔约国，其国内法律在1974年5月21日有此规定的，可以通过向联合国秘书长交存的书面通知声明，为它的目的，第2条第（1）款中出现的“如果首播组织是另一个缔约国的国民”的措词应被认为如同被“如果信号从另一缔约国的领土发射”的措词取代。

（3）（a）任何缔约国，在1974年5月21日对与通过有线、电缆或其他类似通讯渠道向公众中订户成员分播载有节目的信号有关的保护予以限制或拒绝，可以通过向联合国秘书长交存的书面通知声明，在其国内法律限制或拒绝保护的程度上和期间内，将不对此种分播适用本公约。

（b）任何已根据（a）款交存通知的缔约国，应将国内法律中关于不再适用该款之下的保留或更多限制其范围的任何更改，在生效六个月内书面通知联合国秘书长。

第9条

[签署和参加公约]

（1）本公约应向联合国秘书长交存。它应开放供任何是联合国、与联合国有关任何专门机构或国际原子能机构成员的或是国际法院宪章加入方的国家签署，直至1975年3月31日。

（2）本公约应经签署国批准或承认。它应开放供任何第（1）款中提到的国家加入。

（3）批准、承认或加入书应向联合国秘书长交存。

（4）不言而喻，一国开始受本公约约束，应具备条件根据其国内法律实施本公约的条款。

第10条

[公约的生效]

（1）本公约在第五份批准、承认或加入书交存后三个月生效。

（2）对每个在第五份批准、承认或加入书交存后批准、承认或加入本公约的国家，本公约在交存其文书后三个月生效。

第 11 条

[声明公约无效]

（1）任何缔约国可以通过向联合国秘书长交存的书面通知声明本公约无效。

（2）声明无效应在第（1）款中提到的通知被收到之日后十二个月生效。

第 12 条

[语文和通知]

（1）本公约以英文、法文、俄文和西班牙文的独一份签署，四种文本具有同等效力。

（2）应由联合国教育、科学和文化组织总干事和世界知识产权组织总干事在与有关政府磋商后以阿拉伯文、荷兰文、德文、意大利文和葡萄牙文制定正式文本。

（3）联合国秘书长应将以下事项通知第 9 条第（1）款中提到的国家以及联合国教育、科学和文化组织总干事，世界知识产权组织总干事，国际劳工局总干事和国际电信联盟秘书长：

(i) 本公约的签署；

(ii) 批准、承认或加入书的交存；

(iii) 本公约在第 10 条第（1）款之下生效的日期；

(iv) 与第 2 条第（2）款或第 8 条第（2）款或第（3）款有关的任何通知连同其文件的交存；

(v) 声明无效通知的接收。

（4）联合国秘书长应将本公约两份经确认的复本传送所有第 9 条第（1）款中提到的国家。

避免版税双重征税的多边公约

（附带示范双边协议和附加议定书）

马德里，1979年12月13日

目录*

* 为编者所加，原文中无目录。

第 17 条：解释和争议的解决

缔约国，

考虑到版税双重征税损害作者的利益并因此严重阻碍有版权作品的传播，而此种传播是各国人民文化、科学和教育发展中的基本要素之一，

相信通过专门就版税缔结一项多边公约可以改进其有益效果得到普遍承认的、通过双边协议和国内措施防止双重征税的行动已经取得的令人鼓舞的成果，

认为必须解决这些问题，同时尊重各国的合法利益，尤其是尽可能广泛获得人类智力作品为其在文化、科学和教育领域中持续发展的一个基本条件的那些国家特有的需求，

谋求找到旨在尽可能避免版税双重征税并在它存在时消除或减小其影响的有效措施，

达成一致如下：

第一章: 定义

第 1 条

版税

1. 为本公约的目的并以本条第 2 款和第 3 的款规定为条件，版税是根据最初应在其中为使用或有权使用多边版权公约中定义的文学、艺术和科学作品的版权支付这些版税的缔约国的国内版权法进行的任何种类的支付，包括就法定或强制许可或就“追续权”进行的支付。

2. 但是，本公约不得被认为包括利用电影作品或以类似电影摄制的方法制作的作品应支付的版税，此种作品由应向此种作品的制作者或其继承人或承继人支付版税时最初应支付这些版税所在国家的国内版权法限定。

3. 就“追续权”进行的支付除外，为本公约的目的，以下不视为版税：为文学、艺术或科学作品物质载体中权利的购买、出租、出借或其他转让的支付，即

使这一支付的金额系根据应付的版税确定，或如果后者系全部或部分根据该支付的数额确定。当作品物质载体中的权利作为作品版权使用资格转让的附属转让，为本公约的目的，只有酬报这一资格的支付是版税。

4. 在就“追续权”和在本条第3款中提到的作品物质载体权的所有转让中进行支付的情况下，不依赖于所述转让是否免费的事实，为偿付或报销保险费、运输或仓储费、代理人佣金或任何其他服务报酬以及直接或间接由所述物质载体的移动引致的包括关税和其他有关纳税和特别征收进行的支付，为本公约的目的不是版税。

第2条

版税受益人

为本公约的目的，版税的“受益人”是版税全部或部分向其支付的受益所有者，无论他作为作者或其后嗣或合法继承人收取版税，或无论他是否通过适用在与版税双重征税有关双边协议中商定的任何其他相关标准收取它们。

第3条

受益人的居住国

1. 为本公约的目的，版税受益人为其居民的国家应被视为该受益人的居住国。

2. 如果一个人由于其居所、住所、有效经营地或与版税双重征税有关双边协议中商定的任何其他相关标准而在一国有纳税义务，应被视为该国的居民。但是，此条件不包括在该国仅就从其在该国作为资本拥有的资源所得的收入有纳税义务的任何人。

第4条

版税来源国

为本公约的目的，一个国家应被视为版税的来源国，当使用或得到权利使用文学、艺术或科学作品的此种版税的最初支付应：

（a）由该国或该国一个政治或行政分支或地方当局；

（b）由该国的居民，版税由他在另一个国家通过一个常设机构或从一个固定基地从事的活动导致的除外；

（c）由该国的非居民，如果版税由他在该国通过一个常设机构或从一个固定基地进行的活动导致。

第二章：防止版税双重征税行动指导原则

第5条

财政主权和国家权利平等

防止版税双重征税的行动应根据本公约第8条的规定进行，同时给来源国和居住国的财政主权以应有的尊重，并给它们对这些版税征税的平等权利以应有的尊重。

第6条

财政非歧视

防止版税双重征税的措施不得导致基于国籍、种族、性别、语言或宗教的征税歧视。

第7条

信息交换

在实施本公约所需的范围内，缔约国的主管当局将以通过双边协议规定的形式和条件对等地交换信息。

第三章：防止版税双重征税行动指导原则的实施

第8条

实施手段

1. 各缔约国承诺，根据其宪法和上述指导原则，尽可能做出努力避免对版税的双重征税，如果可能，在其存在的情况下消除它或减少其影响。此行动应通过双边协议或国内措施进行。

2. 本条第1款中提到的双边协议包括有关一般双重征税或限于版税双重征税的双边协议。后一种双边协议的选择性范本，包括若干备选，附于本公约而非其一个组成部分。在尊重本公约规定的同时，缔约国可以在每一特定情况下在最为他们接受的准则的基础上缔结双边协议。缔约国实施早先缔结的双边协议完全不受本公约影响。

3. 如果采取国内措施，尽管有本公约第1条的规定，各缔约国可以参照自己的版权立法限定版税。

第四章：一般条款

第9条

外交或领事机构成员

本公约的规定不影响缔约国外交或领事机构成员及其家属在国际法一般规则之下或在专门公约规定之下的财政特权。

第10条

信息

1．联合国教育、科学和文化组织秘书处和世界知识产权组织国际局应汇集并出版与版税征税相关规范有关的信息。

2．各缔约国应尽快将与版税征税有关的任何新定法律以及所有官方文件的文本，包括与涉及一般双重征税的任何双边协议中包含的关于该主题的相关条款有关的任何专门双边协议的文本，传送给联合国教育、科学和文化组织秘书处和世界知识产权组织国际局。

3．应任何缔约国的请求，联合国教育、科学和文化组织秘书处和世界知识产权组织国际局应就与本公约有关的问题向其提供信息；它们还应开展研究和提供服务以便于本公约的适用。

第五章：最后条款

第11条

批准、承认、加入

1．本公约应向联合国组织秘书长交存。它应保持开放至1980年10月31日，供是联合国、联合国任何有关专门机构或国际原子能机构成员或是国际法院宪章参加方的任何国家签署。

2．本公约应经签署国批准或承认。它应开放供任何本条第1款中提到的国家加入。

3．批准、承认或加入书应向联合国秘书长交存。

4．不言而喻，一个国家开始受本公约约束，应具备条件根据其国内法律实施本公约的条款。

第 12 条

保留

缔约国可以在签署本公约时或在批准、承认或加入本公约时就第 1 条至第 4 条、第 9 条和第 17 条中包含的条款的适用条件做出保留。不允许对公约做出其他保留。

第 13 条

生效

1. 本公约在第十份批准、承认或加入书交存后三个月生效。

2. 对每个在第十份批准、承认或加入书交存之后批准、承认或加入本公约的国家，本公约在交存其文书后三个月生效。

第 14 条

声明无效

1. 任何缔约国可以通过给联合国秘书长的通知声明本公约无效。

2. 此种声明无效应在联合国秘书长收到通知之日后十二个月生效。

第 15 条

修订

1. 本公约生效五年后，任何缔约国可以通过给联合国秘书长的通知请求为修订公约的目的召开会议。联合国秘书长应将此请求通知所有缔约国。如果在联合国秘书长的通知之日起六个月时段内，不少于三分之一的缔约国，条件是数目不少于五个，通知同意该请求，秘书长应通知联合国教育、科学和文化组织总干事和世界知识产权组织总干事，他们应召开修订会议以将旨在改进防止版税双重征税行动的更改引入本公约。

2. 通过本公约的任何修订，需要三分之二参加修订会议国家的赞成票，条件是此多数包括在修订会议时为本公约参加方的三分之二。

3. 在整体或部分修订本公约的新公约生效之后参加公约的任何国家，未表示不同意向的，应被认为是：

（a）经修订的公约的参加方；

（b）本公约的参加方，对任何是现公约的参加方但不受经修订的公约约束的国家而言。

4. 本公约对未参加经修订的公约的缔约国之间的或与它们的关系保持有效。

第16条

公约的语文和通知

1. 本公约以阿拉伯文、英文、法文、俄文和西班牙文的独一份签署，五种文字具有同等效力。

2. 由联合国教育、科学和文化组织总干事和世界知识产权组织总干事在与利益相关政府磋商后制定德文、意大利文和葡萄牙文的正式文本。

3. 联合国秘书长应将以下事项通知第11条第1款中提到的国家以及联合国教育、科学和文化组织总干事和世界知识产权组织总干事：

（a）本公约的签署，连同任何附带的文件；

（b）批准、承认和加入书的交存，连同任何附带的文件；

（c）本公约在第13条第1款之下生效的日期；

（d）声明无效通知的接收；

（e）根据第15条送交他的请求以及从缔约国收到的与本公约修订有关的任何信函。

4. 联合国秘书长应将本公约两份经确认的复本送交所有第11条第1款中提到的国家。

第17条

解释和争议的解决

1. 两个或更多缔约国之间与本公约的解释或适用问题有关的争议，谈判解决不成的，应提交国际法院裁定，除非有关国家商定某种其他解决办法。

2. 任何国家在签署本公约或交存批准、承认或加入书时，可以声明不认为自己受第1款规定的约束。该国与任何其他缔约国有争议的，第1款的规定不适用。

3. 任何根据第2款作出声明的国家，可以随时通过给联合国秘书长的通知收回它。

作为有关以上的见证，下方签字人经正式授权已签署本公约。

1979年12月13日制定于马德里

避免版税双重征税的示范双边协议

协议序言

（A 国）政府和（B 国）政府

希望适用《避免版税双重征税多边公约》提出的原则并由此消除双重征税或减小其影响，

达成一致如下：

一、协议的范围

第 I 条：涵盖的人和版税

1. 本协议应适用于是协议国之一或两者的居民的人。
2. 本协议应适用于在一个协议国产生而受益人为另一协议国居民的版税。

第 II 条：涵盖的纳税

选择方案 A

1. 本协议适用于代表每个协议国 [其政治分支或其地方当局] 规定的强制纳税或减除，无论其类型、种类和征收方式，只要它们施加于版税并根据版税数额估算，不包括不参照版税数额计算的固定性质的纳税。
2. 协议适用的现行纳税尤其是：

（a）在（A 国）

（i）[可适用的所得税]

（ii）[可适用的其他纳税]

（iii）……

（b）在（B 国）

（i）[可适用的所得税]

（ii）[可适用的其他纳税]

（iii）……

3. 本协议还适用于与第 1 款中提到的那些相同 [或基本相同] 的、在本协议签定之后规定的另加于或取代现行纳税的未来纳税。
4. 协议国的主管当局应 [在每年开始时] 将各自法律中的任何变动及其 [在前一

年中的] 适用情况通报对方。

选择方案 B

1. 本协议适用于代表每个协议国 [其政治分支或其地方当局] 规定的纳税，无论其类型和征收方式，只要它们施加于版税并根据版税数额估算。

2. 本协议适用的纳税是 :

（a）在（A 国）

（i）[全部所得税]

（ii）[其他所得税]

（iii）......

（b）在（B 国）

（i）[全部所得税]

（ii）[其他所得税]

（iii）......

3. 协议国的主管当局应 [在每年开始时] 将各自税法中的任何变动及其 [在前一年中的] 适用情况通报对方。

二、定义

第 III 条：一般定义

为本协议的目的，除非上下文另有要求 :

（a）“一协议国”和“另一协议国”两词，取决于上下文，应指（A 国）或（B 国）；

（b）“人”一词包括个人、公司和任何其他多人团体 ;

（c）“公司”一词指任何公司团体或为征税目的作为公司团体对待的任何单位 ;

（d）“一协议国的企业”和“另一协议国的企业”两词分别指由一协议国居民经营的企业和由另一协议国居民经营的企业 ;

（e）“国民”一词指 :

（i）拥有一国国籍的所有个人 ;

（ii）由一国的有效法律产生身份的所有法人、合伙和社团。

（f）“主管当局”一词指 :

（i）在（A 国），...... ;

（ii）在（B 国），……；

（g）“版税”一词应根据《避免版税双重征税多边公约》第 1 条中给出的定义解释；

（h）“版税受益人”一词应根据《避免版税双重征税多边公约》第 2 条中给出的定义解释；

（i）“版税来源国”一词应根据《避免版税双重征税多边公约》第 4 条中给出的定义解释；

（j）“受益人的居住国”一词应根据《避免版税双重征税多边公约》第 3 条中给出的由本协议第 IV 条补全的定义解释。

第 IV 条：居民

1. 为本协议的目的，一个人应被视为一个国家的居民，如果他因适用《避免版税双重征税多边公约》第 3 条第 2 款的规定被如此认为。

2. 如果一个个人由于第 1 款的规定被认为同时是两协议国的居民，其身份应按以下确定：

（a）他应被视为他在其中有供他使用的永久性住所的国家的居民。如果他在两国均有供他使用的永久性住所，应被视为与其人身和经济关系更密切的国家（重大利益中心）的居民；

（b）如果不能确定他在其中有重大利益中心的国家，或如果他在任何一国均无供他使用的永久性住所，应被视为他在其中有惯常住所的国家的居民；

（c）如果他在两国均有或均无惯常住所，应被视为他是其国民的国家的居民；

（d）如果他是或不是两国双方的国民，协议国的主管当局应通过相互协议解决此问题。

3. 如果由于第 2 款的规定，一个个人以外的人被视为协议国双方的居民，则[它应被视为其有效经营地所处国家的居民][协议国的主管当局应通过相互协议解决此问题]。

第 V 条：常设机构 — 固定基地

1. 为本协议的目的，“常设机构”一词指一个企业的营业全部或部分通过它进行的固定营业场所。

2. “常设机构”一词特别包括：

（a）经营地；

（b）分支；

（c）办事处；

（d）产业设施；

（e）商店或其他销售点；

（f）接受或征求订单的永久展览；

（g）企业通过雇员或其他人提供包括资讯服务的服务，如果该性质的活动为同一或相关项目在同一国家领土内持续 [达……个月]。

3. 尽管有第 1 款和第 2 款的规定，“常设机构”不得被视为包括：

（a）仅为存储或展示属于企业的货物的目的使用设施；

（b）仅为存储或展示属于企业的货物的目的维持库存；

（c）仅为由另一企业加工的目的维持属于该企业的货物的库存；

（d）仅为为企业购买货物、获得权利或收集信息的目的维持一个固定的业务地；

（e）仅为企业的广告、信息提供、科学研究或具有预备或辅助性质的类似活动的目的维持一个固定的业务地。

4. 尽管有第 1 款和第 2 款的规定，一个在一协议国中代表另一协议国的一个企业行事的人，第 5 款适用的有独立身份的代理人除外，应被视为先提到国家中的“常设机构”：

（a）如果他有并通常在该国行使权力以该企业的名义签订合同，除非他的活动限于为该企业购买货物或获得权利；

（b）如果他没有此种权力但通常在先提到的国家中代表该企业维持一个他从那里定期交付商品的库存。

5. 一协议国的一个企业，不得仅因为它在那里通过经纪人、总委托代理人、文学代理人或任何其他有独立身份的中间人开展业务而被视为在另一协议国中有“常设机构”，如果此种人是在其通常业务过程中行事。但是，当此种中间人的活动完全或几乎完全用于该企业连续超过……个月，不得被视为本条意思中有独立身份的代理人。

6. 一个是一协议国居民的公司，控制或受控于是另一协议国居民的公司，或在该另一协议国开展业务（无论是否通过常设机构），这一事实本身不得构成此公司是另一公司的常设机构。

7. 在本协议中，“固定基地”一词指一处居住或工作地点，或一处一个个人惯常在那里开展其独立性质活动至少一部分的工作地点。

三、征税规则

第 VI 条：征税方法

选择方案之一

第 VI 条 .A：由居住国以在其他国存在常设机构或固定基地为条件征税

1. 在一协议国产生并支付给其他协议国居民的版税，以第 2 款的规定为条件，只应在该其他国家征收，如果此居民是版税的受益所有者。

2. 第 1 款的规定不得适用于所得税，如果版税受益人在产生版税所在其他协议国通过位于该国的常设机构开展工业或商业活动，或在该其他国家从位于该国的固定基地进行独立的个人服务，并且为之支付版税的权利、活动或财产有效地与此种常设机构或固定基地相关联。在此种情况下，只可以在常设机构或固定基地所处的国家对版税征税，但仅在这些版税归属于该机构或该基地的程度上。

3. 在每个协议国中，如果版税受益人建立不同和分立的企业，或如果设立不同和分立的工作地点，在相同或相近条件下，独立于此企业或以此工作地点为常设机构或固定基地的活动中心，从事相同的活动，其可以预期收取的版税应归属于该常设机构或该固定基地。应允许扣除与版税直接关联的和为常设机构或固定基地的目的引致的开支，包括如此引致的一般行政开支，无论在常设机构或固定基地所处的国家或是在其他地方。归属于该常设机构或固定基地的版税，应按同样方法逐年计算，除非有适当和充分的相反理由。

4. 如果版税超过它为之支付的权利的正常、固有价值，第 1 款和第 2 款的规定仅可以适用于与正常、固有价值相称的那部分版税。

选择方案之二

第 VI 条 .B：纳税上限在协议国两方中相同时征税在居住国和来源国之间的分派

1. 在一协议国产生并付给是另一协议国居民的受益所有者的版税，在先提到的国家中，应在（A 国）的情况下免于第 II 条第 2（a）（ii）款 [和第 2（a）（iii）款] 之下涵盖的征税，或在（B 国）的情况下免于第 2 条第 2（b）（ii）款 [和第 2（b）（iii）款] 之下涵盖的征税。

2. 如果在协议的来源国根据该国法律和在受益所有者在其中为居民的协议国对版税征收所得税，此种收税不可以超过来源国中版税数额的“x” % 和居住国中版税总额的“y”%。

3. 如果作为一协议国居民的版税受益人通过位于该国的常设机构开展从中产生版税的工业或商业活动，或在该其他国家从位于该国的固定基地从事独立的个人服务，并且为之支付版税的权利、活动和财产有效地与此种常设机构或固定基地相关联，第1款和第2款的规定不得适用。在此种情况下，版税只可以在常设机构或固定基地所在的国家征税，但只限于其中归属于该常设机构或固定基地的。

4. 在每个协议国中，如果版税受益人建立不同和分立的企业，或如果设立不同和分立的工作地点，在相同或相近条件下，独立于此企业或以此工作地点为常设机构或固定基地的活动中心，从事相同的活动，其可以预期收取的版税应归属于该常设机构或该固定基地。应允许扣除与版税直接关联的和为常设机构或固定基地的目的引致的开支，包括如此引致的一般行政开支，无论在常设机构或固定基地所处的国家或是在其他地方。归属于该常设机构或固定基地的版税，应以同样方法逐年计算，除非有适当和充分的相反理由。

5. 如果版税超过它为之支付的权利的正常、固有价值，第1款、第2款和第3款的规定仅可以适用于与正常、固有价值相称的那部分版税。

选择方案之三

第VI条.C：纳税上限在每个协议国中不相同时征税在居住国和起源国之间的分派

1. 来源在一协议国中并支付给是其他协议国居民的受益人的版税，应可以在协议国两方征税。但是，它们应在（A国）的情况下免于第2条第2(a)(ii)款[和第2(a)(iii)款]涵盖的征税，或在（B国）的情况下免于第2条第2(b)(ii)款[和第2(b)(iii)款]涵盖的征税。

2. 如果在来源所在的协议国根据该国法律和在受益人是其居民的协议国对此种版税征收所得税，此种收税不可以超过：

(a) 在来源在（A国）并支付给（B国）居民的版税的情况下，在（A国）的征税为版税总额的“x”%，在（B国）的征税为版税总额的“y”%。

(b) 在来源在（B国）并支付给（A国）居民的版税的情况下，在（A国）的征税为版税总额的“y”%，在（B国）的征税为版税总额的“y”%。

3. 如果作为一协议国居民的版税受益人通过位于产生版税的另一协议国的常设机构开展业务，或在该另一国家从位于该国的固定基地从事独立的个人服务，并且为之支付版税的权利、活动和财产有效地与此种常设机构或固定基地相关联，第1款和第2款的规定不得适用。在此种情况下，版税只可以在常设机构或固定基地所在的国家中征税，但只限于其中归属于该常设机构或固定基地的。

4. 在每个协议国中，如果版税受益人建立不同和分立的企业，或如果设立不同和分立的工作地点，在相同或相近条件下，独立于此企业或以此工作地点为常设机构或固定基地的活动中心，从事相同的活动，其可以预期收取的版税，应归属于该常设机构或该固定基地。应允许扣除与版税直接关联的和为常设机构或固定基地的目的引致的开支，包括如此引致的一般行政开支，无论在常设机构或固定基地所处的国家或是在其他地方。归属于该常设机构或固定基地的版税，应以同样方法逐年计算，除非有适当和充分的相反理由。

5. 如果版税超过它为之支付的权利的正常、固有价值，第 1 款、第 2 款和第 3 款的规定仅可以适用于与正常、固有价值相称的那部分版税。

选择方案之四

第 VI 条 .D：由来源国征税

来源在一协议国并支付给另一协议国中居民的版税，完全由版税来源国征税。

选择方案之五

第 VI 条 .E：纳税上限在来源国时征税在居住国与来源国之间的分派

1. 在一协议国产生并支付给另一协议国居民的版税，可以在该另一协议国征税。

2. 但是，此种版税亦可以在产生版税的协议国根据该国的法律征税，但是，如果接收人是版税受益人，此种收税不得超过版税总额的“x”%。协议国的主管当局应通过相互协议确定适用这一限制的方式。

选择方案之六

第 VI 条 .F：纳税上限在起源国时征税在来源国和居住国之间的分配

1. 来源在一协议国中并支付给另一协议国的受益所有者居民的版税，应在版税来源国征税。

2. 但是，该版税亦可以在版税受益所有者居住的协议国征税，但不超过版税总额的“x”%。

四、消除双重征税

第 VII 条：避免双重征税的办法

选择方案一

第 VII 条 .A：免除法

选择方案之一：

第 VII 条 .A（i）普通免除

如果一协议国的居民收到根据第 VI 条的规定可以在另一协议国征税的版税，先提到的国家应将此种版税从对此居民收入的征税中免除，并不得在计算此征税的数额时考虑版税。

选择方案之二：

第 VII 条 .A（ii）累进式免除

如果一协议国的居民收到根据第 VI 条的规定可以在另一协议国征税的版税，先提到的国家应将此种版税从对此居民所得的征税中免除。然而，此国家可以在计算对此居民其他所得征税的数额时考虑被免除的版税，并可以如同所涉版税没有被免除一样适用相同的税率。

选择方案之三：

第 VII 条 .A（iii）维持应纳税收入的免除

如果一协议国的居民收到根据第 VI 条的规定可以在另一协议国征税的版税，先提到的国家应允许对从另一协议国收到的版税适用的那部分征税作为从该居民收入所得税的扣除。

选择方案二

第 VII 条 .B：记账法

选择方案之一：

第 VII 条 .B（i）普通记账

1. 如果一协议国的居民收到根据第 VI 条的规定可以在另一协议国征税的版税，

先提到的国家应允许一笔与在另一协议国缴纳的所得税相同的数额作为从该居民所得税的扣除。此种扣除不得超过在扣除前计算的、属于可在另一协议国征税的版税的那部分所得税。

2. 为此扣除的目的，第 2 条第 2（a）（i）款和第 2（b）（i）款中提到的征税应被视为所得税。

选择方案之二：

第 VII 条 .B（ii）全额记账

1. 如果一协议国的居民收到根据第 VI 条的规定可以在另一协议国征税的版税，先提到的国家应允许一笔与在另一协议国缴纳的税相等的数额作为从该居民所得税的扣除。

2. 为此扣除的目的，第 2 条第 2（a）（i）款和第 2（b）（i）款中提到的征税应被视为所得税。

选择方案之三：

第 VII 条 .B（iii）对应记账

1. 如果一协议国的居民收到根据第 VI 条的规定可以在另一协议国征税的版税，先提到的国家应允许一笔与此种版税总额的……% 相等的数额作为从该居民所得税的扣除，无论在版税产生国扣除的数额是否与此百分比相等。

2. 为此扣除的目的，第 2 条第 2（a）（i）款和第 2（b）（i）款中提到的征税应被视为所得税。

选择方案之四：

第 VII 条 .B（iv）减免税记账

1. 如果一协议国的居民收到根据第 VI 条的规定可以在另一协议国征税并在那里有特殊纳税减免之利的版税，先提到的国家应允许一笔与无此减免便须在该另一国作为此种版税的征税缴纳的总额相等的数额，作为从是版税受益人的该居民所得税的扣除。

2. 为此扣除的目的，第 2 条第 2（a）（i）款和第 2（b）（i）款中提到的征税应被视为所得税。

五、杂项规定

第 VIII 条：非歧视

1. 根据《避免版税双重征税多边公约》第 6 条规定的非歧视原则，一协议国的国民不得在另一协议国被使接受该另一国家国民在相同情况下被或可能被使接受的那些以外或较之负担更重的任何根据版税数额估算的征税或任何与之关联的要求。尽管有第 1 条的规定，此原则亦适用于不是协议国之一或两方居民的人。

2. 作为一协议国居民的无国籍人，不得在任一协议国被使接受有关国家国民在相同情况下被或可能被使接受的征税或相关要求以外或负担更重的任何版税征税或任何与之关联的要求。

3. 一协议国企业的常设机构在另一协议国被使接受的版税征税，在该另一协议国征收，不得比该国为税收目的有相同身份并开展相同活动的企业被使接受的对相同种类版税的征税更为不利。本规定不得被解释为使一协议国有义务为另一协议国的居民提供它为征税目的为自己国民提供的任何由于婚姻状况或家庭责任的个人补贴、减免和扣除。

4. 以 [第 VI 条 A 第 4 款][第 VI 条 B 第 5 款或第 VI 条 C] 为条件，一协议国企业支付给另一协议国居民的版税，为确定此一企业的应纳税利润，应以如同版税已被支付给先提到国家的居民一样的条件扣除。

5. 一协议国的企业，其资本全部或部分直接或间接被另一协议国的一个或更多居民拥有或控制的，不得在先提到的国家被使接受先提到国家的其他类似企业被或可能被使接受的征税或相关要求以外或负担更重的任何根据版税估算的征税或任何与之关联的要求。

6. 尽管有第 II 条的规定，本条的规定应适用于每一种类的税收。

第 IX 条：相互协商的程序

1. 如果一个人认为协议方之一或两者的行动对他造成或将造成不符合本协议规定的征税，无论那些国家国内法律规定的救济，可以将他的情况向他是其居民的协议国的主管当局提出，或者，如果他的情况在第 VIII 条第 1 款之下，向他是其国民的协议国的主管当局提出。此情况必须在第一次导致不符合协议规定的征税的行动起三年内提交。

2. 如果在主管当局看来异议有理由，并且如果它自己无法在一个……时段内或在它可能向另一国主管当局通知的一个延长时段内取得令人满意的解决办法，应努力通过与另一协议国主管当局的相互协商解决该情况，以避免不符合本协议规定的征税。任何达成的商定应得到实施，尽管有协议国国内法律中的任何时间限制。
3. 协议国的主管当局应努力通过商定解决就协议的解释或适用产生的困难或疑问。它们亦可以在本协议未规定的情况中为避免双重征税共同磋商。
4. 协议国的主管当局可以为达成第1款、第2款和第3款意思中的商定直接相互通信。当似乎宜通过口头交换意见达成商定，此种交换可以通过一个由协议国主管当局的代表组成的委员会进行。

第X条：信息交换

1. 协议国的主管当局应交换必要的信息以履行本协议的规定，或协议国与本协议涵盖的纳税有关的国内法律的规定，只要在其之下的征税不与本协议相悖。信息交换不受本协议第I条的限制。一协议国收到的任何信息应作为秘密对待，方式与该国在国内法律之下获得的信息相同，并应只披露给参与事关本协议涵盖的纳税的评估、收取、实施或起诉或上诉裁决的人或主管当局，包括法院和行政机关。
2. 第1款的规定无论如何不得被解释为使一个协议国有义务：

（a）采取与该国或另一协议国的法律和行政惯例不一致的行政措施；

（b）提供在该国或另一协议国法律之下或正常行政过程中不能得到的信息；

（c）提供会披露任何行业、业务、工业、商业或专业秘密或商业方法的，或其披露有悖于公共政策（公共秩序）的信息。

第XI条：外交或领事机构成员

本协议任何内容不得影响协议国外交或领事机构的成员及其家属在国际法一般规则之下或在专门公约规定之下的财政特权。

六、最后条款

第XII条：生效

1. 本协议应经批准，批准书应尽快在……交换。
2. 本协议应在交换批准书时生效，其条款生效应：

（a）在（A国）……

（b）在（B国）……

第 XIII 条 : 终止

本协议保持有效直至被一协议国终止。每个协议国均可以通过外交途径以在……之年后的任何历年年底至少六个月之前给予的通知终止协议。在此种情况下，协议应停止生效：

（a）在（A 国）……

（b）在（B 国）……

第 XIV 条 : 解释

事关一协议国对本协议的适用，任何在协议中未予定义的用词，除上下文另有要求，应具有它在《避免版税双重征税多边公约》之下或否则在该国法律之下具有的含义。

第 XV 条 : 本协议与其他有关双重征税的条约之间的关系

如果本协议的规定与协议国达成的另一项关于双重征税的条约的规定有任何不同，对于这些国家之间在与版税征税有关事宜中的关系，本协议的规定应优先。

《避免版税双重征税多边公约》附加议定书

是本议定书参加方的《避免版税双重征税多边公约》（以下称“公约”）参加国，承认以下规定：

1. 公约的规定亦适用于就版权相关权利或“邻接权”向表演者、唱片制作者和广播组织支付的版税的征税，只要后者版税产生于一个参加本议定书的国家并且受益人是另一个参加本议定书的国家的居民。

2.（a）本议定书应经签署并经签署国批准、承认或加入，或可以根据公约第 11 条的规定加入。

（b）本议定书应根据公约第 13 条的规定生效。

（c）任何缔约国可以根据公约第 14 条的规定声明本议定书无效，但是，不言而喻，一缔约国声明公约无效，必须同时亦声明本议定书无效。

（d）公约第 16 条的规定应适用于本议定书。

作为有关以上的证明，下方签字人经正式授权已签署本议定书。

1979 年 12 月 13 日制定于马德里。

视听作品国际注册条约

目录

缔约国，

希望提高与视听作品有关交易中的法律安全度并由此促进视听作品的创作和此种作品的国际流动，

并且有助于与对视听作品和所包含贡献的盗版作斗争；

达成一致如下：

第I章　实质条款

第1条

成立联盟

参加本条约的国家（以下称“缔约国”）为视听作品的国际注册组成一个联盟（以下称“联盟”）。

第2条

“视听作品”

为本条约的目的，“视听作品”指由一系列固定的带有或不带有伴音的相关画面组成的、能够被使看到并在伴有声音的情况下能够被使听到的任何作品。

第3条

国际注册簿

（1）[国际注册簿的建立] 为注册与视听作品和此种作品中权利尤其包括涉及其利用的权利有关的声明，建立国际视听作品国际注册簿（以下称“国际注册簿”）。

（2）[国际注册处的设立和管理] 为维持国际注册簿的目的，设立视听作品国际注册处（以下称“国际注册处”）。它是世界知识产权组织国际局（以下分别称“产权组织”和“国际局”）的一个行政单位。

（3）[国际注册处的地点] 国际注册处应设在奥地利，只要奥地利共和国与产权组织之间一项有此意思的条约在生效中。否则，它应设在日内瓦。

（4）[申请] 在国际注册簿中注册任何声明，应基于一项有此意思的申请，申请由有资格提交申请的自然人或法律实体提交，有规定的内容，以规定的形式，并缴纳规定的费用。

（5）[申请人的资格]

（a）以（b）款为条件，以下人应有资格提交申请：

（i）是一个缔约国的国民、在其中居住、在其中有常住居所或在其中有真实和有效的工业或商业机构的任何自然人；

（ii）在一个缔约国法律之下组建的或在其中有真实和有效的工业或商业机构的任何法律实体。

（b）如果申请涉及一项已进行过的注册，亦可以由一个未满足（a）款中提到的条件的自然人或法律实体提交。

第4条

国际注册的效力

（1）[法律效力] 各缔约国保证承认，一项在国际注册簿中登记的声明被认为真实，直至有相反证明，除非：

（i）该声明在该国版权法或任何其他与视听作品中知识产权有关的法律之下不能有效；

（ii）或者该声明与国际注册簿中另一项声明相矛盾。

（2）[知识产权法和条约的保障] 本条约任何条款的解释，不得影响任何缔约国的版权法或任何其他与视听作品中知识产权有关的法律，或者，如果该国家是《保护文学和艺术作品伯尔尼公约》或任何其他与视听作品中知识产权有关条约的参加方，该国家在所述公约或条约之下的权利和义务。

第II章　行政条款

第5条

大会

（1）[组成]

（a）联盟应有一个由缔约国组成的大会。

（b）各缔约国政府应由一名会议代表作为代表，会议代表可有替补代表、顾问和专家协助。

（2）[费用和代表团] 每个代表团的费用由委派它的政府负担，例外是，每个缔约国一名会议代表的旅行费用和生活补贴由联盟基金支付。

（3）[任务]

（a）大会应：

（i）处理与联盟的维持和发展以及本条约的实施有关的所有事项；

（ii）执行在本条约之下特别分派给它的任务；

（iii）就修订会议的筹备给产权组织总干事（以下称"总干事"）以指示；

（iv）审议和批准产权组织总干事与联盟有关的报告和活动，并就联盟职权范围内的事项对他作出所有必要指示；

（v）决定联盟的计划和通过联盟的双年度预算，并批准其决算；

（vi）通过联盟的财务规章；

（vii）成立一个由利益相关非政府组织的代表组成的顾问委员会，和它为便利联盟及其机构的工作认为适当的其他委员会和工作组，并不时决定其成员；

（viii）管控总干事确定的收费制度和数额；

（ix）决定接受哪些缔约国以外国家以及哪些政府间和非政府间组织作为观察员参加其会议；

（x）采取旨在推进联盟目标的任何其他适当行动和行使本条约之下适当的其他职能。

（b）对于亦与产权组织管理的其他联盟有关的事项，大会应在听取产权组织协调委员会的意见后做出决议。

（4）[行使代表] 一名会议代表只可以代表一个国家和以一个国家的名义投票。

（5）[投票] 每个缔约国拥有一票。

（6）[法定人数]

（a）缔约国的半数构成法定人数。

（b）不够法定人数的，大会可以做出决议，但是，所有此种决议，与大会自身程序有关的决议除外，只有通过信函投票取得法定人数和所需多数才生效。

（7）[多数]

（a）以第 8 条第（2）款（b）项和第 10 条第（2）款（b）项为条件，大会决议需要所投票的多数。

（b）弃权不视为投票。

（8）[大会会议]

（a）大会每两个历年举行一次例会，由总干事召集，如无特殊情况，与产权组织全体大会在同一时段和同一地点举行。

（b）应四分之一缔约国要求或由总干事主动提出，大会由总干事召集举行非常会议。

（9）[程序规则] 大会应通过自己的程序规则。

第6条

国际局

（1）[任务] 国际局应：

（i）通过国际注册处执行所有与维持国际注册簿有关的任务；

（ii）供作修订会议、大会、由大会成立的委员会和工作组以及任何其他由总干事召集和处理与联盟有关事项的会议的秘书处。

（iii）执行在本条约和第8条中提到的细则执行或由大会专门分派给它的所有任务。

（2）[总干事] 总干事是联盟的首席执行官并代表联盟。

（3）[大会会议以外的会议] 总干事得召集大会成立的任何委员会和工作组的会议以及所有其他处理与联盟有关事项的会议。

（4）[国际局在大会和其他会议中的角色]

（a）总干事和由他指定的任何工作人员应参加大会、由大会成立的委员会和工作组的所有会议，以及任何其他由总干事召集和处理与联盟有关事项的会议，但无表决权。

（b）总干事或由他指定的一名工作人员凭借职权是大会、委员会、工作组和（a）项中提到的其他会议的秘书。

（5）[修订会议]

（a）总干事应根据大会指示为修订会议进行筹备。

（b）总干事可以就所述筹备与政府间和非政府组织进行磋商。

（c）总干事和由他指定的工作人员应参与修订会议中的讨论，但无表决权。

（d）总干事或由他指定的一名工作人员凭借职权是任何修订会议的秘书。

第7条

财务

（1）[预算]

（a）联盟应有一部预算。

（b）联盟的预算包括属于联盟的收入和开支，以及它对产权组织管理的联盟的共同预算开支的贡献。

（c）不专属于联盟而亦属于产权组织管理的其他一个或更多联盟的开支，应被视为各联盟的共同开支。联盟在此种共同开支中的份额，应与联盟在其中的利益相称。

（2）[与其他预算的协调] 确定联盟的预算，应适当考虑与产权组织管理的其他联盟的预算相协调的要求。

（3）[收入来源] 联盟预算从以下来源获得经费：

（i）为注册和国际注册处提供的其他服务的付费；

（ii）国际注册处出版物的销售或版税；

（iii）捐赠，尤其是视听作品权利持有人协会的；

（iv）礼品、遗赠和资助；

（v）租金、利息和其他杂项收入。

（4）[自给性财政] 确定国际注册处收费的数额和其出版物的价格，应使它连同任何其他收入足以弥补与管理本条约相关的开支。

（5）[预算的连续；储备基金] 如果预算未在新的财务时段开始前通过，如财务规章规定的，应与前一时段预算的水平相同。如果收入超过支出，差额应划入一个储备基金。

（6）[工作资本基金] 联盟应有一个由联盟收入建立的工作资本基金。

（7）[账目审计] 账目审计，应如财务规章中规定的，由一个或更多缔约国或由外部审计人进行。他们应经自身同意由大会指定。

第8条

细则

（1）[细则的通过] 与本条约同时通过的条例附于本条约。

（2）[更改细则]

（a）大会可以更改细则。

（b）细则的任何更改需要投票的三分之二。

（3）[条约和细则之间的冲突] 本条约的条款和细则的条款之间有冲突的，应以前者为准。

（4）[行政指令] 行政指令的制定由细则规定。

第 III 章　修订和更改

第 9 条

条约的修订

（1）[修订会议] 本条约可以由缔约国会议修订。

（2）[召集] 任何修订会议的召集，应由大会决定。

（3）[亦能由大会更改的条款] 第 10 条第（1）款（a）项中提到的条款，可以由修订会议或根据第 10 条更改。

第 10 条

条约某些条款的更改

（1）[建议]

（a）建议更改第 5 条第（6）款和第（8）款，第 6 条第（4）款和第（5）款以及第 7 条第（1）款至第（3）款和第（5）款至第（7）款，可以由任何缔约国或由总干事提出。

（b）此种建议应由总干事在大会对其作出考虑之前至少六个月通报缔约国。

（2）[通过]

（a）对第（1）款中提到的条款的更改，应经大会通过。

（b）通过需要投票的四分之三。

（3）[生效]

（a）对第（1）款中提到的条款的任何更改，应在总干事从通过更改时大会的缔约国成员的四分之三收到根据其各自宪法程序进行的书面承认通知一个月后生效。

（b）如此承认的对所述条款的任何更改，应约束大会通过更改时为缔约国的所有缔约国。

（c）已得到承认并已根据第（a）款生效的任何更改，应约束所有在大会通过更改之日后成为缔约国的国家。

第 IV 章　最后条款

第 11 条

参加条约

（1）[遵守] 产权组织任何国家成员可以通过以下参加本条约：

（i）签署之后交存批准、承认或同意书；

（ii）或者交存加入书。

（2）[交存文书] 第（1）款中提到的文书应交存于总干事。

第 12 条

条约的生效

（1）[初始生效] 对于最初五个交存批准、承认、一般批准或加入书的国家，本条约应在第五份批准、承认、同意或加入书交存之日后三个月生效。

（2）[初始生效未涵盖的国家] 对于第（1）款未涵盖的任何国家，本条约应在该国交存批准、承认、同意或加入书之日后三个月生效，除非在批准、承认、一般批准或加入书中指明一个更晚日期。在后者情况下，本条约对该国应在如此指明的日期生效。

第 13 条

对条约的保留

（1）[原则] 以第（2）款为条件，不可以对本条约做出保留。

（2）[例外] 任何国家，在参加本条约时，可以通过向总干事交存的通知声明，它不将第 4 条第（1）款的规定适用于与视听作品中知识产权的利用无关的声明。任何作出此种声明的国家，可以通过向总干事交存的通知将其撤回。

第 14 条

声明条约无效

（1）[通知] 任何缔约国可以通过给总干事的通知声明本条约无效。

（2）[生效日] 声明无效应在总干事收到通知之日后一年生效。

（3）[声明无效的延缓] 在本条约对之生效之日起满五年之前，任何缔约国不得行使第（1）款规定的声明本条约无效的权利。

第 15 条

条约的签署和语文

（1）[原始文本] 本条约以英文和法文的独一份原始件签署，两种语文具有同等效力。

（2）[正式文本] 经与利益相关政府协商，总干事应以阿拉伯文、德文、意大利文、日文、葡萄牙文、俄文和西班牙文以及大会可能指定的其他语文制订正式文本。

（3）[签署的时间限制] 本条约在国际局持续开放供签署，直至 1989 年 12 月 31 日。

第 16 条

交存事宜

（1）[原始件的交存] 本条约和细则的原始件应交存于总干事。

（2）[经确认的复本] 总干事应将本条约和细则的两份经他确认的复本送交有资格签署本条约的国家的政府。

（3）[条约的注册] 总干事应将本条约向联合国秘书处注册。

（4）[更改] 总干事应将本条约和细则的任何更改的两份经他确认的复本送交缔约国政府，并根据请求送交任何其他国家。

第 17 条

通知

总干事应将第 8 条第（2）款、第 10 条第（2）款和第（3）款、第 11 条、第 12 条、第 13 条以及第 14 条中提到的任何事件通知产权组织成员国政府。

1989 年 4 月 20 日制定于日内瓦

视听作品国际注册条约细则

（1991年2月28日起生效本）*

目录

细则 1

定义

为本细则的目的，

（i）“条约”指《视听作品国际注册条约》；

（ii）“国际注册簿”指条约设立的视听作品国际注册簿；

（iii）“国际注册处”指国际局维持国际注册簿的行政单位；

（iv）“作品”指视听作品；

（v）“与作品有关的申请”指至少以标题指出一部已有或将有作品，并要求将与被指出的人在该作品中或与之相关的利益有关的声明注册在国际注册簿中的申请；“与作品有关的注册”指根据与作品有关的申请进行的注册；

---

* 1989 年 4 月 18 日通过，1991 年 2 月 28 日修改。

（vi）“与人有关的申请”指至少通过指出制作或拥有或可望制作或拥有作品的自然人或法律实体说明的、未以标题识别的已有或将有作品，并要求将与申请人或申请中指出的第三人的利益有关的声明注册在国际注册簿中的申请；“与人有关的注册”指根据与人有关的申请进行的注册；

（vii）“申请”或“注册”— 除非符合“与作品有关的”或“与人有关的”— 均指与作品有关的或与人有关的申请或注册；

（viii）“申请人”指提交申请的自然人或法律实体；“注册持有者”指申请已被注册的申请人；

（ix）“规定的”指条约、细则或行政指令中规定的；

（x）“顾问委员会”指条约第 5 条第（3）款（a）项（vii）中提到的顾问委员会。

细则 1 之二

数名申请人情况下的资格

一个以上自然人或法律实体提交同一申请，如果其中任何之一有资格在条约第 3 条之下提交申请，第 3 条第（5）款（a）项中规定的要求应被认为得到满足。

细则 2

申请

（1）[表格] 任何申请应使用适当的规定表格提交。

（2）[语文] 任何申请应使用英文或法文。一俟国际注册簿财政自给，大会或可确定提交申请可以使用的其他语文。

（3）[申请人名称和地址] 任何申请应依照规定指明申请人的名称和地址。

（4）[申请中提到的某些第三人的名称和地址] 如果申请在申请人以外提到一项权利由其产生或向其转让、许可或另外移转的自然人或法律实体，应依照规定指明此人或法律实体的名称和地址。

（5）[作品的标题或说明]

（a）任何与作品有关的申请应至少指明作品的标题。当标题使用英文或法文以外的语文或使用拉丁书写体以外的书写体，应视情况附带英文翻译或拉丁书写体音译。

（b）任何与人有关的申请应说明申请人对其享有利益的作品。这样做，应至少指明制作或拥有或可望制作或拥有该作品的自然人或法律实体。

（6）[对已有注册的提述] 当申请涉及的作品是一项已有的与作品有关注册的客体，或在一项已有的与人有关注册中被说明过，只要可能，应指明该注册的编号。如果国际注册处认为指明是可能的但未在申请中提供，可以自己在注册中指明此种编号，条件是在国际注册簿中注明编号系来自国际注册处而不是申请人。

（7）[申请人的利益]

（a）在任何与作品有关的申请中，申请应指明申请人在已有或将有作品中或就其享有的利益。如果利益是一项利用权，还应指明权利的性质和权利属于申请人所在的地域。

（b）在任何与人有关的申请中，申请应指明申请人在被说明的已有或将有作品中或就其享有的利益，尤其是任何为申请人或另一人的利益限制或取消利用作品权的权利。

（c）如果利益有时间限制，申请可以表示此种限制。

（8）[权利来源] 与作品有关的申请涉及作品中一项权利的，如果该权利最初属于申请人，申请应指明此情况，或者，如果权利由申请人以外的自然人或法律实体产生，申请应指明此人或法律实体的名称和地址以及产生权利的法律原因。

（9）[随附文件和识别材料]

（a）任何申请可以随附说明申请中包含的声明的文件。任何此种文件使用英文或法文以外语文的，应以英文随附对文件性质和基本内容的指明；否则，国际注册处应以没有随附文件视之。

（b）任何申请可以随附文件以外的能够识别作品的材料。

（10）[真实性陈述] 申请应包含一项陈述，表示申请中包含的声明据申请人所知为真实，且任何随附文件为原始件或是原始件的真实复本。

（11）[签字] 申请应经申请人或由他依照第（12）款规定任命的代表签字。

（12）[行使代表]

（a）申请人或注册持有者可以由一名代表人作为代表，代表人可在申请中、与特定申请或注册有关的另外委托书中或由申请人或注册持有者签字的总委托书中任命。

（b）总委托书使代表人能够就授予总委托书的人的所有申请或注册代表申请人或注册的持有者。

（c）任何对代表人的任命应有效，直至由作出任命的人签字并发送国际注册处的信函撤销，或直至被代表人以由他签字并发送国际注册处的信函声明无效。

（d）国际注册处应将在细则之下致申请人或注册持有者的任何信函发送代表

人；如此向代表人发送的任何信函，应有同样效力，如同其被发送给申请人或注册持有者。代表人发送国际注册处的任何信函，应有同样效力，如同其出自申请人或注册持有者。

（13）[费用] 为每项申请，申请人应指明为计算收费所需的规定数据并缴纳规定的费用，这些必须不晚于国际注册处收到申请之日到达国际注册处。如果在国际注册处实际收到申请之日起 30 天内，为计算收费所需的规定数据被通报国际注册处，并且规定的缴费到达国际注册处，应认为申请在为计算收费所需的规定数据被通报国际注册处和规定的缴费到达国际注册处之日被国际注册处收到，以较晚发生者为准。

细则 3

申请的审理

（1）[更正] 如果国际注册处在申请中注意到它认为的非故意遗漏、互相冲突的两项或更多项声明、一个抄写错误或另一个明显错误，它应正式请求申请人对申请进行更正。为得到考虑，申请人的任何更正必须在更正申请的正式请求之日起 30 日内到达国际注册处。

（2）[使有消除矛盾的可能]

（a）如果国际注册处认为，一项申请中包含的任何声明与基于早先申请是国际注册簿中一项已有注册的客体的任何声明相矛盾，国际注册处应：

（i）如果申请人亦是已有注册的持有者，向其发送通知，询问他希望更改申请中包含的声明还是申请更改是已有注册的客体的声明。

（ii）如果申请人与已有注册的持有者不是同一人，向申请人发送通知，询问他是否希望更改申请中包含的声明，同时向已有注册的持有者发送通知，询问他在申请人不希望更改申请中出现的声明的情况下是否希望申请更改已有注册中的声明。

申请的注册应被中止，直至提交一项国际注册处认为消除矛盾的更改，但中止不得超过自所述通知之日起 60 天，除非申请人请求一个更长时段，在此情况下申请将被中止直至该更长时段届满。

（b）国际注册处未注意到一项声明的矛盾性质，不得被认为是消除该声明的矛盾性质。

（3）[驳回]

（a）在下列情形中，以第（1）款和第（2）款为条件，国际注册处应驳回申请：

（i）如果申请未包含看起来显示符合条约第 3 条第（5）款要求的声明；

（ii）如果国际注册处认为申请未涉及一部作品，无论已有或将有的；

（iii）如果申请不符合细则 2 第（2）款、第（3）款、第（4）款、第（5）款、第（7）款（a）项和（b）项、第（8）款、第（10）款、第（11）款以及第（13）款的任何要求。

（b）如果申请在形式上未满足规定的条件，国际注册处可以驳回申请。

（c）任何申请不得因（a）项和（b）项中提到以外的任何原因被驳回。

（d）本款之下的任何驳回决定，应由国际注册处以书面通报申请人。申请人可以在通报之日起 30 天内书面请求国际注册处重新考虑其决定。国际注册处应在收到请求之日起 30 天内作出答复。

（4）[国际注册簿中关于收到申请的公告] 如果国际注册处由于任何原因在收到申请之日起三个工作日内未将申请注册，它应在国际注册处的供公众查询的数据库中录入申请的基本项目、未进行注册原因的指明以及，如果原因涉及第（1）款、第（2）款（a）项或第（3）款（d）项，在这些条款任何之下采取的措施的指明。如果并当进行了注册，该录入项目应当被除去。

细则 4

注册的日期和编号

（1）[日期] 国际注册处应以细则 2 第（13）款为条件给每项申请一个申请收到日作为申请日。申请被注册的，应给予申请日作为注册日。

（2）[编号] 国际注册处应给每项申请一个编号。如果申请涉及的作品标题出现在一项已有的与作品有关的注册中，或在一项已有的与人有关的注册中被说明，发给的编号亦应包含该注册的编号。任何注册编号应由申请编号组成。

细则 5

注册

（1）[注册] 申请未被驳回的，其中包含的所有声明应依照规定被在国际注册簿中注册。

（2）[注册的通知和公布] 任何已进行的注册，应依照规定通知申请人并在细则 6 中提到的公报上公布。

细则 6

公报

（1）[公布] 国际注册处应出版一部公报（“公报”），其中应就所有的注册显示规定的项目。公报应使用英文，条件是与以法文提交的申请有关的项目还应使用法文。

（2）[销售] 国际注册处应以付费为条件同时提供公报的年度预订和公报的单本。确定价格数额的方式，应与根据细则 8 第（1）款确定收费数额的相同。

细则 7

问询

（1）[信息和复本] 国际注册处应以支付规定的费用为条件提供与任何注册有关的信息以及任何注册证书或与此种注册有关的文件的经确认的复本。

（2）[证书] 国际注册处应以支付规定的费用为条件提供证书，答复就国际注册簿中是否存在与任何注册中或申请附带的任何文件或材料中具体事项有关的声明提出的问题。

（3）[查阅] 国际注册处应以支付规定的费用为条件允许查阅任何申请，以及申请附带的任何文件或材料。

（4）[跟踪服务] 国际注册处应以支付规定的费用为条件在每次进行注册后迅速提供有关以下的书面信息：

（i）就某一部作品进行的所有注册；

（ii）与要求此种服务的某一自然人或法律实体有关的所有注册，只要其为有关的自然人或法律实体，或经有关的自然人或法律实体授权的第三人。

（5）[计算机存储] 国际注册处可以将国际注册内容的全部或部分输入计算机存储，并可以在进行第（1）款至第（4）款中或细则 3 第（4）款中提到的服务时凭借该存储。

细则 8

费用

（1）[费用的确定] 在确定费用制度和数额之前，以及在对该制度或数额进行变更之前，总干事应与顾问委员会进行磋商。大会可以指示总干事变更该制度、数额或两者。

（2）[为发展中国家的申请减少费用] 如果申请人是一个根据联合国大会既定惯例被视为发展中国家的缔约国的自然人国民，或是在该国法律之下组建的法律实体，费用数额初始应减少15%。大会应阶段性审查提高该减少百分比的可能性。

（3）[费用变更的生效] 费用数额的任何提高不得有追溯力。任何变更的生效日期应由总干事确定，根据大会指令变更的，由大会确定。变更在公报上公布时，应指明此日期。该日期不得早于公报公布后一个月。

（4）[货币和支付方式] 费用应以规定的方式并以规定的货币支付，或者，如果接受数种货币，以申请人从数种货币中选择的货币。

细则9

行政指令

（1）[范围]

（a）行政指令应包含与涉及条约和细则的管理的细节有关的规定。

（b）条约和细则的条款与行政指令的条款之间有冲突的，以前者为准。

（2）[来源]

（a）经与顾问委员会磋商，总干事应制定和可以修改行政指令。

（b）大会可以指示总干事修改行政指令，总干事应据此对其进行修改。

（3）[公布和生效]

（a）行政指令和行政指令的任何修改应在公报上公布。

（b）每次公布应具体说明所公布条款的生效日期。不同的条款，日期可以不同，条件是任何条款不得在于公报上公布之前被宣布生效。

与集成电路有关知识产权条约

(1989 年 5 月 26 日在华盛顿通过)

目录[*]

＊ 为编者所加，原始文本中无目录。

第1条

成立联盟

缔约方自己为本条约的目的组成一个联盟。

第2条

定义

为本条约的目的：

（i）“集成电路”指一种电子产品，终端形式或中间形式的，其中成分至少一个为有源成分，并且一些或全部互连以集成方式构建在一块材料中或之上，作用是执行一项电子功能。

（ii）“布图设计（拓扑图）”指一个集成电路的成分，其中至少一个为有源成分，及其一些或全部互连的无论怎样表现的三维配置，或指为用于制作的集成电路准备的此种三维配置。

（iii）“权利持有人”指根据适用的法律被视为第6条中提到的保护受益人的自然人或法律实体。

（iv）“受保护的布图设计（拓扑图）”指满足本条约中提到的保护条件的布图设计（拓扑图）。

（v）“缔约方”指参加本条约的国家或符合第（x）款要求的政府间组织。

（vi）“缔约方的领土”，缔约方是一个国家的，指该国家的领土，缔约方是一个政府间组织的，指成立该政府间组织的条约适用的领土。

（vii）“联盟”指第1条中提到的联盟。

（viii）“大会”指第9条中提到的大会。

（ix）“总干事”指世界知识产权组织总干事。

（x）“政府间组织”指由世界任何地区国家建立和组成的一个组织，它就本条约规制的事项有主管权，有自己的规定布图设计（拓扑图）知识产权保护的和约束其所有成员国的法律，并根据其内部程序被正式授权签署、批准、承认、通过或加入本条约。

第3条

本条约的主题

（1）[保护布图设计（拓扑图）的义务]

（a）各缔约方有义务根据本条约在其整个领土就布图设计提供知识产权保护。

它尤其应采取适当措施，保证防止在第 6 条之下被视为违法的行为，并在已实施此种行为的情况下提供适当法律救济。

（b）无论集成电路是否结合在一个物件中，与集成电路有关权利持有人的权利均适用。

（c）尽管有第 2 条第（i）款的规定，任何缔约方，其法律将布图设计（拓扑图）的保护限于半导体集成电路布图设计（拓扑图）的，可以自行适用该限制，只要其法律包含此种限制。

（2）[原创性要求]

（a）第（1）款（a）项中提到的义务适用的布图设计（拓扑图）应为原创性的，含义是它们是创作者自己智力付出的结果，并且被创作时对于布图设计（拓扑图）创作者和集成电路制作者并非常见。

（b）由常见成分和互连组合成的布图设计（拓扑图），只有该组合作为整体符合（a）项中提到的条件才受保护。

第 4 条

保护的法律形式

各缔约方可以自行通过有关布图设计（拓扑图）的专门法律或有关版权、专利、实用新型、工业设计、不正当竞争的法律或任何其他法律或这些法律的任何组合履行其在本条约之下的义务。

第 5 条

国民待遇

（1）[国民待遇]

以遵守其在第 3 条第（1）款（a）项中提到的义务为条件，各缔约方应在其领土内就布图设计（拓扑图）的知识产权给予：

（i）是任何其他缔约方国民或在其领土内居住的自然人；

（ii）在任何其他缔约方领土内有真实和有效的创作布图设计（拓扑图）或生产集成电路的机构的法律实体或自然人，与其给予自己国民相同的待遇。

（2）[代理人、送达地址、法院程序]

尽管有第（1）款的规定，只要涉及任命代理人或指定送达地址的义务，或只要涉及法院程序中对外国人适用的专门规定，任何缔约方可以不适用国民待遇。

（3）[第（1）款和第（2）款对政府间组织的适用]

如果缔约方为一个政府间组织，第（1）款中的“国民”指该组织任何成员国的国民。

第6条

保护的范围

（1）[须经权利持有人授权的行为]

（a）任何缔约方应视下列行为为非法，如果未经权利持有人授权而实施：

（i）通过将其整体或任何部分结合进一个集成电路或以另外方式复制受保护布图设计（拓扑图）的行为，复制任何不符合第3条第（2）款中提到的原创性要求之部分的行为除外；

（ii）为商业目的进口、销售或另外发行受保护布图设计（拓扑图）或其中结合受保护布图设计（拓扑图）的集成电路的行为。

（b）任何缔约方亦可以视（a）项中规定以外的行为为非法，如果未经权利持有人授权而实施。

（2）[无须权利持有人授权的行为]

（a）尽管有第（1）款的规定，任何缔约方不得视未经权利持有人授权实施第（1）款（a）（i）项中提到的复制行为为非法，如果该行为由一个第三方为私人目的或仅为评估、分析、研究或教学的目的而实施。

（b）如果（a）项中提到的第三方在评估或分析受保护的布图设计（拓扑图）（“第一布图设计（拓扑图”）的基础上，创作出符合第3条第（2）款中提到的原创性要求的布图设计（拓扑图）（“第二布图设计（拓扑图”），该第三方可以将第二布图设计（拓扑图）结合进一个集成电路或实施第（1）款中提到的任何行为，而不被视为侵犯第一布图设计（拓扑图）中权利持有人的权利。

（c）权利持有人不可以就一个第三方独立创作的相同的原创性布图设计（拓扑图）行使权利。

（3）[与不经权利持有人同意的使用有关的措施]

（a）尽管有第（1）款的规定，任何缔约方可以在法律中规定，在非一般情况下，在一个第三方依照正常商业惯例努力取得权利持有人授权未果之后，其行政或司法当局可以为该第三方不经此种授权实施第（1）款中提到的任何行为发放非专有许可（“非自愿许可”），如果发放当局认为发放非自愿许可为保障该当局视为至关重要的国家目的所必需；非自愿许可应仅供在该国领土内利用，并且以第三方向权利持有人支付公平报酬为条件。

（b）本条约的条款不得影响任何缔约方在适用法律保障自由竞争和防止权利持有人滥用权利时自行采取措施，包括经过正式程序由行政或司法当局发放一项非自愿许可。

（c）发放任何（a）项或（b）项中提到的非自愿许可，应以司法审查为条件。当（a）项中提到的情况停止存在，任何该项中提到的非自愿许可应被撤销。

（4）[善意获得的侵权集成电路的销售和发行]

尽管有第（1）款（a）项（ii）的规定，任何缔约方无须视就一个包含非法复制的布图设计（拓扑图）的集成电路实施该条中提到的任何行为为非法，如果实施或指令此种行为的人在获得该集成电路时不知道或无合理依据知道它包含非法复制的布图设计（拓扑图）。

（5）[权利的穷竭]

尽管有第（1）款（a）项（ii）的规定，任何缔约方可以视不经权利持有人授权实施该款中提到的任何行为为合法，如果实施该行为涉及一个已由权利持有人或经其同意投放市场的受保护布图设计（拓扑图）或其中包含此一布图设计（拓扑图）的集成电路。

第7条

使用；注册，披露

（1）[要求使用的权利]

任何缔约方可以不保护一个布图设计（拓扑图），直至它在世界某地被以通常商业方式单独或包含在一个集成电路中使用。

（2）[要求注册的权利；披露]

（a）任何缔约方可以不保护一个布图设计（拓扑图），直至该布图设计（拓扑图）被以正式形式向主管公共当局提交了注册申请或在该当局进行了注册；可以要求申请时伴随提交布图设计（拓扑图）的复本或图样，和在集成电路已被商业使用的情况下提交该集成电路的样品，连同限定集成电路用以执行的电子功能的信息；但是，申请人可以排除复本或图样中与集成电路制作方法有关的部分，只要提交的部分足以使人指认该布图设计（拓扑图）。

（b）如果要求根据（a）项提交注册申请，缔约方可以要求在自权利持有人首次在世界任何地方以通常商业方式使用一个集成电路的布图设计（拓扑图）之日起某一时段内提交；此时段不得短于自该日期起算的两年。

（c）（a）项之下的注册可以以支付费用为条件。

第8条

保护期限

保护应持续至少八年。

第9条

大会

(1)[组成]

(a) 联盟应有一个由缔约方组成的大会。

(b) 每个缔约方由一名会议代表作为代表，会议代表可有替补代表、顾问和专家协助。

(c) 以(d) 项为条件，各代表团的开支应由委派代表团的缔约方负担。

(d) 大会可以请求世界知识产权组织提供财政援助，以便于依照联合国大会既定惯例被认为是发展中国家的缔约方的代表团参加。

(2)[职能]

(a) 大会应处理与联盟的维持和发展以及本公约的适用和运作有关的事项。

(b) 大会应为修订本条约决定任何外交会议的召集，并为此种会议的筹备给总干事以必要指示。

(c) 大会应履行在第14条之下分派给它的职能，并应制定该条中规定的程序的细节，包括此种程序的经费。

(3)[投票]

(a) 每一个作为国家的缔约方拥有一票并仅以其自己的名义投票。

(b) 任何是一个政府间组织的缔约方应代表其成员国行使投票权，票数与其是本条约参加方并在投票时在场的成员国的数目相等。如果其任何成员国参加投票，此种政府间组织不得行使投票权。

(4)[例会]

大会应每两年由总干事召集举行一次例会。

(5)[程序规则]

大会应制定自己的程序规则，包括非常会议的召集、法定人数的要求以及取决于本条约条款的各种决议所需的多数。

第10条

国际局

（1）[国际局]

（a）世界知识产权组织国际局应：

（i）执行与联盟有关的行政任务以及大会专门分派给它的任何任务。

（ii）以获得资金为条件，根据请求向依照联合国大会既定惯例被认为是发展中国家的缔约方的政府提供技术援助。

（b）任何缔约方均没有任何财政义务；尤其是，任何缔约方均无须因其联盟成员身份向国际局支付任何会费。

（2）[总干事]

总干事是联盟的首席执行官并代表联盟。

第11条

条约某些条款的更改

（1）[由大会更改某些条款]

大会可以更改第2条第（i）项和第（ii）项中包含的定义，以及第3条第（1）款（c）项、第9条第（1）款（c）项和（d）项、第9条第（4）款、第10条第（1）款（a）项以及第14条。

（2）[更改建议的提出和通知]

（a）本条之下更改第（1）款中提到的条款的建议，可以由任何缔约方或由总干事提出。

（b）此种建议应由总干事在大会考虑它之前至少六个月通报缔约方。

（c）任何此种建议不得在本公约在第16条第（1）款之下生效之日起满五年之前提出。

（3）[要求的多数]

大会通过第（1）款之下的任何更改，需要投票的五分之四。

（4）[生效]

（a）第（1）款中提到的对本条约的任何更改，应在总干事从大会通过更改时为大会成员的缔约方的四分之三收到根据其各自宪法程序进行的书面承认通知后三个月生效。如此承认的对所述条款的任何更改，应约束大会通过更改时为缔约方的或在之后成为缔约方的所有国家和政府间组织，在更改生效之前已根据第17

条通知声明本公约无效的缔约方除外。

（b）确定（a）项中提到的所需四分之三时，一个政府间组织作出的通知仅在其任何成员国没有作出通知的情况下才被考虑。

第12条

对巴黎公约和伯尔尼公约的保障

本条约不影响任何缔约方在《保护工业产权巴黎公约》或《保护文学和艺术作品伯尔尼公约》之下可能有的义务。

第13条

保留

不得对本公约做出任何保留。

第14条

争议的解决

（1）[磋商]

（a）如果就本条约的解释或执行发生任何争议，一缔约方可以将此事项提请另一缔约方注意并请求后者与之进行磋商。

（b）被请求的缔约方应及时为请求的磋商提供一个适当机会。

（c）进行磋商的缔约方应争取在一个合理时段内达成共同满意的纠纷解决办法。

（2）[其他解决手段]

如果未在一个合理时段内通过第（1）款中提到的磋商达成共同满意的解决办法，争议当事方可以商定诉诸其他旨在使争议得到友好解决的手段，诸如斡旋、和解、调解和仲裁。

（3）[专家组]

（a）如果争议未得通过第（1）款中提到的磋商满意地解决，或如果第（2）款中提到的手段未被采用或未在一个合理时段内导致友好解决，大会应根据争议任何当事方的书面请求，召集一个三名成员的专家组审查该事项。除非争议当事方另有商定，专家组成员不得来自争议的任何当事方。他们应从大会建立的指定政府专家的名单中选出。专家组的职权范围应经争议当事方同意。如果在三个月内未达成此种同意，大会应在与争议当事方和专家组成员磋商后为专家组确定职权范围。专家组应给争议当事方和任何其他利益相关缔约方发表意见的充分机会。如果争议当事皆有此要求，专家组应停止其程序。

（b）大会应通过规则，用于所述专家名单的建立，应是缔约方政府专家的专家组成员的选择方式，以及专家组程序的进行，包括保障程序的和被程序任何参与者指定为保密的任何材料的保密性。

（c）除非程序当事方在专家组结束其程序之前在自己之间达成一致，专家组应迅速准备一份书面报告，并将其提供给争议当事方审议。争议当事方应有一个长度由专家组确定的合理时段，以就报告向专家组提出任何意见，除非它们在试图就争议达成共同满意的解决办法时同意一个更长的时段。专家组应考虑所提意见并应迅速将其报告送交大会。报告应包含事实和对争议解决办法的建议，并应附带争议方如有的书面意见。

（4）[大会的建议]

大会应迅速对专家组的报告进行考虑。大会应根据其对本条约的解释和专家组的报告，以一致同意向争议当事方提出建议。

第 15 条

参加条约

（1）[资格]

（a）世界知识产权组织或联合国任何成员国可以参加本条约。

（b）任何符合第 2 条第（x）款要求的政府间组织可以参加本条约。该组织应将其与本条约规制的事项有关的主管权和其主管权的任何随后变更通知总干事。该组织及其成员国可以为履行在本条约之下的义务决定其各自的责任，但是不得对在本条约之下的义务有任何减损。

（2）[遵守]

一个国家或政府间组织可以通过以下参加本条约：

（i）签署并随后交存批准、承认或同意书；

（ii）或者交存加入书。

（3）[文书的交存]

第（2）款中提到的文书应向总干事交存。

第16条

条约的生效

（1）[初始生效]

对于最先交存其批准、承认、同意或加入书的五个国家或政府间组织中的每一个，本条约应在第五份批准、承认、同意或加入书交存之日后三个月生效。

（2）[初始生效未涵盖的国家和政府间组织]

对于第（1）款未涵盖的任何国家或政府间组织，本条约应在该国家或政府间组织交存批准、承认、同意或加入书之日后三个月生效，除非文书中指明一个更晚日期；在后者情况下，本条约应在如此指明的日期对该国家或政府间组织生效。

（3）[生效时已存在的布图设计（拓扑图）的保护]

任何缔约方有权不将本条约适用于本条约对该缔约方生效时已存在的布图设计（拓扑图），条件是此规定不影响此种布图设计（拓扑图）当时凭借由本条约产生的以外的国际义务在该缔约方领土可能享有的任何保护。

第17条

声明本条约无效

（1）[通知]

任何缔约方可以通过给总干事的通知声明本条约无效。

（2）[生效日期]

声明无效应在总干事收到声明无效通知之日一年后生效。

第18条

条约的文本

（1）[原始文本]

本条约以英文、阿拉伯文、中文、法文、俄文和西班牙文的独一份原始件签署，所有文本具有同等效力。

（2）[正式文本]

总干事应在与利益相关政府磋商后以大会可能指定的其他语文制定正式文本。

第19条

保管

总干事是本条约的保管人。

第20条

签署

本条约应在1989年5月26日和1989年8月25日之间在美利坚合众国政府，在1989年8月26日和1990年5月25日之间在WIPO总部，开放供签署。

为表明对以上的诚意，经正式授权，下方签字人已签署本条约。

1989年5月25日在华盛顿制定

与贸易有关知识产权协定

（1994年）

目录

各成员，

期望减少对国际贸易的扭曲和阻碍，并考虑到需要促进对知识产权的有效和充分的保护以及保证实施知识产权的措施和程序本身不成为合法贸易的障碍；

承认为此目的需要就以下有新的规则和准则：

（a）1994 年《关税与贸易总协定》（GATT）和有关国际知识产权协定或公约基本原则的适用性；

（b）就与贸易有关知识产权的有效性、范围和使用提供适当的标准和原则；

（c）为实施与贸易有关的知识产权提供有效和适当的手段，其中考虑各国法律制度的差异；

（d）为政府间争端的多边预防和解决提供有效和快捷的程序；以及

（e）旨在最充分分享谈判成果的过渡安排。

承认需要有对付假冒商品国际贸易的原则、规则和管束的多边框架；

承认知识产权为私有权利；

承认保护知识产权的国家制度的根本公共利益目标，包括发展和技术的目标；

亦承认最不发达国家成员在国内实施法律和法规中有最大灵活性的特殊需要，以使它们能够建立健全和可行的技术基础；

强调加强承诺利用多边程序解决与贸易有关知识产权问题上的争端以减少紧张的重要性；

希望在世界贸易组织（WTO）和世界知识产权组织（本协定中称“WIPO”）以及其他有关国际组织之间建立相互支持的关系；

特达成一致如下：

第一部分　一般规定和基本原则

第1条

义务的性质和范围

1. 成员应实施本协定的规定。成员可以，但无须有义务，在其法律中实行比本协定要求更广泛的保护，条件是此种保护不违反本协定的规定。成员可以自行确定在自己法律制度和惯例中实施本协定规定的适当方法。

2. 为本协定的目的，“知识产权”一词指是第二部分第一节至第七节主题的所有类别的知识产权。

3. 成员应将本协定规定的待遇给予其他成员的国民。[①] 对于有关的知识产权，其他成员的国民应被理解为，在所有 WTO 成员是《巴黎公约》（1967）、《伯尔尼公约》（1971）、《罗马公约》和《与集成电路有关知识产权条约》成员的情况下便符合那些公约中规定的保护资格标准的自然人或法人。[②] 任何利用《罗马公约》第5条第3款或第6条第2款规定的可能性的成员，应向与贸易有关知识产权理事会（TRIPS 理事会）作出如那些条款中预设的通知。

① “国民”在本协定中被提到时，在 WTO 单独关税区成员的情况下，应被视为指在该关税区内居住或有真实和有效的工业或商业机构的自然人或法人。

② 在本协定中，“巴黎公约”指“保护工业产权巴黎公约”；“巴黎公约（1967）”指此公约1967年7月14日斯德哥尔摩文本。“伯尔尼公约”指“保护文学和艺术作品伯尔尼公约”；“伯尔尼公约（1971）”指此公约1971年7月24日巴黎文本。“罗马公约”指1961年10月26日在罗马通过的“保护表演者、唱片制作者和广播组织国际公约”。“与集成电路有关知识产权条约”（IPIC 条约）指1989年5月26日在华盛顿通过的“与集成电路有关知识产权条约”。“WTO 条约”指“成立 WTO 的条约”。

第2条

知识产权公约

1. 对于本协定第二部分、第三部分和第四部分，成员应遵守《巴黎公约》（1967）第1条至第12条和第19条。

2. 本协定第一部分至第四部分中任何内容不得减损成员在《巴黎公约》、《伯尔尼公约》、《罗马公约》和《与集成电路有关知识产权条约》之下可能已有的相互义务。

第3条

国民待遇

1. 以已经分别在《巴黎公约》（1967）、《伯尔尼公约》（1971）、《罗马公约》和《与集成电路有关知识产权条约》中规定的例外为条件，就知识产权的保护[③]，每个成员给其他成员国民的待遇，不得低于本国国民。对于表演者、唱片制作者和广播组织，此义务仅适用于本协定之下提供的权利。任何利用《伯尔尼公约》第6条或《罗马公约》第16条第1款（b）项的成员，应向TRIPS理事会作出那些条款中预设的通知。

2. 成员可以利用第1款之下允许的、与包括在成员管辖范围内指定送达地址或任命代理人的司法和行政程序有关的例外，但只有此种例外为确保遵守不与本协定规定不一致的法律和法规所必需，并且适用此种做法不构成对贸易的隐蔽限制。

第4条

最惠国待遇

就知识产权保护，一成员给予任何其他国家国民的任何利益、优惠、特权或豁免，应立即和无条件给予所有其他成员的国民。一成员给予的任何利益、优惠、特权或豁免有以下情况的，免于此义务：

（a）由与一般性质而非特别限于保护知识产权的司法协助或法律实施有关的国际协定产生的；

（b）根据《伯尔尼公约》（1971）或《罗马公约》允许不按国民待遇而按另一国

---

③ 为第3条和第4条的目的，“保护”应包括影响知识产权的有效性、获得、范围、维持和实施的事项，以及影响本协定中专门涉及的知识产权的使用的事项。

给予的给予待遇的条款提供的；

（c）与不在本协定之下提供的表演者、唱片制作者和广播组织的权利有关的；

（d）由在 WTO 协定生效之前生效的与知识产权保护有关国际协定产生的，条件是此种协定被通知 TRIPS 理事会并且不构成对其他成员国民的任意或不正当歧视。

第 5 条

与保护的获得或维持有关的多边协定

第 3 条和第 4 条之下的义务不适用于 WIPO 主持缔结的与知识产权的获得或维持有关的多边协定中规定的程序。

第 6 条

权利穷竭

为本协定之下争端解决的目的，以第 3 条和第 4 条为条件，本协定中任何内容不得被用于涉及知识产权穷竭的问题。

第 7 条

目标

知识产权的保护和实施，应有助于促进技术创新以及技术的转让和传播，使技术知识的生产者和使用者共同受益并以有利于社会和经济福利以及权利与义务平衡的方式。

第 8 条

原则

1. 在制定或修改其法律和法规时，成员可以采用必要措施保护公共卫生和营养，促进对其经济社会和技术发展至关重要部门中的公共利益，条件是此种措施与本协定的规定一致。

2. 可以需要适当措施防止权利持有人滥用知识产权或诉诸过度限制贸易或负面影响国际技术转让的做法，条件是它们与本协定的规定一致。

第二部分　与知识产权的有效性、范围和使用有关的标准

第一节　版权和相关权

第 9 条

与《伯尔尼公约》的关系

1. 成员应遵守《伯尔尼公约》(1971)第 1 条至第 21 条及其附件。但是，对于在该公约第 6 条之 2 之下赋予的或由该条派生的权利，成员不得在本协定之下有权利或义务。

2. 版权保护应延及表达而不延及想法、过程、操作方法或数学概念本身。

第 10 条

计算机程序和数据汇编

1. 计算机程序，无论以源码或目标码，应被作为《伯尔尼公约》(1971)之下的文字作品保护。

2. 数据或其他材料的汇编，无论以机器可读或其他形式，由于内容的选择或编排构成智力创作的，本身应受到保护。此种保护不得延及数据或材料本身，不得损害数据或材料本身中存在的版权。

第 11 条

出租权

至少对于计算机程序和电影作品，成员应给作者及其合法继承人以授权或禁止向公众商业性出租其有版权作品的原始本或复本的权利。对于电影作品，成员应被免于此项义务，除非出租已导致对此种作品的广泛复制而实质损害该成员赋予作者及其合法继承人的专有复制权。对于计算机程序，此义务不适用于出租，如果程序本身不是出租的主要对象。

第 12 条

保护期

摄影作品或实用艺术作品以外的作品，只要保护期在自然人寿命以外的基础上计算，此种保护期不得短于自经授权出版的历年年终起五十年，或者，如果自

该作品制作起五十年内没有经授权出版，自制作的历年年终起五十年。

第 13 条

限制和例外

成员应将对专有权利的限制或例外限于不与作品正常使用相冲突并且不过度损害权利持有人合法利益的某些特殊情况。

第 14 条

对表演者、唱片（声音录制）制作者和广播组织的保护

1. 对于将其表演固定在唱片上，表演者应可以阻止未经其授权而从事的以下行为：固定其未固定的表演和复制此种固定物。表演者还应可以阻止未经其授权而从事的以下行为：以无线手段广播和向公众传播其现场表演。

2. 唱片制作者应有权授权或禁止直接或间接复制其唱片。

3. 广播组织应有权禁止未经其授权而从事的以下行为：对广播进行固定，对固定物进行复制和以无线手段转播广播，以及向公众传播同一组织的电视广播。如果成员不给予广播组织此种权利，它们应以《伯尔尼公约》（1971）的规定为条件为广播内容中版权的所有者提供阻止上述行为的可能性。

4. 第 11 条有关计算机程序的规定，经必要修改应适用于唱片制作者和成员法律中确认的唱片中任何其他权利持有人。如果一成员在

1994 年 4 月 15 日就唱片的出租实行给权利持有人公平报酬的制度，可以保留此种制度，条件是唱片的商业性出租不对权利持有人的专有复制权产生实质性损害。

5. 本协定之下提供表演者和唱片制作者的保护的期限，应至少持续到一个自固定物制作或表演发生的历年年终起计算的五十年时段终止。根据第 3 款提供的保护的期限，应自广播发生的历年年终起至少持续二十年。

6. 任何成员可以在《罗马公约》允许的范围就第 1 款、第 2 款和第 3 款之下赋予的权利规定条件、限制、例外和保留。但是，《伯尔尼公约》（1971）第 18 条经必要修改应适用于表演者和唱片制作者在唱片中的权利。

第二节 商标

第15条

可保护的客体

1. 任何能够将一个企业的商品或服务与其他企业的那些区分开的标记或标记组合，应能够构成商标。此种标记，尤其是包括人名的词、字母、数字、图形要素和色彩组合以及此种标记的任何组合，应合格作为商标注册。如果标记固有地不能区分有关的商品或服务，成员可以根据通过使用获得的独特性确定可注册性。成员可以要求标记能够被视觉感知为注册的一个条件。

2. 第1款不得被理解为阻止成员以其他理由拒绝注册一个商标，条件是它们不减损《巴黎公约》(1967)的规定。

3. 成员可以根据使用确定可注册性。但是，商标的实际使用不得是提交注册申请的一个条件。不得仅以意图的使用未在自申请之日起一个三年时段届满之前发生为由拒绝一项申请。

4. 被申请商标的商品或服务的性质无论如何不构成商标注册的障碍。

5. 成员应在注册之前或在注册之后迅速公布每个商标，并应为请求取消该注册提供合理机会。此外，成员可以提供机会就一项商标注册提出异议。

第16条

赋予的权利

1. 注册商标的所有者应有专有权，阻止所有未经其同意的第三方在贸易过程中为与被注册商标的那些相同或类似的商品或服务使用相同或类似的标记，如果此种使用可能会导致混淆。在为相同商品或服务使用相同标记的情况下，应推定可能存在混淆。上述权利不得损害任何已有的在先权利，也不得影响成员能够基于使用给予权利。

2.《巴黎公约》(1967)第6条之二经必要修改应适用于服务。确认一商标是否知名时，成员应考虑该商标在有关公众群体中的知晓度，包括由于对该商标的推广在有关成员中获得的知晓度。

3.《巴黎公约》(1967)第6条之二经必要修改应适用于不与被注册商标的那些相类似的商品或服务，只要就那些商品或服务使用该商标会表明那些商品或服务与注册商标的所有者之间有一种联系，并且只要注册商标所有者的利益可能因此种使用受到损害。

第 17 条

例外

成员可以对商标赋予的权利规定有限的例外，诸如合理使用描述性语词，条件是此种例外考虑到商标所有者和第三方的合法利益。

第 18 条

保护期

商标的初次注册和注册的每一次续展，应以一个不短于七年的期限。商标注册应可以无限续展。

第 19 条

使用要求

1. 如果维持注册必须使用，注册只可以在至少三年不间断的不使用期之后被取消，除非商标所有者出示以存在使用障碍为依据的正当理由。构成商标使用障碍的不依赖商标所有者意志发生的情况，诸如对受商标保护的商品或服务的进口限制或其他政府要求，应被认为是不使用的正当理由。

2. 在受其所有者控制的情况下，为维持注册的目的，另一人对商标的使用应被认为是使用。

第 20 条

其他要求

贸易过程中对商标的使用不得受特殊要求的不正当妨碍，诸如连同另一商标使用、以特殊形式使用或以有损于其将一企业的商品或服务与其他企业的那些区分开的能力的方式使用。此规定不排除一项要求规定，识别生产商品或服务的企业的商标应与区分该企业的具体有关商品或服务的商标共同但不与之相联系地使用。

第 21 条

许可和转让

成员可以确定商标许可和转让的条件，不言而喻的是，不得允许商标的强制许可，并且注册商标的所有者应有权连同或不连同商标所属的业务转让该商标。

第三节　产地标示

第22条

产地标示的保护

1. 为本协定的目的，产地标示是表明一种商品起源于一成员领土或该领土中一个地区或地点内的标示，如果该商品特定的品质、声誉或其他特点基本上归因于其地理来源。

2. 对于产地标示，成员应为利益相关方提供法律手段以阻止：

（a）在命名或展示一种商品中，使用任何手段，以在商品地理起源上误导公众的方式表明或显示该有关商品起源于真实起源地以外的一个地理区域；

（b）任何构成《巴黎公约》（1967）第10条之2意思中不公平竞争行为的使用。

3. 如果其法律允许或应一个利益相关方的请求，成员应依职权拒绝包含涉及非起源于所标示地域的商品的产地标示或由其组成的商标的注册或使注册无效，如果在该成员内将商标中的标示用于此种商品便具有就真实起源地误导公众的性质。

4. 第1款、第2款和第3款之下的保护，可以适用于针对虽然就地域、地区或地点而言实际真实但虚假地向公众显示该商品起源于另一地域的产地标示。

第23条

对葡萄酒和烈酒产地标示的附加保护

1. 各成员应为利益相关方提供法律手段，以阻止将识别葡萄酒的产地标示用于非从有关产地标示指明的地方起源的葡萄酒，或将识别烈酒的产地标示用于非从有关产地标示指明的地方起源的烈酒，即使指明商品的真实来源，或产地标示用在译文中，或伴随有诸如“类”、“型”、“式”、“仿”或类似的表述。④

2. 对于无此起源的葡萄酒或烈酒，包含或由识别葡萄酒的产地标示组成的葡萄酒商标或包含或由识别烈酒的产地标示组成的烈酒商标的注册，应在成员法律允许的情况下被依职权或应一个利益相关方请求被拒绝或使无效。

3. 在葡萄酒有同名产地标示的情况下，以第22条第4款为条件，应给每一

④　尽管有第42条第一句的规定，就这些义务，成员可以规定通过行政行动实施。

个标示以保护。每个成员应确定将有关同名标示相互区分的可行条件，其中考虑需要保证对有关生产者的平等待遇和消费者不被误导。

4. 为便于葡萄酒产地标示的保护，应在TRIPS理事会中举行谈判，以建立一个通报和注册葡萄酒产地标示的多边机制，用于在参加该机制的成员中符合受保护条件的葡萄酒。

第24条

国际谈判；例外

1. 成员同意参与旨在提高第23条之下对单个产地标示的保护的谈判。以下第4款直至第8款的规定不得被成员用于拒绝进行谈判或缔结双边或多边协定。在此种谈判方面，成员应有意愿考虑将这些条款继续适用于其使用为此种谈判之主题的单个产地标示。

2. TRIPS理事会应保持对本节规定实施情况的检查。首次检查应在WTO协定生效两年内进行。任何影响遵守这些条款之下义务的事项，可以提请理事会注意，理事会应在成员请求下与任何一个或多个成员磋商，讨论尚无法通过有关成员之间双边或多边谈判就其找到满意解决方案的事项。理事会应采取可能商定的行动，以便于本节的运作和其目标的推进。

3. 实施本节时，一成员不得减少对紧接WTO协定生效日期之前在该成员存在的产地标示的保护。

4. 本节任何内容不得要求一成员阻止其任何国民或居民继续和近似地使用另一成员的联系商品和服务识别葡萄酒或烈酒的特定产地标示，如果他们（a）在1994年月15日之前至少十年间或者（b）在该日期之前善意地在该成员领土内就相同或相关的商品或服务连续使用该产地标示。

5. 如果已善意地申请商标注册，或如果已通过善意使用获得商标权，无论：

（a）在这些条款在该成员中如第六部分中限定的适用日期以前；

（b）或者在产地标示在起源国受保护之前；

为实施本节采取的措施，不得以此商标与产地标示相同或相似为依据损害商标注册的资格或有效性或使用商标的权利。

6. 任何其他成员的产地标示，就涉及的商品或服务，与一成员领土内通用语中作为此种商品或服务常用名称的惯用词相同的，本节任何内容不得要求该成员将其条款适用于它。任何其他成员的产地标示，就涉及的葡萄产品，与WTO协定生效之日在一成员地域内存在的葡萄品种的惯用名称相同的，本节任何内容不得要求该成员将其条款适用于它。

7. 成员可以规定，任何在本节之下联系商标的使用或注册作出的请求，必须在受保护标示的有害使用在该成员中成为公知后五年内提交，或者，只要商标至注册日已经公布，如果此日期早于有害使用在该成员中成为公知的日期，在商标在该成员中注册之日后提交，条件是该产地标示未被恶意使用或注册。

8. 本节的规定无论如何不得损害任何人在贸易过程中使用该人的名称或该人业务继受人的名称的权利，此种名称被以误导公众的方式使用的除外。

9. 在本协定之下没有义务保护在起源国不受保护或停止受保护或已在该国被废弃的产地标示。

第四节　工业设计

第25条

保护的要求

1. 成员应规定保护独立创作的新颖或有创意的工业设计。成员可以规定，如果设计与已知设计或已知设计特征的组合无重要区别，便非新颖或有创意。成员可以规定，此种保护不得延及主要由技术或功能方面的考虑决定的设计。

2. 每个成员应保证，对获得纺织品设计保护的要求，尤其是涉及费用、审查或公布的，不过度损害寻求和获得此种保护的机会。成员应可以自行通过工业设计法或通过版权法履行此义务。

第26条

保护

1. 受保护工业设计的所有者应有权阻止未经其同意的第三方制作、销售或进口带有或包含是或实质是受保护设计的复本的设计，如果从事此种行为是为商业目的。

2. 成员可以对工业设计的保护规定有限的例外，条件是此种例外不过度与受保护设计的正常利用相冲突，并且不过度损害受保护设计所有者的合法利益，其中考虑第三方的合法利益。

3. 可提供的保护的期限应至少达到十年。

第五节　专利

第 27 条

可授予专利的客体

1. 与第 2 款和第 3 款的规定为条件，专利应授予所有技术领域内的任何发明，无论是产品或方法，条件是它们新颖、包含发明步骤并能够工业应用。⑤ 以第 65 条第 4 款、第 70 条第 8 款和本条第 3 款为条件，获得专利和享有专利权不得因发明地点、技术领域和产品为进口或本地生产而有差别对待。

2. 对于为保护公共利益或道德，包括保护人、动物或植物的生命和健康或避免对环境的严重损害，而有必要阻止其商业利用的发明，成员可以排除可专利性，条件是此种排除并非仅由于法律禁止该利用。

3. 成员还可以对以下排除可专利性：

（a）用于人或动物的诊断、治疗和外科手术方法；

（b）微生物以外的植物和动物，以及非生物和微生物方法以外的基本为生物的生产植物或动物的方法。但是，成员应通过专利或通过有效的专项制度或通过其任何组合规定对植物品种的保护。本项的规定应在 WTO 协定生效之日后四年进行检查。

第 28 条

赋予的权利

1. 专利应赋予其所有者以下专有权利：

（a）专利客体是产品的，阻止未经所有者同意的第三方的以下行为：制作、使用、许诺销售、销售或为这些目的进口 ⑥ 该产品；

（b）专利客体是方法的，阻止未经所有者同意的第三方使用该方法的行为，以及以下行为：使用、许诺销售、销售或为这些目的进口至少是直接通过该方法获得的产品。

2. 专利所有者还应有权转让或通过继承移转专利以及签订许可合同。

---

⑤　为本条的目的，语词“发明步骤”和“可工业应用”可以被成员视为分别与语词“非显而易见”和“有用”同义。

⑥　此项权利，如同在本协定之下就商品的使用、销售、进口或其他发行赋予的所有其他权利，以第 6 条的规定为条件。

第29条

专利申请人的条件

1. 成员应规定，专利申请人应以足够清楚和完整的方式披露发明以使该领域熟练人员实施该发明，并可以要求申请人指明发明人在申请日或者，如果主张优先权，在申请的优先权日所知的实施该发明的最佳方案。

2. 成员可以要求专利申请人提供与申请人的相应国外申请和批准有关的信息。

第30条

对赋予的权利的例外

成员可以对专利赋予的专有权利规定有限的例外，条件是此种例外不过度与专利的正常利用相冲突，并且不过度损害专利所有者的合法利益，其中考虑第三方的合法利益。

第31条

其他不经权利持有人授权的使用

如果成员的法律允许不经权利持有人授权对专利客体的其他使用[⑦]，包括政府使用或政府授权的第三方使用，应遵守以下规定：

（a）授权此种使用应个案考虑；

（b）只有被提名的使用者在使用之前已经努力以合理的商业条件从权利持有人取得授权，而此种努力在一合理时段内未得成功，才可以允许此种使用。在国家紧急状态或其他极为紧急的情况下，或在公共非商业性使用的情况下，成员可以放弃此要求。然而，在国家紧急状态或其他极为紧急的情况下，应尽合理可行之快通知权利持有人。在公共非商业使用的情况下，如果政府或承包人不经专利检索知道或有明显理由知道一项有效专利正在或将要被或为政府使用，应立即通知权利持有人；

（c）此种使用的范围和期限应限于授权使用所为的目的，而对于半导体技术，应仅为公共非商业性使用或为纠正经司法或行政程序确定为反竞争的做法；

（d）此种使用为非专有的；

（e）此种使用不可以转让，除非与企业或商誉的享有此种使用的那部分一道；

（f）授权任何此种使用应主要为供应授权此种使用的成员的本土市场；

⑦ “其他使用”指第30条之下允许的以外的使用。

（g）如果并当导致授权的情况不复存在并不大可能再发生，以充分保护被授权人的合法利益为条件，应终止此种使用的授权。遇到有动因的请求，主管当局应检查这些情况是否继续存在；

（h）权利持有人应被支付在每次授权情形中为合理的报酬，其中考虑授权的经济价值；

（i）与授权此种使用有关的任何决定的法律有效性，应接受司法审查或该成员中一个明显不同的更高机关的其他独立审查；

（j）与就此种使用规定的报酬有关的任何决定，应接受司法审查或该成员中一个明显不同的更高机关的其他独立审查；

（k）成员无义务适用（b）项和（f）项中陈述的条件，如果允许此种使用是为纠正经司法或行政程序确定为反竞争的做法。在此种情况下确定报酬的数额时，可以考虑纠正反竞争行为的需要。如果并当导致此种授权的情况有可能再度发生，主管当局应有权拒绝终止授权；

（l）如果授权此种使用是允许利用一项不侵犯另一项专利（“第一专利”）便无法被利用的专利（“第二专利”），应适用以下附加条件：

（i）第二专利中主张的发明，相对于第一专利中主张的发明，应包含具有显著经济意义的重要技术进步；

（ii）第一专利的所有者应有权以合理条件得到交叉许可以使用第二专利中主张的发明；

（iii）就第一专利授权的使用应不可转让，除非与第二专利一道转让。

第32条

撤销和剥夺

对于撤销或剥夺专利的任何决定，应有司法审查的机会。

第33条

保护期

提供的保护的期限，不得在一个自申请日[8]起计算的二十年时段届满之前终止。

---

⑧ 兹同意，没有原始批准制度的那些成员可以规定保护期应自原始批准制度中的申请日起算。

第34条

方法专利；举证责任

1. 为与侵犯第28条第1款（b）项中提到的所有者权利有关的民事诉讼的目的，如果一项专利的客体是获得一种产品的方法，司法机关应有权责令被告证明获得相同产品的方法不同于该专利方法。因此，成员应规定：在以下情况至少之一中，任何相同的产品，当未经专利所有者同意而制作，在没有相反证据的情况下，应被视为通过该专利方法获得：

（a）如果通过该专利方法获得的产品是新的；

（b）如果存在通过该方法制作相同产品的重大可能性，而专利所有者无法通过合理努力确定实际使用的方法。

2. 任何成员可以规定，第1款指明的举证责任，只有（a）项中提到的条件得到满足，或只有（b）项中提到的条件得到满足，才应归于被指控的侵权者。

3. 引用相反证据时，应考虑被告保护其制造和商业秘密的合法利益。

第六节　集成电路布图设计（拓扑图）

第35条

与IPIC条约的关系

成员同意根据《与集成电路有关知识产权条约》第2条直至第7条（第6条第3款除外）、第12条和第16条第3款为集成电路布图设计（拓扑图）（本协定中称“布图设计”）提供保护并另外遵守以下规定。

第36条

保护范围

以第37条第1款为条件，成员应将以下行为视为非法，如果未经权利持有人[⑨]授权而从事：为商业目的进口、销售或另外方式发行受保护的布图设计、包含受保护的布图设计的集成电路或者（只要集成电路持续包含非法复制的布图设计）包含此一集成电路的物件。

⑨　本节中“权利持有人”一词应被理解为与IPIC条约中的“权利持有人”具有相同的意思。

第 37 条

无须权利持有人授权的行为

1. 尽管有第 36 条的规定，任何成员不得将从事该条中提到的涉及包含非法复制的布图设计的集成电路或包含此种集成电路的物件的行为视为非法，如果从事或指令此种行为的人在获得该集成电路或包含此种集成电路的物件时不知道并且无合理根据知道它包含非法复制的布图设计。成员应规定，此人在收到该布图设计为非法复制的充分警告之时以后，可以就手上或在此时之前定购的存货从事任何所述的行为，但应有义务向权利持有人支付与在就此布图设计自由谈判的许可证之下应支付的合理版税同等的金额。

2. 在布图设计任何非自愿许可或其不经权利持有人授权被或为政府使用情况下，第 31 条（a）项直至（k）项陈述的条件经必要修改应适用。

第 38 条

保护期

1. 在要求注册作为保护条件的成员中，布图设计的保护期不得在一个自提交注册申请之日或自无论在世界何地发生的首次商业利用起算的十年时段届满之前终止。

2. 在不要求注册作为保护条件的成员中，布图设计的保护期不得短于自无论在世界何地发生的首次商业利用之日起十年。

3. 尽管有第 1 款和第 2 款的规定，成员可以规定，保护在布图设计创作后十五年终止。

第七节　未披露信息的保护

第 39 条

1. 在确保《巴黎公约》（1967）第 10 条之二规定的针对不正当竞争的有效保护的过程中，成员应根据第 2 款保护未披露的信息，并根据第 3 款保护向政府或政府机构提交的数据。

2. 自然人和法人应有可能阻止其合法控制下的信息不经其同意以有悖于诚实

商业做法的方式[⑩]被披露给其他人或被其他人获得或使用，只要此种信息：

（a）是秘密的，意为它作为一体或以其成分的精确编排和组合，在通常处理有关种类信息的业界人员中不被普遍知晓或容易得到；

（b）由于秘密而具有商业价值；

（c）由合法控制信息的人员采取当时情况下的合理步骤为其保密。

3. 如果成员要求提交未披露的试验或其他数据作为批准营销使用新化学实体的医药或农用化学产品的条件，而数据的产生需要大量努力，应保护此种数据免于不正当商业使用。此外，成员应保护此种数据免于被披露，为保护公众而有必要的除外，或除非已采取步骤保证数据受到针对不正当商业使用的保护。

第八节　协议许可证中反竞争做法的控制

第40条

1. 成员同意，有些束缚竞争的与知识产权有关的许可证做法或条件，可能对贸易有不利影响并可能阻碍技术的转让和传播。

2. 本协定任何内容不得阻止成员在其法律中明确特定情况下可能构成对有关市场中的竞争有不利影响的知识产权滥用的许可证做法或条件。如以上规定的，一成员可以在与本协定其他条款一致的情况下，根据该成员的有关法律和法规，采取适当措施阻止或控制此种做法，其中可以包括例如排他性返授条件、阻止对有效性提出质疑的条件以及强迫性一揽子许可。

3. 遇有请求，在不损害任何法律诉讼和任何一方成员作出最终决定的充分自由的情况下，每个成员应与任何其他成员开展磋商，如果该其他成员有理由认为是被请求磋商的成员的国民或居民的知识产权所有者正在进行违反请求方成员与本节主题有关的法律和法规的做法，并希望寻求遵守此种法律。被请求的成员应就与请求方成员磋商给予充分和同情的考虑并应给予适当机会，并应通过向该成员提供与所涉事项有关的可公开得到的非保密信息和其他可提供的信息予以合作。

4. 一成员，其国民或居民就违反一其他成员与本节主题有关的法律和法规的指控而在该其他成员中被提起诉讼的，应在提出请求的情况下被该其他成员根据与第3款预设的那些相同的条件给予一次磋商机会。

---

⑩ 为本条的目的，"有悖于诚实商业做法的方式"应至少指诸如违反合同、违反保密和唆使违反等做法，并包括知道或因严重过失不知道获得过程中涉及此种做法的第三方获得未披露的信息。

第三部分　知识产权的实施

第一节　一般性义务

第41条

1. 成员应保证在其法律之下有本部分规定的实施程序，以使能够针对任何侵犯本协定涵盖的知识产权的行为采用有效措施，包括迅速有效的纠正以阻止侵权和对进一步侵权形成遏制的赔偿。适用这些程序，应避免对合法贸易产生障碍，并提供保障防止其滥用。

2. 与实施知识产权有关的程序应公平和公正。它们不得不必要地复杂或耗费，或导致不合理的时间限制或无正当理由的拖延。

3. 根据案情是非作出的裁决，应以采取书面形式和说明理由为宜。它们应无不当延误地至少使程序当事方得到。根据案情是非作出的裁决，应仅以当事方有机会对其发表意见的证据为基础。

4. 程序当事方应有机会由司法机关对最终行政决定和在遵守成员与案件重要性有关法律中管辖条款的情况下至少对根据案情是非作出的初步司法判决中的法律方面进行审查。但是，对于刑事案件中的无罪宣判，不得有提供审查机会的义务。

5. 不言而喻，本部分既不产生任何义务要求为实施知识产权建立一个与实施一般法律不同的司法制度，也不影响成员实施其一般法律的能力。本部分任何内容不就资源在实施知识产权和实施一般法律之间的分配产生任何义务。

第二节　民事和行政程序及救济

第42条

公平和公正的程序

成员应就本协定涵盖的任何知识产权的实施为权利持有人[⑪]提供民事司法程序。被告人应有权得到及时和其中包含足够细节 包括主张的依据的书面通知。应允许当事方有独立的法律顾问作为代表，程序不得就强制本人到庭施加过重的要求。此种程序中的所有当事方应照章有权证实其主张和提交所有有关证据。程序

⑪　为本部分的目的，“权利持有人”一词包括具有主张此种权利的法律地位的联合会和协会。

应提供手段确认和保护保密信息，除非这有悖于现行宪法的要求。

第43条

证据

1. 如果一当事方已经提交可以合理得到的足以支持其主张的证据，并具体指出与证实其主张有关但处在对方控制下的证据，司法机关应有权责令对方出示此证据，适当情况下取决于保证保护保密信息的条件。

2. 如果一诉讼当事方故意并且无正当理由拒绝开放或不在合理时段内提供必要的信息，或严重妨碍与实施权利的诉讼有关的程序，成员可以给司法机关以权力，根据向其提交的信息，包括因拒绝开放信息而受不利影响的一方提出的诉讼事由或指控，作出初步或最终支持或否决的裁定，条件是为当事方提供一次机会就指控或证据作出陈述。

第44条

禁令

1. 司法机关应有权责令一方停止侵权，尤其是立即在涉及侵犯知识产权的进口商品通过海关后阻止此种商品进入其管辖范围内的商业渠道。对于一人在知道或有合理依据知道经营此种客体必然会涉及侵犯知识产权之前获得或定购的受保护的客体，成员无义务赋予此种权力。

2. 尽管有本部分的其他条款，以遵守第二部分专门涉及政府或政府授权的第三方不经权利持有人授权而使用的条款为条件，成员可以将针对此种使用可有的救济限于根据第31条（h）项支付报酬。在其他情况下，本部分之下的救济应适用，或者，如果这些救济不符合成员的法律，应可以得到法院的陈述性意见和适当补偿。

第45条

损害赔偿

1. 司法机关应有权责令侵权人向权利持有人支付足以赔偿权利持有人因其知识产权被明知或应知而从事侵权活动的侵权人侵犯受到的损失。

2. 司法机关还应有权责令侵权人向权利持有人支付其他开销，其中可以包括适当的律师费。在适当情况下，成员可以授权司法机关责令返还利润或支付预先确定的损害赔偿，即使侵权人并非明知或应知而从事侵权活动。

第46条

其他救济

为对侵权产生有效的遏制，司法机关应有权责令将它们认为侵权的商品不作任何形式的赔偿在商业渠道之外处置以避免对权利持有人造成任何损害，或者，除非此举有悖于现行的宪法要求，将其销毁。司法机关还应有权责令将主要用于产生侵权商品的材料和工具不作任何形式的赔偿在商业渠道之外处置以将进一步侵权的危险减至最小。在考虑此种请求时，应考虑侵权严重程度与责令的救济相称的需要以及第三方的利益。对于假冒商标的商品，除非在特殊情况下，单纯将非法贴加的商标去除应不足以允许将商品放行进入商业渠道。

第47条

获得信息权

成员可以规定，司法机关应有权责令侵权人将参与侵权商品或服务的生产和分销的第三方的身份及其发行渠道告知权利持有人，除非这样做与侵权的严重程度不相称。

第48条

对被告的损害赔偿

1. 司法机关应有权责令请求采取措施和滥用实施程序的一方向误受禁止或限制的一方因此种滥用受到的损害提供适当赔偿。司法机关还应有权责令请求人支付被告的开销，其中可以包括适当的律师费。

2. 对于与知识产权保护或实施有关的任何法律的执行，成员应只有在该法律执行过程中善意地采取或意图采取行动的情况下才使公共机关和官员均免于适当补救措施的责任。

第49条

行政程序

只要行政程序能够导致根据案情是非责令民事救济，此种行政程序应符合与本节陈述的那些实质相同的原则。

第三节　临时措施

第 50 条

1. 司法机关应有权责令采取迅速和有效的临时措施以：

（a）阻止发生对任何知识产权的侵犯，尤其是在其管辖范围阻止包括刚经海关通关的进口商品在内的商品进入商业渠道；

（b）保存与被控的侵权有关的证据。

2. 司法机关应有权在适当情况下不听取对方陈述而采取临时措施，尤其是在任何延误有可能给权利持有人造成不可弥补的损害的情况下，或在显然有证据被销毁之危险的情况下。

3. 司法机关应有权要求请求方提供任何可以合理获得的证据，以使它们自己有足够程度的确定性认为该请求人为权利持有人、请求人的权利正受到侵犯或此种侵权即将发生，并责令请求人提供足以保护被告和防止滥用的保证金或同等的担保。

4. 如果不听取对方陈述而采取了临时措施，应至晚在措施执行后无延迟地通知受影响的各方。在被告请求下，应进行包括有权陈述意见的审查，以在措施通知后一个合理时段内决定这些措施应被修改、撤销或确认。

5. 可以要求申请人提供其他必要信息，以由执行临时措施的机关确认有关商品。

6. 如果未在一合理时段内提起将根据案情是非作出裁定的诉讼，应被告请求，在不损害第 4 款的情况下，根据第 1 款和第 2 款采取的临时措施应被撤销或另行停止有效；在成员法律允许的情况下，该时段由责令采取措施的司法机关确定，或者，无此种确定的，不超过二十个工作日或三十一个历日，以较长者为准。

7. 如果临时措施被撤销，或如果由于申请人的任何行为或疏漏而失效，或如果随后发现不存在对知识产权的侵犯或侵犯的危险，司法机关应有权依被告请求责令申请人为这些措施造成的任何损害向被告提供适当赔偿。

8. 只要行政程序能够导致责令任何临时措施，此种程序应符合与本节陈述的那些实质相同的原则。

第四节　有关边境措施的专门要求[12]

第51条

中止海关当局的放行

成员应依照以下陈述的规定采取程序[13]，使有正当理由怀疑可能发生假冒的商标商品或盗版的版权商品[14]进口的权利持有人能够向司法或行政主管机关书面申请由海关当局中止放行此种商品进入自由流通。成员可以使此种申请能够就对知识产权有其他侵犯的商品提出，只要符合本节的要求。成员亦可以规定相应的程序，用于海关当局中止放行预定从其领土出口的侵权商品。

第52条

申请

任何提起第51条之下程序的权利持有人应被要求提供充分证据，使主管当局相信，根据进口国的法律显然存在对权利持有人知识产权的侵犯，并应被要求提供对其商品的足够详细的描述，使它们可以容易地被海关当局辨认。主管当局应在一合理时段内通知申请人它们是否已经接受申请，以及在由主管当局确定的情况下，海关当局将采取行动的时段。

第53条

保证金或同等保险

1. 主管当局应有权要求申请人提供足以保护被告和主管当局以及防止滥用的

---

⑫　如果一成员基本取消对商品跨其与同属一关税同盟的另一成员的边界流动的所有控制，它不得被要求在该边界适用本节的规定。

⑬　兹同意，不得有义务将此种程序适用于由权利持有人或经其同意投放另一国市场的商品的进口或转运中的商品。

⑭　为本协定的目的：

（a）“假冒的商标商品”指任何商品，包括包装，它们未经授权载有与就此种商品有效注册的商标相同的商标或其基本方面无法与此一商标区分的商标，因而在进口国法律之下侵犯了所涉商标的所有者的权利；

（b）“盗版的版权商品”指任何商品，其是在生产国未经权利持有人或权利持有人正式授权的人同意制作的复本，并直接或间接由一件物品制成，制作该复本在进口国法律之下构成对版权或相关权利的侵犯。

保证金或同等担保。此种保证金或同等担保不得过度阻碍诉诸这些程序。

2. 如果海关当局根据本节之下的一项申请依照非由司法或其他独立机关作出的决定中止将含有工业设计、专利、布图设计或未披露的信息的商品放行进入自由流通，并且第 55 条中规定的时段已届满而经正式授权的机关没有批准临时救济，只要遵守所有其他的进口条件，此种商品的所有者、进口者或收货人，经支付足以就任何侵权保护权利持有人的保证金，应有权使其放行。支付此种保证金不得妨碍权利持有人可有的任何其他救济；不言而喻，如果权利持有人未在合理时段内行使诉讼权，保证金应被放还。

第 54 条

中止的通知

根据第 51 条中止放行商品，应立即通知进口者和申请人。

第 55 条

中止的期限

如果在向申请人送达中止通知后一个不超过十个工作日的时段内，海关当局没有被告知被告以外一方已提起将根据案情是非作出裁定的诉讼，或没有被通知经正式授权的机关已经采取临时措施延长中止商品的放行，该商品应被放行，条件是所有其他进口或出口的条件已得到遵守；在适当情况下，此时间限制可以再延长十个工作日。如果提起将根据案情是非作出裁定的诉讼，在被告请求下，应进行包括有权陈述意见的审查，以在一个合理时段内决定修改、撤销或确认这些措施。尽管有上述规定，如果根据一项临时司法措施中止或继续中止商品的放行，第 50 条第 6 款的规定应适用。

第 56 条

对进口者和商品所有者的赔偿

有关当局应有权责令申请人为因错误地扣押商品或扣押根据第 55 条放行的商品给进口者、收货人和商品所有者造成的任何损害支付适当赔偿。

第 57 条

查看和得到信息的权利

在不损害保密信息的保护的情况下，成员应赋予主管当局权力，给权利持有人足够的机会使任何被海关扣押的商品接受查看，以证实权利持有人的主张。主管当局还应有权给进口者同等的机会，使任何此种商品接受查看。如果根据案情是非作出肯定的确定，成员可以赋予主管当局权力，将发货人、进口者和收货人的名称和地址以及所涉商品的数量通知权利持有人。

第 58 条

依职权的行动

如果成员要求主管当局主动采取行动和中止放行它们就其获得知识产权正受到侵犯的初步证据的商品：

（a）该主管当局可以随时向权利持有人索取任何可能有助于它们行使这些权力的信息；

（b）应迅速将中止通知进口者和权利持有人。如果进口者已就中止向主管当局提出申诉，中止应取决于经必要修改的第 55 条陈述的条件；

（c）成员应只有在善意地采取或意图采取行动的情况下才使公共机关和官员均免于适当救济措施的责任。

第 59 条

救济

不损害权利持有人可有的其他诉讼权，并以被告寻求司法机关审查的权利为条件，主管当局应有权根据第 46 条中陈述的原则责令销毁或处置侵权商品。对于假冒的商标商品，除特殊情况外，主管当局不得允许侵权商品以未改变的状态再出口或对其采取不同的海关程序。

第 60 条

无关紧要的进口

成员可以排除将上述规定适用于旅客个人行李中包含的或以小件寄品发送的非商业性质的商品。

第五节　刑事程序

第 61 条

成员应规定刑事程序和罚责，至少适用于故意假冒商标或商业规模盗用版权。

可以得到的救济应包括足以提供遏制的监禁和/或罚金，程度与适用于严重性相应的犯罪的惩罚一致。在适当情况下，可以得到的救济还应包括没收、剥夺和销毁侵权商品以及主要用于从事违法行为的任何材料和工具。成员可规定刑事程序和罚则，适用于其他侵犯知识产权的情况，尤其是故意和以商业规模从事的。

第四部分　获得和维持知识产权的程序和有关的当事人之间程序

第62条

1. 成员可以要求履行合理的程序和手续，作为获得或维持第二部分第二节直至第六节之下规定的知识产权的条件。此种程序和手续应与本协定的规定一致。

2. 如果获得一项知识产权以该权利的授予或注册为条件，成员应保证授予或注册的程序在履行获得权利的实体条件的前提下使权利在一个合理时段内授予或注册，以避免无正当理由缩短保护期。

3.《巴黎公约》(1967)第4条经必要修改应适用于服务商标。

4. 与知识产权的获得或维持有关的程序以及国内法规定的程序、行政撤销和诸如异议、宣告无效和取消等当事人之间的程序，应由第41条第2款和第3款陈述的一般原则规制。

5. 第4款之下提到的任何程序中的最终行政决定，应接受司法或准司法机关的审查。但是，在异议或行政撤销失败的情况下，不得有义务提供机会对决定作此种审查，条件是能够就此种程序的依据提起无效程序。

第五部分　争端的防止和解决

第63条

透明度

1. 成员实施的与本协定的主题(知识产权的有效性、范围、获得、实施和防止滥用)有关的法律和法规、司法终裁和一般适用的行政裁决，应以能使各政府和权利持有人了解它们的方式以全国性语文公布，或在此种公布不切实的情况下使公众可以得到。一成员的政府或政府机构与另一成员的政府或政府机构之间生效的与本协定主题有关的协定亦应被公布。

2. 成员应将第1款中提到的法律和法规通知TRIPS理事会，以有助于理事会检查本协定的运作。理事会应努力尽量减小成员行使此项义务的负担，并且可以决定不要求将此种法律和法规直接通知理事会的义务，如果就建立包含这些法律和法规的共同注册与WIPO的磋商取得成功。与此相关，理事会还应考虑根据本协定之下源自《巴黎公约》(1967)第6条之三条款的义务就通知要求的任何行动。

3. 每个成员应有意愿应来自另一成员的书面请求提供第1款中提到的信息。一成员有理由相信知识产权领域的一项具体司法裁定或行政裁决或双边协定影响其在本协定之下的权利，也可以书面请求得到或被足够详细地告知此种具体司法裁定、行政裁决或双边协定。

4. 第1款、第2款和第3款中任何内容不得要求成员披露可能妨碍法律实施或另外违背公共利益或损害特定公有或私有企业合法商业利益的保密信息。

第64条

争端解决

1. 由《争端解决协定》详述和适用的GATT(1994)第XXII和XXIII条的规定，应适用于本协定之下的磋商和争端解决，此处另有具体规定的除外。

2. GATT(1994)第XXIII条第1款(b)项和第1款(c)项，在《WTO协定》生效之日起一个五年的时段，不得适用于本协定之下的争端解决。

3. 在第2款中提到的时段期间，TRIPS理事会应审查根据本协定提出的GATT(1994)第XXIII条第1款(b)项和第1款(c)项之下规定种类的控告的范围和形式，并将其建议提交部长级会议批准。部长级会议批准此种建议或延长第2款中的时段的任何决议，应只能通过一致同意作出，经批准的建议应对所有成员有效，无需进一步正式承认的过程。

第六部分　过渡协定

第65条

过渡安排

1. 以第2款、第3款和第4款为条件，任何成员无须在《WTO协定》生效之日起一个一年的一般时段届满之前适用本协定的规定。

2. 发展中国家成员可以将本协定第3条、第4条和第5条以外各条的在第1款中限定的适用日期再延缓四年。

3. 处在从中央计划向自由企业市场经济转型过程中和正在对其知识产权制度进行结构改革并在准备和实施知识产权法律和法规中面临特殊问题的任何其他成员，也可以受益于第 2 款中预设的延缓时段。

4. 只要一发展中国家成员根据本协定有义务将产品专利保护延及在第 2 款限定的本协定对该成员开始适用的一般日期在其领土内不受此保护的技术领域，可以将第二部分第五节关于产品专利的规定的适用再延缓一个五年时段。

5. 在第 1 款、第 2 款、第 3 款或第 4 款之下利用过渡时段的成员，应保证该时段中其法律、法规和惯例中的任何变更不导致降低与本协定条款的一致性。

第 66 条

最不发达国家成员

1. 考虑最不发达国家成员有特殊需要和要求，有经济、财政和行政上的限制，以及需要灵活性以建立可行的技术基础，此种成员在自第 65 条第 1 款之下限定的适用日期起一个十年时段中，无须适用本协定第 3 条、第 4 条和第 5 条以外的条款。应最不发达国家成员有适当动因的请求，TRIPS 理事会应准予延长此时段。

2. 发达国家成员应为其领土内的企业和机构提供激励，以促进和鼓励向最不发达国家转让技术，使它们能够建立健全和可行的技术基础。

第 67 条

技术合作

为便于本协定的实施，发达国家成员应根据请求并以互相商定的期限和条件，为发展中和最不发达国家成员提供技术和财政合作。此种合作应包括协助制定保护和实施知识产权以及防止其滥用的法律和法规，并应包括对建立或加强与这些事项有关的国内机关和机构的支持，包括人员的培训。

第七部分　机构安排; 最后条款

第 68 条

与贸易有关知识产权理事会

TRIPS 理事会应监督本协定的运作，尤其是成员对协定之下义务的履行，并应给予成员就涉及与贸易有关知识产权的事项进行磋商的机会。它应履行成员赋予的其他责任，尤其是，应向成员提供在争端解决程序方面请求的任何帮助。在履行其职责中，TRIPS 理事会可以咨询它认为适当的任何来源并从其寻求信息。在与 WIPO 的磋商中，理事会应在第一次会谈一年内努力达成与该组织的机构进行合作的适当安排。

第 69 条

国际合作

成员同意相互合作以消除侵犯知识产权的商品的国际贸易。为此目的，它们应建立和通告其行政部门中的联系点，并愿意交换与侵权商品贸易有关的信息。它们尤其应促进海关当局之间就假冒的商标商品和盗版的版权商品的贸易交换信息和开展合作。

第 70 条

对已有客体的保护

1. 本协定不就协定对有关成员适用之日以前发生的行为产生义务。

2. 除本协定中另有规定，本协定就协定对有关成员适用之日存在并于该日在该成员中受保护的，或在本协定的期限下符合或随后将符合保护条件的所有客体产生义务。就本款及第 3 款和第 4 款，与已有作品有关的版权义务，应只根据《伯尔尼公约》(1971) 第 18 条确定，与已有唱片中唱片制作者和表演者的权利有关的义务，应只根据在本协定第 14 条第 6 款之下规定适用的《伯尔尼公约》(1971) 第 18 条确定。

3. 不得有义务恢复保护在本协定对有关成员适用之日已经进入公有领域的客体。

4. 与在符合本协定的法律规定之下构成侵权的包含受保护客体的特定物有关的行为，在该成员承认 WTO 协定之日以前开始或已就其作出重大投资的，任何成员可以对权利持有人就本协定对该成员适用之日以后继续从事的此种行为可有的救济规定限制。但是，在此种情况下，成员应至少规定支付公平报酬。

5. 成员无义务就在本协定对该成员适用之日以前购买的原始本或复本适用第 11 条和第 14 条第 4 款的规定。

6. 成员不得被要求将第 31 条或第 27 条第 1 款中关于享有专利权不得因技术领域而受差别待遇的要求适用于不经权利人授权的使用，如果政府在本协定公开之日以前批准授权此种使用。

7. 在知识产权保护以注册为条件的情况下，本协定对有关成员适用之日正在办理中的保护申请，应被允许修改以主张本协定之下提供的任何提高的保护。此种修改不得包含新的事项。

8. 如果一成员在 WTO 协定生效之日不为医药和农用化工产品提供与其在第 27 条之下的义务相称的专利保护，该成员应：

（a）尽管有第六部分的规定，自 WTO 协定生效之日起提供手段以能够为此种发明提交专利申请；

（b）自本协定适用之日起，将本协定规定的可专利性标准适用于这些申请，如同那些标准在该成员中在申请日，或者，如果提供并主张优先权，在申请的优先权日正在适用；

（c）自授予专利起，并在根据本协定第 33 条自申请日起计算的专利期限的剩余部分中，根据本协定为这些申请中符合（b）项中提到的保护标准的那些提供专利保护。

9. 如果一种产品在一个成员中根据第 8 款（a）项是一项专利申请的客体，尽管有第六部分的规定，应授予专有营销权，期限为在该成员中获得营销批准后五年，或直至产品专利在该成员中被授予或被拒绝，以较短者为准，条件是，在 WTO 协定生效后，在另一成员中提交了一项专利申请并为该产品授予了专利，并且在此另一成员中获得了营销批准。

第 71 条

检查和修改

1. TRIPS 理事会应在第 65 条第 2 款中提到的过渡时段届满之后检查本协定的实施。理事会应在该日期之后两年，并在其后以相同间隔，根据实施中取得的经验进行检查。理事会还可以根据可能使本协定有必要更动或修改的有关新发展进行检查。

2. 单纯为调整至在其他多边协定中取得和生效的、并在那些协定之下经所有 WTO 成员承认的更高水平的知识产权保护的目的进行修改，可以提交部长级会议根据 WTO 协定第 X 条第 6 款在 TRIPS 理事会一致建议的基础上采取行动。

第 72 条

保留

未经其他成员同意，不可以对本协定中的任何条款提出保留。

第73条

安全例外

本协定中任何内容不得被解释为：

（a）要求成员提供它认为披露有悖于其至关重要的安全利益的信息。

（b）阻止成员采取它认为于保护其至关重要的安全利益有必要的任何行动：

（i）涉及可裂变材料或从中产生它们的材料的；

（ii）涉及武器、弹药和战争工具交易的，以及涉及直接或间接为供给军事设施的目的进行的其他商品和材料的交易的；

（iii）在战时或国际关系中其他紧急情况时采取的。

（c）阻止成员根据其在联合国宪章之下的义务为维护国际和平与安全采取任何行动。

世界知识产权组织版权条约（WCT）[*, **]

（1996年）

目录[*]

---

* 本条约于1996年12月20日由关于版权和邻接权若干问题外交会议在日内瓦通过。

**（通过本条约的）外交会议关于WCT某些条款的一致声明以脚注形式抄录在有关条款之下。

序言

缔约方，

希望以尽可能有效和一致的方式开展和维持对文学和艺术作品中作者权利的保护，

承认需要启用新的国际规则和澄清对某些现有规则的解释，以为经济、社会、文化和技术的新发展引起的问题提供适当的解决办法，

承认信息和通信技术的发展与交汇对文学和艺术作品的创作和使用的重大影响，

强调版权保护作为对文学和艺术创作的一种激励的显著重要性，

承认需要保持《伯尔尼公约》中体现的作者权利与更大的尤其是教育、研究和获得信息的公众利益之间的一种平衡，

达成一致如下：

第 1 条

与《伯尔尼公约》的关系

（1）对于是《保护文学和艺术作品伯尔尼公约》建立的联盟的成员的缔约方，本条约是该公约第 20 条意思中的一项特别协议。本条约不得与《伯尔尼公约》以

外的条约有任何关联，亦不得损害任何其他条约之下的任何权利和义务。

（2）本条约任何内容不得减损缔约方在《保护文学和艺术作品伯尔尼公约》之下现有的相互义务。

（3）以下，“伯尔尼公约”指《保护文学和艺术作品伯尔尼公约》1971 年 7 月 24 日巴黎文本。

（4）缔约方应遵守《伯尔尼公约》第 1 条至第 21 条和附件。①

第 2 条

版权保护的范围

版权保护延及表达，而非思想、过程、操作方法或数学概念本身。

第 3 条

《伯尔尼公约》第 2 条至第 6 条的适用

缔约方应就本条约规定的保护经必要修改适用《伯尔尼公约》第 2 条至第 6 条的规定。②

第 4 条

计算机程序

计算机程序作为《伯尔尼公约》第 2 条意思中的文字作品受保护。此种保护适用于计算机程序，无论其以什么方式或形式表达。③

---

① 关于第 1 条第（4）款的一致声明：《伯尔尼公约》第 9 条列举的复制权和该条之下允许的例外，完全适用于数字环境，尤其是以数字形式对作品的使用。兹同意，以数字形式在电子媒介中存储受保护的作品，构成《伯尔尼公约》第 9 条意思中的复制。

② 关于第 3 条的一致声明：兹同意，适用本条约第 3 条时，《伯尔尼公约》第 2 条至第 6 条中的“联盟国家”一语，在就本条约规定的保护适用《伯尔尼公约》的那些条款时，将被理解为如同它是对本条约一缔约方的提述。还同意，《伯尔尼公约》那些条款中的“联盟外国家”一语，在同样情况下，将被理解为如同它是对一个不是本条约缔约方的国家的提述，而《伯尔尼公约》第 2 条第（8）款、第 2 条之二第（2）款、第 3 条、第 4 条和第 5 条中的“本公约”，将被理解为如同它是对《伯尔尼公约》和本条约的提述。最后，兹同意，《伯尔尼公约》第 3 条至第 6 条中“联盟国家之一的国民”的提述，在这些条款被适用于本条约时，对作为本条约缔约方的政府间组织而言，将指该组织成员国之一的国民。

③ 关于第 4 条的一致声明：本条约第 4 条之下的计算机的保护的范围，与第 2 条连读，符合《伯尔尼公约》第 2 条并与 TRIPS 协议的有关规定相同。

第 5 条

数据汇编（数据库）

数据或其他材料的任何形式的汇编，由于内容的选择或编排构成智力创作物的，本身受保护。此种保护不延及数据或材料本身，并且不损害汇编包含的数据或材料中存在的任何版权。④

第 6 条

发行权

（1）文学和艺术作品的作者享有专有权利，授权通过销售或其他形式转让所有权向公众提供其作品的原件和复本。

（2）本条约任何内容不得影响缔约方自行确定，在原始本或复本经作者授权首次销售或以其他方式转让所有权后，若有的话以何条件适用第（1）款中权利的用尽。⑤

第 7 条

出租权

（1）以下项的作者

（i）计算机程序；

（ii）电影作品；

（iii）缔约方国内法律确定的唱片中包含的作品，享有授权向公众商业性出租其作品的原件或复本的专有权利。

（2）本条第（1）款不适用于：

（i）计算机程序，如果程序本身不是出租的主要对象；

（ii）电影作品，除非商业性出租导致此种作品的严重损害专有复制权的广泛复制。

（3）尽管有第（1）款的规定，一缔约方在 1994 年 4 月 15 日已有并继续实行作者因出租其包含在唱片中的作品的复本获得公平报酬的制度，可以保留该制度，

---

④ 关于第 5 条的一致声明：本条约第 5 条之下的数据汇编（数据库）的保护的范围，与第 2 条连读，符合《伯尔尼公约》第 2 条并与 TRIPS 协定的有关规定相同。

⑤ 关于第 6 条和第 7 条的一致声明：用在这些条款中，“复本”和“原件和复本”，以所述条款之下的发行权和出租权为条件，专指可以作为有形物品投入流通的固定的复本。

条件是商业性出租唱片中包含的作品不导致对作者专有复制权的严重损害。⑥⑦

第8条

向公众传播的权利

不损害《伯尔尼公约》第11条第（1）款（ii）项、第11条之二第（1）款（i）和（ii）项、第11条之三第（1）款（ii）项、第14条第（1）款（ii）项和第14条之二第（1）款的规定，文学和艺术作品的作者应享有专有权利，授权通过有线或无线手段将其作品向公众进行任何传播，包括以公众成员可以在个人选择的地点和时间获得这些作品的方式向公众提供其作品。⑧

第9条

摄影作品的保护期限

对于摄影作品，缔约方不得适用《伯尔尼公约》第7条第（4）款的规定。

第10条

限制和例外

（1）缔约方可以在某些特殊情况下在其国内法律中对本条约之下赋予文学和艺术作品作者的权利规定不与作品的正常使用相冲突并且不过度损害作者合法利益的限制或例外。

（2）在适用《伯尔尼公约》时，缔约方应将对该公约中规定的权利的任何限制或例外，限于某些不与作品的正常使用相冲突并且不过度损害作者合法利益的

---

⑥ 关于第6条和第7条的一致声明：用在这些条款中，“复本”和“原件和复本”，以所述条款之下的发行权和出租权为条件，专指可以作为有形物品投入流通的固定的复本。

⑦ 关于第7条的一致声明：兹同意，第7条第（1）款之下的义务，不要求一缔约方为在该缔约方法律之下不就唱片享有权利的作者提供专有商业出租权。兹同意，此义务符合TRIPS协议第14条第（4）款。

⑧ 关于第8条的一致声明：兹同意，单纯提供有形设备以使能够或进行传播，本身不构成本条约或《伯尔尼公约》意思中的传播。进一步同意，第8条任何内容不得阻止缔约方适用第11条之二第（2）款。

特殊情况。[⑨]

第11条

与技术措施有关的义务

缔约方应提供充分的法律保护和有效的法律救济，防止规避作者为行使其在本条约或《伯尔尼公约》之下的权利和限制未经有关作者授权的或法律不允许的与其作品有关行为使用的有效技术措施。

第12条

与权利管理信息有关的义务

（1）缔约方应提供充分和有效的法律救济，防止任何人，在知道或就民事救济而言有合理依据知道其会导致、促成、便利或隐瞒对本条约或《伯尔尼公约》涵盖的任何权利的侵犯的情况下，故意实施任何下列行为：

（i）擅自除去或更改任何电子权利管理信息；

（ii）擅自发行、为发行而进口、广播或向公众传播作品或作品的复本，明知电子权利管理信息被擅自除去或更改。

（2）用在本条中，“权利管理信息”指识别作品、作品的作者、作品中任何权利的所有者的信息，或有关使用作品的期限和条件的信息，以及构成此种信息的任何数字或代码，如果这些信息项目中的任何被附加于作品的复本，或与向公众传播作品相关而出现。[⑩]

第13条

及时实施

缔约方应将《伯尔尼公约》第18条的规定适用于本条约规定的所有保护。

---

⑨ 关于第10条的一致声明：兹同意，第10条的规定允许缔约方继续实行其国内法律中被认为可在《伯尔尼公约》之下接受的限制和例外并适当延伸到数字环境中。同样，这些条款应被理解为允许缔约方制定数字网络环境中恰当的新例外和限制。

还同意，第10条第（2）款既不减小也不扩大《伯尔尼公约》允许的限制和例外的适用范围。

⑩ 关于第12条的一致声明：兹同意，“对本条约或《伯尔尼公约》涵盖的任何权利的侵犯”的提述，包括专有权利和报酬权两者。

进一步同意，缔约方不会凭借本条建立或实行《伯尔尼公约》或本条约之下不允许的具有强加手续效果的权利管理制度而阻止货物自由流动或妨碍享有本条约之下的权利。

第14条

关于权利实施的规定

（1）缔约方承诺根据其法律制度采取必要措施保证本条约的适用。

（2）缔约方应保证其法律之下有实施程序，以使能对侵犯本条约涵盖的权利的任何行为采取有效行动，包括阻止侵权的迅速救济和对进一步侵权构成遏制的救济。

第15条

大会

（1）（a）缔约方应有一个大会。

（b）每个缔约方应有一名会议代表作为代表，会议代表可有替补代表、顾问和专家协助。

（c）每个代表团的费用由委派它的缔约方负担。大会可以要求世界知识产权组织（以下称“WIPO”）提供资金援助，以便于按照联合国大会既定惯例被认为是发展中国家或向市场经济转型国家的缔约方的代表团参加。

（2）（a）大会应处理与本条约的维持和发展以及本条约的适用和运作有关的事项。

（b）大会应就接受某些政府间组织参加本公约履行在第17条第（2）款之下赋予它的职能。

（c）大会应决定任何修订本条约的外交会议的召集，并为此种外交会议的筹备给WIPO总干事以必要指示。

（3）（a）每个作为国家的缔约方拥有一票，并应仅以自己的名义投票。

（b）任何作为政府间组织的缔约方可以代替其成员国参加表决，票数与其是本条约参加方的成员国的数目相等。如果其成员国任何之一行使表决权，此种政府间组织不得参加表决，反之亦然。

（4）大会应经WIPO总干事召集每两年举行一次例会。

（5）大会应制定自己的程序规则，包括特别会议的召集、法定人数要求和以本条约条款为条件的各种决议的所需多数。

第16条

国际局

WIPO国际局应执行与本条约有关的行政任务。

第 17 条

参加本条约的资格

（1）WIPO 的任何成员国可以参加本条约。

（2）任何政府间组织，声明就本条约涵盖的事项拥有权限并有自己的约束所有成员国的法律，并根据其内部程序被正式授权的，大会可以决定接受其参加本条约。

（3）欧洲共同体，经在通过本条约的外交会议上作出前款提到的声明，可以参加本条约。

第 18 条

本条约之下的权利和义务

以本条约中任何明确相反的规定为条件，每个缔约方应享有和承担本条约之下的所有权利和所有义务。

第 19 条

条约的签署

本条约应开放供任何 WIPO 成员国和供欧洲共同体签署，直至 1997 年 12 月 31 日。

第 20 条

条约的生效

本条约于三十个国家向 WIPO 总干事交存批准书或加入书三个月之后生效。

第 21 条

参加本条约的生效日期

本条约应约束：

（i）第 20 条中提到的三十个国家，自本条约生效之日起；

（ii）其他每个国家，自该国向 WIPO 总干事交存文书之日起满三个月；

（iii）欧洲共同体，如果在本条约根据第 29 条生效后交存批准书或加入书，自交存此种文书后满三个月起，或者，如果在本条约生效之前已交存此种文书，本条约生效后三个月；

（iv）任何其他被接受参加本条约的政府间组织，自交存加入书后满三个月起。

第 22 条

不得对条约做出保留

不允许对本条约做出保留。

第 23 条

声明条约无效

本条约可以由任何缔约方通过给 WIPO 总干事的通知声明无效。任何声明无效于 WIPO 总干事收到通知之日起一年生效。

第 24 条

条约的语文

（1）本条约以英文、阿拉伯文、中文、法文、俄文和西班牙文的独一份原始件签署，所有这些语文的文本具有同等效力。

（2）应一个利益相关方请求，WIPO 总干事应在与所有利益相关方磋商后，以第（1）款中提到那些以外的任何语文制定一个官方文本。为本款的目的，“利益相关方”指其官方语文或官方语文之一被涉及的任何 WIPO 成员国，以及欧洲共同体和任何其他可以参加本条约的政府间组织，如果其官方语文之一被涉及。

第 25 条

保管人

WIPO 总干事为本条约的保管人。

世界知识产权组织表演和唱片条约（WPPT）*, **

（1996年）

目录*

---

* 本条约于1996年12月20日在日内瓦由关于某些版权和邻接权问题的WIPO外交会议通过。

**（通过本条约的）外交会议关于WPPT某些条款的一致声明以脚注形式抄录在有关条款之下。

序言

缔约方，

希望以尽可能有效和一致的方式开展和维持对表演者和唱片制作者权利的保护，

承认需要启用新的国际规则为经济、社会、文化和技术发展带来的问题提供适当的解决办法，

承认信息和通信技术的发展与交汇对表演和唱片的制作和使用的重大影响，

承认需要在表演者和唱片制作者权利与更大的尤其是教育、研究和获得信息的公众利益之间保持一种平衡，

达成一致如下：

第Ⅰ章 总则

第1条

与其他公约的关系

（1）本条约任何内容不得减损缔约方在1961年10月26日于罗马签署的《保护表演者、唱片制作者和广播组织国际公约》（以下称“罗马公约”）之下现有的相互义务。

（2）在本条约之下给予的保护，不得触动并无论如何不得影响对文学和艺术作品的版权的保护。因而，本条约任何条款不可以作有损于此种保护的解释。[①]

（3）本条约不得与任何其他条约有任何关联，亦不得损害在任何其他条约之下的任何权利和义务。

第2条

定义

为本条约的目的：

（a）“表演者”是演员、歌唱者、演奏者、舞蹈者和其他演出、歌唱、讲述、朗诵、演奏、诠释或以另外方式表演文学或艺术作品或民间文艺表达形式的人；

（b）“唱片”指表演的声音，或其他声音或声音表现的固定物，包含在电影或其他视听作品中的固定物除外；[②]

（c）“固定物”指声音或声音表现的载体，由之声音能够通过装置被感知、复制或传播；

① 关于第1条第（2）款的一致声明：兹同意，第1条第（2）款澄清本条约之下唱片中的权利与唱片中包含的作品中版权之间的关系。在需要唱片中包含的作品的作者和对唱片拥有权利的表演者或制作者两者授权的情况下，不因为还要求表演者或制作者授权而不再需要作者授权，反之亦然。进一步同意，第1条第（2）款无内容阻止缔约方为表演者或唱片制作者提供本条约之下要求提供的那些以外的专有权利。

② 关于第2条（b）款的一致声明：兹同意，第2条（b）款中规定的唱片的定义，不表示唱片中的权利因唱片被包含在电影或其他视听作品中而受任何影响。

（d）“唱片制作者”指主动和负责对表演的声音，或其他声音或声音表现进行首次固定的自然人或法人；

（e）“出版”固定的表演或唱片，指经权利人同意向公众提供固定的表演或唱片的复本，只要复本以合理数量向公众提供；[③]

（f）“广播”指通过无线手段为公众接收发送声音，或图像和声音，或它们的表现；通过卫星的此种发送亦是“广播”；发送密码形式的信号是“广播”，如果广播组织或经其同意向公众提供解码手段；

（g）“向公众传播”表演或唱片，指通过广播以外的任何媒介向公众传送以唱片固定的表演的声音，或声音或声音表现。为第15条的目的，“向公众传播”包括使公众听到以唱片固定的声音或声音表现。

第3条

本条约之下的保护受益人

（1）缔约方应将本条约之下规定的保护给予是其他缔约方国民的表演者和唱片制作者。

（2）其他缔约方的国民应被理解为，在本条约所有缔约方是《罗马公约》缔约方的情况下便符合《罗马公约》保护资格标准的表演者或唱片制作者。就这些资格标准，缔约方应适用本条约第2条中的有关定义。[④]

（3）任何利用《罗马公约》第5条第（3）款规定的，或为同一公约第5条的目的利用其第17条规定的可能性的缔约方，应如那些条款预设的向世界知识产权组织（WIPO）总干事作出通知。[⑤]

第4条

国民待遇

（1）就本条约明确赋予的专有权利和本条约第15条规定的公平报酬权，每个

③　关于第2条（e）款、第8条、第9条、第12条和第13条的一致声明：使用在这些条款中，“复本”和“原始本和复本”等语，以所述条款之下的发行权和出租权为条件，专指能够作为有形物品投入流通的固定的复本。

④　关于第3条第（2）款的一致声明：为适用第3条第（2）款，兹同意，固定指原带（“母带”）的最终完成。

⑤　关于第3条的一致声明：兹同意，《罗马公约》第5条（a）款和第16条（a）款（iv）中“另一缔约国的国民”的提述，在适用于本条约时，就作为本条约一缔约方的政府间组织而言，指该组织成员国之一的国民。

缔约方应将给予本国国民的待遇给予符合第3条第（2）款定义的其他缔约方的国民。

（2）第（1）款中规定的义务，在另一缔约方利用本条约第15条第（3）款允许的保留的程度上不适用。

第II章　表演者的权利

第5条

表演者的精神权利

（1）不依赖于表演者的经济权利，即使在那些权利转让后，表演者就其现场表演或以唱片固定的表演享有要求被指明为其表演的表演者的权利，表演的使用方式决定省略的除外，并且，应有权反对对其表演的任何有损其声誉的歪曲、篡改或其他更改。

（2）根据本条第（1）款赋予表演者的权利，在他去世后至少保留到经济权利终止，并可以由主张保护所在缔约方法律授权的个人或机构行使。但是，批准或加入本条约时法律不规定在表演者去世后保护前款列举的所有权利的那些缔约方，可以规定这些权利中的一些在他去世后停止保留。

（3）保障本条之下赋予的权利的救济手段，由主张保护所在缔约方的法律规制。

第6条

表演者对其未固定的表演的经济权利

表演者就其表演享有授权以下的专有权利：

（i）广播和向公众传播其未固定的表演，表演是已经广播过的除外；

（ii）固定其未固定的表演。

第7条

复制权

表演者享有专有权利，授权以任何方式或形式直接或间接复制其以唱片固定的表演。⑥

⑥　关于第7条、第11条和第16条的一致声明：第7条和第11条列举的复制权和该条之下直到第16条允许的例外，完全适用于数字环境，尤其是以数字形式对表演和唱片的使用。兹同意，在电子媒介中以数字形式储存受保护的表演或唱片，构成这些条款意思中的复制。

第 8 条

发行权

（1）表演者享有专有权利，授权通过销售或其他形式的所有权转让向公众提供其以唱片固定的表演的原件或复本。

（2）本条约任何内容不得影响缔约方自行确定，固定的表演的原始本或复本在经表演者授权首次销售或以其他方式转让所有权后，若有的话以何条件适用第（1）款中权利的用尽。⑦

第 9 条

出租权

（1）表演者享有专有权利，授权向公众商业出租其以缔约方国内法律中确定的唱片固定的表演的原始本和复本，即使在它们由或根据表演者授权发行之后。

（2）尽管有本条第（1）款的规定，一缔约方在 1994 年 4 月 15 日已有并继续实行表演者因出租其以唱片固定的表演的复本获得公平报酬的制度，可以保留该制度，条件是唱片的商业性出租不导致对表演者专有复制权的严重损害。⑧

第 10 条

提供已固定的表演的权利

表演者享有专有权利，授权通过有线或无线手段以公众成员可以在个人选择的地点和时间获得它们的方式向公众提供其以唱片固定的表演。

---

⑦ 关于第 2 条（e）款、第 8 条、第 9 条、第 12 条和第 13 条的一致声明：使用在这些条款中，“复本”和“原始本和复本”等语，以所述条款之下的发行权和出租权为条件，专指能够作为有形物品投入流通的固定的复本。

⑧ 关于第 2 条（e）款、第 8 条、第 9 条、第 12 条和第 13 条的一致声明：使用在这些条款中，“复本”和“原始本和复本”等语，以所述条款之下的发行权和出租权为条件，专指能够作为有形物品投入流通的固定的复本。

第III章　唱片制作者的权利

第11条

复制权

唱片制作者享有授权以任何方式或形式直接或间接复制其唱片的专有权利。⑨

第12条

发行权

（1）唱片制作者享有专有权利，授权通过销售或其他形式的所有权转让向公众提供其唱片的原始本或复本。

（2）本条约任何内容不得影响缔约方自行确定，固定的表演的原始本或复本在经表演者授权首次销售或以其他方式转让所有权后，若有的话以何条件适用第（1）款中权利的用尽。⑩

第13条

出租权

（1）唱片制作者享有专有权利，授权向公众商业性出租其唱片的原始本和复本，即使在它们由或根据制作者授权发行之后。

（2）尽管有第（1）款的规定，一缔约方如在1994年4月15日已有并继续实行唱片制作者因出租其唱片的复本获得公平报酬的制度，可以保留该制度，条件是唱片的商业性出租不导致对唱片制作者专有复制权的严重损害。⑪

---

⑨　关于第7条、第11条和第16条的一致声明：第7条和第11条列举的复制权和该条之下直到第16条允许的例外，完全适用于数字环境，尤其是以数字形式对表演和唱片的使用。兹同意，在电子媒介中以数字形式储存受保护的表演或唱片，构成这些条款意思中的复制。

⑩　关于第2条（e）款、第8条、第9条、第12条和第13条的一致声明：用在这些条款中，“复本”和“原始本和复本”等语，以所述条款之下的发行权和出租权为条件，专指能够作为有形物品投入流通的固定的复本。

⑪　关于第2条（e）款、第8条、第9条、第12条和第13条的一致声明：用在这些条款中，“复本”和“原始本和复本”等语，以所述条款之下的发行权和出租权为条件，专指能够作为有形物品投入流通的固定的复本。

第 14 条

提供唱片的权利

唱片制作者应享有专有权利，授权通过有线或无线手段以公众成员可以在个人选择的地点和时间获得它们的方式向公众提供其唱片。

第 IV 章　共同条款

第 15 条

广播和公共传播的报酬权

（1）为广播或为任何公共传播而直接或间接使用为商业目的出版的唱片，表演者和唱片制作者应享有单笔公平报酬的权利。

（2）缔约方可在其国内法律中规定，单笔公平报酬应由表演者或唱片制作者或两者向使用者主张。缔约方可以制定国内法律，在表演者和唱片制作者之间没有协议的情况下，确定表演者和唱片制作者分享单笔公平报酬的条件。

（3）任何缔约方可以在向 WIPO 总干事交存的通知书中声明，它将仅就某些使用适用本条第（1）款的规定，或将以某种其他方式限制它们的适用，或将根本不适用这些规定。

（4）为本条的目的，通过有线或无线手段以公众成员可以在个人选择的地点和时间获得它们的方式向公众提供的唱片，应被认为已经为商业目的出版。[⑫][⑬]

第 16 条

限制和例外

（1）就表演者和唱片制作者的保护，缔约方可以在国内法律中规定与在国内法律中就文学和艺术作品的版权保护规定的种类相同的限制或例外。

（2）缔约方应将对本条约规定的权利的任何限制或例外，限于某些不与表演

⑫　关于第 15 条的一致声明：兹同意，第 15 条不是解决表演者和唱片制作者在数字时代应享有的广播和公共传播权的水平的完全办法。对于某些情况下的专有性规定或提供无保留可能的权利，有不同建议，各代表团无法达成一致意见，因此将问题留待将来解决。

⑬　关于第 15 条的一致声明：兹同意，第 15 条不阻止将本条赋予的权利给予民间文艺的表演者和记录民间文艺的唱片的制作者，如果此种唱片尚未为商业赢利出版。

的正常利用相冲突和过度损害表演者合法利益的特殊情况。⑭⑮

第17条

保护期

（1）本条约之下给予表演者的保护的期限，至少持续到自表演以唱片固定之年年终起算的一个五十年的时段终止。

（2）本条约之下给予唱片制作者的保护的期限，至少持续到自唱片出版之年年终起算的一个五十年的时段终止，或者，如果自唱片固定起五十年内没有出版，自固定进行之年年终起持续五十年。

第18条

与技术措施有关的义务

缔约方应提供充分的法律保护和有效的法律救济，防止规避表演者或唱片制作者为行使本条约之下的权利和限制未经其授权或法律不允许的与其表演或唱片有关的行为而使用的有效技术措施。

第19条

与权利管理信息有关的义务

（1）缔约方应提供充分和有效的法律救济，防止任何人，在知道或就民事救济而言有合理依据知道其会导致、促成、便利或隐瞒对本条约涵盖的任何权利的侵犯的情况下，故意实施任何下列行为：

（i）擅自除去或更改任何电子权利管理信息；

（ii）擅自发行、为发行而进口、广播、向公众传播或提供表演、固定的表演的复本或唱片的复本，明知电子权利管理信息被擅自除去或更改。

---

⑭ 关于第7条、第11条和第16条的一致声明：第7条和第11条列举的复制权和该条之下直至第16条允许的例外，完全适用于数字环境，尤其是以数字形式对表演和唱片的使用。兹同意，在电子媒介中以数字形式储存受保护的表演或唱片，构成这些条款意思中的复制。

⑮ 关于第16条的一致声明：关于《WIPO版权条约》第10条（限制和例外）的一致声明，经必要修改亦适用于《WIPO表演和唱片条约》第16条（限制和例外）。[关于WCT第10条的一致声明原文如下："兹同意，第10条的规定允许缔约方继续适用其国内法律中被认为可在《伯尔尼公约》之下接受的限制和例外并适当延伸到数字环境中。同样，这些条款应被理解为允许缔约方制定数字网络环境中恰当的新例外和限制。"进一步同意，第10条第（2）款既不缩小也不扩大《伯尔尼公约》允许的限制和例外的适用范围。"]

（2）用在本条中，“权利管理信息”指识别表演者、表演者的表演、唱片制作者、唱片、表演或唱片中任何权利人的信息，或有关使用表演或唱片的期限和条件的信息，以及构成此种信息的任何数字或代码，如果这些信息项目中任何一项被附加于固定的表演或唱片的复本，或与向公众传播或提供固定的表演或唱片相关出现。[16]

第 20 条

手续

享有和行使本条约中规定的权利，不得以任何手续为条件。

第 21 条

保留

以第 15 条第（3）款的规定为条件，不允许对本条约做出任何保留。

第 22 条

及时实施

（1）缔约方应将《伯尔尼公约》第 18 条的规定经必要修改适用于本条约规定的表演者和唱片制作者的权利。

（2）尽管有第（1）款的规定，一缔约方可以将本条约第 5 条的适用限于本条约对该缔约方生效之后发生的表演。

第 23 条

关于权利实施的规定

（1）缔约方承诺根据其法律制度采取必要措施保证本条约的适用。

（2）缔约方应保证其法律之下有实施程序，以使能对任何侵犯本条约涵盖的权利的行为采取有效行动，包括阻止侵权的迅速救济和对进一步侵权构成遏制的救济。

---

⑯ 关于第 19 条的一致声明：关于《WIPO 版权条约》第 12 条（与权利管理信息有关的义务）的一致声明，经必要修改亦适用于《WIPO 表演和唱片条约》第 19 条（与权利管理信息有关的义务）。[关于 WCT 第 12 条的一致声明原文如下：“兹同意，‘侵犯本条约或《伯尔尼公约》涵盖的任何权利’的提述，包括专有权利和获酬权两者。”进一步同意，缔约方不会凭借本条建立或实行《伯尔尼公约》或本条约之下不允许的有手续要求的权利管理制度而阻止货物自由流动或妨碍享有本条约之下的权利。”]

第Ⅴ章　行政和最后条款

第24条

大会

（1）（a）缔约方应有一个大会。

（b）每个缔约方应有一名会议代表作为代表，会议代表可有替补代表、顾问和专家协助。

（c）每个代表团的费用由委派它的缔约方负担。大会可以要求WIPO提供资金援助，以便于按照联合国大会既定惯例被认为是发展中国家或向市场经济转型国家的缔约方的代表团参加。

（2）（a）大会应处理与本条约的维持和发展以及本条约的适用和运作有关的事项。

（b）大会应就接受某些政府间组织参加本公约履行在第26条第（2）款之下赋予它的职能。

（c）大会应决定任何修订本条约的外交会议的召集，并为此种外交会议的筹备给WIPO总干事以必要指示。

（3）（a）每个作为国家的缔约方应有一票，并应仅以其自己的名义投票。

（b）任何作为政府间组织的缔约方可以代替其成员国参加表决，票数与其是本条约参加方的成员国的数目相等。此种政府间组织均不得参加表决，如果其成员国任何之一行使表决权，反之亦然。

（4）大会经WIPO总干事召集每两年以例会开会一次。

（5）大会应制定自己的程序规则，包括特别会议的召集、法定人数要求和以本条约条款为条件的各种决议的所需多数。

第25条

国际局

WIPO国际局执行与本条约有关的行政工作。

第26条

参加本条约的资格

（1）WIPO的任何成员国可以参加本条约。

（2）任何政府间组织，声明就本条约涵盖的事项拥有权限并有自己的约束所有成员国的法律，并根据内部程序被正式授权的，大会可以决定接受其参加本条约。

（3）欧洲共同体，经在通过本条约的外交会议上作出前款提到的声明，可以参加本条约。

第 27 条

本条约之下的权利和义务

以本条约中任何相反的明确规定为条件，每个缔约方享有和承担本条约之下的所有权利和所有义务。

第 28 条

条约的签署

本条约应开放供任何 WIPO 成员国和欧洲共同体签署，直至 1997 年 12 月 31 日。

第 29 条

条约的生效

本条约在三十个国家交存批准书或加入书之后三个月生效。

第 30 条

参加条约的生效日期

本条约应约束：

（i）第 29 条中提到的三十个国家，自本条约生效之日起；

（ii）其他每个国家，自该国向 WIPO 总干事交存文书之日起满三个月；

（iii）欧洲共同体，如果在本条约根据第 29 条生效后交存批准书或加入书，自交存此种文书后满三个月起，或者，如果在本条约生效之前已交存此种文书，本条约生效后三个月；

（iv）任何其他被接受参加本条约的政府间组织，自交存加入书后满三个月起。

第31条

声明条约无效

任何缔约方可以通过给WIPO总干事的通知声明本条约无效。

任何声明无效应于WIPO总干事收到通知之日起一年生效。

第32条

条约的语文

（1）本条约以英文、阿拉伯文、中文、法文、俄文和西班牙文的独一份原始件签署，所有这些语文的文本具有同等效力。

（2）应一个利益相关方请求，WIPO总干事应在与所有利益相关方磋商后，以第（1）款中提到那些以外的任何语文制定一个官方文本。为本款的目的，“利益相关方”指其官方语文或官方语文之一被涉及的任何WIPO成员国，以及欧洲共同体和任何其他可以参加本条约的政府间组织，如果其官方语文之一被涉及。

第33条

保管人

WIPO总干事为本条约的保管人。

视听表演北京条约*

目录

* 本条约于 2012 年 6 月 24 日在北京由保护视听表演外交会议通过。

序言

缔约方，

希望以尽可能有效和一致的方式开展和维持对表演者对其视听表演所享权利的保护，

回顾 2007 年由《成立世界知识产权组织（WIPO）公约》大会通过的旨在保证发展问题成为该组织工作组成部分的发展议程建议的重要性，

承认需要提出新的国际规则为经济、社会、文化和技术发展带来的问题提供适当的解决办法，

承认信息和通信技术的发展和交汇对视听表演的制作和使用的重大影响，

承认需要在表演者对其视听表演的权利与更大的尤其是教育、研究和获得信息的公众利益之间保持一种平衡，

承认 1996 年 12 月 20 日在日内瓦签署的《世界知识产权组织表演和唱片条约》（WPPT）对表演者的保护不延及以视听固定物固定的表演，

追溯到1996年12月20日由版权和邻接权若干问题外交会议通过的《与视听表演有关的决议》，

达成一致如下：

第1条

与其他公约和条约的关系

（1）本条约任何内容不得减损缔约方在WPPT或1961年10月26日在罗马签署的《保护表演者、唱片制作者和广播组织国际公约》之下现有的相互义务。

（2）在本条约之下给予的保护，不得触动并无论如何不得影响对文学和艺术作品的版权的保护。因而，本条约任何条款不可作有损于此种保护的解释。

（3）本条约不得与WPPT以外的条约有任何关联，亦不得损害任何其他条约之下的任何权利和义务[①][②]。

第2条

定义

为本条约的目的：

（a）“表演者”是演员、歌唱者、演奏者、舞蹈者和其他演出、歌唱、讲述、朗诵、演奏、诠释或以另外方式表演文学或艺术作品或民间文艺表达形式的人[③]；

（b）“视听固定物”指伴有或不伴有声音或声音表现的活动图像的载体，由之活动图像能够通过装置被感知、复制或传播[④]；

（c）“广播”指通过无线手段为公众接收传送声音或图像、图像和声音，或它们的表现；通过卫星的此种传送亦是“广播”；传送密码形式的信号是“广播”，

---

① 关于第1条第（1）款的一致声明：兹同意，本条约任何内容不影响《WIPO表演和唱片条约》（WPPT）之下的任何权利或义务或对它们的解释，并进而同意，第（3）款不为本条约缔约方设定任何批准或加入WPPT或遵守其任何条款的义务。

② 关于第1条第（3）款的一致声明：兹同意，作为世界贸易组织（WTO）成员的缔约方承认《与贸易有关知识产权的协议》（TRIPS协议）的所有原则和目标，并同意，本条约任何内容不影响TRIPS协议的条款，包括但不限于与反竞争做法有关的条款。

③ 关于第2条（a）款的一致声明：兹同意，“表演者”的定义包含表演在表演过程中创作或首次固定的文学或艺术作品的人。

④ 关于第2条（b）款的一致声明：兹确认，第2条（b）款中“视听固定物”的定义不损害WPPT第2条（c）款。

如果广播组织或经其同意向公众提供解码手段；

（d）“向公众传播”表演，指通过广播以外的任何媒介向公众传送未固定的表演或以视听固定物固定的表演。为第11条的目的，“向公众传播”包括使公众听到或看到或听到并看到以视听固定物固定的表演。

第3条

保护的受益人

（1）缔约方应将本条约之下规定的保护提供是其他缔约方国民的表演者。

（2）不是缔约方之一的国民但在其中之一有常住居所的表演者，为本条约的目的，应被视同该缔约方的国民。

第4条

国民待遇

（1）就本条约明确赋予的专有权利和本条约第11条规定的公平报酬权，每个缔约方应将给予本国国民的待遇给予其他缔约方的国民。

（2）就本条约第11条第（1）款和第11条第（2）款赋予的权利，一缔约方应有权将在第（1）款之下给予另一缔约方国民的保护的程度和期限，限于自己的国民在其他缔约方享受的那些权利。

（3）第（1）款中规定的义务，在另一缔约方利用本条约第11条第（3）款允许的保留的程度上，不适用于一缔约方；在一缔约方已作出此种保留的程度上，亦不适用于它。

第5条

精神权利

（1）不依赖于表演者的经济权利，并且，即使在那些权利转让后，就其活表演或以视听固定物固定的表演，表演者有权：

（i）要求被指明为其表演的表演者，表演的使用方式决定省略的除外；

（ii）反对对其表演的任何有损其声誉的歪曲、篡改或其他更改，其中适当考虑视听固定物的性质。

（2）根据第（1）款赋予表演者的权利，在他去世后至少保留到经济权利终止，并可以由主张保护所在缔约方法律授权的人或机构行使。但是，批准或加入本条约时法律不规定表演者去世后保护前款列举的所有权利的缔约方，可以规定表演者去世后这些权利中的一些不再保留。

（3）保障本条之下赋予的权利的补救手段，由主张保护所在缔约方的法律规制⑤。

第6条

表演者对其未固定的表演的经济权利

表演者就其表演享有授权以下的专有权利：

（i）广播和向公众传播其未固定的表演，表演是已经广播过的除外；

（ii）固定其未固定的表演。

第7条

复制权

表演者享有专有权利，授权以任何方式或形式直接或间接复制其以视听固定物固定的表演⑥。

第8条

发行权

（1）表演者享有专有权利，授权通过销售或其他方式转让所有权使公众得到其以视听固定物固定的表演的原始本或复本。

（2）本条约任何内容不影响缔约方自行确定，在固定的表演的原始本或复本经表演者授权首次销售或另行转让所有权后，若有的话以何条件适用第（1）款中权利的用尽⑦。

---

⑤　关于第5条的一致声明：为本条约的目的并且不损害任何其他条约，兹同意，考虑到视听固定物及其制作和发行的特点，在对表演进行正常利用，诸如以现有或新的媒介或格式编辑、压缩、配音或格式化，的过程中和在经表演者授权的使用过程中对表演进行的更改，本身不构成第5条第（1）款（ii）项意思中的更改。只有客观上实质性损害表演者声誉的改变，才涉及第5条第（1）款（ii）项之下的权利。还同意，单纯使用新的或改换的技术或媒介，本身不构成第5条第（1）款（ii）项意思中的更改。

⑥　关于第7条的一致声明：第7条规定的复制权和该条直至第13条之下允许的例外，完全适用于数字环境，尤其对表演的数字形式的使用。兹同意，以数字形式在电子媒介中储存受保护的表演，构成本条意思中的复制

⑦　关于第8条和第9条的一致声明：用在这些条款中，“原始本和复本”一语，以所述条款之下的发行权和出租权为条件，专指能够以有形物投入流通的固定的复本。

第 9 条

出租权

（1）表演者享有专有权利，授权向公众商业出租其以缔约方国内法律确定的视听固定物固定的表演的原始本和复本，即使在它们经或根据表演者授权发行之后。

（2）缔约方得免于第（1）款的义务，除非商业出租导致此种固定物的广泛复制而严重损害表演者的专有复制权⑧。

第 10 条

提供经固定的表演的权利

表演者享有专有权利，授权通过有线或无线手段以公众成员可以在个人选择的地点和时间获取它们的方式向公众提供其以视听固定物固定的表演。

第 11 条

广播和向公众传播的权利

（1）表演者享有专有权利，授权广播和向公众传播其以视听固定物固定的表演。

（2）缔约方可以在向 WIPO 总干事交存的通知书中声明，它们将为直接或间接使用以视听固定物固定的表演供广播或向公众传播设立一项公平报酬权，而非第（1）款中规定的授权的权利。缔约方还可以声明，它们将在其法律中为公平报酬权的行使设定条件。

（3）任何缔约方可以声明，它将仅就某些使用适用第（1）或第（2）款的规定，或以某种其他方式限制它们的适用，或根本不适用第（1）和第（2）款的规定。

第 12 条

权利的转让

（1）一缔约方可以在其国内法律中规定，一俟表演者同意他或她的表演以视听固定物固定，本条约第 7 条至第 11 条中规定的授权的专有权利，应由此种视听固定物的制作者拥有或行使或向其转让，表演者和国内法律确定的视听固定物的

⑧ 关于第 8 条和第 9 条的一致声明：用在这些条款中，“原始本和复本”一语，以所述条款之下的发行权和出租权为条件，专指能够以有形物投入流通的固定的复本。

制作者之间可以有任何相反约定。

（2）对于在其国内法律之下制作的视听固定物，缔约方可以要求此种同意或约定以书面形式并经约定双方或其正式授权的代表签字。

（3）不依赖于上述专有权利的转让，国内法律或单个、集体或其他协议可以规定，为本条约之下包括就第 10 条和第 11 条规定的对表演的任何使用，表演者有获得版税或公平报酬的权利。

第 13 条

限制和例外

（1）就表演者的保护，缔约方可以在其国内法律中规定与它们在国内法律中就文学和艺术作品的版权保护规定的种类相同的限制或例外。

（2）缔约方应将对本条约规定的权利的任何限制或例外，限于某些不与表演的正常利用相冲突和不过度损害表演者合法利益的特殊情况[⑨]。

第 14 条

保护期

在本条约之下给予表演者保护的期限，应至少持续到自表演被固定之年年终起算的一个五十年的时段终止。

第 15 条

与技术措施有关的义务

缔约方应提供充分的法律保护和有效的法律救济，防止规避表演者为行使其在本条约之下的权利和限制未经有关表演者授权的或法律不允许的与其表演有关

⑨ 关于第 13 条的一致声明：关于《WIPO 版权条约》（WCT）第 10 条（限制和例外）的一致声明，经必要修改亦适用于本条约第 13 条（限制和例外）。

行为而使用的有效的技术措施。[⑩][⑪]

第16条

与权利管理信息有关的义务

（1）缔约方应提供充分和有效的法律救济，防止任何人，在知道或就民事救济而言有合理依据知道其会导致、促成、便利或隐瞒对本条约涵盖的任何权利的侵犯的情况下，故意实施任何下列行为：

（i）擅自除去或更改任何电子权利管理信息；

（ii）擅自发行、为发行而进口、广播、向公众传播或提供以视听固定物固定的表演或表演的复本，明知电子权利管理信息被擅自除去或更改。

（2）用在本条中，“权利管理信息”指识别表演者、表演者的表演或表演中任何权利的所有者的信息，或有关使用表演的期限和条件的信息，以及构成此种信息的任何数字或代码，如果这些信息项目中任何一项被附加于以视听固定物固定的表演[⑫]。

第17条

手续

享有和行使本条约中规定的权利，不得以任何手续为条件。

第18条

保留和通知

（1）以第11条第（3）款的规定为条件，不得允许对本条约作出任何保留。

---

⑩ 在其与第13条有关时关于第15条的一致声明：兹同意，本条任何内容不阻止缔约方采取有效和必要的措施，在对视听表演使用了技术措施且受益人可以合法使用该表演而权利人未就该表演采取适当和有效的措施使受益人享有该缔约方国内法律之下的例外和限制的情况下，保证受益人可以根据第13条享有该缔约方国内法律规定的限制和例外。不损害对其中固定有表演的视听作品的法律保护，进而同意，第15条之下的义务不适用于在实施本条约的国内法律之下不受或不再受保护的表演。

⑪ 关于第15条的一致声明：“表演者使用的技术措施”一语，涉及WPPT的情况亦同，应被广义理解为亦指代表包括其代理人、被许可人或被转让人的表演者行事的人，包括制作者、服务提供者和基于正式授权使用表演从事传播或广播的人。

⑫ 关于第16条的一致声明：关于WCT第12条（与权利管理信息有关的义务）的一致声明，经必要修改亦适用于本条约第16条（与权利管理信息有关的义务）。

（2）在批准或加入书中可以作出第 11 条第（2）款或第 19 条第（2）款之下的任何通知，通知的生效日期应与本条约对作出通知的缔约方生效的日期相同。任何此种通知亦可以更晚作出，在此情况下，通知在 WIPO 总干事收到后三个月或通知中指明的任何更晚日期生效。

第 19 条

及时实施

（1）缔约方应将本条约之下给予的保护，提供给在本条约生效时存在的已固定的表演和在本条约对每个缔约方生效之后发生的所有表演。

（2）尽管有第（1）款的规定，一缔约方可以在向 WIPO 总干事交存的通知中声明，它将不对本条约对每个缔约方生效时存在的已固定的表演适用本条约第 7 条至第 11 条的规定或其中任何一项或更多项。对此种缔约方，其他缔约方可以限制所述条款对本条约对该缔约方生效后发生的表演的适用。

（3）本条约中规定的保护，不得损害任何在本条约对每个缔约方生效之前实施的行为、达成的协议或获得的权利。

（4）缔约方可以在法律中订立过渡条款，任何在本条约生效之前根据过渡条款就表演从事合法行为的人，可以在本条约对各缔约方生效之后在第 5 条和第 7 条至第 11 条规定的权利范围内就同一表演实施行为。

第 20 条

关于权利实施的规定

（1）缔约方承诺根据其法律制度采取必要措施保证本条约的适用。

（2）缔约方应保证其法律之下有实施程序，以使能对任何侵犯本条约涵盖的权利的行为采取有效行动，包括阻止侵权的迅速救济和对进一步侵权构成遏制的救济。

第 21 条

大会

（1）（a）缔约方应有一个大会。

（b）每个缔约方应在大会有一名会议代表作为代表，会议代表可有替补代表、顾问和专家协助。

（c）每个代表团的费用由委派它的缔约方负担。大会可以要求 WIPO 提供资金援助，以便于按照联合国大会的既定惯例被认为是发展中国家的或是向市场经济转型国家的缔约方的代表团参加。

（2）（a）大会应处理与本条约的维持和发展以及本条约的适用和运作有关的事项。

（b）大会应就接受某些政府间组织参加本公约履行在第 23 条第（2）款之下赋予它的职能。

（c）大会应决定任何修订本条约的外交会议的召集，并为此种外交会议的筹备给 WIPO 总干事以必要指示。

（3）（a）每个作为国家的缔约方拥有一票并应仅以自己的名义投票。

（b）任何作为政府间组织的缔约方可以代替其成员国参加表决，票数与它的是本条约参加方的成员国的数目相等。任何此种政府间组织不得参加表决，如果其成员国任何之一行使表决权，反之亦然。

（4）大会应经总干事召集并且，如无例外情况，与 WIPO 大会在相同时段和相同地点开会。

（5）大会应力求以一致同意作出决定，并应制定自己的程序规则，包括特别会议的召集、法定人数要求和取决于本条约条款的各种决议的所需多数。

第 22 条

国际局

WIPO 国际局执行与本条约有关的行政工作。

第 23 条

参加条约的资格

（1）WIPO 的任何成员国可以参加本条约。

（2）任何政府间组织，声明就本条约涵盖的事项拥有权限并有自己的约束所有成员国的法律，并根据其内部程序被正式授权的，大会可以决定接受其参加本条约。

（3）欧洲共同体，经在通过本条约的外交会议上作出前款提到的声明，可以参加本条约。

第 24 条

条约之下的权利和义务

以本条约中任何明确相反的规定为条件，每个缔约方享有和承担本条约之下的所有权利和所有义务。

第 25 条

条约的签署

本条约在通过后开放一年供任何有资格方在 WIPO 总部签署。

第 26 条

条约的生效

本条约在三十个第23条提到的有资格方交存批准书或加入书之后三个月生效。

第 27 条

参加条约的生效日期

本条约应约束：

（i）三十个第 26 条提到的有资格方，自本条约生效之日起；

（ii）其他每个第 23 条提到的有资格方，自向 WIPO 总干事交存批准书或加入书之日起满三个月。

第 28 条

声明条约无效

任何缔约方可以通过给 WIPO 总干事的通知声明本条约无效。任何声明无效应于 WIPO 总干事收到通知之日起一年生效。

第 29 条

条约的语文

（1）本条约以英文、阿拉伯文、中文、法文、俄文和西班牙文的独一份原始件签署，所有这些语文的文本具有同等效力。

（2）应一个利益相关方请求，WIPO 总干事应在与所有利益相关方磋商后，以第（1）款中提到那些以外的任何语文制定一个官方文本。为本款的目的，“利益相关方”指其官方语文或官方语文之一被涉及的任何 WIPO 成员国，以及欧洲共同体和任何其他可以参加本条约的政府间组织，如果其官方语文之一被涉及。

第30条

保管人

世界知识产权组织总干事为本条约的保管人。

便利失明、视力障碍或阅读失能者利用已出版作品的马拉喀什条约*

目录

* 本条约于2013年6月27日由缔结一项便于有视力障碍和阅读障碍者利用已发表作品的条约的外交会议通过。

序言

缔约方，

回顾《世界人权宣言》和联合国《残疾人权利公约》宣示的非歧视、机会平等、便利性以及充分和有效参与和融入社会的原则，

注意到对视力障碍或其他阅读失能者全面发展不利的挑战，这一挑战限制他们的表达自由，包括与他人平等地寻求、接受和传递各种信息和思想的自由，包括以他们选择的各种交流形式，也限制他们享有教育权和从事研究的机会，

强调版权保护作为对文学和艺术创作的激励和回报的重要性，以及为包括视力障碍或其他阅读失能者的每个人促进参加社群文化生活、享受艺术以及分享科学进步和其益处的机会的重要性，

意识到视力障碍或其他阅读失能者在取得社会机会平等过程中利用已出版作品的障碍，以及同时需要扩大便利格式作品的数量和改善此种作品的流通，

考虑到大多数视力障碍或其他阅读失能者生活在发展中和最不发达国家，

承认尽管有各国版权法中的差异，但新信息和通信技术对视力障碍或其他阅读失能者生活的积极影响可以通过一个改进的国际层面的法律框架得到加强，

承认许多成员国已在国内版权法中为视力障碍或其他阅读失能者规定了限制和例外，但是可提供此种人的便利格式本作品持续匮乏，它们努力使作品能被这些人利用需要大量资源，而便利格式本不能进行跨境交换已造成需要重复这些努力，

承认权利持有人在使视力障碍或其他阅读失能者能够利用其作品中的作用的重要性，也承认尤其在市场无法提供此种便利时适当的限制和例外对于使作品能被这些人利用的重要性，

承认需要在有效保护作者的权利和更大的尤其是教育、研究和获得信息的公

共利益之间保持一种平衡，并承认此种平衡必须便于视力障碍或其他阅读失能者有效和及时地利用作品。

重申缔约方在现有国际版权保护条约之下的义务以及《保护文学和艺术作品伯尔尼公约》第9条第（2）款和其他国际文件中确立的关于限制和例外的三步检验法的重要性和灵活性，

回顾世界知识产权组织（WIPO）大会2007年通过的旨在保证发展问题成为该组织工作组成部分的发展议程建议的重要性，

承认国际版权体系的重要性，并期望使限制和例外协调一致以便于视力障碍或其他阅读失能者获得和使用作品，

达成一致如下：

第1条

与其他公约和条约的关系

本条约任何内容不得减损缔约方在任何其他条约之下拥有的任何相互义务，也不得损害缔约方在任何其他条约之下拥有的任何权利。

第2条

定义

为本条约的目的：

（a）“作品”指《保护文学和艺术作品伯尔尼公约》第2条第（1）款意思中的文字、符号或相关示意图形式的文学和艺术作品，无论已经出版或以任何媒介另外公开提供的[①]。

（b）“便利格式本”指作品的替代方式或形式的复本，它使受益人能够阅读作品，包括使该人与无视力障碍或其他阅读失能的人一样容易和舒适地阅读。便利格式本专为受益人使用，并且，它必须尊重原作的完整性，其中适当考虑为使作品能以替代格式获得所需要的改变以及受益人的便利性需求。

① 关于第2条（a）款的一致声明：兹同意，为本条约的目的，此定义包括有声形式的此种作品，诸如有声读物。

（c）“受权实体”指由政府授权或承认的在非营利基础上向受益人提供教育、指导培训、适应性阅读或信息便利的实体。它还包括以向受益人提供相同服务为主要活动或部门义务的政府机构或非营利组织[②]。

受权实体确定并遵循自己的做法：

（i）确定它服务的人为受益人；

（ii）将便利格式本的发行和提供限于受益人和/或受权实体；

（iii）阻止复制、发行和提供未经授权的复本；

（iv）对作品复本的处理保持应有的谨慎和记录，同时根据第8条尊重受益人的隐私。

第3条

受益人

受益人是以下人：

（a）失明的；

（b）有视力障碍或感知或阅读失能，无法改善达到与无此种障碍或失能的人实质同等的视觉功能，因而无法在与无障碍或失能的人实质相同的程度上阅读印刷的作品的[③]；或者

（c）另外由于身体失能无法把握或操纵一本书，或无法集中或移动目光达到阅读通常要求的程度的。

任何其他残障不在此论。

第4条

国内法律与便利格式本有关的限制和例外

1.（a）缔约方应在国内版权法中对复制权、发行权以及《世界知识产权组织版权条约》（WCT）规定的向公众提供权规定限制或例外，以便于向受益人提供作品的便利格式本。国内法中规定的限制或例外，应允许为使作品能以替代格式利用所需的改变。

---

② 关于第2条（c）款的一致声明：兹同意，为本条约的目的，“政府承认的实体”可以包括接受政府资金支持以在非营利基础上向受益人提供教育、指导性培训、适应性阅读或信息便利的实体。

③ 关于第3条（b）款的一致声明：此语中任何内容不意味着“无法改善”要求使用所有可能的医学诊断方法和治疗。

（b）缔约方还可以对公开表演权规定限制或例外以便于受益人利用作品。

2. 就第 4 条第 1 款中指出的所有权利履行该款，缔约方可以通过在其国内版权法中规定限制或例外，从而：

（a）允许受权实体不经版权持有人授权制作作品的便利格式本，从另一受权实体获得便利格式本，以任何方式，包括非商业性出租或有线或无线手段的电子传播，向受益人提供那些复本，以及采取任何中间步骤实现那些目标，如果满足所有以下条件：

（i）希望进行所述活动的受权实体有合法途径获得该作品或该作品的复本；

（ii）作品被转换成便利格式本，其中可以包括以便利格式浏览信息所需的任何手段，但不采取使作品能被受益人利用所需以外的改变；

（iii）此种便利格式本完全提供受益人使用；

（iv）活动在非营利基础上进行。

并且

（b）受益人或代表他或她的某个人，包括主要看护人或关照人，可以为受益人个人使用而制作作品的便利格式本，或可以帮助受益人制作和使用便利格式本，如果受益人有合法途径利用该作品或该作品的复本。

3. 缔约方可以通过根据第 10 条和第 11 条在其国内法律中规定其他限制或例外的方式履行第 4 条第（1）款④。

4. 缔约方可以将本条之下的限制或例外限于在市场中无法为受益人以合理条件商业性获得的采用特定便利格式的作品。任何利用这一可能的缔约方，应在批准、承认或加入本条约时或之后任何时间向 WIPO 总干事交存的通知中作出这样的声明 。⑤

5. 本条之下的限制或例外是否以支付报酬为条件，由国内法律确定。

第 5 条

便利格式本的跨境交换

1. 缔约方应规定，如果便利格式本是在限制或例外之下或根据法律运作而制作的，该便利格式本可以由一个受权实体向在另一缔约方的受益人或受权实体发

④ 关于第 4 条第 3 款的一致声明：兹同意，对于有视力障碍或其他阅读障碍者，本款既不缩小也不扩大《伯尔尼公约》之下就翻译权允许的限制和例外的适用范围。

⑤ 关于第 4 条第 4 款的一致声明：兹同意，可商业性获得的要求不影响本条之下的限制或例外是否符合三步检验法。

行或提供。⑥

2. 履行第 5 条第 1 款，缔约方可以通过在国内法律中规定限制或例外的方式，从而：

（a）允许受权实体不经权利持有人授权专为受益人使用向在另一缔约方的受权实体发行或提供便利格式本；

（b）允许受权实体不经权利持有人授权并根据第 2 条（c）项向在另一缔约方的受益人发行或提供便利格式本；

条件是在发行或提供之前，最初的受权实体不知道或无合理依据知道便利格式本将被用于受益人以外的人。⑦

3. 缔约方可以通过根据第 5 条第 4 款、第 10 条和第 11 条在国内版权法中规定其他限制或例外的方式履行第 5 条第 1 款。

4.（a）当在一个缔约方的受权实体根据第 5 条第 1 款收到便利格式本而该缔约方没有《伯尔尼公约》第 9 条之下的义务，它将依照自己的法律制度和做法保证便利格式本在该缔约方的管辖范围内仅为受益人使用而复制、发行或提供⑧。

（b）受权实体根据第 5 条第 1 款发行和提供便利格式本，应限于该管辖范围，除非该缔约方是 WCT 的参加方，或将实施本条约的限制和例外限于不与作品正常使用相冲突并且不过度损害权利持有人合法利益的某些特殊情况⑨。

（c）本条任何内容不影响确定什么构成发行的行为或向公众提供的行为。

5. 本条约任何内容不得被用于涉及权利用尽的问题。

第 6 条

便利格式本的进口

只要一缔约方国内法律允许受益人、代表他或她行事的某一人或一个受权实

---

⑥ 关于第 5 条第 1 款的一致声明：进一步同意，本条约中内容不缩小或扩大任何其他条约之下的专有权利的范围。

⑦ 关于第 5 条第 2 款的一致声明：兹同意，为直接向在另一缔约方的受益人发行或提供便利格式本，受权实体采取进一步措施确认它服务的人是受益人和如第 2 条（c）款所述遵循自己的做法，可以是恰当的。

⑧ 关于第 5 条第 4 款（a）项的一致声明：兹同意，本条约任何内容不要求或意味着缔约方在本文件或其他国际条约之下的义务以外采纳或适用三步检验法。

⑨ 关于第 5 条第 4 款（b）项的一致声明：兹同意，本条约任何内容不为缔约方产生任何批准或加入 WCT 或遵守其任何条款的义务，并且，本条约任何内容不损害 WCT 中包含的任何权利、限制和例外。

体制作作品的便利格式本，该缔约方的国内法律还应允许他们不经权利持有人授权为受益人使用而进口便利格式本[⑩]。

第7条

关于技术措施的义务

在规定充分的法律保护和有效的法律救济防止规避有效的技术措施时，缔约方应采取必要的适当措施，保证这一法律保护不妨碍受益人享有本条约规定的限制和例外[⑪]。

第8条

尊重隐私

实施本条约中规定的限制和例外时，缔约方应努力在与其他人平等的基础上保护受益人的隐私。

第9条

开展合作为跨境交换提供便利

1. 缔约方应鼓励自愿的信息共享，帮助受权实体互相识别，以促进便利格式本的跨境交换。WIPO国际局应为此目的建立一个信息获取点。

2. 缔约方承诺，帮助它们从事第5条之下活动的受权实体，通过受权实体之间的信息共享，并通过向利益相关方和适当时向公众成员提供与其政策和做法有关的包括关于便利格式本跨境交换的信息，提供与其根据第2条（c）项所做有关的信息。

3. 邀请WIPO国际局在可提供的情况下分享与本条约的运作有关的信息。

4. 缔约方承认国际合作及其推广对于支持实现本条约的目的和目标的国家努力的重要性[⑫]。

---

⑩ 关于第6条的一致声明：兹同意，缔约方在履行其在第6条之下的义务时有第4条规定的同样的灵活性。

⑪ 关于第7条的一致声明：兹同意，受权实体在各种情况下在制作、发行和提供便利格式本时选择采用技术措施，并且，当符合国内法律，此处无内容妨碍此种做法。

⑫ 关于第9条的一致声明：兹同意，第9条不意味着受权实体的强制登记，也不构成受权实体从事本条约之下承认的活动的前提条件；但它规定可以共享信息以利于便利格式本的跨境交换。

第10条

关于实施的一般原则

1. 缔约方承诺采取必要措施保证本条约的适用。

2. 任何事项不得阻止缔约方确定在自己法律制度和惯例内实施本条约条款的适当办法[13]。

3. 缔约方可以通过其法律制度和惯例内的专为受益人的限制或例外、其他限制或例外或其组合履行它在本条约之下的权利和义务。这些可以包括符合缔约方在《伯尔尼公约》、其他国际条约和第11条之下权利和义务的在公平做法、交易或满足其需求的使用方面有利于受益人的司法、行政和管理决定。

第11条

关于限制和例外的一般义务

采取必要措施保证本条约的适用时，一缔约方可以行使并应遵守该缔约方在《伯尔尼公约》、《与贸易有关知识产权协议》和WCT之下拥有的权利和义务，包括它们的解释性协议，从而：

（a）根据《伯尔尼公约》第9条第（2）款，一缔约方可以允许在某些特殊情况下复制作品，只要此种复制不与作品的正常利用相冲突并且不过度损害作者的合法利益；

（b）根据《与贸易有关知识产权协议》第13条，一缔约方应将对专有权利的限制或例外限于不与作品的正常利用相冲突并且不过度损害权利持有人合法利益的某些特殊情况；

（c）根据WCT第10条第（1）款，一缔约方可以在不与作品的正常利用相冲突并且不过度损害作者合法利益的某些特殊情况下对在《WIPO版权条约》之下赋予作者的权利规定限制或例外；

（d）根据WCT第10条第（2）款，一缔约方应在适用《伯尔尼公约》时将对权利的任何限制或例外限于不与作品的正常利用相冲突并且不过度损害作者合法利益的某些特殊情况。

---

⑬ 关于第10条第2款的一致声明：兹同意，当一部作品具有第2条（a）款之下作品的资格，包括有声形式的此种作品，出于制作、发行和向受益人提供便利格式本的需要，本条约规定的限制和例外经必要修改适用于相关权利。

第12条

其他限制和例外

1. 缔约方承认，一缔约方经考虑它的经济状况以及社会和文化需求，根据该缔约方的国际权利和义务，可以在其国内法律中为受益人实行本条约规定以外的版权限制和例外，并在最不发达国家的情况下考虑其特殊需要以及其特定的国际权利和义务及其灵活性。

2. 本条约不损害国内法律为残障人规定的其他限制和例外。

第13条

大会

1.（a）缔约方应有一个大会。

（b）每个缔约方应在大会由一名会议代表作为代表，会议代表可以有替补代表、顾问和专家协助。

（c）每个代表团的费用由委派它的缔约方负担。大会可以要求 WIPO 提供资金援助，以便于按照联合国大会既定惯例被认为是发展中国家或向市场经济转型国家的缔约方的代表团参加。

2.（a）大会应处理与本条约的维持和发展以及本条约的适用和运作有关的事项。

（b）大会应履行在第 15 条之下委派给它的与接受某些政府间组织参加本条约有关的职能。

（c）大会应就任何修订本条约的外交会议的召开作出决定并就此种外交会议的筹备给 WIPO 总干以必要的指示。

3.（a）每个作为国家的缔约方拥有一票，并仅以自己的名义投票。

（b）任何作为政府间组织的缔约方可以代替其成员国参加表决，票数与其是本条约参加方的成员国的数目相等。如果其成员国任何之一行使表决权，任何此种政府间组织不得参与表决，反之亦然。

4. 大会在总干事召集下开会，如无例外情况，与 WIPO 大会在同一时段和同一地点。

5. 大会应努力通过一致同意做出决议，并制定自己的程序规则，包括特别会议的召集、法定人数要求和取决于本条约条款的各种决议的所需多数。

第 14 条

国际局

WIPO 国际局执行与本条约有关的行政工作。

第 15 条

参加条约的资格

1. WIPO 任何成员国可以参加本条约。

2. 任何政府间组织，声明就本条约涵盖的事项拥有权限并有自己的约束所有成员国的法律，并根据其内部程序被正式授权的，大会可以决定接受其参加本条约。

3. 欧洲联盟，经在通过本条约的外交会议上作出前款提到的声明，可以参加本条约。

第 16 条

本条约之下的权利和义务

以本条约中任何相反的明确规定为条件，每个缔约方享有和承担本条约之下的所有权利和所有义务。

第 17 条

条约的签署

本条约应开放供在马拉喀什外交会议上，并之后在其通过后的一年中在 WIPO 总部，供任何有资格方签署。

第 18 条

条约的生效

本条约在二十个第 15 条中提到的有资格方交存批准或加入书后三个月生效。

第 19 条

参加条约的生效日期

本条约应约束：

（a）第 18 条中提到的二十个国家，自本条约生效之日起；

（b）每个第15条中提到的其他有资格方，自它向WIPO总干事交存批准或加入书之日起满三个月。

第20条

声明条约无效

任何缔约方可以通过给WIPO总干事的通知声明本条约无效。任何声明无效于WIPO总干事收到通知之日起一年生效。

第21条

条约的语文

1. 本条约以英文、阿拉伯文、中文、法文、俄文和西班牙文的独一份原始件签署，所有这些语文的文本具有同等效力。

2. 应一个利益相关方的请求，WIPO总干事应在与所有利益相关方磋商后，以第21条第（1）款中提到那些以外的任何语文制定一个官方文本。为本款的目的，“利益相关方”指其任何官方语文或官方语文之一被涉及的WIPO成员国，以及欧洲联盟和任何其他可以参加本条约的政府间组织，如果其官方语文之一被涉及。

第22条

保管人

WIPO总干事为本条约的保管人。2013年6月27日在马拉喀什签署。

Berne Convention for the Protection of Literary and Artistic Works

(Paris Act of July 24, 1971, as amended on September 28, 1979)

of September 9, 1886,
completed at PARIS on May 4, 1896, revised at BERLIN on November 13, 1908, completed at BERNE on March 20, 1914, revised at ROME on June 2, 1928, at BRUSSELS on June 26, 1948,
at STOCKHOLM on July 14, 1967,
and at PARIS on July 24, 1971,
and amended on September 28, 1979

TABLE OF CONTENTS *

* This Table of Contents is added for the convenience of the reader. It does not appear in the original (English) text of the Convention.

Union: 1. Ratification, accession; possibility of excluding certain provisions; withdrawal of exclusion; 2. Entry into force of Articles 1 to 21 and Appendix; 3. Entry into force of Articles 22 to 38

Article 29: Acceptance and Entry Into Force for Countries Outside the Union: 1. Accession; 2. Entry into force

Article 29bis: Effect of Acceptance of Act for the Purposes of Article 14(2) of the WIPO Convention

Article 30: Reservations: 1. Limits of possibility of making reservations; 2. Earlier reservations; reservation as to the right of translation; withdrawal of reservation

Article 31: Applicability to Certain Territories: 1. Declaration; 2. Withdrawal of declaration; 3. Effective date; 4. Acceptance of factual situations not implied

Article 32: Applicability of this Act and of Earlier Acts: 1. As between countries already members of the Union; 2. As between a country becoming a member of the Union and other countries members of the Union; 3. Applicability of the Appendix in Certain Relations

Article 33: Disputes: 1. Jurisdiction of the International Court of Justice; 2. Reservation as to such jurisdiction; 3. Withdrawal of reservation

Article 34: Closing of Certain Earlier Provisions: 1. Of earlier Acts; 2. Of the Protocol to the Stockholm Act

Article 35: Duration of the Convention; Denunciation: 1. Unlimited duration; 2. Possibility of denunciation; 3. Effective date of denunciation; 4. Moratorium on denunciation

Article 36: Application of the Convention: 1. Obligation to adopt the necessary measures; 2. Time from which obligation exists

Article 37: Final Clauses: 1. Languages of the Act; 2. Signature; 3. Certified copies; 4. Registration; 5. Notifications

Article 38: Transitory Provisions: 1. Exercise of the "five-year privilege"; 2. Bureau of the Union, Director of the Bureau; 3. Succession of Bureau of the Union

Appendix

SPECIAL PROVISIONS REGARDING DEVELOPING COUNTRIES

Article I: Faculties Open to Developing Countries: 1. Availability of certain faculties; declaration; 2. Duration of effect of declaration; 3. Cessation of developing country status; 4. Existing stocks of copies;

5. Declarations concerning certain territories; 6. Limits of reciprocity

Article II: Limitations on the Right of Translation: 1. Licenses grantable by competent authority; 2 to 4. Conditions allowing the grant of such licenses; 5. Purposes for which licenses may be granted; 6. Termination of licenses; 7. Works composed mainly of illustrations; 8. Works withdrawn from circulation; 9. Licenses for broadcasting organizations

Article III: Limitation on the Right of Reproduction: 1. Licenses grantable by competent authority; 2 to 5. Conditions allowing the grant of such licenses; 6. Termination of licenses; 7. Works to which this Article applies

Article IV: Provisions Common to Licenses Under Articles II and III: 1 and 2. Procedure; 3. Indication of author and title of work; 4. Exportation of copies; 5. Notice; 6. Compensation

Article V: Alternative Possibility for Limitation of the Right of Translation: 1. Regime provided for under the 1886 and 1896 Acts; 2. No possibility of change to regime under Article II; 3. Time limit for choosing the alternative possibility

Article VI: Possibilities of applying, or admitting the application of, certain provisions of the Appendix before becoming bound by it: 1. Declaration; 2. Depository and effective date of declaration

The countries of the Union, being equally animated by the desire to protect, in as effective and uniform a manner as possible, the rights of authors in their literary and artistic works,

Recognizing the importance of the work of the Revision Conference held at Stockholm in 1967,

Have resolved to revise the Act adopted by the Stockholm Conference, while maintaining without change Articles 1 to 20 and 22 to 26 of that Act.

Consequently, the undersigned Plenipotentiaries, having presented their full powers, recognized as in good and due form, have agreed as follows:

Article 1
[Establishment of a Union] ①

The countries to which this Convention applies constitute a Union for the protection of the rights of authors in their literary and artistic works.

Article 2
[Protected Works: 1. "Literary and artistic works"; 2. Possible requirement of fixation; 3. Derivative works; 4. Official texts; 5. Collections; 6. Obligation to protect; beneficiaries of protection; 7. Works of applied art and industrial designs; 8. News]

(1) The expression "literary and artistic works" shall include every production in the literary, scientific and artistic domain, whatever may be the mode or form of its expression, such as books, pamphlets and other writings; lectures, addresses, sermons and other works of the same nature; dramatic or dramatico-musical works; choreographic works and entertainments in dumb show; musical compositions with or without words; cinematographic works to which are assimilated works expressed by a process analogous to cinematography; works of drawing, painting, architecture, sculpture, engraving and lithography; photographic works to which are assimilated works expressed by a process analogous to photography; works of applied art; illustrations, maps, plans, sketches and three-dimensional works relative to geography, topography, architecture or science.

(2) It shall, however, be a matter for legislation in the countries of the Union to prescribe that works in general or any specified categories of works shall not be protected unless they have been fixed in some material form.

(3) Translations, adaptations, arrangements of music and other alterations of a literary or artistic work shall be protected as original works without prejudice to the copyright in the original work.

(4) It shall be a matter for legislation in the countries of the Union to determine the protection to be granted to official texts of a legislative, administrative and legal nature, and to official translations of such texts.

(5) Collections of literary or artistic works such as encyclopaedias and anthologies which, by reason of the selection and arrangement of their contents, constitute intellectual creations shall be protected as such, without prejudice to the copyright in each of the works forming part of such collections.

(6) The works mentioned in this Article shall enjoy protection in all countries of the Union. This protection shall operate for the benefit of the author and his successors in title.

---

① Each Article and the Appendix have been given titles to facilitate their identification. There are no titles in the signed (English) text.

(7) Subject to the provisions of Article 7(4) of this Convention, it shall be a matter for legislation in the countries of the Union to determine the extent of the application of their laws to works of applied art and industrial designs and models, as well as the conditions under which such works, designs and models shall be protected. Works protected in the country of origin solely as designs and models shall be entitled in another country of the Union only to such special protection as is granted in that country to designs and models; however, if no such special protection is granted in that country, such works shall be protected as artistic works.

(8) The protection of this Convention shall not apply to news of the day or to miscellaneous facts having the character of mere items of press information.

Article 2bis

[Possible Limitation of Protection of Certain Works: 1. Certain speeches; 2. Certain uses of lectures and addresses; 3. Right to make collections of such works]

(1) It shall be a matter for legislation in the countries of the Union to exclude, wholly or in part, from the protection provided by the preceding Article political speeches and speeches delivered in the course of legal proceedings.

(2) It shall also be a matter for legislation in the countries of the Union to determine the conditions under which lectures, addresses and other works of the same nature which are delivered in public may be reproduced by the press, broadcast, communicated to the public by wire and made the subject of public communication as envisaged in Article 11bis(1) of this Convention, when such use is justified by the informatory purpose.

(3) Nevertheless, the author shall enjoy the exclusive right of making a collection of his works mentioned in the preceding paragraphs.

Article 3

[Criteria of Eligibility for Protection: 1. Nationality of author; place of publication of work; 2. Residence of author; 3. "Published" works; 4. "Simultaneously published" works]

(1) The protection of this Convention shall apply to:

(a) authors who are nationals of one of the countries of the Union, for their works, whether published or not;

(b) authors who are not nationals of one of the countries of the Union, for their works first published in one of those countries, or simultaneously in a country outside the Union and in a country of the Union.

(2) Authors who are not nationals of one of the countries of the Union but who have their habitual residence in one of them shall, for the purposes of this

Convention, be assimilated to nationals of that country.

(3) The expression "published works" means works published with the consent of their authors, whatever may be the means of manufacture of the copies, provided that the availability of such copies has been such as to satisfy the reasonable requirements of the public, having regard to the nature of the work. The performance of a dramatic, dramatico-musical, cinematographic or musical work, the public recitation of a literary work, the communication by wire or the broadcasting of literary or artistic works, the exhibition of a work of art and the construction of a work of architecture shall not constitute publication.

(4) A work shall be considered as having been published simultaneously in several countries if it has been published in two or more countries within thirty days of its first publication.

Article 4

[Criteria of Eligibility for Protection of Cinematographic Works, Works of Architecture and Certain Artistic Works]

The protection of this Convention shall apply, even if the conditions of Article 3 are not fulfilled, to:

(a) authors of cinematographic works the maker of which has his headquarters or habitual residence in one of the countries of the Union;

(b) authors of works of architecture erected in a country of the Union or of other artistic works incorporated in a building or other structure located in a country of the Union.

Article 5

[Rights Guaranteed: 1. and 2. Outside the country of origin; 3. In the country of origin; 4. "Country of origin"]

(1) Authors shall enjoy, in respect of works for which they are protected under this Convention, in countries of the Union other than the country of origin, the rights which their respective laws do now or may hereafter grant to their nationals, as well as the rights specially granted by this Convention.

(2) The enjoyment and the exercise of these rights shall not be subject to any formality; such enjoyment and such exercise shall be independent of the existence of protection in the country of origin of the work. Consequently, apart from the provisions of this Convention, the extent of protection, as well as the means of redress afforded to the author to protect his rights, shall be governed exclusively by the laws of the country where protection is claimed.

(3) Protection in the country of origin is governed by domestic law. However, when the author is not a national of the country of origin of the work for which he is protected under this Convention, he shall enjoy in that country the same rights as

national authors.

(4) The country of origin shall be considered to be:

(a) in the case of works first published in a country of the Union, that country; in the case of works published simultaneously in several countries of the Union which grant different terms of protection, the country whose legislation grants the shortest term of protection;

(b) in the case of works published simultaneously in a country outside the Union and in a country of the Union, the latter country;

(c) in the case of unpublished works or of works first published in a country outside the Union, without simultaneous publication in a country of the Union, the country of the Union of which the author is a national, provided that:

(i) when these are cinematographic works the maker of which has his headquarters or his habitual residence in a country of the Union, the country of origin shall be that country, and

(ii) when these are works of architecture erected in a country of the Union or other artistic works incorporated in a building or other structure located in a country of the Union, the country of origin shall be that country.

Article 6

[Possible Restriction of Protection in Respect of Certain Works of Nationals of Certain Countries Outside the Union: 1. In the country of the first publication and in other countries; 2. No retroactivity; 3. Notice]

(1) Where any country outside the Union fails to protect in an adequate manner the works of authors who are nationals of one of the countries of the Union, the latter country may restrict the protection given to the works of authors who are, at the date of the first publication thereof, nationals of the other country and are not habitually resident in one of the countries of the Union. If the country of first publication avails itself of this right, the other countries of the Union shall not be required to grant to works thus subjected to special treatment a wider protection than that granted to them in the country of first publication.

(2) No restrictions introduced by virtue of the preceding paragraph shall affect the rights which an author may have acquired in respect of a work published in a country of the Union before such restrictions were put into force.

(3) The countries of the Union which restrict the grant of copyright in accordance with this Article shall give notice thereof to the Director General of the World Intellectual Property Organization (hereinafter designated as "the Director General") by a written declaration specifying the countries in regard to which protection is restricted, and the restrictions to which rights of authors who are nationals

of those countries are subjected. The Director General shall immediately communicate this declaration to all the countries of the Union.

Article 6bis

[Moral Rights: 1. To claim authorship; to object to certain modifications and other derogatory actions; 2. After the author's death; 3. Means of redress]

(1) Independently of the author's economic rights, and even after the transfer of the said rights, the author shall have the right to claim authorship of the work and to object to any distortion, mutilation or other modification of, or other derogatory action in relation to, the said work, which would be prejudicial to his honor or reputation.

(2) The rights granted to the author in accordance with the preceding paragraph shall, after his death, be maintained, at least until the expiry of the economic rights, and shall be exercisable by the persons or institutions authorized by the legislation of the country where protection is claimed. However, those countries whose legislation, at the moment of their ratification of or accession to this Act, does not provide for the protection after the death of the author of all the rights set out in the preceding paragraph may provide that some of these rights may, after his death, cease to be maintained.

(3) The means of redress for safeguarding the rights granted by this Article shall be governed by the legislation of the country where protection is claimed.

Article 7

[Term of Protection: 1. Generally; 2. For cinematographic works; 3. For anonymous and pseudonymous works; 4. For photographic works and works of applied art; 5. Starting date of computation; 6. Longer terms; 7. Shorter terms; 8. Applicable law; "comparison" of terms]

(1) The term of protection granted by this Convention shall be the life of the author and fifty years after his death.

(2) However, in the case of cinematographic works, the countries of the Union may provide that the term of protection shall expire fifty years after the work has been made available to the public with the consent of the author, or, failing such an event within fifty years from the making of such a work, fifty years after the making.

(3) In the case of anonymous or pseudonymous works, the term of protection granted by this Convention shall expire fifty years after the work has been lawfully made available to the public. However, when the pseudonym adopted by the author leaves no doubt as to his identity, the term of protection shall be that provided in paragraph (1). If the author of an anonymous or pseudonymous work discloses his

identity during the above-mentioned period, the term of protection applicable shall be that provided in paragraph (1). The countries of the Union shall not be required to protect anonymous or pseudonymous works in respect of which it is reasonable to presume that their author has been dead for fifty years.

(4) It shall be a matter for legislation in the countries of the Union to determine the term of protection of photographic works and that of works of applied art in so far as they are protected as artistic works; however, this term shall last at least until the end of a period of twenty-five years from the making of such a work.

(5) The term of protection subsequent to the death of the author and the terms provided by paragraphs (2), (3) and (4) shall run from the date of death or of the event referred to in those paragraphs, but such terms shall always be deemed to begin on the first of January of the year following the death or such event.

(6) The countries of the Union may grant a term of protection in excess of those provided by the preceding paragraphs.

(7) Those countries of the Union bound by the Rome Act of this Convention which grant, in their national legislation in force at the time of signature of the present Act, shorter terms of protection than those provided for in the preceding paragraphs shall have the right to maintain such terms when ratifying or acceding to the present Act.

(8) In any case, the term shall be governed by the legislation of the country where protection is claimed; however, unless the legislation of that country otherwise provides, the term shall not exceed the term fixed in the country of origin of the work.

Article 7bis

[Term of Protection for Works of Joint Authorship]

The provisions of the preceding Article shall also apply in the case of a work of joint authorship, provided that the terms measured from the death of the author shall be calculated from the death of the last surviving author.

Article 8

[Right of Translation]

Authors of literary and artistic works protected by this Convention shall enjoy the exclusive right of making and of authorizing the translation of their works throughout the term of protection of their rights in the original works.

Article 9

[Right of Reproduction: 1. Generally; 2. Possible exceptions; 3. Sound and visual recordings]

(1) Authors of literary and artistic works protected by this Convention shall

have the exclusive right of authorizing the reproduction of these works, in any manner or form.

(2) It shall be a matter for legislation in the countries of the Union to permit the reproduction of such works in certain special cases, provided that such reproduction does not conflict with a normal exploitation of the work and does not unreasonably prejudice the legitimate interests of the author.

(3) Any sound or visual recording shall be considered as a reproduction for the purposes of this Convention.

Article 10

[Certain Free Uses of Works: 1. Quotations; 2. Illustrations for teaching; 3. Indication of source and author]

(1) It shall be permissible to make quotations from a work which has already been lawfully made available to the public, provided that their making is compatible with fair practice, and their extent does not exceed that justified by the purpose, including quotations from newspaper articles and periodicals in the form of press summaries.

(2) It shall be a matter for legislation in the countries of the Union, and for special agreements existing or to be concluded between them, to permit the utilization, to the extent justified by the purpose, of literary or artistic works by way of illustration in publications, broadcasts or sound or visual recordings for teaching, provided such utilization is compatible with fair practice.

(3) Where use is made of works in accordance with the preceding paragraphs of this Article, mention shall be made of the source, and of the name of the author if it appears thereon.

Article 10bis

[Further Possible Free Uses of Works: 1. Of certain Articles and broadcast works; 2. Of works seen or heard in connection with current events]

(1) It shall be a matter for legislation in the countries of the Union to permit the reproduction by the press, the broadcasting or the communication to the public by wire of articles published in newspapers or periodicals on current economic, political or religious topics, and of broadcast works of the same character, in cases in which the reproduction, broadcasting or such communication thereof is not expressly reserved. Nevertheless, the source must always be clearly indicated; the legal consequences of a breach of this obligation shall be determined by the legislation of the country where protection is claimed.

(2) It shall also be a matter for legislation in the countries of the Union to determine the conditions under which, for the purpose of reporting current events by means of photography, cinematography, broadcasting or communication to the public by wire,

literary or artistic works seen or heard in the course of the event may, to the extent justified by the informatory purpose, be reproduced and made available to the public.

Article 11

[Certain Rights in Dramatic and Musical Works: 1. Right of public performance and of communication to the public of a performance; 2. In respect of translations]

(1) Authors of dramatic, dramatico-musical and musical works shall enjoy the exclusive right of authorizing:

(i) the public performance of their works, including such public performance by any means or process;

(ii) any communication to the public of the performance of their works.

(2) Authors of dramatic or dramatico-musical works shall enjoy, during the full term of their rights in the original works, the same rights with respect to translations thereof.

Article 11bis

[Broadcasting and Related Rights: 1. Broadcasting and other wireless communications, public communication of broadcast by wire or rebroadcast, public communication of broadcast by loudspeaker or analogous instruments; 2. Compulsory licenses; 3. Recording; ephemeral recordings]

(1) uthors of literary and artistic works shall enjoy the exclusive right of authorizing:

(i) the broadcasting of their works or the communication thereof to the public by any other means of wireless diffusion of signs, sounds or images;

(ii) any communication to the public by wire or by rebroadcasting of the broadcast of the work, when this communication is made by an organization other than the original one;

(iii) the public communication by loudspeaker or any other analogous instrument transmitting, by signs, sounds or images, the broadcast of the work.

(2) It shall be a matter for legislation in the countries of the Union to determine the conditions under which the rights mentioned in the preceding paragraph may be exercised, but these conditions shall apply only in the countries where they have been prescribed. They shall not in any circumstances be prejudicial to the moral rights of the author, nor to his right to obtain equitable remuneration which, in the absence of agreement, shall be fixed by competent authority.

(3) In the absence of any contrary stipulation, permission granted in accordance with paragraph (1) of this Article shall not imply permission to record, by means of instruments recording sounds or images, the work broadcast. It shall,

however, be a matter for legislation in the countries of the Union to determine the regulations for ephemeral recordings made by a broadcasting organization by means of its own facilities and used for its own broadcasts. The preservation of these recordings in official archives may, on the ground of their exceptional documentary character, be authorized by such legislation.

Article 11ter

[Certain Rights in Literary Works: 1. Right of public recitation and of communication to the public of a recitation; 2. In respect of translations]

(1) Authors of literary works shall enjoy the exclusive right of authorizing:

(i) the public recitation of their works, including such public recitation by any means or process;

(ii) any communication to the public of the recitation of their works.

(2) Authors of literary works shall enjoy, during the full term of their rights in the original works, the same rights with respect to translations thereof.

Article 12

[Right of Adaptation, Arrangement and Other Alteration]

Authors of literary or artistic works shall enjoy the exclusive right of authorizing adaptations, arrangements and other alterations of their works.

Article 13

[Possible Limitation of the Right of Recording of Musical Works and Any Words Pertaining Thereto: 1. Compulsory licenses; 2. Transitory measures; 3. Seizure on importation of copies made without the author's permission]

(1) Each country of the Union may impose for itself reservations and conditions on the exclusive right granted to the author of a musical work and to the author of any words, the recording of which together with the musical work has already been authorized by the latter, to authorize the sound recording of that musical work, together with such words, if any; but all such reservations and conditions shall apply only in the countries which have imposed them and shall not, in any circumstances, be prejudicial to the rights of these authors to obtain equitable remuneration which, in the absence of agreement, shall be fixed by competent authority.

(2) Recordings of musical works made in a country of the Union in accordance with Article 13(3) of the Conventions signed at Rome on June 2, 1928, and at Brussels on June 26, 1948, may be reproduced in that country without the permission of the author of the musical work until a date two years after that country becomes bound by this Act.

(3) Recordings made in accordance with paragraphs (1) and (2) of this Article and imported without permission from the parties concerned into a country where

they are treated as infringing recordings shall be liable to seizure.

Article 14

[Cinematographic and Related Rights: 1. Cinematographic adaptation and reproduction; distribution; public performance and public communication by wire of works thus adapted or reproduced; 2. Adaptation of cinematographic productions; 3. No compulsory licenses]

(1) Authors of literary or artistic works shall have the exclusive right of authorizing:

(i) the cinematographic adaptation and reproduction of these works, and the distribution of the works thus adapted or reproduced;

(ii) the public performance and communication to the public by wire of the works thus adapted or reproduced.

(2) The adaptation into any other artistic form of a cinematographic production derived from literary or artistic works shall, without prejudice to the authorization of the author of the cinematographic production, remain subject to the authorization of the authors of the original works.

(3) The provisions of Article 13(1) shall not apply.

Article 14bis

[Special Provisions Concerning Cinematographic Works: 1. Assimilation to "original" works; 2. Ownership; limitation of certain rights of certain contributors; 3. Certain other contributors]

(1) Without prejudice to the copyright in any work which may have been adapted or reproduced, a cinematographic work shall be protected as an original work. The owner of copyright in a cinematographic work shall enjoy the same rights as the author of an original work, including the rights referred to in the preceding Article.

(2) (a) Ownership of copyright in a cinematographic work shall be a matter for legislation in the country where protection is claimed.

(b) However, in the countries of the Union which, by legislation, include among the owners of copyright in a cinematographic work authors who have brought contributions to the making of the work, such authors, if they have undertaken to bring such contributions, may not, in the absence of any contrary or special stipulation, object to the reproduction, distribution, public performance, communication to the public by wire, broadcasting or any other communication to the public, or to the subtitling or dubbing of texts, of the work.

(c) The question whether or not the form of the undertaking referred to above should, for the application of the preceding subparagraph (b) , be in a written agreement or a written act of the same effect shall be a matter for the legislation of the country where the maker of the cinematographic work has his headquarters or habitual residence. However, it shall be a matter for the legislation of the country of the Union where protection is claimed to provide that the said undertaking shall be in a written agreement or a written act of the same effect. The countries whose legislation so provides shall notify the Director General by means of a written declaration, which will be immediately communicated by him to all the other countries of the Union.

(d) By "contrary or special stipulation" is meant any restrictive condition which is relevant to the aforesaid undertaking.

(3) Unless the national legislation provides to the contrary, the provisions of paragraph (2)(b) above shall not be applicable to authors of scenarios, dialogues and musical works created for the making of the cinematographic work, or to the principal director thereof. However, those countries of the Union whose legislation does not contain rules providing for the application of the said paragraph (2)(b) to such director shall notify the Director General by means of a written declaration, which will be immediately communicated by him to all the other countries of the Union.

Article 14ter

["Droit de suite" in Works of Art and Manuscripts: 1. Right to an interest in resales; 2. Applicable law; 3. Procedure]

(1) The author, or after his death the persons or institutions authorized by national legislation, shall, with respect to original works of art and original manuscripts of writers and composers, enjoy the inalienable right to an interest in any sale of the work subsequent to the first transfer by the author of the work.

(2) The protection provided by the preceding paragraph may be claimed in a country of the Union only if legislation in the country to which the author belongs so permits, and to the extent permitted by the country where this protection is claimed.

(3) The procedure for collection and the amounts shall be matters for determination by national legislation.

Article 15

[Right to Enforce Protected Rights: 1. Where author's name is indicated or where pseudonym leaves no doubt as to author's identity; 2. In the case of cinematographic works; 3. In the case of anonymous and pseudonymous works; 4. In the case of certain unpublished works of unknown authorship]

(1) In order that the author of a literary or artistic work protected by this Convention shall, in the absence of proof to the contrary, be regarded as such, and

consequently be entitled to institute infringement proceedings in the countries of the Union, it shall be sufficient for his name to appear on the work in the usual manner. This paragraph shall be applicable even if this name is a pseudonym, where the pseudonym adopted by the author leaves no doubt as to his identity.

(2) The person or body corporate whose name appears on a cinematographic work in the usual manner shall, in the absence of proof to the contrary, be presumed to be the maker of the said work.

(3) In the case of anonymous and pseudonymous works, other than those referred to in paragraph (1) above, the publisher whose name appears on the work shall, in the absence of proof to the contrary, be deemed to represent the author, and in this capacity he shall be entitled to protect and enforce the author's rights. The provisions of this paragraph shall cease to apply when the author reveals his identity and establishes his claim to authorship of the work.

(4) (a) In the case of unpublished works where the identity of the author is unknown, but where there is every ground to presume that he is a national of a country of the Union, it shall be a matter for legislation in that country to designate the competent authority which shall represent the author and shall be entitled to protect and enforce his rights in the countries of the Union.

(b) Countries of the Union which make such designation under the terms of this provision shall notify the Director General by means of a written declaration giving full information concerning the authority thus designated. The Director General shall at once communicate this declaration to all other countries of the Union.

Article 16

[Infringing Copies: 1. Seizure; 2. Seizure on importation; 3. Applicable law]

(1) Infringing copies of a work shall be liable to seizure in any country of the Union where the work enjoys legal protection.

(2) The provisions of the preceding paragraph shall also apply to reproductions coming from a country where the work is not protected, or has ceased to be protected.

(3) The seizure shall take place in accordance with the legislation of each country.

Article 17

[Possibility of Control of Circulation, Presentation and Exhibition of Works]

The provisions of this Convention cannot in any way affect the right of the Government of each country of the Union to permit, to control, or to prohibit, by legislation or regulation, the circulation, presentation, or exhibition of any work or production in regard to which the competent authority may find it necessary to exercise that right.

Article 18

[Works Existing on Convention's Entry Into Force: 1. Protectable where protection not yet expired in country of origin; 2. Non-protectable where protection already expired in country where it is claimed; 3. Application of these principles; 4. Special cases]

(1) This Convention shall apply to all works which, at the moment of its coming into force, have not yet fallen into the public domain in the country of origin through the expiry of the term of protection.

(2) If, however, through the expiry of the term of protection which was previously granted, a work has fallen into the public domain of the country where protection is claimed, that work shall not be protected anew.

(3) The application of this principle shall be subject to any provisions contained in special conventions to that effect existing or to be concluded between countries of the Union. In the absence of such provisions, the respective countries shall determine, each in so far as it is concerned, the conditions of application of this principle.

(4) The preceding provisions shall also apply in the case of new accessions to the Union and to cases in which protection is extended by the application of Article 7 or by the abandonment of reservations.

Article 19

[Protection Greater than Resulting from Convention]

The provisions of this Convention shall not preclude the making of a claim to the benefit of any greater protection which may be granted by legislation in a country of the Union.

Article 20

[Special Agreements Among Countries of the Union]

The Governments of the countries of the Union reserve the right to enter into special agreements among themselves, in so far as such agreements grant to authors more extensive rights than those granted by the Convention, or contain other provisions not contrary to this Convention. The provisions of existing agreements which satisfy these conditions shall remain applicable.

Article 21

[Special Provisions Regarding Developing Countries: 1. Reference to Appendix; 2. Appendix part of Act]

(1) Special provisions regarding developing countries are included in the Appendix.

(2) Subject to the provisions of Article 28(1)(b) , the Appendix forms an

integral part of this Act.

Article 22

[Assembly: 1. Constitution and composition; 2. Tasks; 3. Quorum, voting, observers; 4. Convocation; 5. Rules of procedure]

(1) (a) The Union shall have an Assembly consisting of those countries of the Union which are bound by Articles 22 to 26.

(b) The Government of each country shall be represented by one delegate, who may be assisted by alternate delegates, advisors, and experts.

(c) The expenses of each delegation shall be borne by the Government which has appointed it.

(2) (a) The Assembly shall:

(i) deal with all matters concerning the maintenance and development of the Union and the implementation of this Convention;

(ii) give directions concerning the preparation for conferences of revision to the International Bureau of Intellectual Property (hereinafter designated as "the International Bureau") referred to in the Convention Establishing the World Intellectual Property Organization (hereinafter designated as "the Organization"), due account being taken of any comments made by those countries of the Union which are not bound by Articles 22 to 26;

(iii) review and approve the reports and activities of the Director General of the Organization concerning the Union, and give him all necessary instructions concerning matters within the competence of the Union;

(iv) elect the members of the Executive Committee of the Assembly;

(v) review and approve the reports and activities of its Executive Committee, and give instructions to such Committee;

(vi) determine the program and adopt the biennial budget of the Union, and approve its final accounts;

(vii) adopt the financial regulations of the Union;

(viii) establish such committees of experts and working groups as may be necessary for the work of the Union;

(ix) determine which countries not members of the Union and which intergovernmental and international non-governmental organizations shall be admitted to its meetings as observers;

(x) adopt amendments to Articles 22 to 26;

(xi) take any other appropriate action designed to further the objectives of the Union;

(xii) exercise such other functions as are appropriate under this Convention;

(xiii) subject to its acceptance, exercise such rights as are given to it in the Convention establishing the Organization.

(b) With respect to matters which are of interest also to other Unions administered by the Organization, the Assembly shall make its decisions after having heard the advice of the Coordination Committee of the Organization.

(3) (a) Each country member of the Assembly shall have one vote.

(b) One-half of the countries members of the Assembly shall constitute a quorum.

(c) Notwithstanding the provisions of subparagraph (b) , if, in any session, the number of countries represented is less than one-half but equal to or more than one-third of the countries members of the Assembly, the Assembly may make decisions but, with the exception of decisions concerning its own procedure, all such decisions shall take effect only if the following conditions are fulfilled. The International Bureau shall communicate the said decisions to the countries members of the Assembly which were not represented and shall invite them to express in writing their vote or abstention within a period of three months from the date of the communication. If, at the expiration of this period, the number of countries having thus expressed their vote or abstention attains the number of countries which was lacking for attaining the quorum in the session itself, such decisions shall take effect provided that at the same time the required majority still obtains.

(d) Subject to the provisions of Article 26(2), the decisions of the Assembly shall require two-thirds of the votes cast.

(e) Abstentions shall not be considered as votes.

(f) A delegate may represent, and vote in the name of, one country only.

(g) Countries of the Union not members of the Assembly shall be admitted to its meetings as observers.

(4) (a) The Assembly shall meet once in every second calendar year in ordinary session upon convocation by the Director General and, in the absence of exceptional circumstances, during the same period and at the same place as the General Assembly of the Organization.

(b) The Assembly shall meet in extraordinary session upon convocation by the Director General, at the request of the Executive Committee or at the request of one-fourth of the countries members of the Assembly.

(5) The Assembly shall adopt its own rules of procedure.

Article 23

[Executive Committee: 1. Constitution; 2. Composition; 3. Number of members; 4. Geographical distribution; special agreements; 5. Term, limits of re-eligibility, rules of election; 6. Tasks; 7. Convocation; 8. Quorum, voting; 9. Observers; 10. Rules of procedure]

(1) The Assembly shall have an Executive Committee.

(2) (a) The Executive Committee shall consist of countries elected by the Assembly from among countries members of the Assembly. Furthermore, the country on whose territory the Organization has its headquarters shall, subject to the provisions of Article 25(7)(b) , have an *ex officio* seat on the Committee.

(b) The Government of each country member of the Executive Committee shall be represented by one delegate, who may be assisted by alternate delegates, advisors, and experts.

(c) The expenses of each delegation shall be borne by the Government which has appointed it.

(3) The number of countries members of the Executive Committee shall correspond to one-fourth of the number of countries members of the Assembly. In establishing the number of seats to be filled, remainders after division by four shall be disregarded.

(4) In electing the members of the Executive Committee, the Assembly shall have due regard to an equitable geographical distribution and to the need for countries party to the Special Agreements which might be established in relation with the Union to be among the countries constituting the Executive Committee.

(5) (a) Each member of the Executive Committee shall serve from the close of the session of the Assembly which elected it to the close of the next ordinary session of the Assembly.

(b) Members of the Executive Committee may be re-elected, but not more than two-thirds of them.

(c) The Assembly shall establish the details of the rules governing the election and possible re-election of the members of the Executive Committee.

(6) (a) The Executive Committee shall:

(i) prepare the draft agenda of the Assembly;

(ii) submit proposals to the Assembly respecting the draft program and biennial budget of the Union prepared by the Director General;

(iii) [*deleted*]

(iv) submit, with appropriate comments, to the Assembly the periodical reports of the Director General and the yearly audit reports on the accounts;

(v) in accordance with the decisions of the Assembly and having regard to circumstances arising between two ordinary sessions of the Assembly, take all necessary measures to ensure the execution of the program of the Union by the Director General;

(vi) perform such other functions as are allocated to it under this Convention.

(b) With respect to matters which are of interest also to other Unions administered by the Organization, the Executive Committee shall make its decisions after having heard the advice of the Coordination Committee of the Organization.

(7) (a) The Executive Committee shall meet once a year in ordinary session

upon convocation by the Director General, preferably during the same period and at the same place as the Coordination Committee of the Organization.

(b) The Executive Committee shall meet in extraordinary session upon convocation by the Director General, either on his own initiative, or at the request of its Chairman or one-fourth of its members.

(8) (a) Each country member of the Executive Committee shall have one vote.

(b) One-half of the members of the Executive Committee shall constitute a quorum.

(c) Decisions shall be made by a simple majority of the votes cast.

(d) Abstentions shall not be considered as votes.

(e) A delegate may represent, and vote in the name of, one country only.

(9) Countries of the Union not members of the Executive Committee shall be admitted to its meetings as observers.

(10) The Executive Committee shall adopt its own rules of procedure.

Article 24

[International Bureau: 1. Tasks in general, Director General; 2. General information; 3. Periodical; 4. Information to countries; 5. Studies and services; 6. Participation in meetings; 7. Conferences of revision; 8. Other tasks]

(1) (a) The administrative tasks with respect to the Union shall be performed by the International Bureau, which is a continuation of the Bureau of the Union united with the Bureau of the Union established by the International Convention for the Protection of Industrial Property.

(b) In particular, the International Bureau shall provide the secretariat of the various organs of the Union.

(c) The Director General of the Organization shall be the chief executive of the Union and shall represent the Union.

(2) The International Bureau shall assemble and publish information concerning the protection of copyright. Each country of the Union shall promptly communicate to the International Bureau all new laws and official texts concerning the protection of copyright.

(3) The International Bureau shall publish a monthly periodical.

(4) The International Bureau shall, on request, furnish information to any country of the Union on matters concerning the protection of copyright.

(5) The International Bureau shall conduct studies, and shall provide services, designed to facilitate the protection of copyright.

(6) The Director General and any staff member designated by him shall participate, without the right to vote, in all meetings of the Assembly, the Executive Committee and any other committee of experts or working group. The Director General, or a staff member designated by him, shall be *ex officio* secretary of these bodies.

(7) (a) The International Bureau shall, in accordance with the directions of the Assembly and in cooperation with the Executive Committee, make the preparations for the conferences of revision of the provisions of the Convention other than Articles 22 to 26.

(b) The International Bureau may consult with inter-governmental and international non-governmental organizations concerning preparations for conferences of revision.

(c) The Director General and persons designated by him shall take part, without the right to vote, in the discussions at these conferences.

(8) The International Bureau shall carry out any other tasks assigned to it.

Article 25

[Finances: 1. Budget; 2. Coordination with other Unions; 3. Resources; 4. Contributions; possible extension of previous budget; 5. Fees and charges; 6. Working capital fund; 7. Advances by host Government; 8. Auditing of accounts]

(1) (a) The Union shall have a budget.

(b) The budget of the Union shall include the income and expenses proper to the Union, its contribution to the budget of expenses common to the Unions, and, where applicable, the sum made available to the budget of the Conference of the Organization.

(c) Expenses not attributable exclusively to the Union but also to one or more other Unions administered by the Organization shall be considered as expenses common to the Unions. The share of the Union in such common expenses shall be in proportion to the interest the Union has in them.

(2) The budget of the Union shall be established with due regard to the requirements of coordination with the budgets of the other Unions administered by the Organization.

(3) The budget of the Union shall be financed from the following sources:

(i) contributions of the countries of the Union;

(ii) fees and charges due for services performed by the International Bureau in relation to the Union;

(iii) sale of, or royalties on, the publications of the International Bureau concerning the Union;

(iv) gifts, bequests, and subventions;

(v) rents, interests, and other miscellaneous income.

(4) (a) For the purpose of establishing its contribution towards the budget, each country of the Union shall belong to a class, and shall pay its annual contributions on the basis of a number of units fixed as follows:

Class I 25

Class II 20

Class III 15
Class IV 10
Class V 5
Class VI 3
Class VII 1

(b) Unless it has already done so, each country shall indicate, concurrently with depositing its instrument of ratification or accession, the class to which it wishes to belong. Any country may change class. If it chooses a lower class, the country must announce it to the Assembly at one of its ordinary sessions. Any such change shall take effect at the beginning of the calendar year following the session.

(c) The annual contribution of each country shall be an amount in the same proportion to the total sum to be contributed to the annual budget of the Union by all countries as the number of its units is to the total of the units of all contributing countries.

(d) Contributions shall become due on the first of January of each year.

(e) A country which is in arrears in the payment of its contributions shall have no vote in any of the organs of the Union of which it is a member if the amount of its arrears equals or exceeds the amount of the contributions due from it for the preceding two full years. However, any organ of the Union may allow such a country to continue to exercise its vote in that organ if, and as long as, it is satisfied that the delay in payment is due to exceptional and unavoidable circumstances.

(f) If the budget is not adopted before the beginning of a new financial period, it shall be at the same level as the budget of the previous year, in accordance with the financial regulations.

(5) The amount of the fees and charges due for services rendered by the International Bureau in relation to the Union shall be established, and shall be reported to the Assembly and the Executive Committee, by the Director General.

(6) (a) The Union shall have a working capital fund which shall be constituted by a single payment made by each country of the Union. If the fund becomes insufficient, an increase shall be decided by the Assembly.

(b) The amount of the initial payment of each country to the said fund or of its participation in the increase thereof shall be a proportion of the contribution of that country for the year in which the fund is established or the increase decided.

(c) The proportion and the terms of payment shall be fixed by the Assembly on the proposal of the Director General and after it has heard the advice of the Coordination Committee of the Organization.

(7) (a) In the headquarters agreement concluded with the country on the territory of which the Organization has its headquarters, it shall be provided that, whenever the working capital fund is insufficient, such country shall grant advances. The amount of these advances and the conditions on which they are granted shall be the

subject of separate agreements, in each case, between such country and the Organization. As long as it remains under the obligation to grant advances, such country shall have an *ex officio* seat on the Executive Committee.

(b) The country referred to in subparagraph (a) and the Organization shall each have the right to denounce the obligation to grant advances, by written notification. Denunciation shall take effect three years after the end of the year in which it has been notified.

(8) The auditing of the accounts shall be effected by one or more of the countries of the Union or by external auditors, as provided in the financial regulations. They shall be designated, with their agreement, by the Assembly.

Article 26

[Amendments: 1. Provisions susceptible of amendment by the Assembly; proposals; 2. Adoption; 3. Entry into force]

(1) Proposals for the amendment of Articles 22, 23, 24, 25, and the present Article, may be initiated by any country member of the Assembly, by the Executive Committee, or by the Director General. Such proposals shall be communicated by the Director General to the member countries of the Assembly at least six months in advance of their consideration by the Assembly.

(2) Amendments to the Articles referred to in paragraph (1) shall be adopted by the Assembly. Adoption shall require three-fourths of the votes cast, provided that any amendment of Article 22, and of the present paragraph, shall require four-fifths of the votes cast.

(3) Any amendment to the Articles referred to in paragraph (1) shall enter into force one month after written notifications of acceptance, effected in accordance with their respective constitutional processes, have been received by the Director General from three-fourths of the countries members of the Assembly at the time it adopted the amendment. Any amendment to the said Articles thus accepted shall bind all the countries which are members of the Assembly at the time the amendment enters into force, or which become members thereof at a subsequent date, provided that any amendment increasing the financial obligations of countries of the Union shall bind only those countries which have notified their acceptance of such amendment.

Article 27

[Revision: 1. Objective; 2. Conferences; 3. Adoption]

(1) This Convention shall be submitted to revision with a view to the introduction of amendments designed to improve the system of the Union.

(2) For this purpose, conferences shall be held successively in one of the countries of the Union among the delegates of the said countries.

(3) Subject to the provisions of Article 26 which apply to the amendment of Articles 22 to 26, any revision of this Act, including the Appendix, shall require the unanimity of the votes cast.

Article 28

[Acceptance and Entry Into Force of Act for Countries of the Union: 1. Ratification, accession; possibility of excluding certain provisions; withdrawal of exclusion; 2. Entry into force of Articles 1 to 21 and Appendix; 3. Entry into force of Articles 22 to 38]

(1) (a) Any country of the Union which has signed this Act may ratify it, and, if it has not signed it, may accede to it. Instruments of ratification or accession shall be deposited with the Director General.

(b) Any country of the Union may declare in its instrument of ratification or accession that its ratification or accession shall not apply to Articles 1 to 21 and the Appendix, provided that, if such country has previously made a declaration under Article VI(1) of the Appendix, then it may declare in the said instrument only that its ratification or accession shall not apply to Articles 1 to 20.

(c) Any country of the Union which, in accordance with subparagraph (b) , has excluded provisions therein referred to from the effects of its ratification or accession may at any later time declare that it extends the effects of its ratification or accession to those provisions. Such declaration shall be deposited with the Director General.

(2) (a) Articles 1 to 21 and the Appendix shall enter into force three months after both of the following two conditions are fulfilled:

(i) at least five countries of the Union have ratified or acceded to this Act without making a declaration under paragraph (1)(b) ,

(ii) France, Spain, the United Kingdom of Great Britain and Northern Ireland, and the United States of America, have become bound by the Universal Copyright Convention as revised at Paris on July 24, 1971.

(b) The entry into force referred to in subparagraph (a) shall apply to those countries of the Union which, at least three months before the said entry into force, have deposited instruments of ratification or accession not containing a declaration under paragraph (1)(b) .

(c) With respect to any country of the Union not covered by subparagraph (b) and which ratifies or accedes to this Act without making a declaration under paragraph (1)(b) , Articles 1 to 21 and the Appendix shall enter into force three months after the date on which the Director General has notified the deposit of the relevant instrument of ratification or accession, unless a subsequent date has been indicated in the instrument deposited. In the latter case, Articles 1 to 21 and the Appendix shall enter into force with respect to that country on the date thus indicated.

(d) The provisions of subparagraphs (a) to (c) do not affect the application of Article VI of the Appendix.

(3) With respect to any country of the Union which ratifies or accedes to this Act with or without a declaration made under paragraph (1)(b) , Articles 22 to 38 shall enter into force three months after the date on which the Director General has notified the deposit of the relevant instrument of ratification or accession, unless a subsequent date has been indicated in the instrument deposited. In the latter case, Articles 22 to 38 shall enter into force with respect to that country on the date thus indicated.

Article 29

[Acceptance and Entry Into Force for Countries Outside the Union: 1. Accession; 2. Entry into force]

(1) Any country outside the Union may accede to this Act and thereby become party to this Convention and a member of the Union. Instruments of accession shall be deposited with the Director General.

(2) (a) Subject to subparagraph (b) , this Convention shall enter into force with respect to any country outside the Union three months after the date on which the Director General has notified the deposit of its instrument of accession, unless a subsequent date has been indicated in the instrument deposited. In the latter case, this Convention shall enter into force with respect to that country on the date thus indicated.

(b) If the entry into force according to subparagraph (a) precedes the entry into force of Articles 1 to 21 and the Appendix according to Article 28(2)(a) , the said country shall, in the meantime, be bound, instead of by Articles 1 to 21 and the Appendix, by Articles 1 to 20 of the Brussels Act of this Convention.

Article 29bis

[Effect of Acceptance of Act for the Purposes of Article 14(2) of the WIPO Convention]

Ratification of or accession to this Act by any country not bound by Articles 22 to 38 of the Stockholm Act of this Convention shall, for the sole purposes of Article 14(2) of the Convention establishing the Organization, amount to ratification of or accession to the said Stockholm Act with the limitation set forth in Article 28(1)(b)(i) thereof.

Article 30

[Reservations: 1. Limits of possibility of making reservations; 2. Earlier reservations; reservation as to the right of translation; withdrawal of reservation]

(1) Subject to the exceptions permitted by paragraph (2) of this Article, by Article 28(1)(b) , by Article 33(2), and by the Appendix, ratification or accession shall automatically entail acceptance of all the provisions and admission to all the advantages of this Convention.

(2) (a) Any country of the Union ratifying or acceding to this Act may, subject to Article V(2) of the Appendix, retain the benefit of the reservations it has previously formulated on condition that it makes a declaration to that effect at the time of the deposit of its instrument of ratification or accession.

(b) Any country outside the Union may declare, in acceding to this Convention and subject to Article V(2) of the Appendix, that it intends to substitute, temporarily at least, for Article 8 of this Act concerning the right of translation, the provisions of Article 5 of the Union Convention of 1886, as completed at Paris in 1896, on the clear understanding that the said provisions are applicable only to translations into a language in general use in the said country. Subject to Article I(6)(b) of the Appendix, any country has the right to apply, in relation to the right of translation of works whose country of origin is a country availing itself of such a reservation, a protection which is equivalent to the protection granted by the latter country.

(c) Any country may withdraw such reservations at any time by notification addressed to the Director General.

Article 31

[Applicability to Certain Territories: 1. Declaration; 2. Withdrawal of declaration; 3. Effective date;4. Acceptance of factual situations not implied]

(1) Any country may declare in its instrument of ratification or accession, or may inform the Director General by written notification at any time thereafter, that this Convention shall be applicable to all or part of those territories, designated in the declaration or notification, for the external relations of which it is responsible.

(2) Any country which has made such a declaration or given such a notification may, at any time, notify the Director General that this Convention shall cease to be applicable to all or part of such territories.

(3) (a) Any declaration made under paragraph (1) shall take effect on the same date as the ratification or accession in which it was included, and any notification given under that paragraph shall take effect three months after its notification by the Director General.

(b) Any notification given under paragraph (2) shall take effect twelve months after its receipt by the Director General.

(4) This Article shall in no way be understood as implying the recognition or tacit acceptance by a country of the Union of the factual situation concerning a territory to which this Convention is made applicable by another country of the Union by virtue of a declaration under paragraph (1).

Article 32

[Applicability of this Act and of Earlier Acts: 1. As between countries already members of the Union; 2. As between a country becoming a member of the Union and other countries members of the Union; 3. Applicability of the Appendix in Certain Relations]

(1) This Act shall, as regards relations between the countries of the Union, and to the extent that it applies, replace the Berne Convention of September 9, 1886, and the subsequent Acts of revision. The Acts previously in force shall continue to be applicable, in their entirety or to the extent that this Act does not replace them by virtue of the preceding sentence, in relations with countries of the Union which do not ratify or accede to this Act.

(2) Countries outside the Union which become party to this Act shall, subject to paragraph (3), apply it with respect to any country of the Union not bound by this Act or which, although bound by this Act, has made a declaration pursuant to Article 28(1)(b) . Such countries recognize that the said country of the Union, in its relations with them:

(i) may apply the provisions of the most recent Act by which it is bound, and

(ii) subject to Article I(6) of the Appendix, has the right to adapt the protection to the level provided for by this Act.

(3) Any country which has availed itself of any of the faculties provided for in the Appendix may apply the provisions of the Appendix relating to the faculty or faculties of which it has availed itself in its relations with any other country of the Union which is not bound by this Act, provided that the latter country has accepted the application of the said provisions.

Article 33

[Disputes: 1. Jurisdiction of the International Court of Justice; 2. Reservation as to such jurisdiction; 3. Withdrawal of reservation]

(1) Any dispute between two or more countries of the Union concerning the interpretation or application of this Convention, not settled by negotiation, may, by any one of the countries concerned, be brought before the International Court of Justice by application in conformity with the Statute of the Court, unless the countries concerned agree on some other method of settlement. The country bringing the dispute before the Court shall inform the International Bureau; the International

Bureau shall bring the matter to the attention of the other countries of the Union.

(2) Each country may, at the time it signs this Act or deposits its instrument of ratification or accession, declare that it does not consider itself bound by the provisions of paragraph (1). With regard to any dispute between such country and any other country of the Union, the provisions of paragraph (1) shall not apply.

(3) Any country having made a declaration in accordance with the provisions of paragraph (2) may, at any time, withdraw its declaration by notification addressed to the Director General.

Article 34

[Closing of Certain Earlier Provisions: 1. Of earlier Acts; 2. Of the Protocol to the Stockholm Act]

(1) Subject to Article 29bis no country may ratify or accede to earlier Acts of this Convention once Articles 1 to 21 and the Appendix have entered into force.

(2) Once Articles 1 to 21 and the Appendix have entered into force, no country may make a declaration under Article 5 of the Protocol Regarding Developing Countries attached to the Stockholm Act.

Article 35

[Duration of the Convention; Denunciation: 1. Unlimited duration; 2. Possibility of denunciation; 3. Effective date of denunciation; 4. Moratorium on denunciation]

(1) This Convention shall remain in force without limitation as to time.

(2) Any country may denounce this Act by notification addressed to the Director General. Such denunciation shall constitute also denunciation of all earlier Acts and shall affect only the country making it, the Convention remaining in full force and effect as regards the other countries of the Union.

(3) Denunciation shall take effect one year after the day on which the Director General has received the notification.

(4) The right of denunciation provided by this Article shall not be exercised by any country before the expiration of five years from the date upon which it becomes a member of the Union.

Article 36

[Application of the Convention: 1. Obligation to adopt the necessary measures; 2. Time from which obligation exists]

(1) Any country party to this Convention undertakes to adopt, in accordance with its constitution, the measures necessary to ensure the application of this Convention.

(2) It is understood that, at the time a country becomes bound by this Convention, it will be in a position under its domestic law to give effect to the provisions of

this Convention.

Article 37

[Final Clauses: 1. Languages of the Act; 2. Signature; 3. Certified copies; 4. Registration; 5. Notifications]

(1) (a) This Act shall be signed in a single copy in the French and English languages and, subject to paragraph (2), shall be deposited with the Director General.

(b) Official texts shall be established by the Director General, after consultation with the interested Governments, in the Arabic, German, Italian, Portuguese and Spanish languages, and such other languages as the Assembly may designate.

(c) In case of differences of opinion on the interpretation of the various texts, the French text shall prevail.

(2) This Act shall remain open for signature until January 31, 1972. Until that date, the copy referred to in paragraph (1)(a) shall be deposited with the Government of the French Republic.

(3) The Director General shall certify and transmit two copies of the signed text of this Act to the Governments of all countries of the Union and, on request, to the Government of any other country.

(4) The Director General shall register this Act with the Secretariat of the United Nations.

(5) The Director General shall notify the Governments of all countries of the Union of signatures, deposits of instruments of ratification or accession and any declarations included in such instruments or made pursuant to Articles 28(1)(c) , 30(2)(a) and (b) , and 33(2), entry into force of any provisions of this Act, notifications of denunciation, and notifications pursuant to Articles 30(2)(c) , 31(1) and (2), 33(3), and 38(1), as well as the Appendix.

Article 38

[Transitory Provisions: 1. Exercise of the "five-year privilege"; 2. Bureau of the Union, Director of the Bureau; 3. Succession of Bureau of the Union]

(1) Countries of the Union which have not ratified or acceded to this Act and which are not bound by Articles 22 to 26 of the Stockholm Act of this Convention may, until April 26, 1975, exercise, if they so desire, the rights provided under the said Articles as if they were bound by them. Any country desiring to exercise such rights shall give written notification to this effect to the Director General; this notification shall be effective on the date of its receipt. Such countries shall be deemed to be members of the Assembly until the said date.

(2) As long as all the countries of the Union have not become Members of the Organization, the International Bureau of the Organization shall also function as the Bureau of the Union, and the Director General as the Director of the said

Bureau.

(3) Once all the countries of the Union have become Members of the Organization, the rights, obligations, and property, of the Bureau of the Union shall devolve on the International Bureau of the Organization.

APPENDIX

[SPECIAL PROVISIONS REGARDING DEVELOPING COUNTRIES]

Article I

[Faculties Open to Developing Countries: 1. Availability of certain faculties; declaration: 2. Duration of effect of declaration; 3. Cessation of developing country status; 4. Existing stocks of copies; 5. Declarations concerning certain territories; 6. Limits of reciprocity]

(1) Any country regarded as a developing country in conformity with the established practice of the General Assembly of the United Nations which ratifies or accedes to this Act, of which this Appendix forms an integral part, and which, having regard to its economic situation and its social or cultural needs, does not consider itself immediately in a position to make provision for the protection of all the rights as provided for in this Act, may, by a notification deposited with the Director General at the time of depositing its instrument of ratification or accession or, subject to Article V(1)(c) , at any time thereafter, declare that it will avail itself of the faculty provided for in Article II, or of the faculty provided for in Article III, or of both of those faculties. It may, instead of availing itself of the faculty provided for in Article II, make a declaration according to Article V(1)(a) .

(2) (a) Any declaration under paragraph (1) notified before the expiration of the period of ten years from the entry into force of Articles 1 to 21 and this Appendix according to Article 28(2) shall be effective until the expiration of the said period. Any such declaration may be renewed in whole or in part for periods of ten years each by a notification deposited with the Director General not more than fifteen months and not less than three months before the expiration of the ten-year period then running.

(b) Any declaration under paragraph (1) notified after the expiration of the period of ten years from the entry into force of Articles 1 to 21 and this Appendix according to Article 28(2) shall be effective until the expiration of the ten-year period then running. Any such declaration may be renewed as provided for in the second sentence of subparagraph (a) .

(3) Any country of the Union which has ceased to be regarded as a developing country as referred to in paragraph (1) shall no longer be entitled to renew its

declaration as provided in paragraph (2), and, whether or not it formally withdraws its declaration, such country shall be precluded from availing itself of the faculties referred to in paragraph (1) from the expiration of the ten-year period then running or from the expiration of a period of three years after it has ceased to be regarded as a developing country, whichever period expires later.

(4) Where, at the time when the declaration made under paragraph (1) or (2) ceases to be effective, there are copies in stock which were made under a license granted by virtue of this Appendix, such copies may continue to be distributed until their stock is exhausted.

(5) Any country which is bound by the provisions of this Act and which has deposited a declaration or a notification in accordance with Article 31(1) with respect to the application of this Act to a particular territory, the situation of which can be regarded as analogous to that of the countries referred to in paragraph (1), may, in respect of such territory, make the declaration referred to in paragraph (1) and the notification of renewal referred to in paragraph (2). As long as such declaration or notification remains in effect, the provisions of this Appendix shall be applicable to the territory in respect of which it was made.

(6) (a) The fact that a country avails itself of any of the faculties referred to in paragraph (1) does not permit another country to give less protection to works of which the country of origin is the former country than it is obliged to grant under Articles 1 to 20.

(b) The right to apply reciprocal treatment provided for in Article 30(2)(b) , second sentence, shall not, until the date on which the period applicable under Article I(3) expires, be exercised in respect of works the country of origin of which is a country which has made a declaration according to Article V(1)(a) .

Article II

[Limitations on the Right of Translation: 1. Licenses grantable by competent authority; 2. to 4. Conditions allowing the grant of such licenses; 5. Purposes for which licenses may be granted; 6. Termination of licenses; 7. Works composed mainly of illustrations; 8. Works withdrawn from circulation; 9. Licenses for broadcasting organizations]

(1) Any country which has declared that it will avail itself of the faculty provided for in this Article shall be entitled, so far as works published in printed or analogous forms of reproduction are concerned, to substitute for the exclusive right of translation provided for in Article 8 a system of non-exclusive and non-transferable licenses, granted by the competent authority under the following conditions and subject to Article IV.

(2) (a) Subject to paragraph (3), if, after the expiration of a period of three

years, or of any longer period determined by the national legislation of the said country, commencing on the date of the first publication of the work, a translation of such work has not been published in a language in general use in that country by the owner of the right of translation, or with his authorization, any national of such country may obtain a license to make a translation of the work in the said language and publish the translation in printed or analogous forms of reproduction.

(b) A license under the conditions provided for in this Article may also be granted if all the editions of the translation published in the language concerned are out of print.

(3) (a) In the case of translations into a language which is not in general use in one or more developed countries which are members of the Union, a period of one year shall be substituted for the period of three years referred to in paragraph (2)(a) .

(b) Any country referred to in paragraph (1) may, with the unanIntous agreement of the developed countries which are members of the Union and in which the same language is in general use, substitute, in the case of translations into that language, for the period of three years referred to in paragraph (2)(a) a shorter period as determined by such agreement but not less than one year. However, the provisions of the foregoing sentence shall not apply where the language in question is English, French or Spanish. The Director General shall be notified of any such agreement by the Governments which have concluded it.

(4) (a) No license obtainable after three years shall be granted under this Article until a further period of six months has elapsed, and no license obtainable after one year shall be granted under this Article until a further period of nine months has elapsed

(i) from the date on which the applicant complies with the requirements mentioned in Article IV(1), or

(ii) where the identity or the address of the owner of the right of translation is unknown, from the date on which the applicant sends, as provided for in Article IV(2), copies of his application submitted to the authority competent to grant the license.

(b) If, during the said period of six or nine months, a translation in the language in respect of which the application was made is published by the owner of the right of translation or with his authorization, no license under this Article shall be granted.

(5) Any license under this Article shall be granted only for the purpose of teaching, scholarship or research.

(6) If a translation of a work is published by the owner of the right of translation or with his authorization at a price reasonably related to that normally charged in the country for comparable works, any license granted under this Article shall terminate if such translation is in the same language and with substantially the

same content as the translation published under the license. Any copies already made before the license terminates may continue to be distributed until their stock is exhausted.

(7) For works which are composed mainly of illustrations, a license to make and publish a translation of the text and to reproduce and publish the illustrations may be granted only if the conditions of Article III are also fulfilled.

(8) No license shall be granted under this Article when the author has withdrawn from circulation all copies of his work.

(9) (a) A license to make a translation of a work which has been published in printed or analogous forms of reproduction may also be granted to any broadcasting organization having its headquarters in a country referred to in paragraph (1), upon an application made to the competent authority of that country by the said organization, provided that all of the following conditions are met:

(i) the translation is made from a copy made and acquired in accordance with the laws of the said country;

(ii) the translation is only for use in broadcasts intended exclusively for teaching or for the dissemination of the results of specialized technical or scientific research to experts in a particular profession;

(iii) the translation is used exclusively for the purposes referred to in condition (ii) through broadcasts made lawfully and intended for recipients on the territory of the said country, including broadcasts made through the medium of sound or visual recordings lawfully and exclusively made for the purpose of such broadcasts;

(iv) all uses made of the translation are without any commercial purpose.

(b) Sound or visual recordings of a translation which was made by a broadcasting organization under a license granted by virtue of this paragraph may, for the purposes and subject to the conditions referred to in subparagraph (a) and with the agreement of that organization, also be used by any other broadcasting organization having its headquarters in the country whose competent authority granted the license in question.

(c) Provided that all of the criteria and conditions set out in subparagraph (a) are met, a license may also be granted to a broadcasting organization to translate any text incorporated in an audio-visual fixation where such fixation was itself prepared and published for the sole purpose of being used in connection with systematic instructional activities.

(d) Subject to subparagraphs (a) to (c) , the provisions of the preceding paragraphs shall apply to the grant and exercise of any license granted under this paragraph.

Article III

[Limitation on the Right of Reproduction: 1. Licenses grantable by competent authority; 2. to 5. Conditions allowing the grant of such licenses; 6. Termination of licenses; 7. Works to which this Article applies]

(1) Any country which has declared that it will avail itself of the faculty provided for in this Article shall be entitled to substitute for the exclusive right of reproduction provided for in Article 9 a system of non-exclusive and non-transferable licenses, granted by the competent authority under the following conditions and subject to Article IV.

(2) (a) If, in relation to a work to which this Article applies by virtue of paragraph (7), after the expiration of

(i) the relevant period specified in paragraph (3), commencing on the date of first publication of a particular edition of the work, or

(ii)any longer period determined by national legislation of the country referred to in paragraph (1), commencing on the same date,

copies of such edition have not been distributed in that country to the general public or in connection with systematic instructional activities, by the owner of the right of reproduction or with his authorization, at a price reasonably related to that normally charged in the country for comparable works, any national of such country may obtain a license to reproduce and publish such edition at that or a lower price for use in connection with systematic instructional activities.

(b) A license to reproduce and publish an edition which has been distributed as described in subparagraph (a) may also be granted under the conditions provided for in this Article if, after the expiration of the applicable period, no authorized copies of that edition have been on sale for a period of six months in the country concerned to the general public or in connection with systematic instructional activities at a price reasonably related to that normally charged in the country for comparable works.

(3) The period referred to in paragraph (2)(a) (i) shall be five years, except that

(i) for works of the natural and physical sciences, including mathematics, and of technology, the period shall be three years;

(ii) for works of fiction, poetry, drama and music, and for art books, the period shall be seven years.

(4) (a) No license obtainable after three years shall be granted under this Article until a period of six months has elapsed

(i) from the date on which the applicant complies with the requirements mentioned in Article IV(1), or

(ii) where the identity or the address of the owner of the right of reproduction is unknown, from the date on which the applicant sends, as provided for in

Article IV(2), copies of his application submitted to the authority competent to grant the license.

(b) Where licenses are obtainable after other periods and Article IV(2) is applicable, no license shall be granted until a period of three months has elapsed from the date of the dispatch of the copies of the application.

(c) If, during the period of six or three months referred to in subparagraphs (a) and (b) , a distribution as described in paragraph (2)(a) has taken place, no license shall be granted under this Article.

(d) No license shall be granted if the author has withdrawn from circulation all copies of the edition for the reproduction and publication of which the license has been applied for.

(5) A license to reproduce and publish a translation of a work shall not be granted under this Article in the following cases:

(i) where the translation was not published by the owner of the right of translation or with his authorization, or

(ii) where the translation is not in a language in general use in the country in which the license is applied for.

(6) If copies of an edition of a work are distributed in the country referred to in paragraph (1) to the general public or in connection with systematic instructional activities, by the owner of the right of reproduction or with his authorization, at a price reasonably related to that normally charged in the country for comparable works, any license granted under this Article shall terminate if such edition is in the same language and with substantially the same content as the edition which was published under the said license. Any copies already made before the license terminates may continue to be distributed until their stock is exhausted.

(7) (a) Subject to subparagraph (b) , the works to which this Article applies shall be limited to works published in printed or analogous forms of reproduction.

(b) This Article shall also apply to the reproduction in audio-visual form of lawfully made audio-visual fixations including any protected works incorporated therein and to the translation of any incorporated text into a language in general use in the country in which the license is applied for, always provided that the audio-visual fixations in question were prepared and published for the sole purpose of being used in connection with systematic instructional activities.

Article IV

[Provisions Common to Licenses Under Articles II and III: 1 and 2. Procedure; 3. Indication of author and title of work; 4. Exportation of copies; 5. Notice; 6. Compensation]

(1) A license under Article II or Article III may be granted only if the applicant, in accordance with the procedure of the country concerned, establishes either

that he has requested, and has been denied, authorization by the owner of the right to make and publish the translation or to reproduce and publish the edition, as the case may be, or that, after due diligence on his part, he was unable to find the owner of the right. At the same time as making the request, the applicant shall inform any national or international information center referred to in paragraph (2).

(2) If the owner of the right cannot be found, the applicant for a license shall send, by registered airmail, copies of his application, submitted to the authority competent to grant the license, to the publisher whose name appears on the work and to any national or international information center which may have been designated, in a notification to that effect deposited with the Director General, by the Government of the country in which the publisher is believed to have his principal place of business.

(3) The name of the author shall be indicated on all copies of the translation or reproduction published under a license granted under Article II or Article III. The title of the work shall appear on all such copies. In the case of a translation, the original title of the work shall appear in any case on all the said copies.

(4) (a) No license granted under Article II or Article III shall extend to the export of copies, and any such license shall be valid only for publication of the translation or of the reproduction, as the case may be, in the territory of the country in which it has been applied for.

(b) For the purposes of subparagraph (a) , the notion of export shall include the sending of copies from any territory to the country which, in respect of that territory, has made a declaration under Article I(5).

(c) Where a governmental or other public entity of a country which has granted a license to make a translation under Article II into a language other than English, French or Spanish sends copies of a translation published under such license to another country, such sending of copies shall not, for the purposes of subparagraph (a), be considered to constitute export if all of the following conditions are met:

(i) the recipients are individuals who are nationals of the country whose competent authority has granted the license, or organizations grouping such individuals;

(ii) the copies are to be used only for the purpose of teaching, scholarship or research;

(iii) the sending of the copies and their subsequent distribution to recipients is without any commercial purpose; and

(iv) the country to which the copies have been sent has agreed with the country whose competent authority has granted the license to allow the receipt, or distribution, or both, and the Director General has been notified of the agreement by the Government of the country in which the license has been granted.

(5) All copies published under a license granted by virtue of Article II or Article III shall bear a notice in the appropriate language stating that the copies are available for distribution only in the country or territory to which the said license applies.

(6) (a) Due provision shall be made at the national level to ensure

(i) that the license provides, in favour of the owner of the right of translation or of reproduction, as the case may be, for just compensation that is consistent with standards of royalties normally operating on licenses freely negotiated between persons in the two countries concerned, and

(ii) payment and transmittal of the compensation: should national currency regulations intervene, the competent authority shall make all efforts, by the use of international machinery, to ensure transmittal in internationally convertible currency or its equivalent.

(b) Due provision shall be made by national legislation to ensure a correct translation of the work, or an accurate reproduction of the particular edition, as the case may be.

Article V

[Alternative Possibility for Limitation of the Right of Translation: 1. Regime provided for under the 1886 and 1896 Acts; 2. No possibility of change to regime under Article II; 3. Time limit for choosing the alternative possibility]

(1) (a) Any country entitled to make a declaration that it will avail itself of the faculty provided for in Article II may, instead, at the time of ratifying or acceding to this Act:

(i) if it is a country to which Article 30(2)(a) applies, make a declaration under that provision as far as the right of translation is concerned;

(ii) if it is a country to which Article 30(2)(a) does not apply, and even if it is not a country outside the Union, make a declaration as provided for in Article 30(2)(b) , first sentence.

(b) In the case of a country which ceases to be regarded as a developing country as referred to in Article I(1), a declaration made according to this paragraph shall be effective until the date on which the period applicable under Article I(3) expires.

(c) Any country which has made a declaration according to this paragraph may not subsequently avail itself of the faculty provided for in Article II even if it withdraws the said declaration.

(2) Subject to paragraph (3), any country which has availed itself of the faculty provided for in Article II may not subsequently make a declaration according to paragraph (1).

(3) Any country which has ceased to be regarded as a developing country as

referred to in Article I(1) may, not later than two years prior to the expiration of the period applicable under Article I(3), make a declaration to the effect provided for in Article 30(2)(b) , first sentence, notwithstanding the fact that it is not a country outside the Union. Such declaration shall take effect at the date on which the period applicable under Article I(3) expires.

Article VI

[Possibilities of applying, or admitting the application of, certain provisions of the Appendix before becoming bound by it: 1. Declaration; 2. Depository and effective date of declaration]

(1) Any country of the Union may declare, as from the date of this Act, and at any time before becoming bound by Articles 1 to 21 and this Appendix:

(i) if it is a country which, were it bound by Articles 1 to 21 and this Appendix, would be entitled to avail itself of the faculties referred to in Article I(1), that it will apply the provisions of Article II or of Article III or of both to works whose country of origin is a country which, pursuant to (ii) below, admits the application of those Articles to such works, or which is bound by Articles 1 to 21 and this Appendix; such declaration may, instead of referring to Article II, refer to Article V;

(ii) that it admits the application of this Appendix to works of which it is the country of origin by countries which have made a declaration under (i) above or a notification under Article I.

(2) Any declaration made under paragraph (1) shall be in writing and shall be deposited with the Director General. The declaration shall become effective from the date of its deposit.

Universal Copyright Convention

as Revised at Paris on 24 July 1971

The Contracting States,

Moved by the desire to ensure in all countries copyright protection of literary, scientific and artistic works,

Convinced that a system of copyright protection appropriate to all nations of the world and expressed in a universal convention, additional to, and without impairing international systems already in force, will ensure respect for the rights of the individual and encourage the development of literature, the sciences and the arts,

Persuaded that such a universal copyright system will facilitate a wider dissemination of works of the human mind and increase international understanding,

Have resolved to revise the Universal Copyright Convention as signed at Geneva on 6 September 1952 (hereinafter called "the 1952 Convention"), and consequently,

Have agreed as follows:

Article I

Each Contracting State undertakes to provide for the adequate and effective protection of the rights of authors and other copyright proprietors in literary, scientific and artistic works, including writings, musical, dramatic and cinemato graphic works, and paintings, engravings and sculpture.

Article II

1. Published works of nationals of any Contracting State and works first published in that State shall enjoy in each other Contracting State the same protection as that other State accords to works of its nationals first published in its own territory, as well as the protection specially granted by this Convention.

2. Unpublished works of nationals of each Contracting State shall enjoy in each other Contracting State the same protection as that other State accords to unpublished works of its own nationals, as well as the protection specially granted by this Convention.

3. For the purpose of this Convention any Contracting State may, by domestic legislation, assimilate to its own nationals any person domiciled in that State.

Article III

1. Any Contracting State which, under its domestic law, requires as a condition of copyright, compliance with formalities such as deposit, registration, notice, notarial certificates, payment of fees or manufacture or publication in that Contracting State, shall regard these requirements as satisfied with respect to all works protected in accordance with this Convention and first published outside its territory and the author of which is not one of its nationals, if from the time of the first publication all the copies of the work published with the authority of the author or other copyright proprietor bear the symbol © accompanied by the name of the copyright proprietor and the year of first publication placed in such manner and location as to give reasonable notice of claim of copyright.

2. The provisions of paragraph 1 shall not preclude any Contracting State from requiring formalities or other conditions for the acquisition and enjoyment of copyright in respect of works first published in its territory or works of its nationals wherever published.

3. The provisions of paragraph 1 shall not preclude any Contracting State from providing that a person seeking judicial relief must, in bringing the action, comply with procedural requirements, such as that the complainant must appear through domestic counsel or that the complainant must deposit with the court or an administrative office, or both, a copy of the work involved in the litigation; provided that failure to comply with such requirements shall not affect the validity of the copyright, nor shall any such requirement be imposed upon a national of another Contracting State if such requirement is not imposed on nationals of the State in which protection is claimed.

4. In each Contracting State there shall be legal means of protecting without formalities the unpublished works of nationals of other Contracting States.

5. If a Contracting State grants protection for more than one term of copyright and the first term is for a period longer than one of the minimum periods prescribed in Article IV, such State shall not be required to comply with the provisions of paragraph 1 of this Article in respect of the second or any subsequent term of copyright.

Article IV

1. The duration of protection of a work shall be governed, in accordance with

the provisions of Article II and this Article, by the law of the Contracting State in which protection is claimed.

2. (a) The term of protection for works protected under this Convention shall not be less than the life of the author and twenty-five years after his death. However, any Contracting State which, on the effective date of this Convention in that State, has limited this term for certain classes of works to a period computed from the first publication of the work, shall be entitled to maintain these exceptions and to extend them to other classes of works. For all these classes the term of protection shall not be less than twenty-five years from the date of first publication.

(b) Any Contracting State which, upon the effective date of this Convention in that State, does not compute the term of protection upon the basis of the life of the author, shall be entitled to compute the term of protection from the date of the first publication of the work or from its registration prior to publication, as the case may be, provided the term of protection shall not be less than twenty-five years from the date of first publication or from its registration prior to publication, as the case may be.

(c) If the legislation of a Contracting State grants two or more successive terms of protection, the duration of the first term shall not be less than one of the minimum periods specified in sub-paragraphs (a) and (b) .

3. The provisions of paragraph 2 shall not apply to photographic works or to works of applied art; provided, however, that the term of protection in those Contracting States which protect photographic works, or works of applied art in so far as they are protected as artistic works, shall not be less than ten years for each of said classes of works.

4. (a) No Contracting State shall be obliged to grant protection to a work for a period longer than that fixed for the class of works to which the work in question belongs, in the case of unpublished works by the law of the Contracting State of which the author is a national, and in the case of published works by the law of the Contracting State in which the work has been first published.

(b) For the purposes of the application of sub-paragraph (a) , if the law of any Contracting State grants two or more successive terms of protection, the period of protection of that State shall be considered to be the aggregate of those terms. However, if a specified work is not protected by such State during the second or any subsequent term for any reason, the other Contracting States shall not be obliged to protect it during the second or any subsequent term.

5. For the purposes of the application of paragraph 4, the work of a national of a Contracting State, first published in a non-Contracting State, shall be treated as though first published in the Contracting State of which the author is a national.

6. For the purposes of the application of paragraph 4, in case of simultaneous publication in two or more Contracting States, the work shall be treated as though

first published in the State which affords the shortest term; any work published in two or more Contracting States within thirty days of its first publication shall be considered as having been published simultaneously in said Contracting States.

Article IVbis

1. The rights referred to in Article I shall include the basic rights ensuring the author's economic interests, including the exclusive right to authorize reproduction by any means, public performance and broadcasting. The provisions of this Article shall extend to works protected under this Convention either in their original form or in any form recognizably derived from the original.

2. However, any Contracting State may, by its domestic legislation, make exceptions that do not conflict with the spirit and provisions of this Convention, to the rights mentioned in paragraph 1 of this Article. Any State whose legislation so provides, shall nevertheless accord a reasonable degree of effective protection to each of the rights to which exception has been made.

Article V

1. The rights referred to in Article I shall include the exclusive right of the author to make, publish and authorize the making and publication of translations of works protected under this Convention.

2. However, any Contracting State may, by its domestic legislation, restrict the right of translation of writings, but only subject to the following provisions:

(a) If, after the expiration of a period of seven years from the date of the first publication of a writing, a translation of such writing has not been published in a language in general use of the Contracting State, by the owner of the right of translation or with his authorization, any national of such Contracting State may obtain a non-exclusive licence from the competent authority thereof to translate the work into that language and publish the work so translated.

(b) Such national shall in accordance with the procedure of the State concerned, establish either that he has requested, and been denied, authorization by the proprietor of the right to make and publish the translation, or that, after due diligence on his part, he was unable to find the owner of the right. A licence may also be granted on the same conditions if all previous editions of a translation in a language in general use in the Contracting State are out of print.

(c) If the owner of the right of translation cannot be found, then the applicant for a licence shall send copies of his application to the publisher whose name appears on the work and, if the nationality of the owner of the right of translation is known, to the diplomatic or consular representative of the State of which such owner is a national, or to the organization which may have been designated by the government of that State. The licence shall not be granted before the expiration of a period of two months from the date of the dispatch of the copies of the application.

(d) Due provision shall be made by domestic legislation to ensure to the owner of the right of translation a compensation which is just and conforms to international standards, to ensure payment and transmittal of such compensation, and to ensure a correct translation of the work.

(e) The original title and the name of the author of the work shall be printed on all copies of the published translation. The licence shall be valid only for publication of the translation in the territory of the Contracting State where it has been applied for. Copies so published may be imported and sold in another Contracting State if a language in general use in such other State is the same language as that into which the work has been so translated, and if the domestic law in such other State makes provision for such licences and does not prohibit such importation and sale. Where the foregoing conditions do not exist, the importation and sale of such copies in a Contracting State shall be governed by its domestic law and its agreements. The licence shall not be transferred by the licensee.

(f) The licence shall not be granted when the author has withdrawn from circulation all copies of the work.

Article V^{bis}

1. Any Contracting State regarded as a developing country in conformity with the established practice of the General Assembly of the United Nations may, by a notification deposited with the Director-General of the United Nations Educational, Scientific and Cultural Organization (hereinafter called "the Director-General") at the time of its ratification, acceptance or accession or thereafter, avail itself of any or all of the exceptions provided for in Articles V^{ter} and V^{quater}.

2. Any such notification shall be effective for ten years from the date of coming into force of this Convention, or for such part of that ten-year period as remains at the date of deposit of the notification, and may be renewed in whole or in part for further periods of ten years each if, not more than fifteen or less than three months before the expiration of the relevant ten-year period, the Contracting State deposits a further notification with the Director-General. Initial notifications may also be made during these further periods of ten years in accordance with the provisions of this Article.

3. Notwithstanding the provisions of paragraph 2, a Contracting State that has ceased to be regarded as a developing country as referred to in paragraph 1 shall no longer be entitled to renew its notification made under the provisions of paragraph 1 or 2, and whether or not it formally withdraws the notification such State shall be precluded from availing itself of the exceptions provided for in Articles V^{ter} and V^{quater} at the end of the current ten-year period, or at the end of three years after it has ceased to be regarded as a developing country, whichever period expires later.

4. Any copies of a work already made under the exceptions provided for in Articles V^{ter} and V^{quater} may continue to be distributed after the expiration of the period for which notifications under this Article were effective until their stock is exhausted.

5. Any Contracting State that has deposited a notification in accordance with Article XIII with respect to the application of this Convention to a particular country or territory, the situation of which can be regarded as analogous to that of the States referred to in paragraph 1 of this Article, may also deposit notifications and renew them in accordance with the provisions of this Article with respect to any such country or territory. During the effective period of such notifications, the provisions of Articles V^{ter} and V^{quater} may be applied with respect to such country or territory. The sending of copies from the country or territory to the Contracting State shall be considered as export within the meaning of Articles V^{ter} and V^{quater}.

Article V^{ter}

1. (a) Any Contracting State to which Article V^{bis} (I) applies may substitute for the period of seven years provided for in Article V (2) a period of three years or any longer period prescribed by its legislation. However, in the case of a translation into a language not in general use in one or more developed countries that are party to this Convention or only the 1952 Convention, the period shall be one year instead of three.

(b) A Contracting State to which Article V^{bis} (1) applies may, with the unanIn-tous agreement of the developed countries party to this Convention or only the 1952 Convention and in which the same language is in general use, substitute, in the case of translation into that language, for the period of three years provided for in sub-paragraph (a) another period as determined by such agreement but not shorter than one year. However, this sub-paragraph shall not apply where the language in question is English, French or Spanish. Notification of any such agreement shall be made to the Director-General.

(c) The licence may only be granted if the applicant, in accordance with the procedure of the State concerned, establishes either that he has requested, and been denied, authorization by the owner of the right of translation, or that, after due diligence on his part, he was unable to find the owner of the right. At the same time as he makes his request he shall inform either the International Copyright Centre established by the United Nations Educational, Scientific and Cultural Organization or any national or regional information centre which may have been designated in a notification to that effect deposited with the Director-General by the government of the State in which the publisher is believed to have his principal place of business.

(d) If the owner of the right of translation cannot be found, the applicant for a licence shall send, by registered airmail, copies of his application to the publisher whose name appears on the work and to any national or regional information centre as mentioned in sub-paragraph (c) . If no such centre is notified he shall also send a copy to the international copyright information centre established by the United Nations Educational, Scientific and Cultural Organization.

2. (a) Licences obtainable after three years shall not be granted under this Article until a further period of six months has elapsed and licences obtainable after one year until a further period of nine months has elapsed. The further period shall begin either from the date of the request for permission to translate mentioned in paragraph 1 (c) or, if the identity or address of the owner of the right of translation is not known, from the date of dispatch of the copies of the application for a licence mentioned in paragraph 1 (d).

(b) Licences shall not be granted if a translation has been published by the owner of the right of translation or with his authorization during the said period of six or nine months.

3. Any licence under this Article shall be granted only for the purpose of teaching, scholarship or research.

4. (a) Any licence granted under this Article shall not extend to the export of copies and shall be valid only for publication in the territory of the Contracting State where it has been applied for.

(b) Any copy published in accordance with a licence granted under this Article shall bear a notice in the appropriate language stating that the copy is available for distribution only in the Contracting State granting the licence. If the writing bears the notice specified in Article III (1) the copies shall bear the same notice.

(c) The prohibition of export provided for in sub-paragraph (a) shall not apply where a governmental or other public entity of a State which has granted a licence under this Article to translate a work into a language other than English, French or Spanish sends copies of a translation prepared under such licence to another country if:

(i) the recipients are individuals who are nationals of the Contracting State granting the licence, or organizations grouping such individuals;

(ii) the copies are to be used only for the purpose of teaching, scholarship or research;

(iii) the sending of the copies and their subsequent distribution to recipients is without the object of commercial purpose; and

(iv) the country to which the copies have been sent has agreed with the Contracting State to allow the receipt, distribution or both and the Director-General has been notified of such agreement by any one of the governments which have concluded it.

5. Due provision shall be made at the national level to ensure:

(a) that the licence provides for just compensation that is consistent with standards of royalties normally operating in the case of licences freely negociated between persons in the two countries concerned; and

(b) payment and transmittal of the compensation; however, should national currency regulations intervene, the competent authority shall make all efforts, by the use of international machinery, to ensure transmittal in internationally convertible currency or its equivalent.

6. Any licence granted by a Contracting State under this Article shall terminate if a translation of the work in the same language with substantially the same content as the edition in respect of which the licence was granted is published in the said State by the owner of the right of translation or with his authorization, at a price reasonably related to that normally charged in the same State for comparable works. Any copies already made before the licence is terminated may continue to be distributed until their stock is exhausted.

7. For works which are composed mainly of illustrations a licence to translate the text and to reproduce the illustrations may be granted only if the conditions of Article V^{quater} are also fulfilled.

8. (a) A licence to translate a work protected under this Convention, published in printed or analogous forms of reproduction, may also be granted to a broad casting organization having its headquarters in a Contracting State to which Article V^{bis} (1) applies, upon an application made in that State by the said organization under the following conditions:

(i) the translation is made from a copy made and acquired in accordance with the laws of the Contracting State;

(ii) the translation is for use only in broadcasts intended exclusively for teaching or for the dissemination of the results of specialized technical or scientific research to experts in a particular profession;

(iii) the translation is used exclusively for the purposes set out in condition (ii), through broadcasts lawfully made which are intended for recipients on the territory of the Contracting State, including broadcasts made through the medium of sound or visual recordings lawfully and exclusively made for the purpose of such broadcasts;

(iv) sound or visual recordings of the translation may be exchanged only between broadcasting organizations having their headquarters in the Contracting State granting the licence; and

(v) all uses made of the translation are without any commercial purpose.

(b) Provided all of the criteria and conditions set out in sub-paragraph (a) are met, a licence may also be granted to a broadcasting organization to translate any text incorporated in an audio-visual fixation which was itself prepared and published for the sole purpose of being used in connexion with systematic instructional activities.

(c) Subject to sub-paragraphs (a) and (b) , the other provisions of this Article shall apply to the grant and exercise of the licence.

9. Subject to the provisions of this Article, any licence granted under this Article shall be governed by the provisions of Article V, and shall continue to be governed by the provisions of Article V and of this Article, even after the seven-year period provided for in Article V (2) has expired. However, after the said period has expired, the licensee shall be free to request that the said licence be replaced by a new licence governed exclusively by the provisions of Article V.

Article V^{quater}

1. Any Contracting State to which Article V^{bis} (1) applies may adopt the following provisions:

(a) If, after the expiration of (i) the relevant period specified in sub-paragraph (c) commencing from the date of first publication of a particular edition of a literary, scientific or artistic work referred to in paragraph 3, or (ii) any longer period determined by national legislation of the State, copies of such edition have not been distributed in that State to the general public or in connexion with systematic instructional activities at a price reasonably related to that normally charged in the State for comparable works, by the owner of the right of reproduction or with his authorization, any national of such State may obtain a non-exclusive licence from the competent authority to publish such edition at that or a lower price for use in connexion with systematic instructional activities. The licence may only be granted if such national, in accordance with the procedure of the State concerned, establishes either that he has requested, and been denied, authorization by the proprietor of the right to publish such work, or that, after due diligence on his part, he was unable to find the owner of the right. At the same time as he makes his request he shall inform either the international copyright information centre established by the United Nations Educational, Scientific and Cultural Organization or any national or regional information centre referred to in sub-paragraph (d).

(b) A licence may also be granted on the same conditions if, for a period of six months, no authorized copies of the edition in question have been on sale in the State concerned to the general public or in connexion with systematic instructional activities at a price reasonably related to that normally charged in the State for comparable works.

(c) The period referred to in sub-paragraph (a) shall be five years except that:

(i) for works of the natural and physical sciences, including mathematics, and of technology, the period shall be three years;

(ii) for works of fiction, poetry, drama and music, and for art books, the period shall be seven years.

(d) If the owner of the right of reproduction cannot be found, the applicant for a licence shall send, by registered airmail, copies of his application to the publisher whose name appears on the work and to any national or regional information centre identified as such in a notification deposited with the Director-General by the State in which the publisher is believed to have his principal place of business. In the absence of any such notification, he shall also send a copy to the international copyright information centre established by the United Nations Educational, Scientific and Cultural Organization. The licence shall not be granted before the expiration of a period of three months from the date of dispatch of the copies of the application.

(e) Licences obtainable after three years shall not be granted under this Article:

(i) until a period of six months has elapsed from the date of the request for permission referred to in sub-paragraph (a) or, if the identity or address of the owner of the right of reproduction is unknown, from the date of the dispatch of the copies of the application for a licence referred to in sub-paragraph (it);

(ii) if any such distribution of copies of the edition as is mentioned in sub-paragraph (a) has taken place during that period.

(f) The name of the author and the title of the particular edition of the work shall be printed on all copies of the published reproduction. The licence shall not extend to the export of copies and shall be valid only for publication in the territory of the Contracting State where it has been applied for. The licence shall not be transferable by the licensee.

(g) Due provision shall be made by domestic legislation to ensure an accurate reproduction of the particular edition in question.

(h) A licence to reproduce and publish a translation of a work shall not be granted under this Article in the following cases:

(i) where the translation was not published by the owner of the right of translation or with his authorization;

(ii) where the translation is not in a language in general use in the State with power to grant the licence.

2. The exceptions provided for in paragraph 1 are subject to the following additional provisions:

(a) Any copy published in accordance with a licence granted under this Article shall bear a notice in the appropriate language stating that the copy is available for distribution only in the Contracting State to which the said licence applies. If the edition bears the notice specified in Article III (1), the copies shall bear the same notice.

(b) Due provision shall be made at the national level to ensure:

(i) that the licence provides for just compensation that is consistent with standards of royalties normally operating in the case of licences freely negotiated between persons in the two countries concerned; and

(ii) payment and transmittal of the compensation; however, should national currency regulations intervene, the competent authority shall make all efforts, by the use of international machinery, to ensure transmittal in internationally convertible currency or its equivalent.

(c) Whenever copies of an edition of a work are distributed in the Contracting State to the general public or in connexion with systematic instructional activities, by the owner of the right of reproduction or with his authorization, at a price reasonably related to that normally charged in the State for comparable works, any licence granted under this Article shall terminate if such edition is in the same language and is substantially the same in content as the edition published under the licence. Any copies already made before the licence is terminated may continue to be distributed until their stock is exhausted.

(d) No licence shall be granted when the author has withdrawn from circulation all copies of the edition in question.

3. (a) Subject to sub-paragraph (b) , the literary, scientific or artistic works to which this Article applies shall be limited to works published in printed or analogous forms of reproduction.

(b) The provisions of this Article shall also apply to reproduction in audio visual form of lawfully made audio-visual fixations including any protected works incorporated therein and to the translation of any incorporated text into a language in general use in the State with power to grant the licence; always provided that the audio-visual fixations in question were prepared and published for the sole purpose of being used in connexion with systematic instructional activities.

Article VI

"Publication", as used in this Convention, means the reproduction in tangible form and the general distribution to the public of copies of a work from which it can be read or otherwise visually perceived.

Article VII

This Convention shall not apply to works or rights in works which, at the effective date of this Convention in a Contracting State where protection is claimed, are permanently in the public domain in the said Contracting State.

Article VIII

1. This Convention, which shall bear the date of 24 July 1971, shall be deposited with the Director-General and shall remain open for signature by all States party to the 1952 Convention for a period of 120 days after the date of this Convention. It shall be subject to ratification or acceptance by the signatory States.

2. Any State which has not signed this Convention may accede thereto.

3. Ratification, acceptance or accession shall be effected by the deposit of an instrument to that effect with the Director-General.

Article IX

1. This Convention shall come into force three months after the deposit of twelve instruments of ratification, acceptance or accession.

2. Subsequently, this Convention shall come into force in respect of each State three months after that State has deposited its instrument of ratification, acceptance or accession.

3. Accession to this Convention by a State not party to the 1952 Convention shall also constitute accession to that Convention; however, if its instrument of accession is deposited before this Convention comes into force, such State may make its accession to the 1952 Convention conditional upon the coming into force of this Convention. After the coming into force of this Convention, no State may accede solely to the 1952 Convention.

4. Relations between States party to this Convention and States that are party only to the 1952 Convention, shall be governed by the 1952 Convention. However, any State party only to the 1952 Convention may, by a notification deposited with the Director-General, declare that it will admit the application of the 1971 Convention to works of its nationals or works first published in its territory by all States party to this Convention.

Article X

1. Each Contracting State undertakes to adopt, in accordance with its Constitution, such measures as are necessary to ensure the application of this Convention.

2. It is understood that at the date this Convention comes into force in respect of any State, that State must be in a position under its domestic law to give effect to the terms of this Convention.

Article XI

1. An Intergovernmental Committee is hereby established with the following duties:

(a) to study the problems concerning the application and operation of the Universal Copyright Convention;

(b) to make preparation for periodic revisions of this Convention;

(c) to study any other problems concerning the international protection of copyright, in co-operation with the various interested international organizations, such as the United Nations Educational, Scientific and Cultural Organization, the International Union for the Protection of Literary and Artistic Works and the Organization of American States;

(d) to inform States party to the Universal Copyright Convention as to its activities.

2. The Committee shall consist of the representatives of eighteen States party to this Convention or only to the 1952 Convention.

3. The Committee shall be selected with due consideration to a fair balance of national interests on the basis of geographical location, population, languages and stage of development.

4. The Director-General of the United Nations Educational, Scientific and Cultural Organization, the Director-General of the World Intellectual Property Organization and the Secretary-General of the Organization of American States, or their representatives, may attend meetings of the Committee in an advisory capacity.

Article XII

The Intergovernmental Committee shall convene a conference for revision whenever it deems necessary, or at the request of at least ten States party to this Convention.

Article XIII

1. Any Contracting State may, at the time of deposit of its instru ment of ratification, acceptance or accession, or at any time thereafter, declare by notification addressed to the Director-General that this Convention shall apply to all or any of the countries or territories for the international relations of which it is responsible and this Convention shall thereupon apply to the countries or territories named in such notification after the expiration of the term of three months provided for in Article IX. In the absence of such notification, this Convention shall not apply to any such country or territory.

2. However, nothing in this Article shall be understood as implying the recognition or tacit acceptance by a Contracting State of the factual situation concerning a country or territory to which this Convention is made applicable by another Contracting State in accordance with the provisions of this Article.

Article XIV

1. Any Contracting State may denounce this Convention in its own name or on behalf of all or any of the countries or territories with respect to which a notification has been given under Article XIII. The denunciation shall be made by notification addressed to the Director-General. Such denunciation shall also constitute denunciation of the 1952 Convention.

2. Such denunciation shall operate only in respect of the State or of the country or territory on whose behalf it was made and shall not take effect until twelve months after the date of receipt of the notification.

Article XV

A dispute between two or more Contracting States concerning the interpretation or application of this Convention, not settled by negotiation, shall, unless the States concerned agree on some other method of settlement, be brought before the International Court of Justice for determination by it.

Article XVI

1. This Convention shall be established in English, French and Spanish. The three texts shall be signed and shall be equally authoritative.

2. Official texts of this Convention shall be established by the Director-General, after consultation with the governments concerned, in Arabic, German, Italian and Portuguese.

3. Any Contracting State or group of Contracting States shall be entitled to have established by the Director-General other texts in the language of its choice by arrangement with the Director-General.

4. All such texts shall be annexed to the signed texts of this Convention.

Article XVII

1. This Convention shall not in any way affect the provisions of the Berne Convention for the Protection of Literary and Artistic Works or membership in the Union created by that Convention.

2. In application of the foregoing paragraph, a declaration has been annexed to the present Article. This declaration is an integral part of this Convention for the States bound by the Berne Convention on 1 January 1951, or which have or may become bound to it at a later date. The signature of this Convention by such States shall also constitute signature of the said declaration, and ratification, acceptance or accession by such States shall include the declaration, as well as this Convention.

Article XVIII

This Convention shall not abrogate multilateral or bilateral copyright conventions or arrangements that are or may be in effect exclusively between two or more American Republics. In the event of any difference either between the provisions of such existing conventions or arrangements and the provisions of this Convention, or between the provisions of this Convention and those of any new convention or arrangement which may be formulated between two or more American Republics after this Convention comes into force, the convention or arrangement most recently formulated shall prevail between the parties thereto. Rights in works acquired in any Contracting State under existing conventions or arrangements before the date this Convention comes into force in such State shall not be affected.

Article XIX

This Convention shall not abrogate multilateral or bilateral conventions or arrangements in effect between two or more Contracting States. In the event of any difference between the provisions of such existing conventions or arrangements and the provisions of this Convention, the provisions of this Convention shall prevail. Rights in works acquired in any Contracting State under existing conventions or arrangements before the date on which this Convention comes into force in such State shall not be affected. Nothing in this Article shall affect the provisions of Articles XVII and XVIII.

Article XX

Reservations to this Convention shall not be permitted.

Article XXI

1. The Director-General shall send duly certified copies of this Convention to the States interested and to the Secretary-General of the United Nations for registration by him.

2. He shall also inform all interested States of the ratifications, acceptances and accessions which have been deposited, the date on which this Convention comes into force, the notifications under this Convention and denunciations under Article XIV.

Appendix Declaration Relating to Article XVII

The States which are members of the International Union for the Protection of Literary and Artistic Works (hereinafter called "the Berne Union") and which are signatories to this Convention,

Desiring to reinforce their mutual relations on the basis of the said Union and to avoid any conflict which might result from the co-existence of the Berne Convention and the Universal Copyright Convention,

Recognizing the temporary need of some States to adjust their level of copyright protection in accordance with their stage of cultural, social and economic development,

Have, by common agreement, accepted the terms of the following declaration:

(a) Except as provided by paragraph (b) , works which, according to the Berne Convention, have as their country of origin a country which has withdrawn from the Berne Union after 1 January 1951 shall not be protected by the Universal Copyright Convention in the countries of the Berne Union;

(b) Where a Contracting State is regarded as a developing country in conformity with the established practice of the General Assembly of the United Nations, and has deposited with the Director-General of the United Nations Educational, Scientific and Cultural Organization, at the time of its withdrawal from the Berne Union, a notification to the effect that it regards itself as a developing country, the provisions of paragraph (a) shall not be applicable as long as such State may avail itself of the exceptions provided for by this Convention in accordance with Article V^{bis};

(c) The Universal Copyright Convention shall not be applicable to the relationships among countries of the Berne Union in so far as it relates to the protection of works having as their country of origin, within the meaning of the Berne Convention, a country of the Berne Union.

Resolution Concerning Article XI

The Conference for Revision of the Universal Copyright Convention, Having considered the problems relating to the Intergovernmental Committee provided for in Article XI of this Convention, to which this resolution is annexed,

Resolves that:

1. At its inception, the Committee shall include representatives of the twelve States members of the Intergovernmental Committee established under Article XI of the 1952 Convention and the resolution annexed to it, and, in addition, representatives of the following States: Algeria, Australia, Japan, Mexico, Senegal and Yugoslavia.

2. Any States that are not party to the 1952 Convention and have not acceded to this Convention before the first ordinary session of the Committee following the entry into force of this Convention shall be replaced by other States to be selected by the Committee at its first ordinary session in conformity with the provisions of Article XI (2) and (3).

3. As soon as this Convention comes into force the Committee as provided for in paragraph 1 shall be deemed to be constituted in accordance with Article XI of this Convention.

4. A session of the Committee shall take place within one year after the coming into force of this Convention; thereafter the Committee shall meet in ordinary session at intervals of not more than two years.

5. The Committee shall elect its Chairman and two Vice-Chairmen. It shall establish its Rules of Procedure having regard to the following principles:

(a) The normal duration of the term of office of the members represented on the Committee shall be six years with one-third retiring every two years, it being however understood that, of the original terms of office, one-third shall expire at the end of the Committee's second ordinary session which will follow the entry into force of this Convention, a further third at the end of its third ordinary session, and the remaining third at the end of its fourth ordinary session.

(b) The rules governing the procedure whereby the Committee shall fill vacancies, the order in which terms of membership expire, eligibility for re-election, and election procedures, shall be based upon a balancing of the needs for continuity of membership and rotation of representation, as well as the considerations set out in Article XI (3).

Expresses the wish that the United Nations Educational, Scientific and Cultural Organization provide its Secretariat.

IN FAITH WHEREOF the undersigned, having deposited their respective full powers, have signed this Convention.

DONE at Paris, this twenty-fourth day of July 1971, in a single copy.

Protocol 1 annexed for Universal Copyright Convention as revised at Paris on 24 July 1971 concerning the application of that Convention to works of Stateless persons and refugees

The States party hereto, being also party to the Universal Copyright Convention as revised at Paris on 24 July 1971 (hereinafter called "the 1971 Convention"),

Have accepted the following provisions:

1. Stateless persons and refugees who have their habitual residence in a State party to this Protocol shall, for the purposes of the 1971 Convention, be assimilated to the nationals of that State.

2. (a) This Protocol shall be signed and shall be subject to ratification or acceptance, or may be acceded to, as if the provisions of Article VIII of the 1971 Convention applied hereto.

(b) This Protocol shall enter into force in respect of each State, on the date of deposit of the instrument of ratification, acceptance or accession of the State concerned or on the date of entry into force of the 1971 Convention with respect to such State, whichever is the later.

(c) On the entry into force of this Protocol in respect of a State not party to Protocol 1 annexed to the 1952 Convention, the latter Protocol shall be deemed to enter into force in respect of such State.

IN FAITH WHEREOF the undersigned, being duly authorized thereto, have signed this Protocol.

Done at Paris this twenty-fourth day of July 1971, in the English, French and Spanish languages, the three texts being equally authoritative, in a single copy which shall be deposited with the Director-General of the United Nations Educational, Scientific and Cultural Organization. The Director-General shall send certified copies to the signatory States, and to the Secretary-General of the United Nations for registration.

PROTOCOL 2 annexed to the Universal Copyright Convention as revised at Paris on 24 July 1971 concerning the application of that Convention to the works of certain international organizations

The States party hereto, being also party to the Universal Copyright Convention as revised at Paris on 24 July 1971 (hereinafter called "the 1971 Convention"),

Have accepted the following provisions:

1. (a) The protection provided for in Article II (1) of the 1971 Convention shall apply to works published for the first time by the United Nations, by the Specialized Agencies in relationship therewith, or by the Organization of American States.

(b) Similarly, Article II (2) of the 1971 Convention shall apply to the said organization or agencies.

2. (a) This Protocol shall be signed and shall be subject to ratification or acceptance, or may be acceded to, as if the provisions of Article VIII of the 1971 Convention applied hereto.

(b) This Protocol shall enter into force for each State on the date of deposit of the instrument of ratification, acceptance or accession of the State concerned or on the date of entry into force of the 1971 Convention with respect to such State, whichever is the later.

IN FAITH WHEREOF the undersigned, being duly authorized thereto, have signed this Protocol.

DONE at Paris, this twenty-fourth day of July 1971, in the English, French and Spanish languages, the three texts being equally authoritative, in a single copy which shall be deposited with the Director-General of the United Nations

Educational, Scientific and Cultural Organization. The Director-General shall send certified copies to the signatory States, and to the Secretary-General of the United Nations for registration.

Rome Convention, 1961

International Convention For the Protection of Performers, Producers of Phonograms and Broadcasting Organisations

Done at Rome on October 26, 1961

TABLE OF CONTENTS *

* This Table of Contents is added for the convenience of the reader. It does not appear in the original text of the Convention.

The Contracting States, moved by the desire to protect the rights of performers, producers of phonograms, and broadcasting organisations,

Have agreed as follows:

Article 1

[Safeguard of Copyright Proper *]

Protection granted under this Convention shall leave intact and shall in no way affect the protection of copyright in literary and artistic works. Consequently, no provision of this Convention may be interpreted as prejudicing such protection.

Article 2

[Protection given by the Convention. Definition of National Treatment]

1. For the purposes of this Convention, national treatment shall mean the treatment accorded by the domestic law of the Contracting State in which protection is claimed:

(a) to performers who are its nationals, as regards performances taking place, broadcast, or first fixed, on its territory;

* Articles have been given titles to facilitate their identification. There are no titles in the signed text.

(b) to producers of phonograms who are its nationals, as regards phonograms first fixed or first published on its territory;

(c) to broadcasting organisations which have their headquarters on its territory, as regards broadcasts transmitted from transmitters situated on its territory.

2. National treatment shall be subject to the protection specifically guaranteed, and the limitations specifically provided for, in this Convention.

Article 3

[Definitions: (a) Performers; (b) Phonogram; (c) Producers of Phonograms; (d) Publication; (e) Reproduction; (f) Broadcasting; (g) Rebroadcasting]

For the purposes of this Convention:

(a) "performers" means actors, singers, musicians, dancers, and other persons who act, sing, deliver, declaim, play in, or otherwise perform literary or artistic works;

(b) "phonogram" means any exclusively aural fixation of sounds of a performance or of other sounds;

(c) "producer of phonograms" means the person who, or the legal entity which, first fixes the sounds of a performance or other sounds;

(d) "publication" means the offering of copies of a phonogram to the public in reasonable quantity;

(e) "reproduction" means the making of a copy or copies of a fixation;

(f) "broadcasting" means the transmission by wireless means for public reception of sounds or of images and sounds;

(g) "rebroadcasting" means the simultaneous broadcasting by one broadcasting organisation of the broadcast of another broadcasting organisation.

Article 4

[Performances Protected. Points of Attachment for Performers]

Each Contracting State shall grant national treatment to performers if any of the following conditions is met:

(a) the performance takes place in another Contracting State;

(b) the performance is incorporated in a phonogram which is protected under Article 5 of this Convention;

(c) the performance, not being fixed on a phonogram, is carried by a broadcast which is protected by Article 6 of this Convention.

Article 5

[Protected Phonograms: 1. Points of Attachment for Producers of Phonograms; 2. Simultaneous Publication; 3. Power to exclude certain Criteria]

1. Each Contracting State shall grant national treatment to producers of

phonograms if any of the following conditions is met:

(a) the producer of the phonogram is a national of another Contracting State (criterion of nationality);

(b) the first fixation of the sound was made in another Contracting State (criterion of fixation);

(c) the phonogram was first published in another Contracting State (criterion of publication).

2. If a phonogram was first published in a non-contracting State but if it was also published, within thirty days of its first publication, in a Contracting State (simultaneous publication), it shall be considered as first published in the Contracting State.

3. By means of a notification deposited with the Secretary-General of the United Nations, any Contracting State may declare that it will not apply the criterion of publication or, alternatively, the criterion of fixation. Such notification may be deposited at the time of ratification, acceptance or accession, or at any time thereafter; in the last case, it shall become effective six months after it has been deposited.

Article 6

[Protected Broadcasts: 1. Points of Attachment for Broadcasting Organizations; 2. Power to Reserve]

1. Each Contracting State shall grant national treatment to broadcasting organisations if either of the following conditions is met:

(a) the headquarters of the broadcasting organisation is situated in another Contracting State;

(b) the broadcast was transmitted from a transmitter situated in another Contracting State.

2. By means of a notification deposited with the Secretary-General of the United Nations, any Contracting State may declare that it will protect broadcasts only if the headquarters of the broadcasting organisation is situated in another Contracting State and the broadcast was transmitted from a transmitter situated in the same Contracting State. Such notification may be deposited at the time of ratification, acceptance or accession, or at any time thereafter; in the last case, it shall become effective six months after it has been deposited.

Article 7

[Minimum Protection for Performers: 1. Particular Rights; 2. Relations between Performers and Broadcasting Organizations]

1. The protection provided for performers by this Convention shall include the possibility of preventing:

(a) the broadcasting and the communication to the public, without their consent, of their performance, except where the performance used in the broadcasting or the public communication is itself already a broadcast performance or is made from a fixation;

(b) the fixation, without their consent, of their unfixed performance;

(c) the reproduction, without their consent, of a fixation of their performance:

(i) if the original fixation itself was made without their consent;

(ii) if the reproduction is made for purposes different from those for which the performers gave their consent;

(iii) if the original fixation was made in accordance with the provisions of Article 15, and the reproduction is made for purposes different from those referred to in those provisions.

2. (1) If broadcasting was consented to by the performers, it shall be a matter for the domestic law of the Contracting State where protection is claimed to regulate the protection against rebroadcasting, fixation for broadcasting purposes and the reproduction of such fixation for broadcasting purposes.

(2) The terms and conditions governing the use by broadcasting organisations of fixations made for broadcasting purposes shall be determined in accordance with the domestic law of the Contracting State where protection is claimed.

(3) However, the domestic law referred to in sub-paragraphs (1) and (2) of this paragraph shall not operate to deprive performers of the ability to control, by contract, their relations with broadcasting organisations.

Article 8

[Performers acting jointly]

Any Contracting State may, by its domestic laws and regulations, specify the manner in which performers will be represented in connection with the exercise of their rights if several of them participate in the same performance.

Article 9

[Variety and Circus Artists]

Any Contracting State may, by its domestic laws and regulations, extend the protection provided for in this Convention to artists who do not perform literary or artistic works.

Article 10

[Right of Reproduction for Phonogram Producers]

Producers of phonograms shall enjoy the right to authorize or prohibit the direct or indirect reproduction of their phonograms.

Article 11

[Formalities for Phonograms]

If, as a condition of protecting the rights of producers of phonograms, or of performers, or both, in relation to phonograms, a Contracting State, under its domestic law, requires compliance with formalities, these shall be considered as fulfilled if all the copies in commerce of the published phonogram or their containers bear a notice consisting of the symbol Ⓟ, accompanied by the year date of the first publication, placed in such a manner as to give reasonable notice of claim of protection; and if the copies or their containers do not identify the producer or the licensee of the producer (by carrying his name, trade mark or other appropriate designation), the notice shall also include the name of the owner of the rights of the producer; and, furthermore, if the copies or their containers do not identify the principal performers, the notice shall also include the name of the person who, in the country in which the fixation was effected, owns the rights of such performers.

Article 12

[Secondary Uses of Phonograms]

If a phonogram published for commercial purposes, or a reproduction of such phonogram, is used directly for broadcasting or for any communication to the public, a single equitable remuneration shall be paid by the user to the performers, or to the producers of the phonograms, or to both. Domestic law may, in the absence of agreement between these parties, lay down the conditions as to the sharing of this remuneration.

Article 13

[Minimum Rights for Broadcasting Organizations]

Broadcasting organisations shall enjoy the right to authorise or prohibit:

(a) the rebroadcasting of their broadcasts;

(b) the fixation of their broadcasts;

(c) the reproduction:

(i) of fixations, made without their consent, of their broadcasts;

(ii) of fixations, made in accordance with the provisions of Article 15, of their broadcasts, if the reproduction is made for purposes different from those referred to in those provisions;

(d) the communication to the public of their television broadcasts if such communication is made in places accessible to the public against payment of an entrance fee; it shall be a matter for the domestic law of the State where protection of this right is claimed to determine the conditions under which it may be exercised.

Article 14
[Minimum Duration of Protection]

The term of protection to be granted under this Convention shall last at least until the end of a period of twenty years computed from the end of the year in which:

(a) the fixation was made-for phonograms and for performances incorporated therein;

(b) the performance took place-for performances not incorporated in phonograms;

(c) the broadcast took place-for broadcasts.

Article 15
[Permitted Exceptions: 1. Specific Limitations; 2. Equivalents with copyright]

1. Any Contracting State may, in its domestic laws and regulations, provide for exceptions to the protection guaranteed by this Convention as regards:

(a) private use;

(b) use of short excerpts in connexion with the reporting of current events;

(c) ephemeral fixation by a broadcasting organisation by means of its own facilities and for its own broadcasts;

(d) use solely for the purposes of teaching or scientific research.

2. Irrespective of paragraph 1 of this Article, any Contracting State may, in its domestic laws and regulations, provide for the same kinds of limitations with regard to the protection of performers, producers of phonograms and broadcasting organisations, as it provides for, in its domestic laws and regulations, in connexion with the protection of copyright in literary and artistic works. However, compulsory licences may be provided for only to the extent to which they are compatible with this Convention.

Article 16
[Reservations]

1. Any State, upon becoming party to this Convention, shall be bound by all the obligations and shall enjoy all the benefits thereof. However, a State may at any time, in a notification deposited with the Secretary-General of the United Nations, declare that:

(a) as regards Article 12:

(i) it will not apply the provisions of that Article;

(ii) it will not apply the provisions of that Article in respect of certain uses;

(iii) as regards phonograms the producer of which is not a national of another Contracting State, it will not apply that Article;

(iv) as regards phonograms the producer of which is a national of another

Contracting State, it will limit the protection provided for by that Article to the extent to which, and to the term for which, the latter State grants protection to phonograms first fixed by a national of the State making the declaration; however, the fact that the Contracting State of which the producer is a national does not grant the protection to the same beneficiary or beneficiaries as the State making the declaration shall not be considered as a difference in the extent of the protection;

(b) as regards Article 13, it will not apply item (d) of that Article; if a Contracting State makes such a declaration, the other Contracting States shall not be obliged to grant the right referred to in Article 13, item (d), to broadcasting organisations whose headquarters are in that State.

2. If the notification referred to in paragraph 1 of this Article is made after the date of the deposit of the instrument of ratification, acceptance or accession, the declaration will become effective six months after it has been deposited.

Article 17

[Certain countries applying only the "fixation" criterion]

Any State which, on October 26, 1961, grants protection to producers of phonograms solely on the basis of the criterion of fixation may, by a notification deposited with the Secretary-General of the United Nations at the time of ratification, acceptance or accession, declare that it will apply, for the purposes of Article 5, the criterion of fixation alone and, for the purposes of paragraph 1(a) (iii) and (iv) of Article 16, the criterion of fixation instead of the criterion of nationality.

Article 18

[Withdrawal of reservations]

Any State which has deposited a notification under paragraph 3 of Article 5, paragraph 2 of Article 6, paragraph 1 of Article 16 or Article 17, may, by a further notification deposited with the Secretary-General of the United Nations, reduce its scope or withdraw it.

Article 19

[Performers' Rights in Films]

Notwithstanding anything in this Convention, once a performer has consented to the incorporation of his performance in a visual or audio-visual fixation, Article 7 shall have no further application.

Article 20

[Non-retroactivity]

1. This Convention shall not prejudice rights acquired in any Contracting State

before the date of coming into force of this Convention for that State.

2. No Contracting State shall be bound to apply the provisions of this Convention to performances or broadcasts which took place, or to phonograms which were fixed, before the date of coming into force of this Convention for that State.

Article 21

[Protection by other means]

The protection provided for in this Convention shall not prejudice any protection otherwise secured to performers, producers of phonograms and broadcasting organisations.

Article 22

[Special agreements]

Contracting States reserve the right to enter into special agreements among themselves in so far as such agreements grant to performers, producers of phonograms or broadcasting organisations more extensive rights than those granted by this Convention or contain other provisions not contrary to this Convention.

Article 23

[Signature and deposit]

This Convention shall be deposited with the Secretary-General of the United Nations. It shall be open until June 30, 1962, for signature by any State invited to the Diplomatic Conference on the International Protection of Performers, Producers of Phonograms and Broadcasting Organisations which is a party to the Universal Copyright Convention or a member of the International Union for the Protection of Literary and Artistic Works.

Article 24

[Becoming Party to the Convention]

1. This Convention shall be subject to ratification or acceptance by the signatory States.

2. This Convention shall be open for accession by any State invited to the Conference referred to in Article 23, and by any State Member of the United Nations, provided that in either case such State is a party to the Universal Copyright Convention or a member of the International Union for the Protection of Literary and Artistic Works.

3. Ratification, acceptance or accession shall be effected by the deposit of an instrument to that effect with the Secretary-General of the United Nations.

Article 25

[Entry into force]

1. This Convention shall come into force three months after the date of deposit of the sixth instrument of ratification, acceptance or accession.

2. Subsequently, this Convention shall come into force in respect of each State three months after the date of deposit of its instrument of ratification, acceptance or accession.

Article 26

[Implementation of the Convention by the Provision of Domestic Law]

1. Each Contracting State undertakes to adopt, in accordance with its Constitution, the measures necessary to ensure the application of this Convention.

2. At the time of deposit of its instrument of ratification, acceptance or accession, each State must be in a position under its domestic law to give effect to the terms of this Convention.

Article 27

[Applicability of the Convention to Certain Territories]

1. Any State may, at the time of ratification, acceptance or accession, or at any time thereafter, declare by notification addressed to the Secretary-General of the United Nations that this Convention shall extend to all or any of the territories for whose international relations it is responsible, provided that the Universal Copyright Convention or the International Convention for the Protection of Literary and Artistic Works applies to the territory or territories concerned. This notification shall take effect three months after the date of its receipt.

2. The notifications referred to in paragraph 3 of Article 5, paragraph 2 of Article 6, paragraph 1 of Article 16 and Articles 17 and 18, may be extended to cover all or any of the territories referred to in paragraph 1 of this Article.

Article 28

[Denunciation of the Convention]

1. Any Contracting State may denounce this Convention, on its own behalf or on behalf of all or any of the territories referred to in Article 27.

2. The denunciation shall be effected by a notification addressed to the Secretary-General of the United Nations and shall take effect twelve months after the date of receipt of the notification.

3. The right of denunciation shall not be exercised by a Contracting State before the expiry of a period of five years from the date on which the Convention came into force with respect to that State.

4. A Contracting State shall cease to be a party to this Convention from that

time when it is neither a party to the Universal Copyright Convention nor a member of the International Union for the Protection of Literary and Artistic Works.

5. This Convention shall cease to apply to any territory referred to in Article 27 from that time when neither the Universal Copyright Convention nor the International Convention for the Protection of Literary and Artistic Works applies to that territory.

Article 29
[Revision of the Convention]

1. After this Convention has been in force for five years, any Contracting State may, by notification addressed to the Secretary-General of the United Nations, request that a conference be convened for the purpose of revising the Convention. The Secretary-General shall notify all Contracting States of this request. If, within a period of six months following the date of notification by the Secretary-General of the United Nations, not less than one half of the Contracting States notify him of their concurrence with the request, the Secretary-General shall inform the Director-General of the International Labour Office, the Director-General of the United Nations Educational, Scientific and Cultural Organization and the Director of the Bureau of the International Union for the Protection of Literary and Artistic Works, who shall convene a revision conference in co-operation with the Intergovernmental Committee provided for in Article 32.

2. The adoption of any revision of this Convention shall require an affirmative vote by two-thirds of the States attending the revision conference, provided that this majority includes two-thirds of the States which, at the time of the revision conference, are parties to the Convention.

3. In the event of adoption of a Convention revising this Convention in whole or in part, and unless the revising Convention provides otherwise:

(a) this Convention shall cease to be open to ratification, acceptance or accession as from the date of entry into force of the revising Convention;

(b) this Convention shall remain in force as regards relations between or with Contracting States which have not become parties to the revising Convention.

Article 30
[Settlement of disputes]

Any dispute which may arise between two or more Contracting States concerning the interpretation or application of this Convention and which is not settled by negotiation shall, at the request of any one of the parties to the dispute, be referred to the International Court of Justice for decision, unless they agree to another mode of settlement.

Article 31

[Limits on Reservations]

Without prejudice to the provisions of paragraph 3 of Article 5, paragraph 2 of Article 6, paragraph 1 of Article 16 and Article 17, no reservation may be made to this Convention.

Article 32

[Intergovernmental Committee]

1. An Intergovernmental Committee is hereby established with the following duties:

(a) to study questions concerning the application and operation of this Convention; and

(b) to collect proposals and to prepare documentation for possible revision of this Convention.

2. The Committee shall consist of representatives of the Contracting States, chosen with due regard to equitable geographical distribution. The number of members shall be six if there are twelve Contracting States or less, nine if there are thirteen to eighteen Contracting States and twelve if there are more than eighteen Contracting States.

3. The Committee shall be constituted twelve months after the Convention comes into force by an election organized among the Contracting States, each of which shall have one vote, by the Director-General of the International Labour Office, the Director-General of the United Nations Educational, Scientific and Cultural Organization and the Director of the Bureau of the International Union for the Protection of Literary and Artistic Works, in accordance with rules previously approved by a majority of all Contracting States.

4. The Committee shall elect its Chairman and officers. It shall establish its own rules of procedure. These rules shall in particular provide for the future operation of the Committee and for a method of selecting its members for the future in such a way as to ensure rotation among the various Contracting States.

5. Officials of the International Labour Office, the United Nations Educational, Scientific and Cultural Organization and the Bureau of the International Union for the Protection of Literary and Artistic Works, designated by the Directors-General and the Director thereof, shall constitute the Secretariat of the Committee.

6. Meetings of the Committee, which shall be convened whenever a majority of its members deems it necessary, shall be held successively at the headquarters of the International Labour Office, the United Nations Educational, Scientific and Cultural Organization and the Bureau of the International Union for the Protection of Literary and Artistic Works.

7. Expenses of members of the Committee shall be borne by their respective

Governments.

Article 33
[Languages]

1. The present Convention is drawn up in English, French and Spanish, the three texts being equally authentic.

2. In addition, official texts of the present Convention shall be drawn up in German, Italian and Portuguese.

Article 34
[Notifications]

1. The Secretary-General of the United Nations shall notify the States invited to the Conference referred to in Article 23 and every State Member of the United Nations, as well as the Director-General of the International Labour Office, the Director-General of the United Nations Educational, Scientific and Cultural Organization and the Director of the Bureau of the International Union for the Protection of Literary and Artistic Works:

(a) of the deposit of each instrument of ratification, acceptance or accession;

(b) of the date of entry into force of the Convention;

(c) of all notifications, declarations or communications provided for in this Convention;

(d) if any of the situations referred to in paragraphs 4 and 5 of Article 28 arise.

2. The Secretary-General of the United Nations shall also notify the Director-General of the International Labour Office, the Director-General of the United Nations Educational, Scientific and Cultural Organization and the Director of the Bureau of the International Union for the Protection of Literary and Artistic Works of the requests communicated to him in accordance with Article 29, as well as of any communication received from the Contracting States concerning the revision of the Convention.

IN FAITH WHEREOF, the undersigned, being duly authorised thereto, have signed this Convention.

DONE at Rome, this twenty-sixth day of October 1961, in a single copy in the English, French and Spanish languages. Certified true copies shall be delivered by the Secretary-General of the United Nations to all the States invited to the Conference referred to in Article 23 and to every State Member of the United Nations, as well as to the Director-General of the International Labour Office, the Director-General of the United Nations Educational, Scientific and Cultural Organization and the Director of the Bureau of the International Union for the Protection of Literary and Artistic Works.

Convention for the Protection of Producers of Phonograms Against Unauthorized Duplication of Their Phonograms

of October 29, 1971

TABLE OF CONTENTS*

The Contracting States,

concerned at the widespread and increasing unauthorized duplication of phonograms and the damage this is occasioning to the interests of authors, performers and producers of phonograms;

* This Table of Contents is added for the convenience of the reader. It does not appear in the original text of the Convention.

convinced that the protection of producers of phonograms against such acts will also benefit the performers whose performances, and the authors whose works, are recorded on the said phonograms;

recognizing the value of the work undertaken in this field by the United Nations Educational, Scientific and Cultural Organization and the World Intellectual Property Organization;

anxious not to impair in any way international agreements already in force and in particular in no way to prejudice wider acceptance of the Rome Convention of October 26, 1961, which affords protection to performers and to broadcasting organizations as well as to producers of phonograms;

have agreed as follows:

Article 1
[Definitions*]

For the purposes of this Convention:

(a) "phonogram" means any exclusively aural fixation of sounds of a performance or of other sounds;

(b) "producer of phonograms" means the person who, or the legal entity which, first fixes the sounds of a performance or other sounds;

(c) "duplicate" means an article which contains sounds taken directly or indirectly from a phonogram and which embodies all or a substantial part of the sounds fixed in that phonogram;

(d)"distribution to the public" means any act by which duplicates of a phonogram are offered, directly or indirectly, to the general public or any section thereof.

Article 2
[Obligations of Contracting States; Whom they must protect and against what]

Each Contracting State shall protect producers of phonograms who are nationals of other Contracting States against the making of duplicates without the consent of the producer and against the importation of such duplicates, provided that any such making or importation is for the purpose of distribution to the public, and against the distribution of such duplicates to the public.

Article 3
[Means of Implementation by Contracting States]

The means by which this Convention is implemented shall be a matter for

* Articles have been given titles to facilitate their identification. There are no titles in the signed text.

the domestic law of each Contracting State and shall include one or more of the following: protection by means of the grant of a copyright or other specific right; protection by means of the law relating to unfair competition; protection by means of penal sanctions.

Article 4
[Term of Protection]

The duration of the protection given shall be a matter for the domestic law of each Contracting State. However, if the domestic law prescribes a specific duration for the protection, that duration shall not be less than twenty years from the end either of the year in which the sounds embodied in the phonogram were first fixed or of the year in which the phonogram was first published.

Article 5
[Formalities]

If, as a condition of protecting the producers of phonograms, a Contracting State, under its domestic law, requires compliance with formalities, these shall be considered as fulfilled if all the authorized duplicates of the phonogram distributed to the public or their containers bear a notice consisting of the symbol Ⓟ, accompanied by the year date of the first publication, placed in such manner as to give reasonable notice of claim of protection; and, if the duplicates or their containers do not identify the producer, his successor in title or the exclusive licensee (by carrying his name, trademark or other appropriate designation), the notice shall also include the name of the producer, his successor in title or the exclusive licensee.

Article 6
[Limitations on Protection]

Any Contracting State which affords protection by means of copyright or other specific right, or protection by means of penal sanctions, may in its domestic law provide, with regard to the protection of producers of phonograms, the same kinds of limitations as are permitted with respect to the protection of authors of literary and artistic works. However, no compulsory licenses may be permitted unless all of the following conditions are met:

(a) the duplication is for use solely for the purpose of teaching or scientific research;

(b) the license shall be valid for duplication only within the territory of the Contracting State whose competent authority has granted the license and shall not extend to the export of duplicates;

(c) the duplication made under the license gives rise to an equitable remuneration fixed by the said authority taking into account, inter alia, the number of duplicates which will be made.

Article 7

[Savings: 1. Safeguard of Copyright and Neighboring Rights; 2. Protection for Performers; 3. Non-Retroactivity; 4. Substitution of the Criterion of Fixation]

(1) This Convention shall in no way be interpreted to limit or prejudice the protection otherwise secured to authors, to performers, to producers of phonograms or to broadcasting organizations under any domestic law or international agreement.

(2) It shall be a matter for the domestic law of each Contracting State to determine the extent, if any, to which performers whose performances are fixed in a phonogram are entitled to enjoy protection and the conditions for enjoying any such protection.

(3) No Contracting State shall be required to apply the provisions of this Convention to any phonogram fixed before this Convention entered into force with respect to that State.

(4) Any Contracting State which, on October 29, 1971, affords protection to producers of phonograms solely on the basis of the place of first fixation may, by a notification deposited with the Director General of the World Intellectual Property Organization, declare that it will apply this criterion instead of the criterion of the nationality of the producer.

Article 8

[Secretariat]

(1) The International Bureau of the World Intellectual Property Organization shall assemble and publish information concerning the protection of phonograms. Each Contracting State shall promptly communicate to the International Bureau all new laws and official texts on this subject.

(2) The International Bureau shall, on request, furnish information to any Contracting State on matters concerning this Convention, and shall conduct studies and provide services designed to facilitate the protection provided for therein.

(3) The International Bureau shall exercise the functions enumerated in paragraphs (1) and (2) above in cooperation, for matters within their respective competence, with the United Nations Educational, Scientific and Cultural Organization and the International Labour Organisation.

Article 9

[Joining the Convention: 1. Signature and Deposit; 2 and 3. Ratification and Accession; 4. States' Obligations as to their Domestic Law]

(1) This Convention shall be deposited with the Secretary-General of the United Nations. It shall be open until April 30, 1972, for signature by any State that

is a member of the United Nations, any of the Specialized Agencies brought into relationship with the United Nations, or the International Atomic Energy Agency, or is a party to the Statute of the International Court of Justice.

(2) This Convention shall be subject to ratification or acceptance by the signatory States. It shall be open for accession by any State referred to in paragraph (1) of this Article.

(3) Instruments of ratification, acceptance or accession shall be deposited with the Secretary-General of the United Nations.

(4) It is understood that, at the time a State becomes bound by this Convention, it will be in a position in accordance with its domestic law to give effect to the provisions of the Convention.

Article 10
[Reservations]

No reservations to this Convention are permitted.

Article 11
[Entry into Force and Applicability: 1 and 2. Entry into Force of the Convention; 3 and 4. Applicability of the Convention to Certain Territories]

(1) This Convention shall enter into force three months after deposit of the fifth instrument of ratification, acceptance or accession.

(2) For each State ratifying, accepting or acceding to this Convention after the deposit of the fifth instrument of ratification, acceptance or accession, the Convention shall enter into force three months after the date on which the Director General of the World Intellectual Property Organization informs the States, in accordance with Article 13, paragraph (4), of the deposit of its instrument.

(3) Any State may, at the time of ratification, acceptance or accession or at any later date, declare by notification addressed to the Secretary-General of the United Nations that this Convention shall apply to all or any one of the territories for whose international affairs it is responsible. This notification will take effect three months after the date on which it is received.

(4) However, the preceding paragraph may in no way be understood as implying the recognition or tacit acceptance by a Contracting State of the factual situation concerning a territory to which this Convention is made applicable by another Contracting State by virtue of the said paragraph.

Article 12
[Denunciation of the Convention]

(1) Any Contracting State may denounce this Convention, on its own behalf or on behalf of any of the territories referred to in Article 11, paragraph (3), by written

notification addressed to the Secretary-General of the United Nations.

(2) Denunciation shall take effect twelve months after the date on which the Secretary-General of the United Nations has received the notification.

Article 13
[Languages and Notifications]

(1) This Convention shall be signed in a single copy in English, French, Russian and Spanish, the four texts being equally authentic.

(2) Official texts shall be established by the Director General of the World Intellectual Property Organization, after consultation with the interested Governments, in the Arabic, Dutch, German, Italian and Portuguese languages.

(3) The Secretary-General of the United Nations shall notify the Director General of the World Intellectual Property Organization, the Director-General of the United Nations Educational, Scientific and Cultural Organization and the Director-General of the International Labour Office of:

(a) signatures to this Convention;

(b) the deposit of instruments of ratification, acceptance or accession;

(c) the date of entry into force of this Convention;

(d) any declaration notified pursuant to Article 11, paragraph (3);

(e) the receipt of notifications of denunciation.

(4) The Director General of the World Intellectual Property Organization shall inform the States referred to in Article 9, paragraph (1), of the notifications received pursuant to the preceding paragraph and of any declarations made under Article 7, paragraph (4). He shall also notify the Director-General of the United Nations Educational, Scientific and Cultural Organization and the Director-General of the International Labour Office of such declarations.

(5) The Secretary-General of the United Nations shall transmit two certified copies of this Convention to the States referred to in Article 9, paragraph (1).

Vienna Agreement for the Protection of Type Faces and their International Deposit

Done at Vienna on June 12, 1973

TABLE OF CONTENTS *

* This Table of Contents is added for the convenience of the reader. It does not appear in the signed text of the Agreement.

The Contracting States,

Desiring, in order to encourage the creation of type faces, to provide an effective protection thereof,

Conscious of the role which type faces play in the dissemination of culture and of the special requirements which their protection must fulfil,

Have agreed as follows:

Introductory Provisions

Article 1
Establishment of a Union

The States party to this Agreement constitute a Union for the protection of type faces.

Article 2
Definitions

For the purposes of this Agreement and the Regulations,

(i) "type faces" means sets of designs of:

(a) letters and alphabets as such with their accessories such as accents and punctuation marks,

(b) numerals and other figurative signs such as conventional signs, symbols and scientific signs,

(c) ornaments such as borders, fleurons and vignettes,

which are intended to provide means for composing texts by any graphic technique. The term "type faces" does not include type faces of a form dictated by purely technical requirements;

(ii) " International Register" means the International Register of Type Faces;

(iii) "international deposit" means the deposit effected for the purposes of recording in the International Register;

(iv) "applicant" means the natural person who, or the legal entity which, effects an international deposit;

(v) "owner of the international deposit" means the natural person or the legal entity in whose name the inter national deposit is recorded in the International Register;

(vi) "Contracting States" means the States party to this Agreement;

(vii) "Union" means the Union established by this Agreement;

(viii) "Assembly" means the Assembly of the Union;

(ix) "Paris Convention" means the Convention for the Protection of Industrial Property signed on March 20, 1883, including any of its revisions;

(x) "Organization" means the World Intellectual Property Organization;

(xi) "International Bureau" means the International Bureau of the Organization and, as long as it subsists, the United International Bureaux for the Protection of Intellectual Property (BIRPI);

(xii) "Director General" means the Director General of the Organization;

(xiii) "Regulations" means the Regulations under this Agreement.

CHAPTER I

National Protection

Article 3

Principle and Kinds of Protection

The Contracting States undertake, in accordance with the provisions of this Agreement, to ensure the protection of type faces, by establishing a special national deposit, or by adapting the deposit provided for in their national industrial design laws, or by their national copyright provisions. These kinds of protection may be cumulative.

Article 4

Natural Persons and Legal Entities Protected

(1) In Contracting States which declare under Article 34 that they intend to ensure protection by establishing a special national deposit or by adapting their national industrial design laws, the protection of this Agreement shall apply to natural persons who, or legal entities which, are residents or nationals of a Contracting State.

(2) (a) In Contracting States which declare under Article 34 that they intend to ensure protection by their national copyright provisions, the protection of this Agreement shall apply to:

(i) creators of type faces who are nationals of one of the Contracting States;

(ii) creators of type faces who are not nationals of one of the Contracting States but whose type faces are published for the first time in one of such States.

(b) Any Contracting State referred to in subparagraph (a) may assimilate creators of type faces who have their habitual residence or domicile in a Contracting State to creators of type faces who are nationals of that State.

(3) For the purposes of the Agreement, any association of natural persons or legal entities which, under the national law of the State according to which it is constituted, may acquire rights and assume obligations, notwithstanding the fact that it is not a legal entity, shall be assimilated to a legal entity. However, any Contracting State may protect, in lieu of the said association, the natural persons or legal entities constituting it.

Article 5

National Treatment

(1) Each Contracting State shall be obliged to grant to all natural persons and

legal entities entitled to claim the benefits of this Agreement the protection afforded to its nationals according to the kind of protection which such Contracting State declares under Article 34.

(2) If a Contracting State referred to in Article 4(2) requires, under its domestic law, compliance with formalities as a condition of protecting type faces, these should be considered as fulfilled, with respect to type faces whose creators are referred to in Article 4(2), if all the copies of the type faces published with the authority of the creator or other owner entitled to protection are accompanied by or, as the case may be, bear a notice consisting of the symbol @ accompanied by the name of the owner entitled to protection and the year date of the first such publication placed in such a manner as to give reasonable notice of claim of protection.

Article 6

Concepts of Residence and Nationality

(1) (a) Any natural person shall be regarded as a resident of a Contracting State for the purposes of Articles 4(1) and 13 if:

(i) according to the national law of that State be is a resident of that State, or

(ii) he has a real and effective industrial or commercial establishment in that State.

(b) Any natural person shall be regarded as a national of a Contracting State for the purposes of Articles 4(1) and 13 if, according to the national law of that State, he is a national of that State.

(2) (a) Any legal entity shall be regarded as a resident of a Contracting State for the purposes of Articles 4(1) and 13 if it has a real and effective industrial or commercial establishment in that State.

(b) Any legal entity shall be regarded as a national of a Contracting State for the purposes of Articles 4(1) and 13 if it is constituted according to the national law of that State.

(3) Where any natural person or legal entity invoking the benefits of this Agreement is a resident of one State and a national of another State, and where only one of those States is a Contracting State, the Contracting State alone shall be considered for the purposes of this Agreement and the Regulations.

Article 7

Conditions of Protection

(1) The protection of type faces shall be subject to the condition that they be novel, or to the condition that they be original, or to both conditions.

(2) The novelty and the originality of type faces shall be determined in relation to their style or overall appearance, having regard, if necessary, to the criteria recognized by the competent professional circles.

Article 8
Content of Protection

(1) Protection of type faces shall confer upon the owner thereof the right to prohibit:

(i) the making, without his consent, of any reproduction, whether identical or slightly modified, intended to provide means for composing texts by any graphic technique, irrespective of the technical means or material used;

(ii) the commercial distribution or importation of such reproductions without his consent.

(2) (a) Subject to subparagraph (b) , the right defined in paragraph (1) applies irrespective of whether or not the protected type faces have been known to the maker of the reproduction.

(b) Contracting States in which originality is a condition of protection are not required to apply subparagraph (a) .

(3) The right provided for in paragraph (1) shall also cover any reproduction of type faces obtained by the distortion, by any purely technical means, of the protected type faces, where the essential features thereof remain recognizable.

(4) The making of elements of type faces, by a person acquiring type faces, during the ordinary course of the composition of texts, shall not be considered a reproduction within the meaning of paragraph (1) (i).

(5) Contracting States may take legislative measures to avoid abuses which might result from the exercise of the exclusive right provided under this Agreement in cases where, apart from the protected type faces in question, no other type faces are available in order to achieve a particular purpose in the public interest. The legislative measures shall not, however, prejudice the right of the owner to just remuneration for the use of his type faces. Nor shall the protection of type faces under any circumstances be subject to any forfeiture either by reason of failure to work or by reason of the importation of reproductions of the protected type faces.

Article 9
Term of Protection

(1) The term of protection may not be less than fifteen years.

(2) The term of protection may be divided into several periods, each extension being granted only at the request of the owner of the protected type faces.

Article 10
Cumulative Protection

The provisions of this Agreement shall not preclude the making of a claim to the benefit of any more extensive protection granted by national laws and shall in no way affect the protection granted by other international conventions.

Article 11
Right of Priority

For the purposes of the right of priority, if applicable, national deposits of type faces shall be considered deposits of industrial designs.

CHAPTER II

International Deposit

Article 12
International Deposit and Recording

(1) Subject to the provisions of paragraph (2), the international deposit shall be effected direct with the International Bureau, which shall record it in the International Register in accordance with this Agreement and the Regulations.

(2) (a) The national law of any Contracting State may provide that international deposits by natural persons or legal entities residing in the respective State may be effected through the intermediary of the competent Office of that State.

(b) Where an international deposit is effected, as provided for in subparagraph (a), through the intermediary of a competent Office of a Contracting State, that Office shall indicate the date on which it received the international deposit and shall transmit the said deposit in good time to the International Bureau in the manner provided for in the Regulations.

Article 13
Right to Effect International Deposits and to Own Such Deposits

(1) Any natural person who, or legal entity which, is a resident or a national of a Contracting State may effect and be the owner of international deposits.

(2) (a) Any association of natural persons or legal entities which, under the national law of the State according to which it is constituted, may acquire rights and assume obligations, notwithstanding the fact that it is not a legal entity, shall have the right to effect international deposits and to own such deposits if it is a resident or national of a Contracting State.

(b) Subparagraph (a) shall be without prejudice to the application of the national law of any Contracting State. However, no such State shall refuse or cancel the effects provided for in Article 18 with respect to an association of the kind referred to in subparagraph (a) on the ground that it is not a legal entity if, within two months from the date of an invitation addressed to it by the competent Office of that State, the said association files with that Office a list of the names and addresses of all the natural persons or legal entities constituting it, together with a declaration that its members are engaged in a joint enterprise. In such a case, the said State may consider the natural persons or legal entities constituting the said association to be the owners of the international deposit, in lieu of the association itself, provided that the said persons or entities fulfill the conditions set forth in paragraph (1).

Article 14
Contents and Form of the International Deposit

(1) The international deposit shall contain:

(i) a signed instrument of international deposit declaring that the deposit is effected under this Agreement, and indicating the identity, residence, nationality and address of the applicant as well as the name of the creator of the type faces for which protection is sought or that the creator has renounced being mentioned as such;

(ii) a representation of the type faces;

(iii) payment of the prescribed fees.

(2) The instrument of international deposit may contain:

(i) a declaration claiming the priority of one or more earlier deposits effected in or for one or more States party to the Paris Convention;

(ii) an indication of the denomination given to the type faces by the applicant;

(iii) the appointment of a representative;

(iv) such additional indications as are provided for in the Regulations.

(3) The instrument of international deposit shall be in one of the languages prescribed by the Regulations.

Article 15
Recording or Declining of the International Deposit

(1) Subject to paragraph (2), the International Bureau shall promptly record the international deposit in the International Register. The date of the international deposit shall be the date on which it was received by the International Bureau or, if the international deposit has been effected, as provided for in Article 12(2), through the intermediary of the competent Office of a Contracting State, the date on which that Office received the deposit, provided that the deposit reaches the International Bureau before the expiration of a period of one month following that date.

(2) (a) Where the International Bureau finds any of the following defects, it shall invite the applicant, unless it is clearly impossible to reach him, to correct the defect within three months from the date on which it sent the invitation:

(i) the instrument of international deposit does not contain an indication that it is effected under this Agreement;

(ii) the instrument of international deposit does not contain such indications concerning the residence and nationality of the applicant as to permit the conclusion that he has the right to effect international deposits;

(iii) the instrument of international deposit does not contain such indications concerning the applicant as are necessary to permit him to be identified and reached by mail;

(iv) the instrument of international deposit does not contain an indication of the name of the creator of the type faces or of the fact that the creator has renounced being mentioned as such;

(v) the instrument of international deposit is not signed;

(vi) the instrument of international deposit is not in one of the languages prescribed by the Regulations;

(vii) the international deposit does not contain a representation of the type faces;

(viii) the prescribed fees have not been paid.

(b) If the defect or defects are corrected in due time, the International Bureau shall record the international deposit in the International Register, and the date of the international deposit shall be the date on which the International Bureau receives the correction of the said defect or defects.

(c) If the defect or defects are not corrected in due time, the International Bureau shall decline the international deposit, inform the applicant accordingly, and reimburse to him part of the fees paid, as provided in the Regulations. If the international deposit is effected through the intermediary of the competent Office of a Contracting State, as provided for in Article 12(2), the International Bureau shall also inform that Office of the declining.

Article 16

Avoiding Certain Effects of Declining

(1) Where the International Bureau has declined the international deposit, the applicant may, within two months from the date of the notification of the declining effect, in respect of the type faces that were the subject of the international deposit, a national deposit with the competent Office of any Contracting State which ensures the protection of type faces by establishing a special national deposit or by adapting the deposit provided for in its national industrial design law.

(2) If the competent Office or any other competent authority of that Contracting State finds that the International Bureau has declined the international deposit in error, and provided the national deposit complies with all the requirements of the national law of the said State, the said national deposit shall be treated as if it had been effected on the date which would have been the date of the international deposit had that international deposit not been declined.

Article 17
Publication and Notification of the International Deposit

International deposits recorded in the International Register shall be published by the International Bureau and notified by the latter to the competent Offices of the Contracting States.

Article 18
Effect of the International Deposit

(1) In Contracting States which declare in accordance with Article 34 that they intend to ensure the protection of type faces by establishing a special national deposit or by adapting the deposit provided for in their national industrial design laws, the international deposit recorded in the International Register shall have the same effect as a national deposit effected on the same date.

(2) The Contracting States referred to in paragraph(1) may not require that the applicant comply with any additional formality, with the exception of such formalities as may be prescribed by their national laws for the exercise of the rights. However, Contracting States which undertake an ex officio novelty examination or make provision for opposition proceedings may prescribe the formalities required by such examination or such proceedings and charge the fees, with the exception of the publication fee, provided for in their national laws for such examination, the grant of protection and the renewal thereof.

Article 19
Right of Priority

(1) For the purposes of the right of priority, if applicable, the international deposit of type faces shall be considered an industrial design deposit within the meaning of Article 4A of the Paris Convention.

(2) The international deposit shall be a regular filing within the meaning of Article 4A of the Paris Convention if it is not declined pursuant to Article 15(2)(c) of this Agreement, and shall be considered to have been effected on the date accorded to it under Article 15(1) or (2)(b) of this Agreement.

Article 20
Change in the Ownership of the International Deposit

(1) Any change in the ownership of the international deposit shall, on request, be recorded in the International Register by the International Bureau.

(2) The change in the ownership of the international deposit shall not be recorded in the International Register if, according to the indications furnished by the person requesting the recording of the change, the new owner of the international deposit does not have the right to effect international deposits.

(3) The change in the ownership of the international deposit may relate to one or more of the Contracting States referred to in Article 18(1). In such a case, renewal of the international deposit must subsequently be applied for separately by each of the owners of the international deposit as far as he is concerned.

(4) The request for the recording of a change in the ownership of the international deposit shall be presented in the form, and accompanied by the fee, prescribed in the Regulations.

(5) The International Bureau shall record the change in the ownership of the international deposit in the International Register, shall publish it, and shall notify it to the competent Offices of the Contracting States.

(6) The recording of the change in the ownership of the international deposit in the International Register shall have the same effect as if the request for such recording had been filed direct with the competent Office of each of the Contracting States referred to in Article 18(1) which are concerned by the said change in ownership.

Article 21

Withdrawal and Renunciation of the International Deposit

(1) The applicant may withdraw his international deposit by a declaration addressed to the International Bureau.

(2) The owner of the international deposit may at any time renounce his international deposit by a declaration addressed to the International Bureau.

(3) Withdrawal and renunciation may relate to a part or the whole of the type faces which are the subject of the international deposit, or to their denomination, and to one or more of the Contracting States referred to in Article 18(1).

(4) The International Bureau shall record the renunciation in the International Register, shall publish it, and shall notify it to the competent Offices of the Contracting States.

(5) Renunciation recorded in the International Register shall have the same effect as if it had been communicated direct to the competent Office of each of the Contracting States referred to in Article 18(1).

Article 22

Other Amendments to the International Deposit

(1) The owner of the international deposit may at any time amend the indications appearing in the instrument of international deposit.

(2) Type faces which are the subject of an international deposit may not be amended.

(3) Amendments shall be subject to the payment of the fees prescribed in the Regulations.

(4) The International Bureau shall record amendments in the International Register, shall publish them, and shall notify them to the competent Offices of the Contracting States.

(5) Amendments recorded in the International Register shall have the same effect as if they had been communicated direct to the competent Office of each of the Contracting States referred to in Article 18(1).

Article 23

Term and Renewal of the International Deposit

(1) The international deposit shall have effect for an initial term of ten years from the date of such deposit.

(2) The effect of the international deposit may be extended for terms of five years on the basis of demands for renewal submitted by the owner of the international deposit.

(3) Each new term shall commence on the day following that on which the previous term expires.

(4) The demand for renewal shall be presented in the form, and accompanied by the fees, prescribed by the Regulations.

(5) The International Bureau shall record the renewal in the International Register, shall publish it, and shall notify it to the competent Offices of the Contracting States.

(6) Renewal of the international deposit shall replace such renewals as may be provided for in the national laws. However, the international deposit may not, in any Contracting State referred to in Article 18(1), have effect after the maximum term of protection provided for in the national law of that State has expired.

Article 24

Regional Treaties

(1) Two or more Contracting States may notify the Director General that a common Office shall be substituted for the national Office of each of them, and that their territories, as a whole, shall be deemed a single State for the purposes of international deposit.

(2) Such notification shall take effect three months after the date on which the Director General receives it.

Article 25

Representation Before the International Bureau

(1) Applicants and owners of international deposits may be represented before the International Bureau by any person empowered by them to that effect

(hereinafter referred to as "the duly appointed representative").

(2) Any invitation, notification or other communication addressed by the International Bureau to the duly appointed representative shall have the same effect as if it had been addressed to the applicant or the owner of the international deposit. Any deposit, request, demand, declaration or other document whose signature by the applicant or the owner of the international deposit is required in proceedings before the International Bureau, except the document appointing the representative or revoking his appointment, may be signed by his duly appointed representative, and any communication from the duly appointed representative to the International Bureau shall have the same effect as if it had been effected by the applicant or the owner of the international deposit.

(3) (a) Where there are several applicants, they shall appoint a common representative. In the absence of such appointment, the applicant first named in the instrument of international deposit shall be considered the duly appointed representative of all the applicants.

(b) Where there are several owners of an international deposit, they shall appoint a common representative. In the absence of such appointment, the natural person or legal entity first named among the said owners in the International Register shall be considered the duly appointed common representative of all the owners of the international deposit.

(c) Subparagraph (b) shall not apply to the extent that the owners own the international deposit in respect of different Contracting States.

CHAPTER III

Administrative Provisions

Article 26

Assembly

(1) (a) The Assembly shall consist of the Contracting States.

(2) (a) The Assembly shall:

(i) deal with all matters concerning the maintenance and development of the Union and the implementation of this Agreement;

(ii) exercise such rights and perform such tasks as are specially conferred upon it or assigned to it under this Agreement;

(iii) give directions to the Director General concerning the preparation for revision conferences;

(iv) review and approve the reports and activities of the Director General concerning the Union, and give him all necessary instructions concerning matters within the competence of the Union;

(v) determine the program, adopt the triennial budget of the Union, and approve its final accounts;

(vi) adopt the financial regulations of the Union;

(vii) establish such committees and working groups as it deems appropriate to facilitate the work of the Union and of its organs;

(viii) determine which States other than Contracting States and which intergovernmental and international non-governmental organizations shall be admitted to its meetings as observers;

(ix) take any other appropriate action designed to further the objectives of the Union and perform such other functions as are appropriate under this Agreement.

(b) With respect to matters which are of interest also to other Unions administered by the Organization, the Assembly shall make its decisions after having heard the advice of the Coordination Committee of the Organization.

(3) A delegate may represent, and vote in the name of, one Contracting State only.

(4) Each Contracting State shall have one vote.

(5) (a) One-half of the Contracting States shall constitute a quorum.

(b) In the absence of the quorum, the Assembly may make decisions but, with the exception of decisions concerning its own procedure, all such decisions shall take effect only if the quorum and the required majority are attained through voting by correspondence as provided in the Regulations.

(6) (a) Subject to the provisions of Articles 29(3) and 32(2)(b) , the decisions of the Assembly shall require a majority of the votes cast.

(b) Abstentions shall not be considered as votes.

(7) (a) The Assembly shall meet once in every third calendar year in ordinary session upon convocation by the Director General, preferably during the same period and at the same place as the General Assembly of the Organization.

(b) The Assembly shall meet in extraordinary session upon convocation by the Director General, either on his own initiative or at the request of one-fourth of the Contracting States.

(8) The Assembly shall adopt its own rules of procedure.

Article 27
International Bureau

(1) The International Bureau shall:

(i) perform the administrative tasks concerning the Union; in particular, it shall perform such tasks as are specifically assigned to it under this Agreement or by the Assembly;

(ii) provide the secretariat of revision conferences, of the Assembly, of committees and working groups established by the Assembly, and of any other meeting convened by the Director General and dealing with matters of concern to the Union.

(2) The Director General shall be the chief executive of the Union and shall represent the Union.

(3) The Director General shall convene any committee and working group established by the Assembly and all other meetings dealing with matters of concern to the Union.

(4) (a) The Director General and any staff member designated by him shall participate, without the right to vote, in all meetings of the Assembly, the committees and working groups established by the Assembly, and any other meeting convened by the Director General and dealing with matters of concern to the Union.

(b) The Director General, or a staff member designated by him, shall be *ex officio* secretary of the Assembly, and of the committees, working groups and other meetings referred to in subparagraph (a) .

(5) (a) The Director General shall, in accordance with the directions of the Assembly, make the preparations for revision conferences.

(b) The Director General may consult with intergovernmental and international non-governmental organizations concerning the preparations for revision conferences.

(c) The Director General and persons designated by him shall take part, without the right to vote, in the discussions at revision conferences.

(d) The Director General, or a staff member designated by him, shall be *ex officio* secretary of any revision conference.

Article 28
Finances

(1) (a) The Union shall have a budget.

(b) The budget of the Union shall include the income and expenses proper to the Union, its contribution to the budget of expenses common to the Unions administered by the Organization and any sum made available to the budget of the Conference of the Organization.

(c) Expenses not attributable exclusively to the Union but also to one or more other Unions administered by the Organization shall be regarded as expenses common to the Unions. The share of the Union in such common expenses shall be in proportion to the interest the Union has in them.

(2) The budget of the Union shall be established with due regard to the requirements of coordination with the budgets of the other Unions administered by the

Organization.

(3) (a) The budget of the Union shall be financed from the following sources:

(i) fees and other charges due for services rendered by the International Bureau in relation to the Union;

(ii) sale of, or royalties on, the publications of the International Bureau concerning the Union;

(iii) gifts, bequests, and subventions;

(iv) rents, interests, and other miscellaneous income;

(v) the contributions of Contracting States, in so far as income deriving from the sources mentioned under (i) to (iv) is not sufficient to cover the expenses of the Union.

(b) The amounts of fees and charges due to the International Bureau under subparagraph (a) (i) and the prices of its publications shall be so fixed that they should, under normal circumstances, be sufficient to cover the expenses of the International Bureau connected with the administration of this Agreement.

(c) If the income exceeds the expenses, the difference shall be credited to a reserve fund.

(d) If the budget is not adopted before the beginning of a new financial period, it shall be at the same level as the budget of the previous year, as provided in the financial regulations.

(4) (a) For the purpose of establishing its contribution as provided in paragraph (3)(a) (v), each Contracting State shall belong to a class, and shall pay its contribution on the basis of a number of units fixed as follows:

Class I 25
Class I 20
Class III..................................15
Class IV 10
Class V 5
Class VI 3
Class VII 1

(b) Unless it has already done so, each Contracting State shall indicate, concurrently with depositing its instrument of ratification or accession, the class to which it wishes to belong. Any country may change class. If it chooses a lower class, it must announce such change to the Assembly at one of its ordinary sessions. Any such change shall take effect at the beginning of the calendar year following the said session.

(c) The contribution of each Contracting State shall be an amount in the same proportion to the total sum to be contributed as the number of its units is to the total of the units of all the Contracting States.

(d) Contributions shall be payable on the first of January of the year for which they are due.

(5) (a) The Union shall have a working capital fund which shall be constituted by a single payment made by each Contracting State. If the fund becomes insufficient, the Assembly shall arrange to increase it. If part of the fund is no longer needed, it shall be reimbursed.

(b) The amount of the initial payment of each Contracting State to the said fund or of its participation in the increase thereof shall be a proportion of the contribution which that State may be required to pay under paragraph (3)(a) (v) for the year in which the fund is established or the decision to increase it is made.

(c) The proportion and the terms of payment shall be fixed by the Assembly on the proposal of the Director General and after it has heard the advice of the Coordination Committee of the Organization.

(d) Any reimbursement under subparagraph (a) shall be proportionate to the amounts paid by each Contracting State, taking into account the dates at which they were paid.

(e) If a working capital fund of sufficient amount can be constituted by borrowing from the reserve fund, the Assembly may suspend the application of subparagraphs (a) to (d).

(6) (a) In the headquarters agreement concluded with the State on the territory of which the Organization has its headquarters, it shall be provided that, whenever the working capital fund is insufficient, such State shall grant advances. The amount of those advances and the conditions on which they are granted shall be the subject of separate agreements, in each case, between such State and the Organization. As long as it remains under the obligation to grant advances, such State shall have an *ex officio* seat in the Assembly if it is not a Contracting State.

(b) The State referred to in subparagraph (a) and the Organization shall each have the right to denounce the obligation to grant advances, by written notification. Denunciation shall take effect three years after the end of the year in which it has been notified.

(7) The auditing of the accounts shall be effected by one or more of the Contracting States or by external auditors, as provided in the financial regulations. They shall be designated, with their agreement, by the Assembly.

Article 29
Regulations

(1) The Regulations provide rules:

(i) concerning matters in respect of which this Agreement expressly refers to the Regulations or expressly provides that they are or shall be prescribed;

(ii) concerning any administrative requirements, matters or procedures;

(iii) concerning any details useful in the implementation of this Agreement.

(2) The Regulations adopted at the same time as this Agreement are annexed to this Agreement.

(3) The Assembly may amend the Regulations, and such amendments shall require two-thirds of the votes cast.

(4) In the case of conflict between the provisions of this Agreement and those of the Regulations, the provisions of this Agreement shall prevail.

CHAPTER IV

Disputes

Article 30
Disputes

(1) Any dispute between two or more Contracting States concerning the interpretation or application of this Agreement or the Regulations, not settled by negotiation, may, by any of the Contracting States concerned, be brought before the International Court of Justice by application in conformity with the Statute of the Court, unless the Contracting States concerned agree on some other method of settlement. The Contracting State bringing the dispute before the Court shall inform the International Bureau; the International Bureau shall bring the matter to the attention of the other Contracting States.

(2) Each Contracting State may, at the time it signs this Agreement or deposits its instrument of ratification or accession, declare that it does not consider itself bound by the provisions of paragraph (1). With regard to any dispute between any Contracting State having made such a declaration and any other Contracting State, the provisions of paragraph (1) shall not apply.

(3) Any Contracting State having made a declaration in accordance with the provisions of paragraph (2) may, at any time, withdraw its declaration by notification addressed to the Director General.

CHAPTER V

Revision and Amendment

Article 31
Revision of the Agreement

(1) This Agreement may be revised from time to time by a conference of the Contracting States.

(2) The convocation of any revision conference shall be decided by the Assembly.

(3) Articles 26, 27, 28 and 32 may be amended either by a revision conference or according to the provisions of Article 32.

Article 32
Amendment of Certain Provisions of the Agreement

(1) (a) Proposals for the amendment of Articles 26, 27, 28 and the present Article, may be initiated by any Contracting State or by the Director General.

(b) Such proposals shall be communicated by the Director General to the Contracting States at least six months in advance of their consideration by the Assembly.

(2) (a) Amendments to the Articles referred to in paragraph (1) shall be adopted by the Assembly.

(b) Adoption shall require three-fourths of the votes cast, provided that adoption of any amendment to Article 26 and to the present subparagraph shall require four-fifths of the votes cast.

(3) (a) Any amendment to the Articles referred to in paragraph (1) shall enter into force one month after written notifications of acceptance, effected in accordance with their respective constitutional processes, have been received by the Director General from three-fourths of the Contracting States members of the Assembly at the time the Assembly adopted the amendment.

(b) Any amendment to the said Articles thus accepted shall bind all the Contracting States which were Contracting States at the time the amendment was adopted by the Assembly, provided that any amendment increasing the financial obligations of the said Contracting States shall bind only those States which have notified their acceptance of such amendment.

(c) Any amendment which has been accepted and which has entered into force in accordance with the provisions of subparagraph (a) shall bind all States which become Contracting States after the date on which the amendment was adopted by the Assembly.

CHAPTER VI

Final Provisions

Article 33

Becoming Party to the Agreement

(1) (a) Subject to subparagraph (b) , any State member of either the International Union for the Protection of Industrial Property or the International Union for the Protection of Literary and Artistic Works, or party to the Universal Copyright Convention or to the latter Convention as revised, may become party to this Agreement by:

(i) signature followed by the deposit of an instrument of ratification, or

(ii) deposit of an instrument of accession.

(b) States which intend to ensure the protection of type faces by establishing a special national deposit or by adapting the deposit provided for in their national industrial design laws may only become party to this Agreement if they are members of the International Union for the Protection of Industrial Property. States which intend to ensure the protection of type faces by their national copyright provisions may only become party to this Agreement if they are either members of the International Union for the Protection of Literary and Artistic Works or party to the Universal Copyright Convention or to the latter Convention as revised.

(2) Instruments of ratification or accession shall be deposited with the Director General.

(3) The provisions of Article 24 of the Stockholm Act of the Paris Convention for the Protection of Industrial Property shall apply to this Agreement.

(4) Paragraph (3) shall in no way be understood as implying the recognition or tacit acceptance by a Contracting State of the factual situation concerning a territory to which this Agreement is made applicable by another Contracting State by virtue of the said paragraph.

Article 34

Declarations Concerning National Protection

(1) At the time of depositing its instrument of ratification or accession, each State shall, by a notification addressed to the Director General, declare whether it intends to ensure the protection of type faces by establishing a special national deposit, or by adapting the deposit provided for in its national industrial design laws,

or by its national copyright provisions or by more than one of these kinds of protection. Any such State which intends to ensure protection by its national copyright provisions shall declare at the same time whether it intends to assimilate creators of type faces who have their habitual residence or domicile in a Contracting State to creators of type faces who are nationals of that State.

(2) Any subsequent modification of the declarations made in accordance with paragraph (1) shall be indicated by a further notification addressed to the Director General.

Article 35
Entry Into Force of the Agreement

(1) This Agreement shall enter into force three months after five States have deposited their instruments of ratification or accession.

(2) Any State which is not among those referred to in paragraph (1) shall become bound by this Agreement three months after the date on which it has deposited its instrument of ratification or accession, unless a later date has been indicated in the instrument of ratification or accession. In the latter case, this Agreement shall enter into force with respect to that State on the date thus indicated.

(3) The provisions of Chapter II of this Agreement shall become applicable, however, only on the date on which at least three of the States for which this Agreement has entered into force under paragraph (1) afford protection to type faces by establishing a special national deposit or by adapting the deposit provided for in their national industrial design laws. For the purpose of this paragraph, the States party to the same regional treaty which gave notification under Article 24 shall count as one State only.

Article 36
Reservations

No reservations to this Agreement other than the reservation under Article 30(2) are permitted.

Article 37
Loss of Status of Party to the Agreement

Any Contracting State shall cease to be party to this Agreement when it no longer meets the conditions set forth in Article 33(1)(b) .

Article 38
Denunciation of the Agreement

(1) Any Contracting State may denounce this Agreement by notification addressed to the Director General.

(2) Denunciation shall take effect one year after the day on which the Director General has received the notification.

(3) The right of denunciation provided for in paragraph (1) shall not be exercised by any Contracting State before the expiration of five years from the date on which it becomes party to this Agreement.

(4) (a) The effects of this Agreement on type faces enjoying the benefits of Articles 12 to 25 on the day preceding the day on which the denunciation by any Contracting State takes effect shall subsist in that State until the expiration of the term of protection which, subject to Article 23(6) , was running on that date according to Article 23.

(b) The same shall apply in Contracting States other than the denouncing State in respect of international deposits owned by a resident or national of the denouncing State.

Article 39

Signature and Languages of the Agreement

(1) (a) This Agreement shall be signed in a single original in the English and French languages, both texts being equally authentic.

(b) Official texts shall be established by the Director General, after consultation with the interested Governments, in the German, Italian, Japanese, Portuguese, Russian and Spanish languages, and such other languages as the Assembly may designate.

(2) This Agreement shall remain open for signature at Vienna until December 31, 1973.

Article 40

Depositary Functions

(1) The original of this Agreement, when no longer open for signature, shall be deposited with the Director General.

(2) The Director General shall transmit two copies, certified by him, of this Agreement and the Regulations annexed thereto to the Governments of all the States referred to in Article 33(1)(a) and, on request, to the Government of any other State.

(3) The Director General shall register this Agreement with the Secretariat of the United Nations.

(4) The Director General shall transmit two copies, certified by him, of any amendment to this Agreement and to the Regulations to the Governments of the Contracting States and, on request, to the Government of any other State.

Article 41
Notifications

The Director General shall notify the Governments of States referred to in Article 33(1)(a) of:

(i) signatures under Article 39;

(ii) deposits of instruments of ratification or accession under Article 33(2);

(iii) the date of entry into force of this Agreement under Article 35(1) and the date from which Chapter II is applicable in accordance with Article 35 (3);

(iv) declarations concerning national protection notified under Article 34;

(v) notifications concerning regional treaties under Article 24;

(vi) declarations made under Article 30(2);

(vii) withdrawals of any declarations, notified under Article 30(3);

(viii) declarations and notifications made in accordance with Article 33(3);

(ix) acceptances of amendments to this Agreement under Article 32(3);

(x) the dates on which such amendments enter into force;

(xi) denunciations received under Article 38.

Regulations Under the Vienna Agreement for the Protection of Type Faces and their International Deposit

TABLE OF CONTENTS *

* This Table of Contents is added for the convenience of the reader. It does not appear in the original.

5.4 Indications Concerning the Type Faces

5.5 Indications Concerning Fees

5.6 International Deposit Effected Through the Intermediary of the Competent Office of a Contracting State

Rule 6: Optional Contents of the Instrument of International Deposit

6.1 Naming of a Representative

6.2 Claiming of Priority

6.3 Denomination of the Type Faces

Rule 7: Language of the Instrument of International Deposit, Recordings, Notifications and Correspondence

7.1 Language of the Instrument of International Deposit

7.2 Language of Recordings, Notifications and Correspondence

Rule 8: Form of the Instrument of International Deposit

8.1 Model Form

8.2 Copies; Signature

8.3 No Additional Matter

Rule 9: Representation of Type Faces

9.1 Form of Representation

9.2 Other Indications

Rule 10: Fees Payable with the International Deposit

10.1 Kinds and Amounts of Fees

Rule 11: Defects in the International Deposit

11.1 Notification of Declining of International Deposit and Reimhursement of Publication Fee

11.2 Defects Peculiar to an International Deposit Effected Through the Intermediary of the Competent Office of a Contracting State

Rule 12: Procedure Where Avoiding Certain Effects of Declining Is Sought

12.1 Information Available to Competent Offices of Contracting States

Rule 13: International Deposit Certificate

13.1 International Deposit Certificate

Rule 14: Publication of International Deposits

14.1 Contents of Publication of the International Deposit

Rule 15: Notification of International Deposits

15.1 Form of Notification

15.2 Time of Notification

Rule 16: Changes in Ownership

16.1 Request for Recording of Change in Ownership

16.2 Recording, Notification and Publication; Declining of Request for Recording

Rule 17: Withdrawal and Renunciation of International Deposits

Rule Concerning These Regulations

Rule 1
Abbreviated Expressions

1.1 "Agreement"

In these Regulations, the word "Agreement" means the Vienna Agreement for the Protection of Type Faces and their International Deposit.

1.2 "Article"

In these Regulations, the word "Article" refers to the specified Article of the Agreement.

1.3 "Bulletin"

In these Regulations, the word "Bulletin" means the *International Bulletin of Type Faces / Bulletin international des caractères typographiques.*

1.4 "Table of Fees"

In these Regulations, the words "Table of Fees" mean the Table of Fees annexed hereto.

Rules Concerning Chapter II of the Agreement

Rule 2

Representation Before the International Bureau

2.1 Number of Duly Appointed Representatives

(a) The applicant and the owner of the international deposit may appoint only one representative.

(b) Where several natural persons or legal entities have been indicated as representatives by the applicant or the owner of the international deposit, the natural person or legal entity first mentioned in the document in which they are indicated shall be regarded as the only duly appointed representative.

(c) Where the representative is a partnership or firm composed of attorneys or patent or trademark agents, it shall be regarded as one representative.

2.2 Form of Appointment

(a) A representative shall be regarded as a "duly appointed representative" if his appointment complies with the prescriptions of paragraphs (b) to (e).

(b) The appointment of any representative shall require:

(i) that his name appear as that of a representative in the instrum ent of international deposit and that such document bear the signature of the applicant, or

(ii) that a separate power of attorney (i.e., a document appointing the representative), signed by the applicant or the owner of the international deposit, be filed with the International Bureau.

(c) Where there are several applicants or owners of the international deposit, the document containing or constituting the appointment of their common representative shall be signed by all of them.

(d) Any document containing or constituting the appointment of a representative shall indicate his name and his address. Where the representative is a natural person, his name shall be indicated by his family name and given name(s), the family name being indicated before the given name(s). Where the representative is a legal entity or a partnership or firm of attorneys or patent or trademark agents, "name" shall mean the complete name of the legal entity or partnership or firm. The address of the representative shall be indicated in the same manner as that provided for in respect of the applicant in Rule 5.2(c) .

(e) The document containing or constituting the appointment shall contain no words which, contrary to Article 25 (2), wonld limit the powers of the representative to certain matters or exclude certain matters from the powers of the representative or limit such powers in time.

(f) Where the appointment does not comply with the requirements referred to in paragraphs (b) to (e), it shall be treated by the International Bureau as if it had not been made, and the applicant or the owner of the international deposit as well as the natural person, the legal entity, the partnership or firm which was indicated as the representative in the purported appointment shall be informed of this fact by the International Bureau.

(g) The Administrative Instructions shall provide recommended wording for the appointment.

2.3 Revocation or Renunciation of Appointment

(a) The appointment of any representative may be revoked at any time by the natural person who, or legal entity which, has appointed that representative. The revocation shall be effective even if only one of the natural persons who, or legal entities which, have appointed the representative revokes the appointment.

(b) Revocation shall require a written document signed by the natural person or the legal entity referred to in paragraph (a) .

(c) The appointment of a representative as provided in Rule 2.2 shall be regarded as the revocation of any earlier appointment of any other representative. The appointment shall preferably indicate the name of the other earlier appointed representative.

(d) Any representative may renounce his appointment by means of a notification signed by him and addressed to the International Bureau.

2.4 General Powers of Attorney

The appointment of a representative in a separate power of attorney (i.e., a document appointing the representative) may be general in the sense that it relates to more than one instrument of international deposit and more than one international deposit in respect of the same natural person or legal entity. The identification of such instruments of international deposit and such international deposits, as well as other details in respect of such general power of attorney and of its revocation or renunciation, shall be provided in the Administrative Instructions. The Administrative Instructions may provide for a fee payable in connection with the filing of general powers of attorney.

2.5 Substitute Representative

(a) The appointment of the representative referred to in Rule 2.2(b) may indicate also one or more natural persons as substitute representatives.

(b) For the purposes of the second sentence of Article 25(2), substitute representatives shall be considered as representatives.

(c) The appointment of any substitute representative may be revoked at any time by the natural person who, or legal entity which, has appointed the representative or by the representative. Revocation shall require a written document signed by the said natural person, legal entity or representative. It shall be effective, as far as the International Bureau is concerned, as from the date of receipt of the said document by that Bureau.

2.6 Recording, Notification and Publication

Each appointment of a representative or of a substitute representative, its revocation and its renunciation, shall be recorded, notified to the applicant or owner of the international deposit, published and notified to the competent Offices of the Contracting States.

Rule 3
The International Register

3.1 Contents of the International Register; Keeping of the International Register

(a) The International Register shall contain, in respect of each international deposit recorded therein:

(i) all the indications that must or may be furnished under the Agreement or these Regulations, and that have in fact been furnished, to the International Bureau, and, where relevant, the date on which such indications were received by that Bureau;

(ii) the representation of the deposited type faces;

(iii) the number and the date of the international deposit and the numbers, if any, and the dates of all recordings relating to that deposit;

(iv) the amount of all fees received and the date or dates on which they were received by the International Bureau;

(v) any other indication whose recording is provided for by the Agreement or these Regulations.

(b) The Administrative Instructions shall regulate the establishment of the International Register, and, subject to the Agreement and these Regulations, shall specify the form in which it shall be kept and the procedure which the International Bureau shall follow for making recordings therein and for preserving it from loss or other damage.

Rule 4
Applicants; Owners of International Deposits

4.1 Several Applicants; Several Owners of the International Deposit

(a) If there are several applicants, they shall have the right to effect an international deposit only if all of them are residents or nationals of Contracting States.

(b) If there are several owners of an international deposit, they shall have the right to own such a deposit only if all of them are residents or nationals of Contracting States.

Rule 5

Mandatory Contents of the Instrument of International Deposit

5.1 Declaration that the International Deposit is Effected Under the Agreement

(a) The declaration referred to in Article 14(1) (i) shall be worded as follows:

"The undersigned requests that the deposit of the type faces of which a representation is enclosed herewith be recorded in the International Register established under the Vienna Agreement for the Protection of Type Faces and their International Deposit."

(b) The declaration may, however, be worded differently if it has the same effect.

5.2 Indications Concerning the Applicant

(a) The applicant's identity shall be indicated by his name. If the applicant is a natural person, his name shall be indicated by his family name and given name(s), the family name being indicated before the given name(s). If the applicant is a legal entity, its name shall be indicated by the full, official designation of the said entity.

(b) The applicant's residence and nationality shall be indicated by the name(s) of the State(s) of which he is a resident and of which he is a national.

(c) The applicant's address shall be indicated in such a way as to satisfy the customary requirements for prompt postal delivery at the indicated address and shall, in any case, consist of all the relevant administrative units up to, and including, the house number, if any. Any telegraphic and teletype address and telephone number that the applicant may have should preferably be indicated. For each applicant, only one address shall be indicated; if several addresses are indicated, only the one first mentioned in the instrument of international deposit shall be considered.

(d) Where the applicant bases his right to effect international deposits on the fact that he has a real and effective industrial or commercial establishment in a Contracting State, he shall mention that fact and specify the State in question.

5.3 Name of the Creator of the Type Faces

The creator of the type faces should be indicated by name. His name shall comprise the family name and given name(s), the family name being indicated before the given name(s).

5.4 Indications Concerning the Type Faces

The instrument of international deposit shall indicate the number of sheets bearing representations of the type faces which are the subject of the deposit.

5.5 Indications Concerning Fees

The instrument of international deposit shall indicate the amount paid and contain the other indications prescribed by Rule 22.5.

5.6 International Deposit Effected Through the Intermediary of the Competent Office of a Contracting State

The indication referred to in Article 12(2)(b) shall be worded as follows:

"The ... (1) certifies that the present international deposit was received by it on ... (2)."

(1) Indicate the name of the competent Office. (2) Indicate the date.

Rule 6

Optional Contents of the Instrument of International Deposit

6.1 Naming of a Representative

The instrument of international deposit may indicate a representative.

6.2 Claiming of Priority

(a) The declaration referred to in Article 14(2) (i) shall consist of a statement to the effect that the priority of an earlier deposit is claimed and shall indicate:

(i) where the earlier deposit is not an International deposit, the State in which such earlier deposit was effected;

(ii) where the earlier deposit is not an international deposit, the nature of that deposit (type face deposit or industrial design deposit);

(iii) the date of the earlier deposit;

(iv) the number of the earlier deposit.

(b) If the declaration does not contain the indications referred to in paragraph (a) (i) to (iii), the International Bureau shall treat the declaration as if it had not been made.

(c) If the earlier deposit number referred to in paragraph (a) (iv) is not indicated in the declaration but is furnished by the applicant or the owner of the International deposit to the International Bureau prior to the expiration of the tenth month from the date of the earlier deposit, it shall be considered to have been included in the declaration and shall be published by the International Bureau.

(d) If the date of the earlier deposit as indicated in the declaration precedes the date of the international deposit by more than six months, the International Bureau shall treat the declaration as if it had not been made.

(e) If the declaration referred to in Article 14(2) (i) claims the priority of more than one earlier deposit, the provisions of paragraphs (a) to (d) shall apply to each of them.

6.3 Denomination of the Type Faces

Where a denomination relates only to a part of the type faces, the instrument of international deposit shall clearly indicate those to which it does relate. The same shall apply where more than one denomination is indicated.

Rule 7

Language of the Instrument of International Deposit, Recordings, Notifications and Correspondence

7.1 Language of the Instrument of International Deposit

(a) The instrument of international deposit shall be in the English or in the French language.

(b) The Administrative Instructions may provide that the headings of the model form referred to in Rule 8.1 shall also be in languages other than English and French.

7.2 Language of Recordings, Notifications and Correspondence

(a) Recordings and notifications by the International Bureau shall be in the same language as that of the instrument of international deposit.

(b) Correspondence between the International Bureau and the applicant or the owner of the international deposit shall be in the same language as that of the instrument of international deposit.

(c) Letters or other written communications from the competent Offices of Contracting States to the International Bureau shall be in the English or in the French language.

(d) Letters from the International Bureau to any competent Office of a Contracting State shall be in English or French according to the wish of that Office; any matter in such letters quoted from the International Register shall be in the language in which such matter appears in that Register.

(e) Where the International Bureau is under the obligation to forward to the applicant or the owner of the international deposit any of the communications referred to in paragraph (c) , it shall forward them in the language in which it received them.

Rule 8

Form of the Instrument of International Deposit

8.1 Model Form

(a) The instrument of international deposit shall be established in accordance with the model form issued by the International Bureau. Printed copies of the model form shall be furnished free of charge, on request, by the International Bureau.

(b) The form shall be filled in preferably by typewriter and shall be easily legible.

8.2 Copies; Signature

(a) The instrument of international deposit shall be filed in one copy.

(b) The instrument of international deposit shall be signed by the applicant.

8.3 No Additional Matter

(a) The instrument of international deposit shall not contain any matter and shall not be accompanied by any document other than those prescribed or permitted by the Agreement and these Regulations.

(b) If the instrument of international deposit contains matter other than matter so prescribed or permitted, the International Bureau shall delete it *ex officio*; and if it is accompanied by any document other than those prescribed or permitted, the International Bureau shall treat it as if it had not been transmitted to it and shall return the said document to the applicant.

Rule 9
Representation of Type Faces

9.1 Form of Representation

(a) Type faces which are the subject of an international deposit shall be represented on one side only of one or more sheets of paper of A4 size (29.7 cm × 21 cm.), separate from the instrument of international deposit. A margin shall be left of at least 1.5 cm. from all four edges of each sheet.

(b) Letters and signs shall be presented in such a way that the tallest letter or sign within a set shall be not less than 10 mm., and they shall be separated from one another by their normal inter-letter spacing.

(c) The representation of the type faces shall also include a text of not less than three lines composed with the characters which are the subject of the international deposit. The text need not necessarily be in English or French or in the minimum dimensions required under paragraph (b) .

(d) The representation of the type faces shall be of a quality admitting of direct reproduction by photography and printing processes.

9.2 Other Indications

The sheet bearing the representation of the type faces shall also bear the name of the applicant and his signature. If there are several sheets, each shall contain the same indications and each shall be numbered.

Rule 10
Fees Payable with the International Deposit

10.1 Kinds and Amounts of Fees

(a) The fees payable with the international deposit shall be:

(i) a deposit fee;

(ii) a publication fee.

(b) The amount of each of those fees is indicated in the Table of Fees.

Rule 11

Defects in the International Deposit

11.1 Notification of Declining of International Deposit and Reimbursement of Publication Fee

Where, under Article 15(2)(c) , the International Bureau declines the international deposit, it shall notify the applicant, stating the grounds for declining, and shall reimburse to him the publication fee which has been paid.

11.2 Defects Peculiar to an International Deposit Effected Through the Intermediary of the Competent Office of a Contracting State

Where the instrument of international deposit presented through the intermediary of the competent Office of a Contracting State under Article 12(2):

(i) does not indicate that the applicant is a resident of the State through the intermediary of whose Office the international deposit was effected, or

(ii) does not contain a statement by the said Office indicating the date on which that Office received the said deposit, or

(iii) contains the said statement indicating a date which precedes by more than one month the date on which the International Bureau received the international deposit,

the international deposit shall be treated as if it had been effected direct with the International Bureau on the date it reached the Bureau. The International Bureau shall inform accordingly the Office through the intermediary of which the international deposit was effected.

Rule 12

Procedure Where Avoiding Certain Effects of Declining Is Sought

12.1 Information Available to Competent Offices of Contracting States

At the request of the applicant or of the interested competent Office, the International Bureau shall send to that Office a copy of the file of the declined international deposit, together with a memorandum setting out the grounds for and the various steps leading to the declining of the said application.

Rule 13

International Deposit Certificate

13.1 International Deposit Certificate

Once the International Bureau has recorded the international deposit, it shall issue to the owner thereof an international deposit certificate, the contents of which are provided for in the Administrative Instrutions.

Rule 14

Publication of International Deposits

14.1 Contents of Publication of the International Deposit

The publication of any international deposit shall contain:

(i) the name and address of the applicant and, if he bases his right to effect international deposits on the fact that he is a resident or national of, or has a real and effective industrial or commercial establishment in, a State other than that in which he has his address, the name of the State of which he is a resident or national or in which he has a real and effective industrial or commercial establishment;

(ii) the name of the creator of the type faces or an indication that the creator has renounced being mentioned as such;

(iii) the representation of the type faces, including the text referred to in Rule 9.1(c) , in the same presentation and dimensions as those in which they were deposited;

(iv) the date of the international deposit;

(v) the number of the international deposit;

(vi) where priority is claimed, the indications listed in Rule 6.2(a) ;

(vii) where a representative is appointed, the name and address of that representative;

(viii) where a denomination is indicated for the type faces, that denomination.

Rule 15

Notification of International Deposits

15.1 Form of Notification

The notification referred to in Article 17 shall be effected separately for each competent Office and shall consist of separate reprints of the publication by the International Bureau of each international deposit.

15.2 Time of Notification

The notification shall be effected on the same date as that of the issue of the Bulletin in which the international deposit is published.

Rule 16

Changes in Ownership

16.1 Request for Recording of Change in Ownership

(a) The request for recording referred to in Article 20(1) shall indicate its purpose and contain:

(i) the name of the owner of the international deposit (hereinafter referred to as "the earlier owner") who appears as such in the International Register;

(ii) the name, residence, nationality and address of the new owner of the international deposit (hereinafter referred to as “the new owner”), in the manner provided for indications to be furnished in respect of the applicant under Rule 5.2;

(iii) the number of the international deposit;

(iv) where the change in ownership relates to fewer than all the Contracting States referred to in Article 18(1), identification of those States to which it relates.

(b) The request shall be signed by the earlier owner or, if his signature cannot be obtained, by the new owner, provided that if it is signed by the new owner the request shall be accompanied by an attestation by the competent Office of the Contracting State of which the earlier owner, at the time of the change of ownership, was a national or, if at that time the earlier owner was not a national of a Contracting State, by the competent Office of the Contracting State of which, at the said time, the earlier owner was a resident. The competent Office shall attest that, according to evidence produced before it, the new owner appears to be the successor in title of the earlier owner to the extent described in the request and the conditions prescribed in the preceding sentence are fulfilled. The attestation shall be dated and shall bear the stamp or seal of the competent Office and the signature of an official thereof. The attestation shall be given for the sole purpose of allowing the change of ownership to be recorded in the International Register.

(c) The amount of the fee referred to in Article 20(4) is indicated in the Table of Fees.

16.2 Recording, Notification and Publication; Declining of Request for Recording

(a) Where, according to the indications furnished in the request for recording of the change in ownership, the new owner is a person entitled to own international deposits and the request complies with the other prescribed requirements, the International Bureau shall record the change in ownership in respect of all the Contracting States or those specified in the request, as the case may be. Such recording shall contain the indications referred to in Rule 16.1(a) (ii) and (iv) and shall mention the date on which it was effected.

(b) The International Bureau shall notify the recording of the change in ownership to the earlier and to the new owners.

(c) The publication and the notification referred to in Article 20(5) shall contain the indications referred to in Rule 16.1(a) and the date of the recording.

(d) Where, according to the indications furnished in the request for recording of the change in ownership, the new owner is a person not entitled to own international deposits, or where the request does not comply with the other prescribed requirements, the International Bureau shall decline it and notify the person who has signed the request, stating the grounds for declining.

Rule 17

Withdrawal and Renunciation of International Deposits

17.1 Withdrawal of the International Deposit

Any withdrawal of an international deposit shall be treated as such by the International Bureau if the declaration of withdrawal reaches it before preparations for publication have been completed. If the said declaration reaches the International Bureau later, it shall be treated as a renunciation of the international deposit.

17.2 Procedure

(a) Withdrawals and renunciations shall be effected by means of a written declaration addressed to the International Bureau and signed by the applicant or the owner of the international deposit, as the case may be.

(b) If withdrawal or renunciation is only partial, the States or type faces to which it relates shall be clearly indicated, failing which it shall not be taken into consideration.

(c) The International Bureau shall acknowledge receipt of the declaration of withdrawal. If withdrawal is total, the International Bureau shall reimburse to the applicant the publication fee which has been paid.

(d) The International Bureau shall record the renunciation, notify the said recording to the owner of the international deposit, publish such renunciation and notify it to the competent Offices of the Contracting States.

Rule 18

Other Amendments to International Deposits

18.1 Permissible Amendments

The owner of the international deposit may amend the mandatory and optional indications appearing in the instrument of international deposit in accordance with Rules 5.2, 5.3, 6.1 and 6.3.

18.2 Procedure

(a) Any amendment referred to in Rule 18.1 shall be effected by means of a written communication addressed to the International Bureau and signed by the owner of the international deposit.

(b) The fees referred to in Article 22(3) are indicated in the Table of Fees.

(c) The International Bureau shall record the amendment, notify the said recording to the owner of the international deposit, publish such amendment and notify it to the competent Offices of the Contracting States.

Rule 19

Renewal of International Deposits

19.1 Reminder by the International Bureau

The International Bureau shall send a letter to the owner of the international deposit before the expiration of the term, initial or renewal, which is in effect, reminding him that such term is about to expire. Further details concerning the contents of the reminder shall be provided in the Administrative Instructions. The reminder shall be sent at least six months prior to the expiration date. Failure to send or receive the reminder, or the fact of sending or receiving it outside the said period, or any error in the reminder, shall not affect the expiration date.

19.2 Demand for Renewal

The demand for renewal referred to in Article 23(4) shall preferably be made on a printed form furnished free of charge by the International Bureau together with the reminder referred to in Rule 19.1. The demand shall, in any case, indicate its purpose and contain:

(i) the name and address of the owner of the international deposit;

(ii) the number of the international deposit.

19.3 Time Limits; Fees

(a) Subject to paragraph (b) , the demand for renewal and the fees referred to in Article 23(4) must reach the International Bureau not later than six months after the expiration of the term of protection.

(b) If the demand for renewal or the fees due reach the International Bureau after the expiration of the term of protection, renewal shall be subject to the payment of a surcharge, which must be paid within the time limit fixed in paragraph (a) .

(c) Where, within the time limit fixed in paragraph(a) , the International Bureau receives:

(i) a demand for renewal which does not conform to the requirements of Rule 19.2, or

(ii) a demand for renewal but no payment or insufficient payment to cover the fees due, or

(iii) money which appears to be intended to cover fees connected with renewal but no demand for renewal,

it shall promptly invite the owner of the international deposit to present a correct demand, to pay or complete the fees due, or to present a demand, as the case may be. The invitation shall indicate the applicable time limits.

(d) Failure to send or receive the invitation referred to in paragraph (c) , or any delay in dispatching or receiving such invitation, or any errors in the invitation, shall not prolong the time limits fixed in paragraphs (a) and (b) .

(e) The amounts of the fees prescribed under this Rule are indicated in the Table of Fees.

19.4 Recording, Notification and Publication of the Renewal

Where the demand is presented and the fees are paid as prescribed, the International Bureau shall record the renewal, notify the said recording to the owner of the international deposit, publish the indications referred to in Rule 19.2 together with an indication of the date on which the renewal expires, and notify the competent Offices of the Contracting States of the said indications and the said date.

19.5 Declining the demand

(a) where the time limit fixed in Rule 19.3(a) is not respected or where the demand does not conform to the requirements of Rule 19.2 or the fees due are not paid as prescribed, the International Bureau shall decline the demand and shall notify the owner of the international deposit, stating the grounds for declining the demand.

(b) The International Bureau shall not decline any demand before the expiration of six months after the starting date of the term of renewal.

19.6 Recording, Notification and Publication of Lack of Demand

Where, by the expiration of six months after the starting date of the term of renewal, no demand for renewal is presented to the International Bureau, the International Bureau shall record such fact, notify it to the owner of the international deposit, publish it and notify it to the competent Offices of the Contracting States.

Rule 20

Transmittal of Documents to the International Bureau

20.1 Place and Mode of Transmittal

Instruments of international deposit and their annexes, demands, notifications and any other documents intended for filing, notification or other communication to the International Bureau shall be deposited with the competent service of that Bureau during the office hours fixed in the Administrative Instructions, or mailed to that Bureau.

20.2 Date of Receipt of Documents

Any docum ent received by the International Bureau through deposit or mail shall be considered to have been received on the day on which it is actually received by that Bureau, provided that, when it is actually received after office hours, or on a day when the Bureau is closed for business, it shall be considered to have been received on the next subsequent day on which the Bureau is open for business.

20.3 Legal Entity; Partnerships and Firms

(a) Where any document submitted to the International Bureau is required to be signed by a legal entity, the name of the legal entity shall be indicated in the place reserved for signature and shall be accompanied by the signature of the natural person or persons entitled to sign for such legal entity according to the national law of the country under whose law the legal entity was established.

(b) The provisions of paragraph(a) shall apply, mutatis mutandis, to partnerships or firms composed of attorneys or patent or trademark agents but which are not legal entities.

20.4 Exemption from Certification

No authentication, legalization or other certification of the signature shall be required for documents submitted to the International Bureau under the Agreement or these Regulations.

Rule 21
Calendar; Computation of Time Limits

21.1 Calendar

The International Bureau, competent Offices of Contracting States, applicants and owners of international deposits shall, for the purposes of the Agreement and these Regulations, express any date in terms of the Christian era and the Gregorian calendar.

21.2 Periods Expressed in Years, Months or Days

(a) When a period is expressed as one year or a certain number of years, computation shall start on the day following the day on which the relevant event occurred, and the period shall expire in the relevant subsequent year in the month having the same name and on the day having the same number as the month and the day on which the said event occurred, provided that if the relevant subsequent month has no day with the same number the period shall expire on the last day of that month.

(b) When a period is expressed as one month or a certain number of months, computation shall start on the day following the day on which the relevant event occurred, and the period shall expire in the relevant subsequent month on the day which has the same number as the day on which the said event occurred, provided that if the relevant subsequent month has no day with the same number the period shall expire on the last day of that month.

(c) When a period is expressed as a certain number of days, computation shall start on the day following the day on which the relevant event occurred, and the period shall expire on the day on which the last day of the count has been reached.

21.3 Local Dates

(a) The date which is taken into consideration as the starting date of the computation of any period shall be the date which prevails in the locality at the time when the relevant event occurred.

(b) The date on which any period expires shall be the date which prevails in the locality in which the required document is filed or the required fee is paid.

21.4 Expiration on a Non-Working Day

If the expiration of any period during which any document or fee must reach the International Bureau falls on a day on which that Bureau is not open for business, or on which ordinary mail is not delivered in Geneva, the period shall expire on the next subsequent day on which neither of the said two circumstances exists.

Rule 22
Fees

22.1 Fees Due

(a) Fees due under the Agreement and these Regulations are fixed in the Table of Fees and in the Administrative Instructions.

(b) The fees payable shall be:

(i) where they concern an international deposit, the fees in force on the date on which the international deposit is received by the International Bureau or, where the deposit has been filed through the intermediary of a competent Office of a Contracting State, the fees in force on the date on which it was received by that Office;

(ii) where they concern a demand for renewal, the fees in force on the date which precedes by six months the starting date of the term of renewal.

22.2 Payment to the International Bureau

All fees due shall be payable to the International Bureau.

22.3 Currency

All fees due shall be payable in Swiss currency.

22.4 Deposit Accounts

(a) Any natural person or legal entity may open a deposit account with the International Bureau.

(b) The details concerning deposit accounts shall be provided in the Administrative Instructions.

22.5 Indication of the Mode of Payment

(a) Unless the payment is made in cash to the cashier of the International Bureau, the international deposit, the demand, and any other request or other document filed with the International Bureau in connection with any international deposit, subject to the payment of any fee, shall indicate:

(i) the name and address, as provided in Rule 5.2(a) and (c) , of the natural person or legal entity making the payment, unless the payment is made by a cheque attached to the document;

(ii) the mode of payment, which may be by an authorization to debit the amount of the fee to the deposit account of such person, or by transfer to a bank account or to the postal cheque account of the International Bureau, or by cheque. The Administrative Instructions shall provide the details, in particular those governing the kind of cheques that shall be accepted in payment.

(b) Where the payment is made pursuant to an authorization to debit the amount of the fee to a deposit account, the authorization shall specify the transaction to which it relates, unless there is a general authorization to debit to a specified deposit account any fee concerning a certain applicant, owner of an international deposit, or duly appointed representative.

(c) Where the payment is made by transfer to a bank account or to the postal cheque account of the International Bureau, or by a cheque not attached to the instrument of international deposit, the demand for renewal or any other request or other document, the notification of the transfer or cheque (or paper accompanying it) shall identify the transaction to which the payment relates, in the manner to be provided for in the Administrative Instructions.

22.6 Effective Date of Payment

Any payment shall be considered to have been received by the International Bureau on the date indicated herein below:

(i) if the payment is made in cash to the cashier of the International Bureau, on the date on which such payment is made;

(ii) if the payment is made by debiting a deposit account with the International Bureau pursuant to a general authorization to debit, on the date on which the instrument of international deposit, the demand for renewal, or any other request or other document entailing the obligation to pay fees is received by the International Bureau, or, in the case of a specific authorization to debit, on the date on which the specific authorization is received by the International Bureau;

(iii) if the payment is made by transfer to a bank account or to the postal cheque account of the International Bureau, on the date on which such account is credited;

(iv) if the payment is made by cheqne, on the date on which the cheque is received by the International Bureau, provided that it is honored upon presentation to the bank on which the cheque is drawn.

Rule 23
The Bulletin

23.1 Contents

(a) All matters which, according to the Agreement or these Regulations, the International Bureau is obliged to publish shall be published in the Bulletin.

(b) The Administrative Instructions may provide for the inclusion of other matters in the Bulletin.

23.2 Frequency

The Bulletin shall be issued according to requirements, so that any deposit or communication requiring to be published shall be published within three months.

23.3 Languages

(a) The Bulletin shall be issued in a bilingual (English and French) edition.

(b) The Administrative Instructions shall identify those portions which require translation and those portions which do not require translation.

(c) Where matters are published in both languages, the Bulletin shall indicate which is the original language. Translations shall be prepared by the International Bureau. In case of any divergence between the original and the translation, all legal effects shall be governed by the original.

23.4 Sale

The sale prices of the Bulletin shall be fixed in the Administrative Instructions.

23.5 Copies of the Bulletin for Competent Offices of Contracting States

(a) Before July 1 of each year, the competent Office of each Contracting State shall notify the International Bureau of the number of copies of the Bulletin which it wishes to receive in the next subsequent year.

(b) The International Bureau shall make the requested number of copies available to each competent Office:

(i) free of charge, up to the same number as the number of units corresponding to the class chosen under Article 28(4) by the Contracting State of which it is the competent Office;

(ii) at half the sale price for copies in excess of the said number.

(c) Copies given free of charge or sold under paragraph (b) shall be for the internal use of the competent Office which has requested them.

Rule 24

Copies, Extracts and Information; Certification of Documents Issued by the International Bureau

24.1 Copies, Extracts and Information Concerning International Deposits

(a) Any person may obtain from the International Bureau, against payment of a fee whose amount shall be fixed in the Administrative Instructions, certified or uncertified copies or extracts of recordings in the International Register or of any document in the file of any international deposit. Each copy or extract shall reflect the situation of the international deposit on a specified date; such date shall be indicated in the said copy or extract.

(b) On request and against payment of a fee whose amount shall be fixed in the Administrative Instructions, any person may obtain from the International Bureau oral or written information, or information by telecopier devices, on any fact appearing in the International Register or in any document in the file of any international deposit.

(c) Notwithstanding paragraphs (a) and (b) , the Administrative Instructions may waive the obligation to pay any fee where the work or the expense connected with the furnishing of a copy, extract, or information is minimal.

24.2 Certification of Documents Issued by the International Bureau

Where any document issued by the International Bureau bears the seal of that

Bureau and the signature of the Director General or a person acting on his behalf, no authority of any Contracting State shall require authentication, legalization or any other certification of such document, seal or signature, by any other person or authority.

Rules Concerning Chapter III of the Agreement

Rule 25

Expenses of Delegations

25.1 Expenses Borne by Governments

The expenses of each delegation participating in any session of the Assembly and of any committee, working group or other body dealing with matters of concern to the Union shall be borne by the Government which has appointed it.

Rule 26

Absence of Quorum in the Assembly

26.1 Voting by Correspondence

(a) In the case provided for in Article 26(5)(b) , the International Bureau shall communicate any decision of the Assembly, other than decisions relating to the Assembly's own procedure, to the Contracting States which were not represented when the decision was made and shall invite them to express in writing their vote or abstention within a period of three months from the date of the communication.

(b) If, at the expiration of the said period, the number of Contracting States having thus expressed their vote or abstention attains the number of Contracting States which was lacking for attaining the quorum when the decision was made, that decision shall take effect provided that at the same time the required majority still obtains.

Rule 27

Administrative Instructions

27.1 Establishment of Administrative Instructions; Matters Governed by Them

(a) The Director General shall establish Administrative Instructions. He may modify them. He shall consult the competent Offices of the Contracting States which have a direct interest in the proposed Administrative Instructions or their proposed modification.

(b) The Administrative Instructions shall deal with matters in respect of which these Regulations expressly refer to such Instructions and with details in respect of the application of these Regulations.

(c) All forms of interest to applicants and owners of international deposits shall be included in the Administrative Instructions.

27.2 Control by the Assembly

The Assembly may invite the Director General to modify any provision of the Administrative Instructions, and the Director General shall proceed accordingly.

27.3 Publication and Effective Date

(a) The Administrative Instructions and any modification thereof shall be published in the Bulletin.

(b) Each publication shall specify the date on which the published provisions become effective. The date need not be the same for all the provisions, provided that no provision may be declared effective prior to the expiration of a period of one month after the publication date of that issue of the Bulletin in which it has been published.

27.4 Conflict with the Agreement and the Regulations

In the case of conflict between any provision of the Administrative Instructions and any provision of the Agreement or of these Regulations, the latter shall prevail.

Final Clanse

Rule 28

Entry Into Force

28.1 Entry Into Force of the Regulations

These Regulations shall enter into force at the same time as Chapter Ⅱ of the Agreement, with the exception of Rules 25 and 26, which shall enter into force at the same time as the Agreement itself.

Annex to the Regulations

Table of Fees

The International Bureau shall collect the following fees:

I. Deposit *Swiss francs*

1. (a) Deposit fee, up to 75 letters or signs 500

(b) Complementary fee for each additional block or part of a block of 10 letters or signs 100

2. Publication fee for each standard space unit used (26.7×18 cm), being the minimum publication fee 200

II. Renewal

1. Renewal fee 600

2. Surcharge (Rule 19.3(b)) 300

III. Other Fees

1. Fee for recording a total or partial change in ownership 100

2. Fee for recording a change in the name or address of the owner of the International deposit or in other indications concerning the owner: per deposit........... 100

3. Fee for recording the appointment of a representative, a change of representative, or a change in his name or address: per deposit 50

4. Fee for recording any other amendment: per deposit 50

Protocol

to the Vienna Agreement for the Protection of Type Faces and Their International Deposit Concerning the Term of Protection

The States party to the Vienna Agreement for the Protection of Type Faces and Their International Deposit (hereinafter referred to as "the Agreement"), and party to this Protocol

Have agreed to the following provisions:

1. The term of protection shall be a minimum of twenty-five years instead of the minimum of fifteen years referred to in Article 9(1) of the Agreement.

2. (a) This Protocol shall be open for signature by the States which have signed the Agreement.

(b) This Protocol may be ratified by the States which have signed the Protocol and ratified the Agreement.

(c) This Protocol shall be open to accession by States which have not signed the Protocol but have ratified or acceded to the Agreement.

(d) This Protocol shall enter into force three months after three States have deposited their instruments of ratification of or accession to this Protocol, but not before the Agreement itself enters into force.

(e) This Protocol may be revised by conferences of the States party to the Protocol which shall be convened by the Director General at the request of at least one-half of those States. The expenses attributable to any conference for the revision of this Protocol which is not held during the same period and at the same place as a conference for the revision of the Agreement shall be borne by the States party to this Protocol.

(f) The provisions of Articles 30, 33, 35(2), 36, 37, 38, 39, 40 and 41 (i), (ii), (iii), (vi), (vii), (viii) and (xi) of the Agreement shall apply *mutatis mutandis*.

Convention Relating to the Distribution of Programme-Carrying Signals Transmitted by Satellite

Done at Brussels on May 21, 1974

The Contracting States,

Aware that the use of satellites for the distribution of programme-carrying signals is rapidly growing both in volume and geographical coverage;

Concerned that there is no world-wide system to prevent distributors from distributing programme-carrying signals transmitted by satellite which were not intended for those distributors, and that this lack is likely to hamper the use of satellite communications;

Recognizing, in this respect, the importance of the interests of authors, performers, producers of phonograms and broadcasting organizations;

Convinced that an international system should be established under which measures would be provided to prevent distributors from distributing programme-carrying signals transmitted by satellite which were not intended for those distributors;

Conscious of the need not to impair in any way international agreements already in force, including the International Telecommunication Convention and the Radio Regulations annexed to that Convention, and in particular in no way to prejudice wider acceptance of the Rome Convention of October 26, 1961, which affords protection to performers, producers of phonograms and broadcasting organizations,

Have agreed as follows:

Article 1

For the purposes of this Convention:

(i) "signal" is an electronically-generated carrier capable of transmitting programmes;

(ii) "programme" is a body of live or recorded material consisting of images, sounds or both, embodied in signals emitted for the purpose of ultimate distribution;

(iii) "satellite" is any device in extraterrestrial space capable of transmitting signals;

(iv) "emitted signal" or "signal emitted" is any programme-carrying signal that goes to or passes through a satellite;

(v) "derived signal" is a signal obtained by modifying the technical characteristics of the emitted signal, whether or not there have been one or more intervening fixations;

(vi) "originating organization" is the person or legal entity that decides what programme the emitted signals will carry;

(vii) "distributor" is the person or legal entity that decides that the transmission of the derived signals to the general public or any section thereof should take place;

(viii) "distribution" is the operation by which a distributor transmits derived signals to the general public or any section thereof.

Article 2

(1) Each Contracting State undertakes to take adequate measures to prevent the distribution on or from its territory of any programme-carrying signal by any distributor for whom the signal emitted to or passing through the satellite is not intended. This obligation shall apply where the originating organization is a national of another Contracting State and where the signal distributed is a derived signal.

(2) In any Contracting State in which the application of the measures referred to in paragraph (1) is limited in time, the duration thereof shall be fixed by its domestic law. The Secretary-General of the United Nations shall be notified in writing of such duration at the time of ratification, acceptance or accession, or if the domestic law comes into force or is changed thereafter, within six months of the coming into force of that law or of its modification.

(3) The obligation provided for in paragraph (1) shall not apply to the distribution of derived signals taken from signals which have already been distributed by a distributor for whom the emitted signals were intended.

Article 3

This Convention shall not apply where the signals emitted by or on behalf of the originating organization are intended for direct reception from the satellite by the general public.

Article 4

No Contracting State shall be required to apply the measures referred to in Article 2(1) where the signal distributed on its territory by a distributor for whom the emitted signal is not intended

(i) carries short excerpts of the programme carried by the emitted signal, consisting of reports of current events, but only to the extent justified by the informatory purpose of such excerpts, or

(ii) carries, as quotations, short excerpts of the programme carried by the emitted signal, provided that such quotations are compatible with fair practice and are justified by the informatory purpose of such quotations, or

(iii) carries, where the said territory is that of a Contracting State regarded as a developing country in conformity with the established practice of the General Assembly of the United Nations, a programme carried by the emitted signal, provided that the distribution is solely for the purpose of teaching, including teaching in the framework of adult education, or scientific research.

Article 5

No Contracting State shall be required to apply this Convention with respect to any signal emitted before this Convention entered into force for that State.

Article 6

This Convention shall in no way be interpreted to limit or prejudice the protection secured to authors, performers, producers of phonograms, or broadcasting organizations, under any domestic law or international agreement.

Article 7

This Convention shall in no way be interpreted as limiting the right of any Contracting State to apply its domestic law in order to prevent abuses of monopoly.

Article 8

(1) Subject to paragraphs (2) and (3), no reservation to this Convention shall be permitted.

(2) Any Contracting State whose domestic law, on May 21, 1974, so provides may, by a written notification deposited with the Secretary-General of the United Nations, declare that, for its purposes, the words "where the originating organization is a national of another Contracting State" appearing in Article 2(1) shall be considered as if they were replaced by the words "where the signal is emitted from the territory of another Contracting State."

(3) (a) Any Contracting State which, on May 21, 1974, limits or denies

protection with respect to the distribution of programme-carrying signals by means of wires, cable or other similar communications channels to subscribing members of the public may, by a written notification deposited with the Secretary-General of the United Nations, declare that, to the extent that and as long as its domestic law limits or denies protection, it will not apply this Convention to such distributions.

(b) Any State that has deposited a notification in accordance with subparagraph (a) shall notify the Secretary-General of the United Nations in writing, within six months of their coming into force, of any changes in its domestic law whereby the reservation under that subparagraph becomes inapplicable or more limited in scope.

Article 9

(1) This Convention shall be deposited with the Secretary-General of the United Nations. It shall be open until March 31, 1975, for signature by any State that is a member of the United Nations, any of the Specialized Agencies brought into relationship with the United Nations, or the International Atomic Energy Agency, or is a party to the Statute of the International Court of Justice.

(2) This Convention shall be subject to ratification or acceptance by the signatory States. It shall be open for accession by any State referred to in paragraph (1).

(3) Instruments of ratification, acceptance or accession shall be deposited with the Secretary-General of the United Nations.

(4) It is understood that, at the time a State becomes bound by this Convention, it will be in a position in accordance with its domestic law to give effect to the provisions of the Convention.

Article 10

(1) This Convention shall enter into force three months after the deposit of the fifth instrument of ratification, acceptance or accession.

(2) For each State ratifying, accepting or acceding to this Convention after the deposit of the fifth instrument of ratification, acceptance or accession, this Convention shall enter into force three months after the deposit of its instrument.

Article 11

(1) Any Contracting State may denounce this Convention by written notification deposited with the Secretary-General of the United Nations.

(2) Denunciation shall take effect twelve months after the date on which the notification referred to in paragraph (1) is received.

Article 12

(1) This Convention shall be signed in a single copy in English, French, Russian and Spanish, the four texts being equally authentic.

(2) Official texts shall be established by the Director-General of the United Nations Educational, Scientific and Cultural Organization and the Director General of the World Intellectual Property Organization, after consultation with the interested Governments, in the Arabic, Dutch, German, Italian and Portuguese languages.

(3) The Secretary-General of the United Nations shall notify the States referred to in Article 9(1), as well as the Director-General of the United Nations Educational, Scientific and Cultural Organization, the Director General of the World Intellectual Property Organization, the Director-General of the International Labour Office and the Secretary-General of the International Telecommunication Union, of

(i) signatures to this Convention;

(ii) the deposit of instruments of ratification, acceptance or accession;

(iii) the date of entry into force of this Convention under Article 10(1);

(iv) the deposit of any notification relating to Article 2(2) or Article 8(2) or (3), together with its text;

(v) the receipt of notifications of denunciation.

(4) The Secretary-General of the United Nations shall transmit two certified copies of this Convention to all States referred to in Article 9(1).

Multilateral Convention for the Avoidance of Double Taxation of Copyright Royalties, with model bilateral agreement and additional Protocol. 1979

Madrid, 13 December 1979

The Contracting States,

Considering that the double taxation of copyright royalties is prejudicial to the interests of authors and thus constitutes a serious impediment to the dissemination of copyrighted works, which is one of the basic factors in the development of the culture, science and education of all peoples,

Believing that the encouraging results already achieved by action against double taxation, through bilateral agreements and domestic measures, whose beneficial effects are generally recognized, can be improved by the conclusion of a multilateral convention specific to copyright royalties,

Being of the opinion that these problems must be solved while respecting the legitimate interests of States and particularly the needs specific to those where the widest possible access to works of the human mind is an essential condition to their continuing development in the fields of culture, science and education,

Seeking to find effective measures designed to avoid double taxation of copyright royalties where possible and, should it subsist, to eliminate it or to reduce its effect,

Have agreed on the following provisions

Chapter I: Definitions

Article 1: Copyright royalties

1. For the purposes of this Convention and subject to the provisions of paragraphs 2 and 3 of this Article, copyright royalties are payments of any kind made on the basis of the domestic copyright laws of the Contracting State in which these

royalties are originally due, for the use of, or the right to use, a copyright in a literary, artistic or scientific work, as defined in the multilateral copyright conventions, including such payments made in respect of legal or compulsory licences or in respect of the "droit de suite".

2. This Convention shall not, however, be taken to cover royalties due in respect of the exploitation of cinematographic works or works produced by a process analogous to cinematography as defined in the domestic copyright laws of the Contracting State in which these royalties are originally due when the said royalties are due to the producers of such works or their heirs or successors-in-title.

3. With the exception of payments made in respect of the "droit de suite" the following shall not be considered as copyright royalties for the purposes of this Convention: payments for the purchase, rental, loan or any other transfers of a right in the material base of a literary, artistic or scientific work, even if the amount of this payment is fixed in the light of the copyright royalties due or if the latter are determined, in whole or in part, by that of the said payment. When a right in the material base of work is transferred as an accessory to the transfer of the entitlement to use a copyright in the work, only the payments in return for this entitlement are copyright royalties for the purposes of this Convention.

4. In the case of payments made in respect of the "droit de suite" and in all cases of the transfer of a right in the material base of a work referred to, in paragraph 3 of this Article and independently of the fact that the transfer in question is or is not free of charge, any payment made in settlement of or as a reimbursement for an insurance premium, transport or warehousing costs, agent's commission or any other remuneration for a service, and any other expenses incurred, directly or indirectly, by the removal of the material base in question, including customs duties and other related taxes and special levies, shall not be a copyright royalty for the purposes of this Convention.

Article 2: Beneficiary of copyright royalties

For the purposes of this Convention, the "beneficiary" of copyright royalties is the beneficial owner thereof to whom all or a part of such royalties is paid, whether he collects them as author, or heir or successor-in-title of the author, or whether he collects them in application of any other relevant criterion as agreed to in a bilateral agreement concerning double taxation of copyright royalties.

Article 3: State of residence of the beneficiary

1. For the purposes of this Convention, the State of which the beneficiary of the copyright royalties is a resident shall be deemed to be the State of residence of the beneficiary.

2. A person shall be deemed to be a resident of a State if he is liable to tax

therein by reason of his domicile, residence, place of effective management or any other relevant criterion as agreed to in a bilateral agreement concerning double taxation of copyright royalties. But this term does not include any person who is liable to tax in that State in respect only of income from sources in that State as capital he possesses there.

Article 4: State of source of royalty

For the purposes of this Convention, a State shall be deemed to be the State of source of copyright royalties when such royalties for the use of, or the right to use, a copyright in a literary, artistic or scientific work are originally due:

(a) by that State or by a political or administrative subdivision or local authority of that State;

(b) by a resident of that State except where they result from an activity carried on by him in another State through a permanent establishment or from a fixed base;

(c) by a non-resident of that State, where they result from an activity carried on by him through a permanent establishment or from a fixed base.

Chapter II: Guiding principles for action against double taxation of copyright royalties

Article 5: Fiscal sovereignty and equality of rights of States

Action against double taxation of copyright royalties shall be carried out, in accordance with the provisions of Article 8 of this Convention, with due respect for the fiscal sovereignty of the State of source and the State of residence, and due respect for the equality of their right to tax these royalties.

Article 6: Fiscal non-discrimination

The measures against double taxation of copyright royalties shall not give rise to any tax discrimination based on nationality, race, sex, language or religion.

Article 7: Exchange of information

In so far as it is necessary for the implementation of this Convention, the competent authorities of the Contracting States will exchange reciprocally information in the form and under the conditions which shall be laid down by means of bilateral agreement.

Chapter III: Implementation of the guiding principles for the action against double taxation of copyright royalties

Article 8: Means of implementation

1. Each Contracting State undertakes to make every possible effort, in accordance with its Constitution and the guiding principles set out above, to avoid double taxation of copyright royalties, where possible, and, should it subsist, to eliminate it or to reduce its effect. This action shall be carried out by means of bilateral agreements or by way of domestic measures.

2. The bilateral agreements referred to in paragraph 1 of this Article include those which deal with double taxation in general or those which are limited to double taxation of copyright royalties. An optional model of a bilateral agreement of the latter category, comprising several alternatives, is attached to this Convention of which it does not form an integral part. The Contracting States, while respecting the provisions of this Convention, may conclude bilateral agreements based on the norms that are most acceptable to them in each particular case. The application of bilateral agreements concluded earlier by the Contracting States is in no way affected by this Convention.

3. In case of adoption of domestic measures, each Contracting State may, notwithstanding the provisions of Article 1 of this Convention, define copyright royalties by reference to its own copyright legislation.

Chapter IV: General provisions

Article 9: Members of diplomatic or consular missions

The provisions of this Convention do not affect the fiscal privileges of members of diplomatic or consular missions of the Contracting States, as well as of their families, either under the general rules of international law or under the provisions of special conventions.

Article 10: Information

1. The Secretariat of the United Nations Educational, Scientific and Cultural Organization and the International Bureau of the World Intellectual Property Organization shall assemble and publish relevant normative information concerning taxation of copyright royalties.

2. Each Contracting State shall communicate, as soon as possible, to the Secretariat of the United Nations Educational, Scientific and Cultural Organization and to

the International Bureau of the World Intellectual Property Organization, the text of any new law, as well as all official texts concerning the taxation of copyright royalties, including the text of any specific bilateral agreement on the relevant provisions on the said subject contained in any bilateral agreement dealing with double taxation in general.

3. The Secretariat of the United Nations Educational, Scientific and Cultural Organization and the International Bureau of the World Intellectual Property Organization shall furnish to any Contracting State, upon its request, information on questions relating to this Convention; they shall also carry out studies and provide services in order to facilitate the application of this Convention.

Chapter V: Final clauses

Article 11: Ratification, acceptance, accession

1. This Convention shall be deposited with the Secretary-General of the United Nations Organization. It shall remain open until October 31, 1980, for signature by any State that is a member of the United Nations, any of the Specialized Agencies brought into relationship with the United Nations or the International Atomic Energy Agency, or is a party to the Statute of the International Court of Justice.

2. This Convention shall be subject to ratification or acceptance by the signatory States. It shall be open for accession by any State referred to in paragraph 1 of this Article.

3. Instruments of ratification, acceptance or accession shall be deposited with the Secretary-General of the United Nations.

4. It is understood that, at the time a State becomes bound by this Convention, it will be in a position in accordance with its domestic law to give effect to the provisions of this Convention.

Article 12: Reservations

The Contracting States may, either at the time of signature of this Convention or at the time of ratification, acceptance or accession, make reservations as regards the conditions of application of the provisions contained in Articles 1 to 4, 9 and 17. No other reservation to the Convention shall be permitted.

Article 13: Entry into force

1. This Convention shall enter into force three months after the deposit of the tenth instrument of ratification, acceptance or accession.

2. For each State ratifying, accepting, or acceding to this Convention after the deposit of the tenth instrument of ratification, acceptance or accession, this Convention shall enter into force three months after the deposit of its instrument.

Article 14: Denunciation

1. Any Contracting State may denounce this Convention by a written notification addressed to the Secretary-General of the United Nations.

2. Such denunciation shall take effect twelve months after the date of receipt of the notification by the Secretary-General of the United Nations.

Article 15: Revision

1. After this Convention has been in force for five years, any Contracting State may, by notification addressed to the Secretary-General of the United Nations, request that a conference be convened for the purpose of revising the Convention. The Secretary-General shall notify all Contracting States of this request. If, within a period of six months following the date of notification by the Secretary-General of the United Nations, not less than one-third of the Contracting States, provided the number is not less than five, notify him of their concurrence with the request, the Secretary-General shall inform the Director-General of the United Nations Educational, Scientific and Cultural Organization and the Director-General of the World Intellectual Property Organization, who shall convene a revision conference with a view to introducing into this Convention amendments designed to improve action against double taxation of copyright royalties.

2. The adoption of any revision of this Convention shall require an affirmative vote by two-thirds of the States attending the revision conference, provided that this majority includes two-thirds of the States which, at the time of the revision conference, are parties to the Convention.

3. Any State which becomes a party to the Convention after the entry into force of a new Convention wholly or partially revising this Convention shall, failing an expression of a different intention by that State, be considered as:

(a) a party to the revised convention;

(b) a party to this Convention in relation to any State which is a party to the present Convention but is not bound by the revised convention.

4. This Convention shall remain in force as regards relations between or with the Contracting States, which have not become parties to the revised convention.

Article 16: Languages of the convention and notifications

1. This Convention shall be signed in a single copy in Arabic, English, French, Russian and Spanish, the five texts being equally authoritative.

2. Official texts shall be established by the Director-General of the United Nations Educational, Scientific and Cultural Organization and the Director-General of the World Intellectual Property Organization, after consultation with the interested Governments concerned, in the German, Italian and Portuguese languages.

3. The Secretary-General of the United Nations shall notify the States referred

to in Article 11, paragraph 1, as well as the Director-General of the United Nations Educational, Scientific and Cultural Organization and the Director-General of the World Intellectual Property Organization of

(a) signature of this Convention, together with any accompanying text;

(b) the deposit of instruments of ratification, acceptance of accession, together with any accompanying text;

(c) the date of entry into force of this Convention under Article 13, paragraph 1;

(d) the receipt of notifications of denunciation;

(e) the requests communicated to him in accordance with Article 15, as well as any communication received from the Contracting States concerning the revision of this Convention.

4. The Secretary-General of the United Nations shall transmit two certified copies of this Convention to all States referred to in Article 11, paragraph 1.

Article 17: Interpretation and settlement of disputes

1. A dispute between two or more Contracting States concerning the interpretation or in the matter of application of this Convention, not settled by negotiation, shall, unless the States concerned agree on some other method of settlement, be brought before the International Court of Justice for determination by it.

2. Any State may, at the time of signing this Convention or depositing its instrument of ratification, acceptance or accession, declare that it does not consider itself bound by the provisions of paragraph 1. In the event of a dispute between that State and any other Contracting State, the provisions of paragraph 1 shall not apply.

3. Any State that has made a declaration in accordance with paragraph 2 may at any time withdraw it by notification addressed to the Secretary-General of the United Nations.

IN WITNESS WHEREOF, the undersigned, being duly authorized, have signed this Convention.

Done at Madrid on December 13, 1979.

Model bilateral agreement for the avoidance of double taxation of copyright royalties

Preamble of agreement

The Government of (State A) and the Government of (State B) ,

Wishing to apply the principles set out in the Multilateral Convention for the Avoidance of Double Taxation of Copyright Royalties and thus to eliminate such double taxation or to reduce its effect.

Have agreed on the following provisions:

I: Scope of the agreement

Article I: Persons and royalties covered

1. This Agreement shall apply to persons who are residents of one or both of the Contracting States.
2. This Agreement shall apply to copyright royalties when they arise in one Contracting State and their beneficiary is a resident of the other Contracting State.

Article II: Taxes covered

Alternative A

1. This Agreement shall apply to compulsory taxes or deductions imposed on behalf of each Contracting State, [of its political subdivisions or its local authorities], irrespective of their description, their kind and the manner in which they are levied, provided that they are imposed on copyright royalties and are assessed on the amount of royalties, excluding taxes of a fixed nature calculated without reference to the amount of the royalty.
2. The existing taxes to which the Agreement shall apply, are in particular:
   (a) in (State A)
      (i) [income tax applicable]
      (ii) [other taxes applicable]
      (iii) ...
   (b) in (State B)
      (i) [income tax applicable]
      (ii) [other taxes applicable]
      (iii) ...

3. This Agreement shall apply also to future taxes identical [or substantially similar] to those referred to in paragraph 1, which are imposed after the date of signature of this Agreement in addition to, or in place of, existing taxes.
4. The competent authorities of Contracting States shall communicate [at the beginning of each year] any changes in their respective laws and their application [made during the preceding year].

Alternative B

1. This Agreement shall apply to taxes imposed on behalf of each Contracting State [of its political subdivisions or its local authorities], irrespective of their description or the manner in which they are levied, provided that they are imposed on copyright royalties and are assessed on the amount of the royalties.
2. The taxes to which this Agreement shall apply are:
   (a) in (State A)
      (i) [total income tax]
      (ii) [other income taxes]
      (iii) ...
   (b) in (State B)
      (i) [total income tax]
      (ii) [other income taxes]
      (iii) ...
3. The competent authorities of Contracting States shall communicate [at the beginning of each year] any changes in their respective tax laws and their application [made during the preceding year].

II: Definitions

Article III: General definitions

For the purposes of this Agreement, unless the context otherwise requires:
   (a) the terms "a Contracting State" and "the other Contracting State" shall, depending on the context, refer to (State A) or (State B) ;
   (b) the term "person" includes an individual, a company and any other body of persons;
   (c) the term "company" means any body corporate or any entity which is treated as a body corporate for tax purposes;
   (d) the terms "enterprise of a Contracting State" and "enterprise of the other Contracting State" mean respectively an enterprise carried on by a resident of a Contracting State and an enterprise carried on by a resident of the other Contracting State;
   (e) the term "nationals" means

(i) all individuals possessing the nationality of a State;

(ii) all legal persons, partnerships and associations deriving their status as such from the law in force in a State;

(f) the term "competent authority" means

(i) in (State A) , ... and,

(ii) in (State B) , ...;

(g) the term "copyright royalties" shall be interpreted in accordance with the definition given in Article 1 of the Multilateral Convention for the Avoidance of Double Taxation of Copyright Royalties;

(h) the term "beneficiary of copyright royalties" shall be interpreted in accordance with the definition given in Article 2 of the Multilateral Convention for the Avoidance of Double Taxation of Copyright Royalties;

(i) the term "State of source of royalties" shall be interpreted in accordance with the definition given in Article 4 of the Multilateral Convention for the Avoidance of Double Taxation of Copyright Royalties;

(j) the term "state of residence of the beneficiary" shall be interpreted in accordance with the definition given in Article 3 of the Multilateral Convention for the Avoidance of Double Taxation of Copyright Royalties completed by Article IV of this Agreement.

Article IV: Resident

1. For the purposes of this Agreement, a person shall be deemed to be a resident of a State if he is so considered in application of the provisions of Article 3, paragraph 2, of the Multilateral Convention for the Avoidance of Double Taxation of Copyright Royalties.

2. Where by reason of the provision of paragraph 1 an individual is deemed to be a resident of both Contracting States, then his status shall be determined as follows:

(a) he shall be deemed to be a resident of the State in which he has a permanent home available to him. If he has a permanent home available to him in both States, he shall be deemed to be a resident of the State with which his personal and economic relations are closer (center of vital interests);

(b) if the State in which he has his center of vital interests cannot be determined, or if he has not a permament home available to him in either State, he shall be deemed to be a resident of the State in which he has an habitual abode;

(c) if he has an habitual abode in both States or in neither of them, he shall be deemed to be a resident of the State of which he is a national;

(d) if he is a national of both States or of neither of them, the competent authorities of the Contracting States shall settle the question by mutual agreement.

3. Where by reason of the provisions of paragraph 2 a person other than an individual is deemed to be a resident of both Contracting States, [it shall be deemed to

be a resident of the Contracting State in which its place of effective management is situated] [the competent authorities of the Contracting States shall settle the question by mutual agreement].

Article V: Permanent establishment-fixed base

1. For the purposes of this Agreement, the term "permanent establishment" means a fixed place of business through which the business of an enterprise is wholly or partly carried on.

2. The term "permanent establishment" includes especially:

(a) a place of management;

(b) a branch;

(c) an office;

(d) an industrial installation;

(e) a store or other sales outlet;

(f) a permanent exhibition at which orders are received or solicited;

(g) the furnishing of services, including consultancy services, by an entreprise through employees or other personnel, where activities of that nature continue, for the same or a connected project, in the territory of the same State [for ... months].

3. Notwithstanding the provisions of paragraphs 1 and 2, a "permanent establishment" shall not be deemed to include:

(a) the use of facilities solely for the purpose of storage or display of goods belonging to the enterprise;

(b) the maintenance of a stock of goods belonging to the enterprise solely for the purpose of storage or display;

(c) the maintenance of a stock of goods belonging to the enterprise solely for the purpose of processing by another enterprise;

(d) the maintenance of a fixed place of business solely for the purpose of purchasing goods, acquiring rights or collecting information for the enterprise;

(e) the maintenance of a fixed place of business solely for the purpose of advertising, for the supply of information, for scientific research or for similar activities which have a preparatory or auxiliary character, for the enterprise.

4. Notwithstanding the provisions of paragraphs 1 and 2, a person acting in a Contracting State on behalf of an enterprise of the other Contracting State other than an agent of an independent status, to whom paragraph 5 applies, shall be deemed to be a "permanent establishment" in the first-mentioned State:

(a) if he has, and habitually exercises in that State, an authority to conclude contracts in the name of the enterprise, unless his activities are limited to the purchase of goods, or to the acquisition of rights, for the enterprise; or

(b) if he has no such authority but habitually maintains in the first-mentioned State a stock from which he regularly delivers merchandise on behalf of the enterprise.

5. An enterprise of a Contracting State shall not be deemed to have a permanent establishment in the other Contracting State merely because it carries on business there through a broker, general commission agent, literary agent, or any other intermediary of an independent status, where such persons are acting in the ordinary course of their business. However, when the activities of such an intermediary are devoted exclusively or almost exclusively to that enterprise for more than ... consecutive months, he shall not be deemed an agent of an independent status within the meaning of this Article.

6. The fact that a company which is a resident of a Contracting State controls or is controlled by a company which is a resident of another Contracting State, or which carries on business in that other State (whether through a permanent establishment or otherwise), shall not in itself constitute such a company as a permanent establishment of the other.

7. In this Agreement, the term "fixed base" means a place of residence and of work, or a place of work, where an individual habitually carries on a part at least of his activities of an independent nature.

III: Rules of taxation

Article VI: Taxation methods

1ST ALTERNATIVE

Article VI. A: Taxation by the State of residence subject to the existence of a permanent establishment or fixed base in the other State

1. Copyright royalties arising in a Contracting State and paid to a resident of the other Contracting State shall, subject to the provisions of paragraph 2, be taxable only in that other State if such resident is the beneficial owner of the royalties.

2. The provisions of paragraph 1 shall not apply with respect to taxes on income if the beneficiary of the royalties carries on an industrial or commercial activity in the other Contracting State in which the royalties arise, through a permanent establishment situated therein, or performs in that other State independent personal services from a fixed base situated therein, and the right, activity or property in respect of which the royalties are paid is effectively connected with such permanent establishment or fixed base. In such a case, the royalties may be taxed solely in the State where the permanent establishment or the fixed base is situated, but only to the extent that these are attributed to that establishment or that base.

3. In each, Contracting State, the royalties that the beneficiary might have been

expected to collect if he had created a distinct and separate enterprise or if he had installed a distinct and separate place of work engaged in the same activities under the same or similar conditions independently of the center of activity of which this enterprise or this place of work constitutes a permanent establishment or a fixed base, shall be attributed to that permanent establishment or that fixed base. There shall be allowed as deductions expenses directly connected with the copyright royalties and incurred for the purposes of the permanent establishment or fixed base, including executive and general administrative expenses so incurred, whether in the State in which the permanent establishment or the fixed base is situated, or elsewhere. The royalties attributed to the permanent establishment or the fixed base shall be calculated by the same method year by year, unless there is good and sufficient reason to the contrary.

[4. If a royalty is more than the normal, intrinsic value of the rights in respect of which it is paid, the provisions in paragraphs 1 and 2 may be applied only to that part of the royalty corresponding to this normal, intrinsic value.]

2ND ALTERNATIVE

Article VI. B: Allocation of taxation between the State of residence and the State of source with the same tax ceiling in both Contracting States

1. Copyright royalties arising in a Contracting State and paid to a beneficial owner who is a resident of the other Contracting State shall be exempt in the first-mentioned State from the taxes covered under paragraph[s] 2(a) (ii) [and 2(a) (iii)] of Article II in the case of (State A) or under paragraph[s] 2(b) (ii) [and 2(b) (iii)] of Article II in the case of (State B) .

2. Where royalties are subject to income tax in the Contracting State of source according to the law of that State and in the Contracting State in which the beneficial owner is resident, the tax so charged may not exceed "*x*"% of the amount of the royalty in the State of source and "*y*"% of the gross amount of the royalty in the State of residence.

3. The provisions of paragraphs 1 and 2 shall not apply if the beneficiary of royalties, being a resident of a Contracting State, carries on an industrial or commercial activity in which the royalties arise through a permanent establishment situated therein, or performs in that other State independent personal services from a fixed base situated therein, and the right, activity or property in respect of which the royalties are paid is effectively connected with such permanent establishment or fixed base. In such a case the royalties may be taxed solely in the State where the permanent establishment or the fixed base is situated, but only so much of them as is attributable to that permanent establishment or fixed base.

4. In each Contracting State, the royalties that the beneficiary might have been

expected to collect if he had created a distinct and separate enterprise or if he had installed a distinct and separate place of work engaged in the same or similar activities under the same or similar conditions independently of the center of activity of which this enterprise or this place of work constitutes a permanent establishment or a fixed base, shall be attributed to that permanent establishment or that fixed base. There shall be allowed as deductions expenses incurred for the purpose of the permanent establishment or fixed base, including executive and general administrative expenses so incurred, whether in the State in which the permanent establishment or the fixed base is situated, or elsewhere. The royalties attributed to the permanent establishment or the fixed base shall be calculated by the same method year by year, unless there is good and sufficient reason to the contrary. [5. If a royalty is more than the normal, intrinsic value of the rights in respect of which it is paid, the provisions in paragraphs 1, 2 and 3, may be applied only to that part of the royalty corresponding to this normal, intrinsic value.]

3RD ALTERNATIVE

Article VI. C: Allocation of taxation between the State of residence and the State of source with different tax ceilings in each Contracting State

1. Copyright royalties whose source is in a Contracting State and paid to a beneficial owner who is a resident of the other Contracting State shall be taxable in both Contracting States. They shall, however, be exempt from the taxes covered by paragraph[s] 2(a) (ii) [and 2(a) (iii)] of Article II in the case of (State A) or in paragraph[s] 2(b) (ii) [and 2(b) (iii)] of Article II in the case of (State B) .

2. Where such royalties are subject to income tax in the Contracting State in which they have their source, according to the law of that State, and in the Contracting State of which the beneficiary is a resident, the tax so charged may not exceed:

(a) in the case of royalties whose source is in (State A) and paid to a resident of (State B) "*x*"% of the gross amount of the royalties in the case of the tax levied in (State A) and "*y*"% of the gross amount of the royalties in the case of the tax levied in (State B) .

(b) in the case of royalties whose source is in (State B) and paid to a resident of (State A) "*y*"% of the gross amount of the royalties in the case of the tax levied in (State A) and "*y*"% of the gross amount of the royalties in the case of the tax levied in (State B) .

3. The provisions of paragraphs 1 and 2 shall not apply if the beneficiary of the royalties, being a resident of a Contracting State, carries on business in the other Contracting State in which the royalties arise, through a permanent establishment situated therein, or performs in that other State independent personal services from a fixed base situated therein, and the right, activity or property in respect of which

the royalties are paid is effectively connected with such permanent establishment or fixed base. In such a case the royalties may be taxed solely in the State where the permanent establishment or the fixed base is situated, but only so much of them as is attributable to that permanent establishment or fixed base.

4. In each Contracting State, the royalties that the beneficiary might have been expected to collect if he had created a distinct and separate enterprise or if he had installed a distinct and separate place of work engaged in the same or similar activities under the same or similar conditions independently of the center of activity of which this enterprise or this place of work constitutes a permanent establishment or fixed base, shall be attributed to that permanent establishment or that fixed base. There shall be allowed as deductions expenses directly connected with the copyright royalties and incurred for the purposes of the permanent establishment or fixed base, including executive and general administrative expenses so incurred, whether in the State in which the permanent establishment or the fixed base is situated, or elsewhere. The royalties attributed to the permanent establishment or the fixed base shall be calculated by the same method year by year, unless there is good and sufficient reason to the contrary.

[5. If a royalty is more than the normal, intrinsic value of the rights in respect of which it is paid, the provisions in paragraphs 1, 2 and 3, may be applied only to that part of the royalty corresponding to this normal, intrinsic value.]

4TH ALTERNATIVE

Article VI. D: Taxation by the State of source

Copyright royalties whose source is in, a Contracting State and paid to a resident in the other Contracting State are taxable exclusively in the State of source of the royalties.

5TH ALTERNATIVE

Article VI. E: Allocation of taxation between the State of residence and the State of source with the tax ceiling in the State of source

1. Copyright royalties arising in a Contracting State and paid to a resident of the other Contracting State may be taxed in that other State.

2. However, such royalties may also be taxed in the Contracting State in which they arise and according to the laws of that State, but if the recipient is the beneficiary of the royalties, the tax so charged shall not exceed "*x*" % of the gross amount of the royalties. The competent authorities of the Contracting States shall by mutual

agreement settle the mode of application of this limitation.

6TH ALTERNATIVE

Article VI. F: Allocation of taxation between the State of source and that of residence with the tax ceiling in the State of residence

1. Copyright royalties whose source is in a Contracting State and which are paid to a beneficial owner resident of the other Contracting State, shall be taxable in the State of source of the royalties.

2. However, said royalties may also be taxed in the Contracting State where the beneficial owner of the royalties resides, but not to exceed "*x*"% of the gross amount of the royalties.

IV: Elimination of double taxation

Article VII: Methods for avoidance of double taxation

1st Alternative:

Article VII. A: Exemption Method

1st Alternative: Article VII. A(i) Ordinary exemption

Where a resident of a Contracting State receives royalties which, in accordance with the provisions of Article VI, may be taxed in the other Contracting State, the first-mentioned State shall exempt such royalties from the tax on the income of this resident and shall not take them into account in calculating the amount of this tax.

2nd Alternative: Article VII. A(ii) Exemption with progression

Where a resident of a Contracting State receives royalties which, in accordance with the provisions of Article VI, may be taxed in the other Contracting State, the first-mentioned State shall exempt such royalties from the tax on the income of this resident. Such State may nevertheless take into account the exempted royalties in calculating the amount of tax on the other income of this resident and may apply the same rate of tax as if the royalties in question had not been exempted.

3rd Alternative: Article VII. A(iii) Exemption maintaining taxable income

Where a resident of a Contracting State receives royalties which, in accordance with the provisions of Article VI, may be taxed in the other Contracting State, the first-mentioned State shall allow as a deduction from tax on the income of that resident, that part of the tax which is applicable to the royalties received from the other Contracting State.

2ND ALTERNATIVE

Article VII. B: Credit method

1st Alternative: Article VII. B(i) Ordinary credit

1. Where a resident of a Contracting State receives royalties which, in accordance with the provisions of Article VI, may be taxed in the other Contracting State, the first-mentioned State shall allow as a deduction from the tax on the income of that resident, an amount equal to the income tax paid in the other Contracting State. Such deduction shall not exceed that part of the income tax, as computed before the deduction is given, which is attributable to the royalties which may be taxed in the other Contracting State.
2. For the purposes of this deduction, the taxes referred to in paragraphs 2(a) (i) and 2(b) (i) of Article II shall be deemed to be income tax.

2nd Alternative: Article VII. B(ii) Full credit

1. Where a resident of a Contracting State receives royalties which, in accordance with the provisions of Article VI, may be taxed in the other Contracting State, the first-mentioned State shall allow as a deduction from the tax on the income of that resident an amount equal to the tax paid in the other Contracting State.
2. For the purposes of this deduction, the taxes referred to in paragraphs 2(a) (i) and 2(b) (i) of Article II shall be deemed to be income tax.

3rd Alternative: Article VII. B(iii) Matching credit

1. Where a resident of a Contracting State receives royalties which, in accordance with the provisions of Article VI, may be taxed in the other Contracting State, the first-mentioned State shall allow as a deduction from the tax on the income of that resident, an amount equal to ... % of the gross amount of such royalties, whether or not the amount deducted in the State where the royalties arise equals this percentage.
2. For the purpose of this deduction, the taxes referred to in paragraphs 2(a) (i) and 2(b) (i) of Article II shall be deemed to be income tax.

4th Alternative: Article VII. B(iv) Tax sparing credit

1. Where a resident of a Contracting State received royalties which, in accordance

with the provisions of Article VI, may be taxed in the other Contracting State and benefit there from special tax relief, the first-mentioned State shall allow as a deduction from the tax on the income of that resident, who is the beneficiary of royalties, an amount equal to the total sum which, without this relief, would have had to be paid in that other State as tax on such royalties.

2. For the purposes of this deduction, the taxes referred to in paragraphs 2(a) (i) and 2(b) (i) of Article II shall be deemed to be income tax.

V: Miscellaneous provisions

Article VIII: Non-discrimination

1. In accordance with the principle of non-discrimination set out in Article 6 of the Multilateral Convention for the Avoidance of Double Taxation of Copyright Royalties, the nationals of a Contracting State shall not be subjected in the other Contracting State to any taxation assessed on the amount of a copyright royalty or any requirement connected therewith, which is other or more burdensome than those to which nationals of that other State in the same circumstances are or may be subjected. Notwithstanding the provisions of Article I, this principle also applies to persons who are not residents of one or both Contracting States.

2. Stateless persons who are residents of a Contracting State shall not be subjected in either Contracting State to any taxation on copyright royalties or any requirement connected therewith, which is other or more burdensome than the taxation and connected requirements to which nationals of the State concerned in the same circumstances are or may be subjected.

3. The taxation on copyright royalties to which a permanent establishment of an enterprise of a Contracting State is subjected in the other Contracting State shall not be less favourably levied in that other State than the taxation on the same kind of copyright royalties to which enterprises of that State having the same status for tax purposes and carrying on the same activities are subjected. This provision shall not be construed as obliging a Contracting State to grant to residents of the other Contracting State any personal allowances, reliefs and reductions for taxation purposes on account of civil status or family responsibilities which it grants to its own residents.

4. Subject to the provisions of [paragraph 4 of Article VI A] [paragraph 5 of Article VI B or VI C], the royalties paid by an enterprise of a Contracting State to a resident of the other Contracting State shall, for the purpose of determining the taxable prof its of such an enterprise, be deductible under the same conditions as if they had been paid to a resident of the first-mentioned State.

5. Enterprises of a Contracting State, the capital of which is wholly or partly owned

or controlled, directly or indirectly, by one or more residents of the other Contracting State, shall not be subjected in the first-mentioned State to any taxation assessed on copyright royalties or any requirement connected therewith, which is other or more burdensome than the taxation and connected requirements to which other similar enterprises of the first-mentioned State are or may be subjected.

6. The provisions of this Article shall, notwithstanding the provisions of Article II, apply to taxes of every kind and description.

Article IX: Mutual agreement procedure

1. Where a person considers that the actions of one or both of the Contracting States result or will result for him in taxation not in accordance with the provisions of this Agreement, he may, irrespective of the remedies provided by the domestic law of those States, present his case to the competent authority of the Contracting State of which he is a resident or, if his case comes under Article VIII(1), to that of the Contracting State of which he is a national. This case must be presented within three years from the first notification of the action resulting in taxation not in accordance with the provisions of the Agreement.

2. The competent authority shall endeavour, if the objection appears to it to be justified and if it is not itself able to arrive at a satisfactory solution within a period of ... or such extended period as may be communicated by it to the competent authority of the other State, to resolve the case by mutual agreement with the competent authority of the other Contracting State, with a view to the avoidance of taxation which is not in accordance with this Agreement. Any agreement reached shall be implemented notwithstanding any time limits in the domestic law of the Contracting States.

3. The competent authorities of the Contracting States shall endeavour to resolve by agreement any difficulties or doubts arising as to the interpretation or application of the Agreement. They may also consult together for the avoidance of double taxation in cases not provided for in this Agreement.

4. The competent authorities of the Contracting States may communicate with each other directly for the purpose of reaching an agreement in the sense of paragraphs 1, 2 and 3. When it seems advisable in order to reach agreement to have an oral exchange of opinions, such exchange may take place through a Commission consisting of representatives of the competent authorities of the Contracting States.

Article X: Exchange of information

1. The competent authorities of the Contracting State shall exchange such information as is necessary for carrying out the provisions of this Agreement or of the domestic laws of the Contracting States concerning taxes covered by this Agreement in so far as the taxation thereunder is not contrary to the Agreement. The exchange

of information is not restricted by Article I of this Agreement. Any information received by a Contracting State shall be treated as secret in the same manner as information obtained under the domestic laws of that State and shall be disclosed only to persons or authorities, including courts and administrative bodies, involved in the assessment or collection of, the enforcement or prosecution in respect of, or the determination of appeals in relation to the taxes covered by this Agreement. Such persons or authorities shall use the information only for such purposes. They may disclose the information in public court proceedings or in judicial decisions.

2. In no case shall the provisions of paragraph 1 be construed so as to impose on a Contracting State the obligation:

(a) to carry out administrative measures at variance with the laws and administrative practice of that or of the other Contracting State;

(b) to supply information which is not obtainable under the laws or in the normal course of the administration of that or of the other Contracting State;

(c) to supply information which would disclose any trade, business, industrial, commercial or professional secret or trade process, or information, the disclosure of which would be contrary to public policy (ordre public) .

Article XI: Members of diplomatic or consular missions

Nothing in this Agreement shall affect the fiscal privileges of members of diplomatic or consular missions of the Contracting States as well as of their families, either under the general rules of international law or under the provisions of special conventions.

Article XII: Entry into force

1. This Agreement shall be ratified and the instruments of ratification shall be exchanged at ... as soon as possible.

2. The Agreement shall enter into force upon the exchange of instruments of ratification and its provisions shall have effect:

(a) in (State A) ...

(b) in (State B) ...

Article XIII: Termination

This Agreement shall remain in force until terminated by a Contracting State. Either Contracting State may terminate the Agreement, through diplomatic channels, by giving notice of termination at least six months before the end of any calendar year after the year ... In such event, the Agreement shall cease to have effect:

(a) in (State A) ...

(b) in (State B) ...

Article XIV: Interpretation

As regards the application of this Agreement by a Contracting State, any term not defined therein shall, unless the context otherwise requires, have the meaning which it has under the Multilateral Convention for the Avoidance of Double Taxation of Copyright Royalties or, failing this, under the law of that State.

Article XV: Relations between this agreement and other treaties on double taxation

In the event of any difference between the provisions of this Agreement and those of another treaty on double taxation concluded by the Contracting States, the provisions of this Agreement shall take precedence in the relations between these States in matters relating to the taxation of copyright royalties.

Additional protocol to the Multilateral Convention for the Avoidance of Double Taxation of Copyright Royalties

The States party to the Multilateral Convention for the Avoidance of Double Taxation of Copyright Royalties (hereinafter called "the Convention") that are party to this Protocol have accepted the following provisions:

1. The provisions of the Convention also apply to the taxation of royalties paid to performers, producers of phonograms and broadcasting organizations in respect of rights related to copyright or "neighboring" rights, in so far as the latter royalties arise in a State party to this Protocol and their beneficiaries are residents of another State party to this Protocol.

2. (a) This Protocol shall be signed and shall be subject to ratification, acceptance or accession by the signatory States, or may be acceded to, in accordance with the provisions of Article 11 of the Convention.

(b) This Protocol shall enter into force in accordance with the provisions of Article 13 of the Convention.

(c) Any Contracting State may denounce this Protocol in accordance with provisions of Article 14 of the Convention, it being understood, however, that a Contracting State denouncing the Convention must at the same time also denounce this Protocol.

(d) The provisions of Article 16 of the Convention shall apply to this Protocol.

IN WITNESS WHEREOF, the undersigned, being duly authorized, have signed this Protocol.

Done at Madrid on December 13, 1979.

Treaty on the International Registration of Audiovisual Works

Contents

The Contracting States

Desirous to increase the legal security in transactions relating to audiovisual works and thereby

to enhance the creation of audiovisual works and the international flow of such works and to contribute to the fight against piracy of audiovisual works and contributions contained therein;

Have agreed as follows:

CHAPTER I

SUBSTANTIVE PROVISIONS

Article 1
Establishment of the Union

The States party to this Treaty (hereinafter called "the Contracting States") constitute a Union for the international registration of audiovisual works (hereinafter referred to as "the Union").

Article 2
"Audiovisual Work"

For the purposes of this Treaty, "audiovisual work" means any work that consists of a series of fixed related images, with or without accompanying sound, susceptible of being made visible and, where accompanied by sound, susceptible of being made audible.

Article 3
The International Register

(1) [*Establishment of the International Register*] The International Register of Audiovisual Works (hereinafter referred to as "the International Register") is hereby established for the purpose of the registration of statements concerning audiovisual works and rights in such works, including, in particular, rights relating to their exploitation.

(2) [*Setting Up and Administration of the International Registry*] The International Registry of Audiovisual Works (hereinafrer referred to as "the International Registry") is hereby set up for the purpose of keeping the International Register. It is an administrative unit of the International Bureau of the World Intellectual Property Organization (hereinafter referred to as "the International Bureau" and "the Organization," respectively).

(3) [*Location of the International Registry*] The International Registry shall be located in Austria as long as a treaty to that effect between the Republic of Austria and the Organization is in force. Otherwise, it shall be located in Geneva.

(4) [*Applications*] The registration of any statement in the International

Register shall be based on an application filed to this effect, with the prescribed contents, in the prescribed form and subject to the payment of the prescribed fee, by a natural person or legal entity entitled to file an application.

(5) [*Eligibility for Being an Applicant*] (a) Subject to subparagraph (b) , the following shall be entitled to file an application:

(i) any natural person who is a national of, is domiciled in, has his habitual residence in, or has a real and effective industrial or commercial establishment in, a Contracting State;

(ii) any legal entity which is organized under the laws of, or has a real and effective industrial or commercial establishment in, a Contracting State.

(b) If the application concerns a registration already effected, it may also be filed by a natural person or legal entity not satisfying the conditions referred to in subparagraph (a) .

Article 4

Legal Effect of the International Register

(1) [*Legal Effect*] Each Contracting State undertakes to recognize that a statement recorded in the International Register shall be considered as true until the contrary is proved, except

(i) where the statement cannot be valid under the copyright law, or any other law concerning intellectual property rights in audiovisual works, of that State, or

(ii) where the statement is contradicted by another statement recorded in the International Register.

(2) [*Safeguard of Intellectual Property Laws and Treaties*] No provision of this Treaty shall be interpreted as affecting the copyright law, or any other law concerning intellectual property rights in audiovisual works, of any Contracting State or, if that State is party to the Berne Convention for the Protection of Literary and Artistic Works or any other treaty concerning intellectual property rights in audiovisual works, the rights and obligations of the said State under the said Convention or treaty.

CHAPTER II

ADMINISTRATIVE PROVISIONS

Article 5

Assembly

(1) [*Composition*] (a) The Union shall have an Assembly that shall consist of the Contracting States.

(b) The Government of each Contracting State shall be represented by one delegate, who may be assisted by alternate delegates, advisors and experts.

(2) [*Expenses of Delegations*] The expenses of each delegation shall be borne by the Government which has appointed it, except for the travel expenses and the subsistence allowance of one delegate for each Contraaing State, which shall be paid from the funds of the Union.

(3) [*Tasks*] (a) The Assembly shall:

(i) deal with all matters concerning the maintenance and development of the Union and the implementation of this Treaty;

(ii) exercise such tasks as are specially assigned to it under this Treaty;

(iii) give directions to the Director General of the Organization (hereinafter referred to as "the Director General"), concerning the preparation for revision conferences;

(iv) review and approve the reports and activities of the Director General concerning the Union, and give him all necessary instructions concerning matters within the competence of the Union;

(v) determine the program and adopt the biennial budget of the Union, and approve its final accounts;

(vi) adopt the financial regulations of the Union;

(vii) establish, and decide from time to time the membership of, a consultative committee consisting of representatives of interested non-governmental organizations and such other committees and working groups as it deems appropriate to facilitate the work of the Union and of its organs;

(viii) control the system and amounts of the fees determined by the Director General;

(ix) determine which States other than Contracting States and which intergovernmental and non-governmental organizations shall be admitted to its meetings as observers;

(x) take any other appropriate action designed to further the objectives of the Union and perform such other functions as are appropriate under this Treaty.

(b) With respect to matters which are of interest also to other Unions administered by the Organization, the Assembly shall make its decisions afier having heard the advice of the Coordination Committee of the Organization.

(4) [*Representation*] A delegate may represent, and vote in the name of, one State only.

(5) [*Vote*] Each Contracting State shall have one vote.

(6) [*Quorum*] (a) One-half of the Contracting States shall constitute a quorum.

(b) In the absence of the quorum, the Assembly may make decisions but, with the exception of the decisions concerning its own procedure, all such decisions shall take effect only if the quorum and the required majority are attained through voting by correspondence.

(7) [*Majority*] (a) Subject to Article 8(2)(b) and Article 10(2)(b) , the decisions of the Assembly shall require a majority of the votes cast.

(b) Abstentions shall not be considered as votes.

(8) [*Sessions*] (a) The Assembly shall meet once in every second calendar year in ordinary session upon convocation by the Director General and, in the absence of exceptional circumstances, during the same period and at the same place as the General Assembly of the Organization.

(b) The Assembly shall meet in extraordinary session upon convocation by the Director General, either at the request of one-fourth of the Contracting States or on the Director General's own initiative.

(9) [*Rules of Procedure*] The Assembly shall adopt its own rules of procedure.

Article 6
International Bureau

(1) [*Tasks*] The International Bureau shall:

(i) perform, through the International Registry, all the tasks related to the keeping of the International Register;

(ii) provide the secretariat of revision conferences, of the Assembly, of the committees and working groups established by the Assembly, and of any other meeting convened by the Director General and dealing with matters of concern to the Union;

(iii) perform all other tasks specially assigned to it under this Treaty and the Regulations referred to in Article 8 or by the Assembly.

(2) [*Director General*] The Director General shall be the chief executive of the Union and shall represent the Union.

(3) [*Meetings Other Than Sessions of the Assembly*] The Director General shall convene any committee and working group established by the Assembly and all other meetings dealing with matters of concern to the Union.

(4) [*Role of the International Bureau in the Assembly and Other Meetings*] (a) The Director General and any staff member designated by him shall participate, without the right to vote, in all meetings of the Assembly, the committees and working groups established by the Assembly, and any other meeting convened by the Director General and dealing with matters of concern to the Union.

(b) The Director General or a staff member designated by him shall be *ex officio* secretary of the Assembly, and of the committees, working groups and other meetings referred to in subparagraph (a) .

(5) [*Revision Conferences*] (a) The Director General shall, in accordance with the directions of the Assembly, make the preparations for revision conferences.

(b) The Director General may consult with Intergovernmental and non-governmental organizations concerning the said preparations.

(c) The Director General and staff members designated by him shall take part, without the right to vote, in the discussions at revision conferences.

(d) The Director General or a staff member designated by him shall be *ex officio* secretary of any revision conference.

Article 7
Finances

(l) [*Budget*] (a) The Union shall have a budget.

(b) The budget of the Union shall include the income and expenses proper to the Union, and its contribution to the budget of expenses common to the Unions administered by the Organization.

(c) Expenses not attributable exclusively to the Union but also to one or more other Unions administered by the Organization shall be considered as expenses common to the Unions. The share of the Union in such common expenses shall be in proportion to the interest the Union has in them.

(2) [*Coordination with Other Budgets*] The budget of the Union shall be established with due regard to the requirements of coordination with the budgets of the other Unions administered by the Organization.

(3) [*Sources of Income*] The budget of the Union shall be financed from the following sources:

(i) fees due for registrations and other services rendered by the International Registry;

(ii) sale of, or royalties on, the publications of the International Registry;

(iii) donations, particularly by associations of rights holders in audiovisual works;

(iv) gifts, bequests, and subventions;

(v) rents, interests, and other miscellaneous income.

(4) [*Self Supporting Financing*] The amounts of fees due to the International Registry and the prices of its publications shall be so fixed that they, together with any other income, should be sufficient to cover the expenses connected with the administration of this Treaty.

(5) [*Continuation of Budget; Reserve Fund*] If the budget is not adopted before the beginning of a new financial period, it shall be at the same level as the budget of the previous period, as provided in the financial regulations. If the income exceeds the expenses, the difference shall be credited to a reserve fund.

(6) [*Working Capital Fund*] The Union shall have a working capital fund which shall be constituted from the income of the Union.

(7) [*Auditing of Accounts*] The auditing of the accounts shall be effected by one

or more of the Contracting States or by external auditors, as provided in the financial regulations. They shall be designated, with their agreement, by the Assembly.

Article 8
Regulations

(1) [*Adoption of Regulations*] The Regulations adopted at the same time as this Treaty are annexed io this Treaty.

(2) [*Amending the Regulations*] (a) The Assembly may amend the Regulations.

(b) Any amendment of the Regulations shall require two-thirds of the votes cast.

(3) [*Conflict between the Treaty and the Regulations*] In the case of conflict between the provisions of this Treaty and those of the Regulations, the former shall prevail.

(4) [*Administrative Instructions*] The Regulations provide for the establishment of Administrative Instructions.

CHAPTER III

REVISION AND AMENDMENT

Article 9
Revision of the Treaty

(1) [*Revision Conferences*] This Treaty may be revised by a conference of the Contracting States.

(2) [*Convocation*] The convocation of any revision conference shall be decided by the Assembly.

(3) [*Provisions That Can Be Amended Also by the Assembly*] The provisions referred to in Article 10(l)(a) may be amended either by a revision conference or according to Article 10.

Article 10
Amendment of Certain Provisions of the Treaty

(l) [*Proposals*] (a) Proposals for the amendment of Article 5(6) and (8), Article 6(4) and (5) and Article 7(1) to (3) and (5) to (7) may be initiated by any Contracting State or by the Director General.

(b) Such proposals shall be communicated by the Director General to the Contracting States at least six months in advance of their consideration by the Assembly.

(2) [*Adoption*] (a) Amendments to the provisions referred to in paragraph (1) shall be adopted by the Assembly.

(b) Adoption shall require three-fourths of the votes cast.

(3) [*Enty Into Force*] (a) Any amendment to the provisions referred to in paragraph (1) shall enter into force one month after written notifications of acceptance, effected in accordance with their respective constitutional processes, have been received by the Director General from three-fourths of the Contracting States members of the Assembly at the time the Assembly adopted the amendment.

(b) Any amendment to the said Articles thus accepted shall bind all the Contracting States which were Contracting States at the time the amendment was adopted by the Assembly.

(c) Any amendment which has been accepted and which has entered into force in accordance with subparagraph (a) shall bind all States which become Contracting States after the date on which the amendment was adopted by the Assembly.

CHAPTER IV

FINAL PROVISIONS

Article 11

Becoming Party to the Treaty

(1) [*Adherence*] Any State member of the Organization may become party to this Treaty by:

(i) signature followed by the deposit of an instrument of ratification, acceptance or approval, or

(ii) the deposit of an instrument of accession.

(2) [*Deposit of Instruments*] The instruments referred to in paragraph (1) shall be deposited with the Director General.

Article 12

Entry Into Force of the Treaty

(1) [*Initial Entry Into Force*] This Treaty shall enter into force, with respect to the first five States which have deposited their instruments of ratification, acceptance, approval or accession, three months after the date on which the fifth instrument of ratification, acceptance, approval or accession has been deposited.

(2) [*States Not Covered by the Initial Entry Into Force*] This Treaty shall enter into force with respect to any State not covered by paragraph (1) three months after the date on which that State has deposited its instrument of ratification, acceptance, approval or accession unless a later date has been indicated in the instrument of ratification, acceptance, approval or accession. In the latter case, this Treaty shall enter into force with respect to the said State on the date thus indicated.

Article 13

Reservations to the Treaty

(1) [*Principle*] Subject to paragraph (2), no reservation may be made to this Treaty.

(2) [*Exception*] Any State, upon becoming party to this Treaty, may, in a notification deposited with the Director General, declare that it will not apply the provisions of Article 4(1) in respect of statements which do not concern the exploitation of intellectual property rights in audiovisual works. Any State that has made such a declaration may, by a notification deposited with the Director General, withdraw it.

Article 14

Denunciation of the Treaty

(1) [*Notification*] Any Contracting State may denounce this Treaty by notification addressed to the Director General.

(2) [*Effective Date*] Denunciation shall take effect one year after the day on which the Director General has received the notification.

(3) [*Moratorium on Denunciation*] The right of denouncing this Treaty provided for in paragraph (1) shall not be exercised by any Contracting State before the expiration of five years from the date on which this Treaty enters into force with respect to it.

Article 15

Signature and Languages of the Treaty

(1) [*Original Texts*] This Treaty shall be signed in a single original in the English and French languages, both texts being equally authentic.

(2) [*Official Texts*] Official texts shall be established by the Director General, after consultation with the interested Governments, in the Arabic, German, Italian, Japanese, Portuguese, Russian and Spanish languages, and such other languages as the Assembly may designate.

(3) [*Time Limit for Signature*] This Treaty shall remain open for signature at the International Bureau until December 31, 1989.

Article 16

Depositary Functions

(1) [*Deposit of the Original*] The original of this Treaty and the Regulations shall be deposited with the Director General.

(2) [*Certified Copies*] The Director General shall transmit two copies, certified by him, of this Treaty and the Regulations, to the Governments of States entitled to sign this Treaty.

(3) [*Registration of the Treaty*] The Director General shall register this Treaty

with the Secretariat of the United Nations.

(4) [*Amendments*] The Director General shall transmit two copies, certified by him, of any amendment to this Treaty and the Regulations to the Governments of the Contracting States and, on request, to the Government of any other State.

Article 17
Notifications

The Director General shall notify the Governments of the States members of the Organization of any of the events referred to in Articles 8(2), 10(2) and (3), 11, 12, 13 and 14.

Done at Geneva, on April 20, 1989.

Regulations under the Treaty on the International Registration of Audiovisual Works

(as in force since February 28, 1991)*

Contents

Rule 1
Definitions

For the purposes of these Regulations,

(i) "Treaty" means the Treaty on the International Registration of Audiovisual Works;

(ii) "International Register" means the International Register of Audiovisual Works established by the Treaty;

---

* Adopted on April 18, 1989, as modified on February 28, 1991.

(iii) "International Registry" means the administrative unit of the International Bureau that keeps the International Register;

(iv) "work" means audiovisual work;

(v) "work-related application" means an application that identifies an existing or future work at least by its title or titles and requests that statements in respect of the interest of an identified person or identified persons in or concerning that work be registered in the International Register; "work-related registration" means a registration effected pursuant to a work-related application;

(vi) "person-related application" means an application that describes one or more existing or future work or works, not identified by its or their title or titles, at least by indicating the natural person who or legal entity which has made, or owns, or is expected to make or own, the work or works, and requests that statements in respect of the interest of the applicant, or of a third person identified in the application, be registered in the International Register; "person-related registration" means a registration effected pursuant to a person-related application;

(vii) "application" or "registration"—unless qualified as "work-related" or "person-related"—means both a work-related and a person-related application or registration;

(viii) "applicant" means the natural person who or the legal entity which filed the application; "holder of the registration" means the applicant once the application has been registered;

(ix) "prescribed" means as prescribed in the Treaty, in these Regulations or in the Administrative Instructions;

(x) "Consultative Committee" means the consultative committee referred to in Article 5(3)(a) (vii) of the Treaty.

Rule 1bis

Eligibility in the Case of Several Applicants

Where more than one natural person or legal entity files the same application, the requirements specified in Article 3(5)(a) of the Treaty shall be considered as fulfilled if any of them is entitled to file an application under the said Article.

Rule 2

Application

(1) [*Forms*] Any application shall be filed by using the appropriate prescribed form.

(2) [*Language*] Any application shall be in the English language or in the French language. As soon as the International Register is financially

self-supporting, the Assembly may determine the other languages in which applications may be filed.

(3) [*Name and Address of Applicant*] Any application shall indicate, as prescribed, the name and address of the applicant.

(4) [*Name and Address of Certain Third Persons Referred to in the Application*] Where an application refers to a natural person or legal entity, other than the applicant, from whom or from which a right of exploitation is derived, or to whom or to which such a right is assigned, licensed or otherwise transferred, the application shall indicate, as prescribed, the name and address of such person or entity.

(5) [*Title or Description of the Work*] (a) Any work-related application shall indicate at least the title or titles of the work. When a title is in a language other than English or French or in a script other than the Latin script, it shall be accompanied by a literal translation into English or a transliteration into Latin script, as the case may be.

(b) Any person-related application shall describe the work or works in which the applicant has an interest. It shall do so by at least indicating the natural person who or the legal entity which has made or owns, or is expected to make or own, the work or works.

(6) [*Reference to Existing Registration*] When the application relates to a work which is the subject matter of an existing work-related registration, or to a work which is described in an existing person-related registration, the said application shall, whenever possible, indicate the registration number of the said registration. If the International Registry finds that such an indication would be possible but was not given in the application, it may, itself, indicate such number in the registration, subject to noting in the International Register that the indication comes from the International Registry rather than the applicant.

(7) [*Interest of the Applicant*] (a) In any work-related application, the application shall indicate the interest of the applicant in or concerning the work, whether existing or future. Where the interest consists of a right of exploitation of the work, the nature of the right and the territory for which the right belongs to the applicant shall also be indicated.

(b) In any person-related application, the application shall indicate the interest of the applicant in or concerning the described, existing or future, work or works, in particular any right that limits or negates, for the benefit of the applicant or another person, the right of exploitation of the work or works.

(c) Where the interest is limited in time, the application may express such a limit.

(8) [*Source of Rights*] Where a work-related application concerns a right in the work, the application shall indicate, where the right originally vested in the applicant, that fact, or, where the right is derived from a natural person or legal entity

other than the applicant, the name and address of such person or entity and the legal cause of the derivation.

(9) [*Accompanying Documents and Identifying Material*] (a) Any application may be accompanied by documents supporting the statements contained in the application. Any such document in a language other than English or French shall be accompanied, in English, by an indication of the nature and essence of the document; otherwise, the International Registry shall treat the document as if it had not been attached.

(b) Any application may be accompanied by material, other than documents, susceptible of identifying the work.

(10) [*Statement of Veracity*] The application shall contain a statement to the effect that the statements contained therein are, to the knowledge of the applicant, true, and that any accompanying document is an original or is a true copy of an original.

(11) [*Signature*] The application shall be signed by the applicant or by his representative appointed as provided in paragraph (12).

(12) [*Representation*] (a) Any applicant or holder of the registration may be represented by a representative who may be appointed in the application, in a separate power of attorney relating to a specific application or registration, or in a general power of attorney, signed by the applicant or holder of the registration.

(b) A general power of attorney enables the representative to represent the applicant or holder of the registration in connection with all the applications or registrations of the person having given the general power of attorney.

(c) Any appointment of a representative shall be in force until it is revoked in a communication signed by the person who made the appointment and addressed to the International Registry or until it is renounced by the representative in a communication signed by the representative and addressed to the International Registry.

(d) The International Registry shall address to the representative any communication intended for the applicant or holder of the registration under these Regulations; any communication so addressed to the representative shall have the same effect as if it had been addressed to the applicant or holder of the registration. Any communication addressed to the International Registry by the representative shall have the same effect as if it had originated with the applicant or holder of the registration.

(13) [*Fees*] For each application, the applicant shall indicate the prescribed data necessary for the calculation of the fee and pay the prescribed fee, which must reach the International Registry not later than the day on which the application is received by the International Registry. If the prescribed data necessary for the calculation of the fee is communicated to the International Registry and the prescribed fee reaches the International Registry within 30 days from the date on which the application

was actually received by the International Registry, the application shall be considered as having been received by the International Registry on the date on which the prescribed data necessary for the calculation of the fee had been communicated to the International Registry and the prescribed fee has reached the International Registry, whichever occurs later.

Rule 3
Processing of the Application

(1) [*Corrections*] If the International Registry notices what it believes to be an inadvertent omission, two or more statements conflicting with each other, a mistake of transcription, or another obvious error, in the application, it shall invite the applicant to correct the application. Any correction by the applicant must, in order to be taken into consideration, reach the International Registry within 30 days from the date of the invitation to correct the application.

(2) [*Giving Possibility to Remove Contradictions*] (a) Where, in the opinion of the International Registry, any statement contained in an application is in contradiction to any statement that, on the basis of an earlier application, is the subject matter of an existing registration in the International Register, the International Registry shall immediately,

(i) where the applicant is also the holder of the existing registration, send him a notification asking him whether he wishes to either modify the statement contained in the application or apply for the modification of the statement that is subject matter of the existing registration,

(ii) where the applicant and the holder of the existing registration are not the same, send a notification to the applicant asking him whether he wishes to modify the statement contained in the application and, at the same time, send a notification to the holder of the existing registration asking the said holder whether—in case the applicant does not wish to modify the statement appearing in the application—he wishes to apply for the modification of the statement in the existing registration.

The registration of the application shall be suspended until a modification is submitted that, in the opinion of the International Registry, removes the contradiction, but for no longer than 60 days from the date of the said notification or notifications, unless the applicant asks for a longer period, in which case it will be suspended until the expiration of that longer period.

(b) The fact that the International Registry failed to notice the contradictory nature of a statement shall not be considered as removing that nature of the statement.

(3) [*Rejection*] (a) In the following cases, the International Registry shall, subject to paragraphs (1) and (2), reject the application:

(i) where the application does not contain a statement which, on the face of it, shows that the requirements of Article 3(5) of the Treaty are met;

(ii) where, in the opinion of the International Registry, the application does not relate to a work, whether existing or future;

(iii) where the application does not meet any of the requirements of Rule 2(2), (3), (4), (5), (7)(a) and (b) , (8), (10), (11) and(13)

(b) The International Registry may reject the application where the application does not fulfill the prescribed conditions as to its form.

(c) No application shall be rejected for any reason other than those referred to in subparagraphs (a) and (b) .

(d) Any decision of rejection under this paragraph shall be communicated in writing by the International Registry to the applicant. The applicant may, within 30 days from the date of the communication, request in writing the International Registry to reconsider its decision. The International Registry shall reply to the request within 30 days from the date of receipt of the said request.

(4) [*Notice in the International Register of Receipt of the Application*] If, for any reason, the International Registry, within three working days from the receipt of the application, does not register the application, it shall enter into the data base of the International Registry, open for consultation to the public, the essential elements of the application, and an indication of the reason for which no registration has taken place and, if the reason is related to paragraphs (1), (2)(a) or (3)(d), an indication of the measures taken under any of those provisions. If and when the registration is effected, the said entry in the data base shall be erased.

Rule 4

Date and Number of the Registration

(1) [*Date*] The International Registry shall allot, subject to Rule 2(13), as the filing date, to each application, the date of receipt of the application. Where the application is registered, it shall be given, as registration date, the filing date.

(2) [*Number*] The International Registry shall allot a number to each application. If the application refers to a work whose title appears in an existing work-related registration, or which is described in an existing person-related registration, the number allotted shall also contain the number of that registration. Any registration number shall consist of the application number.

Rule 5

Registration

(1) [*Registration*] Where an application is not rejected, all the statements contained therein shall, as prescribed, be registered in the International Register.

(2) [*Notification and Publication of the Registration*] Any registration effected

shall, as prescribed, be notified to the applicant and published in the Gazette referred to in Rule 6.

Rule 6
The Gazette

(1) [*Publication*] The International Registry shall publish a gazette ("the Gazette") in which it shall indicate the prescribed elements in respect of all registrations. The Gazette shall be in English, provided that elements concerning applications that were filed in French shall also be in French.

(2) [*Sale*] The International Registry shall offer, against payment, both yearly subscriptions to the Gazette and single copies of the Gazette. The amount of the prices shall be fixed in the same manner as the amount of the fees is fixed according to Rule 8(1).

Rule 7
Inquiries

(1) [*Information and Copies*] The International Registry shall, against the payment of the prescribed fee, furnish information concerning any registration and certified copies of any registration certificate or document concerning such registration.

(2) [*Certificates*] The International Registry shall, against the payment of the prescribed fee, furnish a certificate answering questions about the existence, in the International Register, of statements concerning specific matters in any registration or any document or material that has been attached to the application.

(3) [*Inspection*] The International Registry shall, against the payment of the prescribed fee, allow the inspection of any application, as well as of any document or material that has been attached to the application.

(4) [*Monitoring Service*] The International Registry shall, against the payment of the prescribed fee, give written information, promptly after each registration is effected,

(i) on all registrations effected in respect of a given work;

(ii) in respect of all registrations that concern a given natural person or legal entity, provided that it is the person or entity concerned, or a third person authorized by the person or entity concerned, who or which requests such a service.

(5) [*Computerized Memory*] The International Registry may input into computer memory all or part of the contents of the International Register, and, in performing any of the services referred to in paragraphs (1) to (4) or in Rule 3(4), it may rely on that memory.

Rule 8

Fees

(1) [*Fixing of the Fees*] Before determining the system and amounts of the fees, and before making any changes in that system or amounts, the Director General shall consult the Consultative Committee. The Assembly may instruct the Director General to change the said system, the said amounts, or both.

(2) [*Reduction of Fees for Applicants from Developing Countries*] The amounts of the fees shall be reduced initially by 15% where the applicant is a natural person who is a national of, or a legal entity which is organized under the laws of, a Contracting State that is regarded as a developing country in conformity with the established practice of the General Assembly of the United Nations. The Assembly shall periodically examine the possibility of increasing the percentage of the said reduction.

(3) [*Entry into Effect of Changes in the Fees*] Any increase in the amounts of the fees shall not be retroactive. The date of the entry into effect of any change shall be fixed by the Director General or, where the change is on instruction by the Assembly, by the Assembly. Such date shall be indicated when the change is published in the Gazette. It shall not be sooner than one month after the publication in the Gazette.

(4) [*Currency and Manner of Payment*] The fees shall be paid in the prescribed manner and in the prescribed currency or, if several currencies are admitted, in the currency that the applicant chooses among the said currencies.

Rule 9

Administrative Instructions

(1) [*Scope*] (a) The Administrative Instructions shall contain provisions concerning details in respect of the administration of the Treaty and these Regulations.

(b) In the case of conflict between the provisions of the Treaty or these Regulations and those of the Administrative Instructions, the former shall prevail.

(2) [*Source*] (a) The Administrative Instructions shall be drawn up, and may be modified, by the Director General after consultation of the Consultative Committee.

(b) The Assembly may instruct the Director General to modify the Administrative Instructions, and the Director General shall modify them accordingly.

(3) [*Publication and Entry into Force*] (a) The Administrative Instructions and any modification thereof shall be published in the Gazette.

(b) Each publication shall specify the date on which the published provisions come into effect. The dates may be different for different provisions, provided that no provision may be declared effective prior to its publication in the Gazette.

Treaty on Intellectual Property in Respect of Integrated Circuits

Adopted at Washington, on May 26, 1989

Contents

Article 1
Establishment of a Union

The Contracting Parties constitute themselves into a Union for the purposes of this Treaty.

Article 2
Definitions

For the purposes of this Treaty:

(i) "integrated circuit" means a product, in its final form or an intermediate form, in which the elements, at least one of which is an active element, and some or all of the interconnections are integrally formed in and/or on a piece of material and which is intended to perform an electronic function,

(ii) "layout-design (topography)" means the three-dimensional disposition, however expressed, of the elements, at least one of which is an active element, and of some or all of the interconnections of an integrated circuit, or such a three-dimensional disposition prepared for an integrated circuit intended for manufacture,

(iii) "holder of the right" means the natural person who, or the legal entity which, according to the applicable law, is to be regarded as the beneficiary of the protection referred to in Article 6,

(iv) "protected layout-design (topography)" means a layout-design (topography) in respect of which the conditions of protection referred to in this Treaty are fulfilled,

(v) "Contracting Party" means a State, or an Intergovernmental Organization meeting the requirements of item (x), party to this Treaty,

(vi) "territory of a Contracting Party" means, where the Contracting Party is a State, the territory of that State and, where the Contracting Party is an Intergovernmental Organization, the territory in which the constituting treaty of that Intergovernmental Organization applies,

(vii) "Union" means the Union referred to in Article l,

(viii) "Assembly" means the Assembly referred to in Article 9,

(ix) "Director General" means the Director General of the World Intellectual Property Organization,

(x) "Intergovernmental Organization" means an organization constituted by, and composed of, States of any region of the world, which has competence in respect of matters governed by this Treaty, has its own legislation providing for intellectual property protection in respect of layout-designs (topographies) and binding on all its member States, and has been duly authorized, in accordance with its internal procedures, to sign, ratify, accept, approve or accede to this Treaty.

Article 3
The Subject Matter of the Treaty

(1) [*Obligation to Protect Layout-Designs (Topographies)*]

(a) Each Contracting Party shall have the obligation to secure, throughout its territory, intellectual property protection in respect of layout-designs (topographies) in accordance with this Treaty. It shall, in particular, secure adequate measures to ensure the prevention of acts considered unlawful under Article 6 and appropriate legal remedies where such acts have been committed.

(b) The right of the holder of the right in respect of an integrated circuit applies whether or not the integrated circuit is incorporated in an article.

(c) Notwithstanding Article 2(i), any Contracting Party whose law limits the protection of layout-designs (topographies) to layout-designs (topographies) of semi-conductor integrated circuits shall be free to apply that limitation as long as its law contains such limitation.

(2) [*Requirement of Originality*]

(a) The obligation referred to in paragraph (l)(a) shall apply to layout-designs (topographies) that are original in the sense that they are the result of their creators' own intellectual effort and are not commonplace among creators of lavout-designs (topographies) and manufacturers of integrated circuits at the time of their creation.

(b) A layout-design (topography) that consists of a combination of elements and interconnections that are commonplace shall be protected only If the combination, taken as a whole, fulfills the conditions referred to in subparagraph (a) .

Article 4

The Legal Form of the Protection

Each Contracting Party shall be free to implement its obligations under this Treaty through a special law on layout-designs (topographies) or its law on copy-right, patents, utility models, industrial designs, unfair competition or any other law or a combination of any of those laws.

Article 5

National Treatment

(1) [*National Treatment*]

Subject to compliance with its obligation referred to in Article 3(l)(a) , each Contracting Party shall, in respect of the intellectual property protection of layout-designs (topographies), accord, within its territory,

(i) to natural persons who are nationals of, or are domiciled in the territory of, any of the other Contracting Parties, and

(ii) to legal entities which or natural persons who, in the territory of any of the other Contracting Parties, have a real and effective establishment for the creation of layout-designs (topographies) or the production of integrated circuits,

the same treatment that it accords to its own nationals.

(2) [*Agents, Addresses for Service, Court Proceedings*]

Notwithstanding paragraph (1), any Contracting Party is free not to apply national treatment as far as any obligations to appoint an agent or to designate an address for service are concerned or as far as the special rules applicable to foreigners in court proceedings are concerned.

(3) [*Application of Paragraphs (1) and (2) to Intergovernmental Organizations*]

Where the Contracting Party is an Intergovernmental Organization, "nationals" in paragraph (1) means nationals of any of the States members of that Organization.

Article 6
The Scope of the Protection

(1) [*Acts Requiring the Authorization of the Holder of the Right*]

(a) Any Contracting Party shall consider unlawful the following acts if performed without the authorization of the holder of the right:

(i) the act of reproducing, whether by incorporation in an integrated circuit or otherwise, a protected layout-design (topography) in its entirety or any part there of, except the act of reproducing any part that does not comply with the requirement of originality referred to in Article 3(2),

(ii) the act of importing, selling or otherwise distributing for commercial purposes a protected layout-design (topography) or an integrated circuit in which a protected layout-design (topography) is incorporated.

(b) Any Contracting Party shall be free to consider unlawful also acts other than those specified in subparagraph (a) if performed without the authorization of the holder of the right.

(2) [*Acts Not Requiring the Authorization of the Holder of the Right*]

(a) Notwithstanding paragraph (1), no Contracting Party shall consider unlawful the performance, without the authorization of the holder of the right, of the act of reproduction referred to in paragraph (1)(a) (i) where that act is performed by a third party for private purposes or for the sole purpose of evaluation, analysis, research or teaching.

(b) Where the third party referred to in subparagraph (a), on the basis of evaluation or analysis of the protected layout-design (topography) ("the first layout-design (topography)"), creates a layout-design (topography) complying with the requirement of originality referred to in Article 3(2) ("the second layout-design (topography)"), that third party may incorporate the second layout-design (topography) in an integrated circuit or perform any of the acts referred to in paragraph (1) in respect of the second layout-design (topography) without being regarded as infringing the rights of the holder of the right in the first layout-design (topography).

(c) The holder of the right may not exercise his right in respect of an identical original layout-design (topography) that was independently created by a third party.

(3) [*Measures Concerning Use Without the Consent of the Holder of the Right*]

(a) Notwithstanding paragraph (1), any Contracting Party may, in its legislation, provide for the possibility of its executive or judicial authority granting a non-exclusive license, in circumstances that are not ordinary, for the performance of any of the acts referred to in paragraph (1) by a third party without the authorization of the holder of the right ("non-voluntary license"), after unsuccessful efforts, made by the said third party in line with normal commercial practices, to obtain such authorization, where the granting of the non-voluntary license is found, by the granting authority, to be necessary to safeguard a national purpose deemed to be vital by that authority; the non-voluntary license shall be available for exploitation only in the territory of that country and shall be subject to the payment of an equitable remuneration by the third party to the holder of the right.

(b) The provisions of this Treaty shall not affect the freedom of any Contracting Party to apply measures, including the granting, after a formal proceeding by its executive or judicial authority, of a non-voluntary license, in application of its laws in order to secure free competition and to prevent abuses by the holder of the right.

(c) The granting of any non-voluntary license referred to in subparagraph (a) or subparagraph (b) shall be subject to judicial review. Any non-voluntary license referred to in subparagraph (a) shall be revoked when the conditions referred to in that subparagraph cease to exist.

(4) [*Sale and Distribution of Infringing Integrated Circuits Acquired Innocently*]

Notwithstanding paragraph (l)(a) (ii), no Contracting Party shall be obliged to consider unlawful the performance of any of the acts referred to in that paragraph in respect of an integrated circuit incorporating an unlawfully reproduced layout-design (topography) where the person performing or ordering such acts did not know and had no reasonable ground to know, when acquiring the said integrated circuit, that it incorporates an unlawfully reproduced layout-design (topography).

(5) [*Exhaustion of Rights*]

Notwithstanding paragraph (l)(a) (ii), any Contracting Party may consider lawful the performance, without the authorization of the holder of the right, of any of the acts referred to in that paragraph where the act is performed in respect of a protected layout-design (topography), or in respect of an integrated circuit in which such a layout-design (topography) is incorporated, that has been put on the market by, or with the consent of, the holder of the right.

Article 7
Exploitation; Registration, Disclosure

(1) [*Faculty to Require Exploitation*]

Any Contracting Party shall be free not to protect a layout-design (topography) until it has been ordinarily commercially exploited, separately or as incorporated in an integrated circuit, somewhere in the world.

(2) [*Faculty to Require Registration; Disclosure*]

(a) Any Contracting Party shall be free not to protect a layout-design (topography) until the layout-design (topography) has been the subject of an application for registration, filed in due form with the competent public authority, or of a registration with that authority; it may be required that the application be accompanied by the filing of a copy or drawing of the layout-design (topography) and, where the integrated circuit has been commercially exploited, of a sample of that integrated circuit, along with information defining the electronic function which the integrated circuit is intended to perform; however, the applicant may exclude such parts of the copy or drawing that relate to the manner of manufacture of the integrated circuit, provided that the parts submitted are sufficient to allow the identification of the layout-design (topography).

(b) Where the filing of an application for registration according to subparagraph (a) is required, the Contracting Party may require that such filing be effected within a certain period of time from the date on which the holder of the right first exploits ordinarily commercially anywhere in the world the layout-design (topography) of an integrated circuit; such period shall not be less than two years counted from the said date.

(c) Registration under subparagraph (a) may be subject to the payment of a fee.

Article 8
The Duration of the Protection

Protection shall last at least eight years.

Article 9
Assembly

(1) [*Composition*]

(a) The Union shall have an Assembly consisting of the Contracting Parties.

(b) Each Contracting Party shall be represented by one delegate who may be assisted by alternate delegates, advisors and experts.

(c) Subject to subparagraph (d), the expenses of each delegation shall be borne by the Contracting Party that has appointed the delegation.

(d) The Assembly may ask the World Intellectual Property Organization to grant financial assistance to facilitate the participation of delegations of Contracting Parties that are regarded as developing countries in conformity with the established practice of the General Assembly of the United Nations.

(2) [*Functions*]

(a) The Assembly shall deal with matters concerning the maintenance and development of the Union and the application and operation of this Treaty.

(b) The Assembly shall decide the convocation of any diplomatic conference for the revision of this Treaty and give the necessary instructions to the Director General for the preparation of such diplomatic conference.

(c) The Assembly shall perform the functions allocated to it under Article 14 and shall establish the details of the procedures provided for in that Article, including the financing of such procedures.

(3) [*Voting*]

(a) Each Contracting Party that is a State shall have one vote and shall vote only in its own name.

(b) Any Contracting Party that is an Intergovernmental Organization shall exercise its right to vote, in place of its member States, with a number of votes equal to the number of its member States which are party to this Treaty and which are present at the time the vote is taken. No such Intergovernmental Organization shall exercise its right to vote if any of its member States participates in the vote.

(4) [*Ordinary Sessions*]

The Assembly shall meet in ordinary session once every two years upon convocation by the Director General.

(5) [*Rules of Procedure*]

The Assembly shall establish its own rules of procedure, including the convocation of extraordinary sessions, the requirements of a quorum and, subject to the provisions of this Treaty, the required majority for various kinds of decisions.

Article 10
International Bureau

(1) [*International Bureau*]

(a) The International Bureau of the World Intellectual Property Organization shall:

(i) perform the administrative tasks concerning the Union, as well as any tasks specially assigned to it by the Assembly;

(ii) subject to the availability of funds, provide technical assistance, on request, to the Governments of Contracting Parties that are States and are regarded as developing countries in conformity with the established practice of the General Assembly of the United Nations.

(b) No Contracting Party shall have any financial obligations; in particular, no Contracting Party shall be required to pay any contributions to the International Bureau on account of its membership in the Union.

(2) [*Director General*]

The Director General shall be the chief executive of the Union and shall represent the Union.

Article 11

Amendment of Certain Provisions of the Treaty

(1) [*Amending of Certain Provisions by the Assembly*]

The Assembly may amend the definitions contained in Article 2(i) and (ii), as well as Articles 3(1)(c) , 9(1)(c) and (d), 9(4), 10(1)(a) and 14.

(2) [*Initiation and Notice of Proposals for Amendment*]

(a) Proposals under this Article for amendment of the provisions of this Treaty referred to in paragraph (1) may be initiated by any Contracting Party or by the Director General.

(b) Such proposals shall be communicated by the Director General to the Contracting Parties at least six months in advance of their consideration by the Assembly.

(c) No such proposal shall be made before the expiration of five vears from the date of entry into force of this Treaty under Article 16(1).

(3) [*Required Majority*]

Adoption by the Assembly of any amendment under paragraph (1) shall require four-fifths of the votes cast.

(4) [*Entry Into Force*]

(a) Any amendment to the provisions of this Treaty referred to in paragraph (1) shall enter into force three months after written notifications of acceptance, effected in accordance with their respective constitutional processes, have been received by the Director General from three-fourths of the Contracting Parties members of the Assembly at the time the Assembly adopted the amendment. Any amendment to the said provisions thus accepted shall bind all States and Intergovernmental Organizations that were Contracting Parties at the time the amendment was adopted by the Assembly or that become Contracting Parties thereafter, except Contracting Parties which have notified their denunciation of this Treaty in accordance with Article 17 before the entry into force of the amendment.

(b) In establishing the required three-fourths referred to in subparagraph (a) , a notification made by an Intergovernmental Organization shall only be taken into account if no notification has been made by any of its member States.

Article 12

Safeguard of Paris and Berne Conventions

This Treaty shall not affect the obligations that any Contracting Party may have under the Paris Convention for the Protection of Industrial Property or the Berne Convention for the Protection of Literary and Artistic Works.

Article 13
Reservations

No reservations to this Treaty shall be made.

Article 14
Settlement of Disputes

(1) [*Consultations*]

(a) Where any dispute arises concerning the interpretation or implementation of this Treaty, a Contracting Party may bring the matter to the attention of another Contracting Party and request the latter to enter into consultations with it.

(b) The Contracting Party so requested shall provide promptly an adequate opportunity for the requested consultations.

(c) The Contracting Parties engaged in consultations shall attempt to reach, within a reasonable period of time, a mutually satisfactory solution of the dispute.

(2) [*Other Means of Settlement*]

If a mutually satisfactory solution is not reached within a reasonable period of time through the consultations referred to in paragraph (1), the parties to the dispute may agree to resort to other means designed to lead to an amicable settlement of their dispute, such as good offices, conciliation, mediation and arbitration.

(3) [*Panel*]

(a) If the dispute is not satisfactorily settled through the consultations referred to in paragraph (1), or if the means referred to in paragraph (2) are not resorted to, or do not lead to an amicable settlement within a reasonable period of time, the Assembly, at the written request of either of the parties to the dispute, shall convene a panel of three members to examine the matter. The members of the panel shall not, unless the parties to the dispute agree otherwise, be from either party to the dispute. They shall be selected from a list of designated governmental experts established by the Assembly. The terms of reference for the panel shall be agreed upon by the parties to the dispute. If such agreement is not achieved within three months, the Assembly shall set the terms of reference for the panel after having consulted the parties to the dispute and the members of the panel. The panel shall give full opportunity to the parties to the dispute and any other interested Contracting Parties to present to it their views. If both parties to the dispute so request, the panel shall stop its proceedings.

(b) The Assembly shall adopt rules for the establishment of the said list of experts, and the manner of selecting the members of the panel, who shall be governmental experts of the Contracting Parties, and for the conduct of the panel proceedings, including provisions to safeguard the confidentiality of the proceedings and of any material designated as confidential by any participant in the proceedings.

(c) Unless the parties to the dispute reach an agreement between themselves prior to the panel's concluding its proceedings, the panel shall promptly prepare a written report and provide it to the parties to the dispute for their review. The parties to the dispute shall have a reasonable period of time, whose length will be fixed by the panel, to submit any comments on the report to the panel, unless they agree to a longer time in their attempts to reach a mutually satisfactory resolution to their dispute. The panel shall take into account the comments and shall promptly transmit its report to the Assembly. The report shall contain the facts and recommendations for the resolution of the dispute, and shall be accompanied by the written comments, if any, of the parties to the dispute.

(4) [*Recommendation by the Assembly*]

The Assembly shall give the report of the panel prompt consideration. The Assembly shall, by consensus, make recommendations to the parties to the dispute, based upon its interpretation of this Treaty and the report of the panel.

Article 15
Becoming Party to the Treaty

(1) [*Eligibility*]

(a) Any State member of the World Intellectual Property Organization or of the United Nations may become party to this Treaty.

(b) Any Intergovernmental Organization which meets the requirements of Article 2(x) may become party to this Treaty. The Organization shall inform the Director General of its competence, and any subsequent changes in its competence, with respect to the matters governed by this Treaty. The Organization and its member States may, without, however, any derogation from the obligations under this Treaty, decide on their respective responsibilities for the performance of their obligations under this Treaty.

(2) [*Adherence*]

A State or Intergovernmental Organization shall become party to this Treaty by:

(i) signature followed by the deposit of an instrument of ratification, acceptance or approval. or

(ii) the deposit of an instrument of accession.

(3) [*Deposit of Instruments*]

The instruments referred to in paragraph (2) shall be deposited with the Director General.

Article 16
Entry Into Force of the Treaty

(1) [*Initial Entry Into Force*]

This Treaty shall enter into force, with respect to each of the first five States or

Intergovernmental Organizations which have deposited their instruments of ratification, acceptance, approval or accession, three months after the date on which the fifth instrument of ratification, acceptance, approval or accession has been deposited.

(2) [*States and Intergovernmental Organizations Not Covered by the Initial Entry Into Force*]

This Treaty shall enter into force with respect to any State or Intergovernmental Organization not covered by paragraph (1) three months after the date on which that State or Intergovernmental Organization has deposited its instrument of ratification, acceptance, approval or accession unless a later date has been indicated in the instrument; in the latter case, this Treaty shall enter into force with respect to the said State or Intergovernmental Organization on the date thus indicated.

(3) [*Protection of Layout-Designs (Topographies) Existing at Time of Entry Into Force*]

Any Contracting Party shall have the right not to apply this Treaty to any layout-design (topography) that exists at the time this Treaty enters into force in respect of that Contracting Party, provided that this provision does not affect any protection that such layout-design (topography) may, at that time, enjoy in the territory of that Contracting Party by virtue of international obligations other than those resulting from this Treaty or the legislation of the said Contracting Party.

Article 17
Denunciation of the Treaty

(1) [*Notification*]

Any Contracting Party may denounce this Treaty by notification addressed to the Director General.

(2) [*Effective Date*]

Denunciation shall take effect one year after the day on which the Director General has received the notification of denunciation.

Article 18
Texts of the Treaty

(1) [*Original Texts*]

This Treaty is established in a single original in the English, Arabic, Chinese, French, Russian and Spanish languages, all texts being equally authentic.

(2) [*Official Texts*]

Official texts shall be established by the Director General, after consultation with the interested Governments, in such other languages as the Assembly may designate.

Article 19
Depositary

The Director General shall be the depositary of this Treaty.

Article 20
Signature

This Treaty shall be open for signature between May 26, 1989, and August 25, 1989, with the Government of the United States of America, and between August 26, 1989, and May 25, 1990, at the headquarters of WIPO.

IN WITNESS THEREOF the undersigned, being duly authorized thereto, have signed this Treaty.

Done at Washington, May 26, 1989.

Agreement on Trade-Related Aspects of Intellectual Property Rights

Members,

Desiring to reduce distortions and impediments to international trade, and taking into account the need to promote effective and adequate protection of intellectual property rights, and to ensure that measures and procedures to enforce intellectual property rights do not themselves become barriers to legitimate trade;

Recognizing, to this end, the need for new rules and disciplines concerning:

(a) the applicability of the basic principles of GATT 1994 and of relevant international intellectual property agreements or conventions;

(b) the provision of adequate standards and principles concerning the availability, scope and use of trade-related intellectual property rights;

(c) the provision of effective and appropriate means for the enforcement of trade-related intellectual property rights, taking into account differences in national legal systems;

(d) the provision of effective and expeditious procedures for the multilateral prevention and settlement of disputes between governments; and

(e) transitional arrangements aiming at the fullest participation in the results of the negotiations;

Recognizing the need for a multilateral framework of principles, rules and disciplines dealing with international trade in counterfeit goods;

Recognizing that intellectual property rights are private rights;

Recognizing the underlying public policy objectives of national systems for the protection of intellectual property, including developmental and technological objectives;

Recognizing also the special needs of the least-developed country Members in respect of maximum flexibility in the domestic implementation of laws and regulations in order to enable them to create a sound and viable technological base;

Emphasizing the importance of reducing tensions by reaching strengthened commitments to resolve disputes on trade-related intellectual property issues through multilateral procedures;

Desiring to establish a mutually supportive relationship between the WTO and the World Intellectual Property Organization (referred to in this Agreement as "WIPO") as well as other relevant international organizations;

Hereby agree as follows:

PART I

GENERAL PROVISIONS AND BASIC PRINCIPLES

Article 1

Nature and Scope of Obligations

1. Members shall give effect to the provisions of this Agreement. Members may, but shall not be obliged to, implement in their law more extensive protection than is required by this Agreement, provided that such protection does not contravene the provisions of this Agreement. Members shall be free to determine the appropriate method of implementing the provisions of this Agreement within their own legal system and practice.

2. For the purposes of this Agreement, the term "intellectual property" refers to all categories of intellectual property that are the subject of Sections 1 through 7 of Part II.

3. Members shall accord the treatment provided for in this Agreement to the nationals of other Members.① In respect of the relevant intellectual property right, the nationals of other Members shall be understood as those natural or legal persons that would meet the criteria for eligibility for protection provided for in the Paris Convention (1967), the Berne Convention (1971), the Rome Convention and the Treaty on Intellectual Property in Respect of Integrated Circuits, were all Members of the WTO members of those conventions.② Any Member availing itself of the possibilities provided in paragraph 3 of Article 5 or paragraph 2 of Article 6 of the Rome Convention shall make a notification as foreseen in those provisions to the Council for Trade-Related Aspects of Intellectual Property Rights (the "Council for TRIPS").

---

① When "nationals" are referred to in this Agreement, they shall be deemed, in the case of a separate customs territory Member of the WTO, to mean persons, natural or legal, who are domiciled or who have a real and effective industrial or commercial establishment in that customs territory.

② In this Agreement, "Paris Convention" refers to the Paris Convention for the Protection of Industrial Property; "Paris Convention (1967)" refers to the Stockholm Act of this Convention of 14 July 1967. "Berne Convention" refers to the Berne Convention for the Protection of Literary and Artistic Works; "Berne Convention (1971)" refers to the Paris Act of this Convention of 24 July 1971. "Rome Convention" refers to the International Convention for the Protection of Performers, Producers of Phonograms and Broadcasting Organizations, adopted at Rome on 26 October 1961. "Treaty on Intellectual Property in Respect of Integrated Circuits" (IPIC Treaty) refers to the Treaty on Intellectual Property in Respect of Integrated Circuits, adopted at Washington on 26 May 1989. "WTO Agreement" refers to the Agreement Establishing the WTO.

Article 2

Intellectual Property Conventions

1. In respect of Parts II, III and IV of this Agreement, Members shall comply with Articles 1 through 12, and Article 19, of the Paris Convention (1967).

2. Nothing in Parts I to IV of this Agreement shall derogate from existing obligations that Members may have to each other under the Paris Convention, the Berne Convention, the Rome Convention and the Treaty on Intellectual Property in Respect of Integrated Circuits.

Article 3

National Treatment

1. Each Member shall accord to the nationals of other Members treatment no less favourable than that it accords to its own nationals with regard to the protection[3] of intellectual property, subject to the exceptions already provided in, respectively, the Paris Convention (1967), the Berne Convention (1971), the Rome Convention or the Treaty on Intellectual Property in Respect of Integrated Circuits. In respect of performers, producers of phonograms and broadcasting organizations, this obligation only applies in respect of the rights provided under this Agreement. Any Member availing itself of the possibilities provided in Article 6 of the Berne Convention (1971) or paragraph 1(b) of Article 16 of the Rome Convention shall make a notification as foreseen in those provisions to the Council for TRIPS.

2. Members may avail themselves of the exceptions permitted under paragraph 1 in relation to judicial and administrative procedures, including the designation of an address for service or the appointment of an agent within the jurisdiction of a Member, only where such exceptions are necessary to secure compliance with laws and regulations which are not inconsistent with the provisions of this Agreement and where such practices are not applied in a manner which would constitute a disguised restriction on trade.

Article 4

Most-Favoured-Nation Treatment

With regard to the protection of intellectual property, any advantage, favour, privilege or immunity granted by a Member to the nationals of any other country shall be accorded immediately and unconditionally to the nationals of all other Members. Exempted from this obligation are any advantage, favour, privilege or immunity accorded by a Member:

(a) deriving from international agreements on judicial assistance or law

---

③ For the purposes of Articles 3 and 4, "protection" shall include matters affecting the availability, acquisition, scope, maintenance and enforcement of intellectual property rights as well as those matters affecting the use of intellectual property rights specifically addressed in this Agreement.

enforcement of a general nature and not particularly confined to the protection of intellectual property;

(b) granted in accordance with the provisions of the Berne Convention (1971) or the Rome Convention authorizing that the treatment accorded be a function not of national treatment but of the treatment accorded in another country;

(c) in respect of the rights of performers, producers of phonograms and broadcasting organizations not provided under this Agreement;

(d) deriving from international agreements related to the protection of intellectual property which entered into force prior to the entry into force of the WTO Agreement, provided that such agreements are notified to the Council for TRIPS and do not constitute an arbitrary or unjustifiable discrimination against nationals of other Members.

Article 5

Multilateral Agreements on Acquisition or Maintenance of Protection

The obligations under Articles 3 and 4 do not apply to procedures provided in multilateral agreements concluded under the auspices of WIPO relating to the acquisition or maintenance of intellectual property rights.

Article 6

Exhaustion

For the purposes of dispute settlement under this Agreement, subject to the provisions of Articles 3 and 4 nothing in this Agreement shall be used to address the issue of the exhaustion of intellectual property rights.

Article 7

Objectives

The protection and enforcement of intellectual property rights should contribute to the promotion of technological innovation and to the transfer and dissemination of technology, to the mutual advantage of producers and users of technological knowledge and in a manner conducive to social and economic welfare, and to a balance of rights and obligations.

Article 8

Principles

1. Members may, in formulating or amending their laws and regulations, adopt measures necessary to protect public health and nutrition, and to promote the public interest in sectors of vital importance to their socio-economic and technological development, provided that such measures are consistent with the provisions of this Agreement.

2. Appropriate measures, provided that they are consistent with the provisions of this Agreement, may be needed to prevent the abuse of intellectual property rights by right holders or the resort to practices which unreasonably restrain trade or adversely affect the international transfer of technology.

PART II

STANDARDS CONCERNING THE AVAILABILITY, SCOPE AND USE OF INTELLECTUAL PROPERTY RIGHTS

SECTION 1: COPYRIGHT AND RELATED RIGHTS

Article 9
Relation to the Berne Convention

1. Members shall comply with Articles 1 through 21 of the Berne Convention (1971) and the Appendix thereto. However, Members shall not have rights or obligations under this Agreement in respect of the rights conferred under Article 6bis of that Convention or of the rights derived therefrom.

2. Copyright protection shall extend to expressions and not to ideas, procedures, methods of operation or mathematical concepts as such.

Article 10
Computer Programs and Compilations of Data

1. Computer programs, whether in source or object code, shall be protected as literary works under the Berne Convention (1971).

2. Compilations of data or other material, whether in machine readable or other form, which by reason of the selection or arrangement of their contents constitute intellectual creations shall be protected as such. Such protection, which shall not extend to the data or material itself, shall be without prejudice to any copyright subsisting in the data or material itself.

Article 11
Rental Rights

In respect of at least computer programs and cinematographic works, a Member shall provide authors and their successors in title the right to authorize or to prohibit the commercial rental to the public of originals or copies of their copyright works. A Member shall be excepted from this obligation in respect of cinematographic works unless such rental has led to widespread copying of such works which is materially impairing the exclusive right of reproduction conferred in that Member on authors and their successors in title. In respect of computer programs, this obligation does not apply to rentals where the program itself is not the essential object of the rental.

Article 12
Term of Protection

Whenever the term of protection of a work, other than a photographic work or a work of applied art, is calculated on a basis other than the life of a natural person, such term shall be no less than 50 years from the end of the calendar year of authorized publication, or, failing such authorized publication within 50 years from the making of the work, 50 years from the end of the calendar year of making.

Article 13
Limitations and Exceptions

Members shall confine limitations or exceptions to exclusive rights to certain special cases which do not conflict with a normal exploitation of the work and do not unreasonably prejudice the legitimate interests of the right holder.

Article 14
Protection of Performers, Producers of Phonograms(Sound Recordings) and Broadcasting Organizations

1. In respect of a fixation of their performance on a phonogram, performers shall have the possibility of preventing the following acts when undertaken without their authorization: the fixation of their unfixed performance and the reproduction of such fixation. Performers shall also have the possibility of preventing the following acts when undertaken without their authorization: the broadcasting by wireless means and the communication to the public of their live performance.

. 2. Producers of phonograms shall enjoy the right to authorize or prohibit the direct or indirect reproduction of their phonograms.

3. Broadcasting organizations shall have the right to prohibit the following acts when undertaken without their authorization: the fixation, the reproduction of fixations, and the rebroadcasting by wireless means of broadcasts, as well as the communication to the public of television broadcasts of the same. Where Members do not grant such rights to broadcasting organizations, they shall provide owners of copyright in the subject matter of broadcasts with the possibility of preventing the above acts, subject to the provisions of the Berne Convention (1971).

4. The provisions of Article 11 in respect of computer programs shall apply *mutatis mutandis* to producers of phonograms and any other right holders in

phonograms as determined in a Member's law. If on 15 April 1994 a Member has in force a system of equitable remuneration of right holders in respect of the rental of phonograms, it may maintain such system provided that the commercial rental of phonograms is not giving rise to the material impairment of the exclusive rights of reproduction of right holders.

5. The term of the protection available under this Agreement to performers and producers of phonograms shall last at least until the end of a period of 50 years computed from the end of the calendar year in which the fixation was made or the performance took place. The term of protection granted pursuant to paragraph 3 shall last for at least 20 years from the end of the calendar year in which the broadcast took place.

6. Any Member may, in relation to the rights conferred under paragraphs 1, 2 and 3, provide for conditions, limitations, exceptions and reservations to the extent permitted by the Rome Convention. However, the provisions of Article 18 of the Berne Convention (1971) shall also apply, *mutatis mutandis*, to the rights of performers and producers of phonograms in phonograms.

SECTION 2: TRADEMARKS

Article 15
Protectable Subject Matter

1. Any sign, or any combination of signs, capable of distinguishing the goods or services of one undertaking from those of other undertakings, shall be capable of constituting a trademark. Such signs, in particular words including personal names, letters, numerals, figurative elements and combinations of colours as well as any combination of such signs, shall be eligible for registration as trademarks. Where signs are not inherently capable of distinguishing the relevant goods or services, Members may make registrability depend on distinctiveness acquired through use. Members may require, as a condition of registration, that signs be visually perceptible.

2. Paragraph 1 shall not be understood to prevent a Member from denying registration of a trademark on other grounds, provided that they do not derogate from the provisions of the Paris Convention (1967).

3. Members may make registrability depend on use. However, actual use of a trademark shall not be a condition for filing an application for registration. An application shall not be refused solely on the ground that intended use has not taken place before the expiry of a period of three years from the date of application.

4. The nature of the goods or services to which a trademark is to be applied shall in no case form an obstacle to registration of the trademark.

5. Members shall publish each trademark either before it is registered or promptly after it is registered and shall afford a reasonable opportunity for petitions to cancel the registration. In addition, Members may afford an opportunity for the registration of a trademark to be opposed.

Article 16
Rights Conferred

1. The owner of a registered trademark shall have the exclusive right to prevent all third parties not having the owner's consent from using in the course of trade identical or similar signs for goods or services which are identical or similar to those in respect of which the trademark is registered where such use would result in a likelihood of confusion. In case of the use of an identical sign for identical goods or services, a likelihood of confusion shall be presumed. The rights described above shall not prejudice any existing prior rights, nor shall they affect the possibility of Members making rights available on the basis of use.

2. Article 6bis of the Paris Convention (1967) shall apply, *mutatis mutandis*, to services. In determining whether a trademark is well-known, Members shall take account of the knowledge of the trademark in the relevant sector of the public, including knowledge in the Member concerned which has been obtained as a result of the promotion of the trademark.

3. Article 6bis of the Paris Convention (1967) shall apply, *mutatis mutandis*, to goods or services which are not similar to those in respect of which a trademark is registered, provided that use of that trademark in relation to those goods or services would indicate a connection between those goods or services and the owner of the registered trademark and provided that the interests of the owner of the registered trademark are likely to be damaged by such use.

Article 17
Exceptions

Members may provide limited exceptions to the rights conferred by a trademark, such as fair use of descriptive terms, provided that such exceptions take account of the legitimate interests of the owner of the trademark and of third parties.

Article 18
Term of Protection

Initial registration, and each renewal of registration, of a trademark shall be for a term of no less than seven years. The registration of a trademark shall be renewable indefinitely.

Article 19

Requirement of Use

1. If use is required to maintain a registration, the registration may be cancelled only after an uninterrupted period of at least three years of non-use, unless valid reasons based on the existence of obstacles to such use are shown by the trademark owner. Circumstances arising independently of the will of the owner of the trademark which constitute an obstacle to the use of the trademark, such as import restrictions on or other government requirements for goods or services protected by the trademark, shall be recognized as valid reasons for non-use.

2. When subject to the control of its owner, use of a trademark by another person shall be recognized as use of the trademark for the purpose of maintaining the registration.

Article 20

Other Requirements

The use of a trademark in the course of trade shall not be unjustifiably encumbered by special requirements, such as use with another trademark, use in a special form or use in a manner detrimental to its capability to distinguish the goods or services of one undertaking from those of other undertakings. This will not preclude a requirement prescribing the use of the trademark identifying the undertaking producing the goods or services along with, but without linking it to, the trademark distinguishing the specific goods or services in question of that undertaking.

Article 21

Licensing and Assignment

Members may determine conditions on the licensing and assignment of trademarks, it being understood that the compulsory licensing of trademarks shall not be permitted and that the owner of a registered trademark shall have the right to assign the trademark with or without the transfer of the business to which the trademark belongs.

SECTION 3: GEOGRAPHICAL INDICATIONS

Article 22

Protection of Geographical Indications

1. Geographical indications are, for the purposes of this Agreement, indications which identify a good as originating in the territory of a Member, or a region or locality in that territory, where a given quality, reputation or other characteristic of the good is essentially attributable to its geographical origin.

2. In respect of geographical indications, Members shall provide the legal

means for interested parties to prevent:

(a) the use of any means in the designation or presentation of a good that indicates or suggests that the good in question originates in a geographical area other than the true place of origin in a manner which misleads the public as to the geographical origin of the good;

(b) any use which constitutes an act of unfair competition within the meaning of Article 10bis of the Paris Convention (1967).

3. A Member shall, *ex officio* if its legislation so permits or at the request of an interested party, refuse or invalidate the registration of a trademark which contains or consists of a geographical indication with respect to goods not originating in the territory indicated, if use of the indication in the trademark for such goods in that Member is of such a nature as to mislead the public as to the true place of origin.

4. The protection under paragraphs 1, 2 and 3 shall be applicable against a geographical indication which, although literally true as to the territory, region or locality in which the goods originate, falsely represents to the public that the goods originate in another territory.

Article 23

Additional Protection for Geographical Indications for Wines and Spirits

1. Each Member shall provide the legal means for interested parties to prevent use of a geographical indication identifying wines for wines not originating in the place indicated by the geographical indication in question or identifying spirits for spirits not originating in the place indicated by the geographical indication in question, even where the true origin of the goods is indicated or the geographical indication is used in translation or accompanied by expressions such as "kind", "type", "style", "imitation" or the like. ④

2. The registration of a trademark for wines which contains or consists of a geographical indication identifying wines or for spirits which contains or consists of a geographical indication identifying spirits shall be refused or invalidated, *ex officio* if a Member's legislation so permits or at the request of an interested party, with respect to such wines or spirits not having this origin.

3. In the case of homonymous geographical indications for wines, protection shall be accorded to each indication, subject to the provisions of paragraph 4 of Article 22. Each Member shall determine the practical conditions under which the homonymous indications in question will be differentiated from each other, taking into account the need to ensure equitable treatment of the producers concerned and that consumers are not misled.

4. In order to facilitate the protection of geographical indications for wines,

④ Notwithstanding the first sentence of Article 42, Members may, with respect to these obligations, instead provide for enforcement by administrative action.

negotiations shall be undertaken in the Council for TRIPS concerning the establishment of a multilateral system of notification and registration of geographical indications for wines eligible for protection in those Members participating in the system.

Article 24

International Negotiations; Exceptions

1. Members agree to enter into negotiations aimed at increasing the protection of individual geographical indications under Article 23. The provisions of paragraphs 4 through 8 below shall not be used by a Member to refuse to conduct negotiations or to conclude bilateral or multilateral agreements. In the context of such negotiations, Members shall be willing to consider the continued applicability of these provisions to individual geographical indications whose use was the subject of such negotiations.

2. The Council for TRIPS shall keep under review the application of the provisions of this Section; the first such review shall take place within two years of the entry into force of the WTO Agreement. Any matter affecting the compliance with the obligations under these provisions may be drawn to the attention of the Council, which, at the request of a Member, shall consult with any Member or Members in respect of such matter in respect of which it has not been possible to find a satisfactory solution through bilateral or plurilateral consultations between the Members concerned. The Council shall take such action as may be agreed to facilitate the operation and further the objectives of this Section.

3. In implementing this Section, a Member shall not diminish the protection of geographical indications that existed in that Member immediately prior to the date of entry into force of the WTO Agreement.

4. Nothing in this Section shall require a Member to prevent continued and similar use of a particular geographical indication of another Member identifying wines or spirits in connection with goods or services by any of its nationals or domiciliaries who have used that geographical indication in a continuous manner with regard to the same or related goods or services in the territory of that Member either (a) for at least 10 years preceding 15 April 1994 or (b) in good faith preceding that date.

5. Where a trademark has been applied for or registered in good faith, or where rights to a trademark have been acquired through use in good faith either:

(a) before the date of application of these provisions in that Member as defined in Part VI; or

(b) before the geographical indication is protected in its country of origin; measures adopted to implement this Section shall not prejudice eligibility for or the validity of the registration of a trademark, or the right to use a trademark, on the basis that such a trademark is identical with, or similar to, a geographical indication.

6. Nothing in this Section shall require a Member to apply its provisions in respect of a geographical indication of any other Member with respect to goods or services for which the relevant indication is identical with the term customary in common language as the common name for such goods or services in the territory of that Member. Nothing in this Section shall require a Member to apply its provisions in respect of a geographical indication of any other Member with respect to products of the vine for which the relevant indication is identical with the customary name of a grape variety existing in the territory of that Member as of the date of entry into force of the WTO Agreement.

7. A Member may provide that any request made under this Section in connection with the use or registration of a trademark must be presented within five years after the adverse use of the protected indication has become generally known in that Member or after the date of registration of the trademark in that Member provided that the trademark has been published by that date, if such date is earlier than the date on which the adverse use became generally known in that Member, provided that the geographical indication is not used or registered in bad faith.

8. The provisions of this Section shall in no way prejudice the right of any person to use, in the course of trade, that person's name or the name of that person's predecessor in business, except where such name is used in such a manner as to mislead the public.

9. There shall be no obligation under this Agreement to protect geographical indications which are not or cease to be protected in their country of origin, or which have fallen into disuse in that country.

SECTION 4: INDUSTRIAL DESIGNS

Article 25

Requirements for Protection

1. Members shall provide for the protection of independently created industrial designs that are new or original. Members may provide that designs are not new or original if they do not significantly differ from known designs or combinations of known design features. Members may provide that such protection shall not extend to designs dictated essentially by technical or functional considerations.

2. Each Member shall ensure that requirements for securing protection for textile designs, in particular in regard to any cost, examination or publication, do not unreasonably impair the opportunity to seek and obtain such protection. Members shall be free to meet this obligation through industrial design law or through copyright law.

Article 26

Protection

1. The owner of a protected industrial design shall have the right to prevent third parties not having the owner's consent from making, selling or importing articles bearing or embodying a design which is a copy, or substantially a copy, of the protected design, when such acts are undertaken for commercial purposes.

2. Members may provide limited exceptions to the protection of industrial designs, provided that such exceptions do not unreasonably conflict with the normal exploitation of protected industrial designs and do not unreasonably prejudice the legitimate interests of the owner of the protected design, taking account of the legitimate interests of third parties.

3. The duration of protection available shall amount to at least 10 years.

SECTION 5: PATENTS

Article 27

Patentable Subject Matter

1. Subject to the provisions of paragraphs 2 and 3, patents shall be available for any inventions, whether products or processes, in all fields of technology, provided that they are new, involve an inventive step and are capable of industrial application.[⑤] Subject to paragraph 4 of Article 65, paragraph 8 of Article 70 and paragraph 3 of this Article, patents shall be available and patent rights enjoyable without discrimination as to the place of invention, the field of technology and whether products are imported or locally produced.

2. Members may exclude from patentability inventions, the prevention within their territory of the commercial exploitation of which is necessary to protect *ordre public* or morality, including to protect human, animal or plant life or health or to avoid serious prejudice to the environment, provided that such exclusion is not made merely because the exploitation is prohibited by their law.

3. Members may also exclude from patentability:

(a) diagnostic, therapeutic and surgical methods for the treatment of humans or animals;

(b) plants and animals other than micro-organisms, and essentially biological processes for the production of plants or animals other than non-biological and microbiological processes. However, Members shall provide for the protection of plant varieties either by patents or by an effective *sui generis* system or by any

---

⑤ For the purposes of this Article, the terms "inventive step" and "capable of industrial application" may be deemed by a Member to be synonymous with the terms "non-obvious" and "useful" respectively.

combination thereof. The provisions of this subparagraph shall be reviewed four years after the date of entry into force of the WTO Agreement.

Article 28

Rights Conferred

1. A patent shall confer on its owner the following exclusive rights:

(a) where the subject matter of a patent is a product, to prevent third parties not having the owner's consent from the acts of: making, using, offering for sale, selling, or importing ⑥ for these purposes that product;

(b) where the subject matter of a patent is a process, to prevent third parties not having the owner's consent from the act of using the process, and from the acts of: using, offering for sale, selling, or importing for these purposes at least the product obtained directly by that process.

2. Patent owners shall also have the right to assign, or transfer by succession, the patent and to conclude licensing contracts.

Article 29

Conditions on Patent Applicants

1. Members shall require that an applicant for a patent shall disclose the invention in a manner sufficiently clear and complete for the invention to be carried out by a person skilled in the art and may require the applicant to indicate the best mode for carrying out the invention known to the inventor at the filing date or, where priority is claimed, at the priority date of the application.

2. Members may require an applicant for a patent to provide information concerning the applicant's corresponding foreign applications and grants.

Article 30

Exceptions to Rights Conferred

Members may provide limited exceptions to the exclusive rights conferred by a patent, provided that such exceptions do not unreasonably conflict with a normal exploitation of the patent and do not unreasonably prejudice the legitimate interests of the patent owner, taking account of the legitimate interests of third parties.

Article 31

Other Use Without Authorization of the Right Holder

Where the law of a Member allows for other use ⑦ of the subject matter of a patent without the authorization of the right holder, including use by the government or third parties authorized by the government, the following provisions shall

⑥ This right, like all other rights conferred under this Agreement in respect of the use, sale, importation or other distribution of goods, is subject to the provisions of Article 6.

⑦ "Other use" refers to use other than that allowed under Article 30.

be respected:

(a) authorization of such use shall be considered on its individual merits;

(b) such use may only be permitted if, prior to such use, the proposed user has made efforts to obtain authorization from the right holder on reasonable commercial terms and conditions and that such efforts have not been successful within a reasonable period of time. This requirement may be waived by a Member in the case of a national emergency or other circumstances of extreme urgency or in cases of public non-commercial use. In situations of national emergency or other circumstances of extreme urgency, the right holder shall, nevertheless, be notified as soon as reasonably practicable. In the case of public non-commercial use, where the government or contractor, without making a patent search, knows or has demonstrable grounds to know that a valid patent is or will be used by or for the government, the right holder shall be informed promptly;

(c) the scope and duration of such use shall be limited to the purpose for which it was authorized, and in the case of semi-conductor technology shall only be for public non-commercial use or to remedy a practice determined after judicial or administrative process to be anti-competitive;

(d) such use shall be non-exclusive;

(e) such use shall be non-assignable, except with that part of the enterprise or goodwill which enjoys such use;

(f) any such use shall be authorized predominantly for the supply of the domestic market of the Member authorizing such use;

(g) authorization for such use shall be liable, subject to adequate protection of the legitimate interests of the persons so authorized, to be terminated if and when the circumstances which led to it cease to exist and are unlikely to recur. The competent authority shall have the authority to review, upon motivated request, the continued existence of these circumstances;

(h) the right holder shall be paid adequate remuneration in the circumstances of each case, taking into account the economic value of the authorization;

(i) the legal validity of any decision relating to the authorization of such use shall be subject to judicial review or other independent review by a distinct higher authority in that Member;

(j) any decision relating to the remuneration provided in respect of such use shall be subject to judicial review or other independent review by a distinct higher authority in that Member;

(k) Members are not obliged to apply the conditions set forth in subparagraphs (b) and (f) where such use is permitted to remedy a practice determined after judicial or administrative process to be anti-competitive. The need to correct anti-competitive practices may be taken into account in determining the amount of remuneration in such cases. Competent authorities shall have the authority to refuse termination of authorization if and when the conditions which led to such authorization are likely to recur;

(l) where such use is authorized to permit the exploitation of a patent ("the second patent") which cannot be exploited without infringing another patent ("the first patent"), the following additional conditions shall apply:

(i) the invention claimed in the second patent shall involve an important technical advance of considerable economic significance in relation to the invention claimed in the first patent;

(ii) the owner of the first patent shall be entitled to a cross-licence on reasonable terms to use the invention claimed in the second patent; and

(iii) the use authorized in respect of the first patent shall be non-assignable except with the assignment of the second patent.

Article 32
Revocation/Forfeiture

An opportunity for judicial review of any decision to revoke or forfeit a patent shall be available.

Article 33
Term of Protection

The term of protection available shall not end before the expiration of a period of twenty years counted from the filing date. [8]

Article 34
Process Patents: Burden of Proof

1. For the purposes of civil proceedings in respect of the infringement of the rights of the owner referred to in paragraph 1(b) of Article 28, if the subject matter of a patent is a process for obtaining a product, the judicial authorities shall have the authority to order the defendant to prove that the process to obtain an identical product is different from the patented process. Therefore, Members shall provide, in at least one of the following circumstances, that any identical product when produced without the consent of the patent owner shall, in the absence of proof to the contrary, be deemed to have been obtained by the patented process:

(a) if the product obtained by the patented process is new;

(b) if there is a substantial likelihood that the identical product was made by the process and the owner of the patent has been unable through reasonable efforts to determine the process actually used.

2. Any Member shall be free to provide that the burden of proof indicated in

⑧ It is understood that those Members which do not have a system of original grant may provide that the term of protection shall be computed from the filing date in the system of original grant.

paragraph 1 shall be on the alleged infringer only if the condition referred to in subparagraph (a) is fulfilled or only if the condition referred to in subparagraph (b) is fulfilled.

3. In the adduction of proof to the contrary, the legitimate interests of defendants in protecting their manufacturing and business secrets shall be taken into account.

SECTION 6: LAYOUT-DESIGNS (TOPOGRAPHIES) OF INTEGRATED CIRCUITS

Article 35

Relation to the IPIC Treaty

Members agree to provide protection to the layout-designs (topographies) of integrated circuits (referred to in this Agreement as "layout-designs") in accordance with Articles 2 through 7 (other than paragraph 3 of Article 6), Article 12 and paragraph 3 of Article 16 of the Treaty on Intellectual Property in Respect of Integrated Circuits and, in addition, to comply with the following provisions.

Article 36

Scope of the Protection

Subject to the provisions of paragraph 1 of Article 37, Members shall consider unlawful the following acts if performed without the authorization of the right holder:[⑨] importing, selling, or otherwise distributing for commercial purposes a protected layout-design, an integrated circuit in which a protected layout-design is incorporated, or an article incorporating such an integrated circuit only in so far as it continues to contain an unlawfully reproduced layout-design.

Article 37

Acts Not Requiring the Authorization of the Right Holder

1. Notwithstanding Article 36, no Member shall consider unlawful the performance of any of the acts referred to in that Article in respect of an integrated circuit incorporating an unlawfully reproduced layout-design or any article incorporating such an integrated circuit where the person performing or ordering such acts did not know and had no reasonable ground to know, when acquiring the integrated circuit or article incorporating such an integrated circuit, that it incorporated an unlawfully reproduced layout-design. Members shall provide that, after the time that such person has received sufficient notice that the layout-design was unlawfully reproduced, that person may perform any of the acts with respect to the stock on hand or ordered

⑨ The term "right holder" in this Section shall be understood as having the same meaning as the term "holder of the right" in the IPIC Treaty.

before such time, but shall be liable to pay to the right holder a sum equivalent to a reasonable royalty such as would be payable under a freely negotiated licence in respect of such a layout-design.

2. The conditions set out in subparagraphs (a) through (k) of Article 31 shall apply *mutatis mutandis* in the event of any non-voluntary licensing of a layout-design or of its use by or for the government without the authorization of the right holder.

Article 38
Term of Protection

1. In Members requiring registration as a condition of protection, the term of protection of layout-designs shall not end before the expiration of a period of 10 years counted from the date of filing an application for registration or from the first commercial exploitation wherever in the world it occurs.

2. In Members not requiring registration as a condition for protection, layout-designs shall be protected for a term of no less than 10 years from the date of the first commercial exploitation wherever in the world it occurs.

3. Notwithstanding paragraphs 1 and 2, a Member may provide that protection shall lapse 15 years after the creation of the layout-design.

SECTION 7: PROTECTION OF UNDISCLOSED INFORMATION

Article 39

1. In the course of ensuring effective protection against unfair competition as provided in Article 10bis of the Paris Convention (1967), Members shall protect undisclosed information in accordance with paragraph 2 and data submitted to governments or governmental agencies in accordance with paragraph 3.

2. Natural and legal persons shall have the possibility of preventing information lawfully within their control from being disclosed to, acquired by, or used by others without their consent in a manner contrary to honest commercial practices [⑩] so long as such information:

(a) is secret in the sense that it is not, as a body or in the precise configuration and assembly of its components, generally known among or readily accessible to persons within the circles that normally deal with the kind of information in question;

(b) has commercial value because it is secret; and

⑩ For the purpose of this provision, "a manner contrary to honest commercial practices" shall mean at least practices such as breach of contract, breach of confidence and inducement to breach, and includes the acquisition of undisclosed information by third parties who knew, or were grossly negligent in failing to know, that such practices were involved in the acquisition.

(c) has been subject to reasonable steps under the circumstances, by the person lawfully in control of the information, to keep it secret.

3. Members, when requiring, as a condition of approving the marketing of pharmaceutical or of agricultural chemical products which utilize new chemical entities, the submission of undisclosed test or other data, the origination of which involves a considerable effort, shall protect such data against unfair commercial use. In addition, Members shall protect such data against disclosure, except where necessary to protect the public, or unless steps are taken to ensure that the data are protected against unfair commercial use.

SECTION 8: CONTROL OF ANTI-COMPETITIVE PRACTICES IN CONTRACTUAL LICENCES

Article 40

1. Members agree that some licensing practices or conditions pertaining to intellectual property rights which restrain competition may have adverse effects on trade and may impede the transfer and dissemination of technology.

2. Nothing in this Agreement shall prevent Members from specifying in their legislation licensing practices or conditions that may in particular cases constitute an abuse of intellectual property rights having an adverse effect on competition in the relevant market. As provided above, a Member may adopt, consistently with the other provisions of this Agreement, appropriate measures to prevent or control such practices, which may include for example exclusive grantback conditions, conditions preventing challenges to validity and coercive package licensing, in the light of the relevant laws and regulations of that Member.

3. Each Member shall enter, upon request, into consultations with any other Member which has cause to believe that an intellectual property right owner that is a national or domiciliary of the Member to which the request for consultations has been addressed is undertaking practices in violation of the requesting Member's laws and regulations on the subject matter of this Section, and which wishes to secure compliance with such legislation, without prejudice to any action under the law and to the full freedom of an ultimate decision of either Member. The Member addressed shall accord full and sympathetic consideration to, and shall afford adequate opportunity for, consultations with the requesting Member, and shall cooperate through supply of publicly available non-confidential information of relevance to the matter in question and of other information available to the Member, subject to domestic law and to the conclusion of mutually satisfactory agreements concerning the safeguarding of its confidentiality by the requesting Member.

4. A Member whose nationals or domiciliaries are subject to proceedings in

another Member concerning alleged violation of that other Member's laws and regulations on the subject matter of this Section shall, upon request, be granted an opportunity for consultations by the other Member under the same conditions as those foreseen in paragraph 3.

PART III

ENFORCEMENT OF INTELLECTUAL PROPERTY RIGHTS

SECTION 1: GENERAL OBLIGATIONS

Article 41

1. Members shall ensure that enforcement procedures as specified in this Part are available under their law so as to permit effective action against any act of infringement of intellectual property rights covered by this Agreement, including expeditious remedies to prevent infringements and remedies which constitute a deterrent to further infringements. These procedures shall be applied in such a manner as to avoid the creation of barriers to legitimate trade and to provide for safeguards against their abuse.

2. Procedures concerning the enforcement of intellectual property rights shall be fair and equitable. They shall not be unnecessarily complicated or costly, or entail unreasonable time-limits or unwarranted delays.

3. Decisions on the merits of a case shall preferably be in writing and reasoned. They shall be made available at least to the parties to the proceeding without undue delay. Decisions on the merits of a case shall be based only on evidence in respect of which parties were offered the opportunity to be heard.

4. Parties to a proceeding shall have an opportunity for review by a judicial authority of final administrative decisions and, subject to jurisdictional provisions in a Member's law concerning the importance of a case, of at least the legal aspects of initial judicial decisions on the merits of a case. However, there shall be no obligation to provide an opportunity for review of acquittals in criminal cases.

5. It is understood that this Part does not create any obligation to put in place a judicial system for the enforcement of intellectual property rights distinct from that for the enforcement of law in general, nor does it affect the capacity of Members to enforce their law in general. Nothing in this Part creates any obligation with respect to the distribution of resources as between enforcement of intellectual property rights and the enforcement of law in general.

SECTION 2: CIVIL AND ADMINISTRATIVE PROCEDURES AND REMEDIES

Article 42

Fair and Equitable Procedures

Members shall make available to right holders ⑪ civil judicial procedures concerning the enforcement of any intellectual property right covered by this Agreement. Defendants shall have the right to written notice which is timely and contains sufficient detail, including the basis of the claims. Parties shall be allowed to be represented by independent legal counsel, and procedures shall not impose overly burdensome requirements concerning mandatory personal appearances. All parties to such procedures shall be duly entitled to substantiate their claims and to present all relevant evidence. The procedure shall provide a means to identify and protect confidential information, unless this would be contrary to existing constitutional requirements.

Article 43

Evidence

1. The judicial authorities shall have the authority, where a party has presented reasonably available evidence sufficient to support its claims and has specified evidence relevant to substantiation of its claims which lies in the control of the opposing party, to order that this evidence be produced by the opposing party, subject in appropriate cases to conditions which ensure the protection of confidential information.

2. In cases in which a party to a proceeding voluntarily and without good reason refuses access to, or otherwise does not provide necessary information within a reasonable period, or significantly impedes a procedure relating to an enforcement action, a Member may accord judicial authorities the authority to make preliminary and final determinations, affirmative or negative, on the basis of the information presented to them, including the complaint or the allegation presented by the party adversely affected by the denial of access to information, subject to providing the parties an opportunity to be heard on the allegations or evidence.

Article 44

Injunctions

1. The judicial authorities shall have the authority to order a party to desist from an infringement, *inter alia* to prevent the entry into the channels of commerce

⑪ For the purpose of this Part, the term "right holder" includes federations and associations having legal standing to assert such rights.

in their jurisdiction of imported goods that involve the infringement of an intellectual property right, immediately after customs clearance of such goods. Members are not obliged to accord such authority in respect of protected subject matter acquired or ordered by a person prior to knowing or having reasonable grounds to know that dealing in such subject matter would entail the infringement of an intellectual property right.

2. Notwithstanding the other provisions of this Part and provided that the provisions of Part II specifically addressing use by governments, or by third parties authorized by a government, without the authorization of the right holder are complied with, Members may limit the remedies available against such use to payment of remuneration in accordance with subparagraph (h) of Article 31. In other cases, the remedies under this Part shall apply or, where these remedies are inconsistent with a Member's law, declaratory judgments and adequate compensation shall be available.

Article 45
Damages

1. The judicial authorities shall have the authority to order the infringer to pay the right holder damages adequate to compensate for the injury the right holder has suffered because of an infringement of that person's intellectual property right by an infringer who knowingly, or with reasonable grounds to know, engaged in infringing activity.

2. The judicial authorities shall also have the authority to order the infringer to pay the right holder expenses, which may include appropriate attorney's fees. In appropriate cases, Members may authorize the judicial authorities to order recovery of prof its andfor payment of pre-established damages even where the infringer did not knowingly, or with reasonable grounds to know, engage in infringing activity.

Article 46
Other Remedies

In order to create an effective deterrent to infringement, the judicial authorities shall have the authority to order that goods that they have found to be infringing be, without compensation of any sort, disposed of outside the channels of commerce in such a manner as to avoid any harm caused to the right holder, or, unless this would be contrary to existing constitutional requirements, destroyed. The judicial authorities shall also have the authority to order that materials and implements the predominant use of which has been in the creation of the infringing goods be, without compensation of any sort, disposed of outside the channels of commerce in such a manner as to minimize the risks of further infringements. In considering such requests, the need for proportionality between the seriousness of the infringement and the remedies ordered as well as the interests of third parties shall be taken into account. In regard to counterfeit trademark goods, the simple removal of the trademark unlawfully affixed shall not be sufficient, other than in exceptional cases, to permit release of the goods into the channels of commerce.

Article 47
Right of Information

Members may provide that the judicial authorities shall have the authority, unless this would be out of proportion to the seriousness of the infringement, to order the infringer to inform the right holder of the identity of third persons involved in the production and distribution of the infringing goods or services and of their channels of distribution.

Article 48
Indemnification of the Defendant

1. The judicial authorities shall have the authority to order a party at whose request measures were taken and who has abused enforcement procedures to provide to a party wrongfully enjoined or restrained adequate compensation for the injury suffered because of such abuse. The judicial authorities shall also have the authority to order the applicant to pay the defendant expenses, which may include appropriate attorney's fees.

2. In respect of the administration of any law pertaining to the protection or enforcement of intellectual property rights, Members shall only exempt both public authorities and officials from liability to appropriate remedial measures where actions are taken or intended in good faith in the course of the administration of that law.

Article 49
Administrative Procedures

To the extent that any civil remedy can be ordered as a result of administrative procedures on the merits of a case, such procedures shall conform to principles equivalent in substance to those set forth in this Section.

SECTION 3: PROVISIONAL MEASURES

Article 50

1. The judicial authorities shall have the authority to order prompt and effective provisional measures:

(a) to prevent an infringement of any intellectual property right from occurring, and in particular to prevent the entry into the channels of commerce in their jurisdiction of goods, including imported goods immediately after customs clearance;

(b) to preserve relevant evidence in regard to the alleged infringement.

2. The judicial authorities shall have the authority to adopt provisional measures *inaudita altera parte* where appropriate, in particular where any delay is likely to cause irreparable harm to the right holder, or where there is a demonstrable risk of evidence being destroyed.

3. The judicial authorities shall have the authority to require the applicant to provide any reasonably available evidence in order to satisfy themselves with a sufficient degree of certainty that the applicant is the right holder and that the applicant's right is being infringed or that such infringement is imminent, and to order the applicant to provide a security or equivalent assurance sufficient to protect the defendant and to prevent abuse.

4. Where provisional measures have been adopted *inaudita altera parte*, the parties affected shall be given notice, without delay after the execution of the measures at the latest. A review, including a right to be heard, shall take place upon request of the defendant with a view to deciding, within a reasonable period after the notification of the measures, whether these measures shall be modified, revoked or confirmed.

5. The applicant may be required to supply other information necessary for the identification of the goods concerned by the authority that will execute the provisional measures.

6. Without prejudice to paragraph 4, provisional measures taken on the basis of paragraphs 1 and 2 shall, upon request by the defendant, be revoked or otherwise cease to have effect, if proceedings leading to a decision on the merits of the case are not initiated within a reasonable period, to be determined by the judicial authority ordering the measures where a Member's law so permits or, in the absence of such a determination, not to exceed 20 working days or 31 calendar days, whichever is the longer.

7. Where the provisional measures are revoked or where they lapse due to any act or omission by the applicant, or where it is subsequently found that there has been no infringement or threat of infringement of an intellectual property right, the judicial authorities shall have the authority to order the applicant, upon request of the defendant, to provide the defendant appropriate compensation for any injury caused by these measures.

8. To the extent that any provisional measure can be ordered as a result of administrative procedures, such procedures shall conform to principles equivalent in substance to those set forth in this Section.

SECTION 4: SPECIAL REQUIREMENTS RELATED TO BORDER MEASURES [12]

Article 51

Suspension of Release by Customs Authorities

Members shall, in conformity with the provisions set out below, adopt procedures [13] to enable a right holder, who has valid grounds for suspecting that the importation of counterfeit trademark or pirated copyright goods [14] may take place, to lodge an application in writing with competent authorities, administrative or judicial, for the suspension by the customs authorities of the release into free circulation of such goods. Members may enable such an application to be made in respect of goods which involve other infringements of intellectual property rights, provided that the requirements of this Section are met. Members may also provide for corresponding procedures concerning the suspension by the customs authorities of the release of infringing goods destined for exportation from their territories.

Article 52

Application

Any right holder initiating the procedures under Article 51 shall be required to provide adequate evidence to satisfy the competent authorities that, under the laws of the country of importation, there is *prima facie* an infringement of the right holder's intellectual property right and to supply a sufficiently detailed description of the goods to make them readily recognizable by the customs authorities. The competent authorities shall inform the applicant within a reasonable period whether they have accepted the application and, where determined by the competent authorities, the period for which the customs authorities will take action.

---

⑫ Where a Member has dismantled substantially all controls over movement of goods across its border with another Member with which it forms part of a customs union, it shall not be required to apply the provisions of this Section at that border.

⑬ It is understood that there shall be no obligation to apply such procedures to imports of goods put on the market in another country by or with the consent of the right holder, or to goods in transit.

⑭ For the purposes of this Agreement:

(a) "counterfeit trademark goods" shall mean any goods, including packaging, bearing without authorization a trademark which is identical to the trademark validly registered in respect of such goods, or which cannot be distinguished in its essential aspects from such a trademark, and which thereby infringes the rights of the owner of the trademark in question under the law of the country of importation;

(b) "pirated copyright goods" shall mean any goods which are copies made without the consent of the right holder or person duly authorized by the right holder in the country of production and which are made directly or indirectly from an article where the making of that copy would have constituted an infringement of a copyright or a related right under the law of the country of importation.

Article 53

Security or Equivalent Assurance

1. The competent authorities shall have the authority to require an applicant to provide a security or equivalent assurance sufficient to protect the defendant and the competent authorities and to prevent abuse. Such security or equivalent assurance shall not unreasonably deter recourse to these procedures.

2. Where pursuant to an application under this Section the release of goods involving industrial designs, patents, layout-designs or undisclosed information into free circulation has been suspended by customs authorities on the basis of a decision other than by a judicial or other independent authority, and the period provided for in Article 55 has expired without the granting of provisional relief by the duly empowered authority, and provided that all other conditions for importation have been complied with, the owner, importer, or consignee of such goods shall be entitled to their release on the posting of a security in an amount sufficient to protect the right holder for any infringement. Payment of such security shall not prejudice any other remedy available to the right holder, it being understood that the security shall be released if the right holder fails to pursue the right of action within a reasonable period of time.

Article 54

Notice of Suspension

The importer and the applicant shall be promptly notified of the suspension of the release of goods according to Article 51.

Article 55

Duration of Suspension

If, within a period not exceeding 10 working days after the applicant has been served notice of the suspension, the customs authorities have not been informed that proceedings leading to a decision on the merits of the case have been initiated by a party other than the defendant, or that the duly empowered authority has taken provisional measures prolonging the suspension of the release of the goods, the goods shall be released, provided that all other conditions for importation or exportation have been complied with; in appropriate cases, this time-limit may be extended by another 10 working days. If proceedings leading to a decision on the merits of the case have been initiated, a review, including a right to be heard, shall take place upon request of the defendant with a view to deciding, within a reasonable period, whether these measures shall be modified, revoked or confirmed. Notwithstanding the above, where the suspension of the release of goods is carried out or continued in accordance with a provisional judicial measure, the provisions of paragraph 6 of Article 50 shall apply.

Article 56

Indemnification of the Importer and of the Owner of the Goods

Relevant authorities shall have the authority to order the applicant to pay the importer, the consignee and the owner of the goods appropriate compensation for any injury caused to them through the wrongful detention of goods or through the detention of goods released pursuant to Article 55.

Article 57

Right of Inspection and Information

Without prejudice to the protection of confidential information, Members shall provide the competent authorities the authority to give the right holder sufficient opportunity to have any goods detained by the customs authorities inspected in order to substantiate the right holder's claims. The competent authorities shall also have authority to give the importer an equivalent opportunity to have any such goods inspected. Where a positive determination has been made on the merits of a case, Members may provide the competent authorities the authority to inform the right holder of the names and addresses of the consignor, the importer and the consignee and of the quantity of the goods in question.

Article 58

Ex Officio Action

Where Members require competent authorities to act upon their own initiative and to suspend the release of goods in respect of which they have acquired *prima facie* evidence that an intellectual property right is being infringed:

(a) the competent authorities may at any time seek from the right holder any information that may assist them to exercise these powers;

(b) the importer and the right holder shall be promptly notified of the suspension. Where the importer has lodged an appeal against the suspension with the competent authorities, the suspension shall be subject to the conditions, *mutatis mutandis*, set out at Article 55;

(c) Members shall only exempt both public authorities and officials from liability to appropriate remedial measures where actions are taken or intended in good faith.

Article 59

Remedies

Without prejudice to other rights of action open to the right holder and subject to the right of the defendant to seek review by a judicial authority, competent authorities shall have the authority to order the destruction or disposal of infringing goods in accordance with the principles set out in Article 46. In regard to counterfeit trademark goods, the authorities shall not allow the re-exportation of the infringing goods in an unaltered state or subject them to a different customs procedure, other than in exceptional circumstances.

Article 60

De Minimis Imports

Members may exclude from the application of the above provisions small quantities of goods of a non-commercial nature contained in travellers' personal luggage or sent in small consignments.

SECTION 5: CRIMINAL PROCEDURES

Article 61

Members shall provide for criminal procedures and penalties to be applied at least in cases of wilful trademark counterfeiting or copyright piracy on a commercial scale. Remedies available shall include imprisonment andfor monetary fines sufficient to provide a deterrent, consistently with the level of penalties applied for crimes of a corresponding gravity. In appropriate cases, remedies available shall also include the seizure, forfeiture and destruction of the infringing goods and of any materials and implements the predominant use of which has been in the commission of the offence. Members may provide for criminal procedures and penalties to be applied in other cases of infringement of intellectual property rights, in particular where they are committed wilfully and on a commercial scale.

PART IV

ACQUISITION AND MAINTENANCE OF INTELLECTUAL PROPERTY RIGHTS AND RELATED *INTER-PARTES* PROCEDURES

Article 62

1. Members may require, as a condition of the acquisition or maintenance of the intellectual property rights provided for under Sections 2 through 6 of Part II, compliance with reasonable procedures and formalities. Such procedures and formalities shall be consistent with the provisions of this Agreement.

2. Where the acquisition of an intellectual property right is subject to the right being granted or registered, Members shall ensure that the procedures for grant or registration, subject to compliance with the substantive conditions for acquisition of the right, permit the granting or registration of the right within a reasonable period of time so as to avoid unwarranted curtailment of the period of protection.

3. Article 4 of the Paris Convention (1967) shall apply *mutatis mutandis* to service marks.

4. Procedures concerning the acquisition or maintenance of intellectual property rights and, where a Member's law provides for such procedures, administrative revocation and *inter partes* procedures such as opposition, revocation and cancellation, shall be governed by the general principles set out in paragraphs 2 and 3 of Article 41.

5. Final administrative decisions in any of the procedures referred to under paragraph 4 shall be subject to review by a judicial or quasi-judicial authority. However, there shall be no obligation to provide an opportunity for such review of decisions in cases of unsuccessful opposition or administrative revocation, provided that the grounds for such procedures can be the subject of invalidation procedures.

PART V

DISPUTE PREVENTION AND SETTLEMENT

Article 63

Transparency

1. Laws and regulations, and final judicial decisions and administrative rulings of general application, made effective by a Member pertaining to the subject matter of this Agreement (the availability, scope, acquisition, enforcement and prevention of the abuse of intellectual property rights) shall be published, or where such publication is not practicable made publicly available, in a national language, in such a manner as to enable governments and right holders to become acquainted with them. Agreements concerning the subject matter of this Agreement which are in force between the government or a governmental agency of a Member and the government or a governmental agency of another Member shall also be published.

2. Members shall notify the laws and regulations referred to in paragraph 1 to the Council for TRIPS in order to assist that Council in its review of the operation of this Agreement. The Council shall attempt to minimize the burden on Members in carrying out this obligation and may decide to waive the obligation to notify such laws and regulations directly to the Council if consultations with WIPO on the establishment of a common register containing these laws and regulations are successful. The Council shall also consider in this connection any action required regarding notifications pursuant to the obligations under this Agreement stemming from the provisions of Article 6*ter* of the Paris Convention (1967).

3. Each Member shall be prepared to supply, in response to a written request from another Member, information of the sort referred to in paragraph 1. A

Member, having reason to believe that a specific judicial decision or administrative ruling or bilateral agreement in the area of intellectual property rights affects its rights under this Agreement, may also request in writing to be given access to or be informed in sufficient detail of such specific judicial decisions or administrative rulings or bilateral agreements.

4. Nothing in paragraphs 1, 2 and 3 shall require Members to disclose confidential information which would impede law enforcement or otherwise be contrary to the public interest or would prejudice the legitimate commercial interests of particular enterprises, public or private.

Article 64
Dispute Settlement

1. The provisions of Articles XXII and XXIII of GATT 1994 as elaborated and applied by the Dispute Settlement Understanding shall apply to consultations and the settlement of disputes under this Agreement except as otherwise specifically provided herein.

2. Subparagraphs 1(b) and 1(c) of Article XXIII of GATT 1994 shall not apply to the settlement of disputes under this Agreement for a period of five years from the date of entry into force of the WTO Agreement.

3. During the time period referred to in paragraph 2, the Council for TRIPS shall examine the scope and modalities for complaints of the type provided for under subparagraphs 1(b) and 1(c) of Article XXIII of GATT 1994 made pursuant to this Agreement, and submit its recommendations to the Ministerial Conference for approval. Any decision of the Ministerial Conference to approve such recommendations or to extend the period in paragraph 2 shall be made only by consensus, and approved recommendations shall be effective for all Members without further formal acceptance process.

PART VI

TRANSITIONAL ARRANGEMENTS

Article 65
Transitional Arrangements

1. Subject to the provisions of paragraphs 2, 3 and 4, no Member shall be obliged to apply the provisions of this Agreement before the expiry of a general period of one year following the date of entry into force of the WTO Agreement.

2. A developing country Member is entitled to delay for a further period of four years the date of application, as defined in paragraph 1, of the provisions of this

Agreement other than Articles 3, 4 and 5.

3. Any other Member which is in the process of transformation from a centrally-planned into a market, free-enterprise economy and which is undertaking structural reform of its intellectual property system and facing special problems in the preparation and implementation of intellectual property laws and regulations, may also benefit from a period of delay as foreseen in paragraph 2.

4. To the extent that a developing country Member is obliged by this Agreement to extend product patent protection to areas of technology not so protectable in its territory on the general date of application of this Agreement for that Member, as defined in paragraph 2, it may delay the application of the provisions on product patents of Section 5 of Part II to such areas of technology for an additional period of five years.

5. A Member availing itself of a transitional period under paragraphs 1, 2, 3 or 4 shall ensure that any changes in its laws, regulations and practice made during that period do not result in a lesser degree of consistency with the provisions of this Agreement.

Article 66
Least-Developed Country Members

1. In view of the special needs and requirements of least-developed country Members, their economic, financial and administrative constraints, and their need for flexibility to create a viable technological base, such Members shall not be required to apply the provisions of this Agreement, other than Articles 3, 4 and 5, for a period of 10 years from the date of application as defined under paragraph 1 of Article 65. The Council for TRIPS shall, upon duly motivated request by a least-developed country Member, accord extensions of this period.

2. Developed country Members shall provide incentives to enterprises and institutions in their territories for the purpose of promoting and encouraging technology transfer to least-developed country Members in order to enable them to create a sound and viable technological base.

Article 67
Technical Cooperation

In order to facilitate the implementation of this Agreement, developed country Members shall provide, on request and on mutually agreed terms and conditions, technical and financial cooperation in favour of developing and least-developed country Members. Such cooperation shall include assistance in the preparation of laws and regulations on the protection and enforcement of intellectual property rights as well as on the prevention of their abuse, and shall include support regarding the establishment or reinforcement of domestic offices and agencies relevant to these matters, including the training of personnel.

PART VII

INSTITUTIONAL ARRANGEMENTS; FINAL PROVISIONS

Article 68

Council for Trade-Related Aspects of Intellectual Property Rights

The Council for TRIPS shall monitor the operation of this Agreement and, in particular, Members' compliance with their obligations hereunder, and shall afford Members the opportunity of consulting on matters relating to the trade-related aspects of intellectual property rights. It shall carry out such other responsibilities as assigned to it by the Members, and it shall, in particular, provide any assistance requested by them in the context of dispute settlement procedures. In carrying out its functions, the Council for TRIPS may consult with and seek information from any source it deems appropriate. In consultation with WIPO, the Council shall seek to establish, within one year of its first meeting, appropriate arrangements for cooperation with bodies of that Organization.

Article 69

International Cooperation

Members agree to cooperate with each other with a view to eliminating international trade in goods infringing intellectual property rights. For this purpose, they shall establish and notify contact points in their administrations and be ready to exchange information on trade in infringing goods. They shall, in particular, promote the exchange of information and cooperation between customs authorities with regard to trade in counterfeit trademark goods and pirated copyright goods.

Article 70

Protection of Existing Subject Matter

1. This Agreement does not give rise to obligations in respect of acts which occurred before the date of application of the Agreement for the Member in question.

2. Except as otherwise provided for in this Agreement, this Agreement gives rise to obligations in respect of all subject matter existing at the date of application of this Agreement for the Member in question, and which is protected in that Member on the said date, or which meets or comes subsequently to meet the criteria for protection under the terms of this Agreement. In respect of this paragraph and paragraphs 3 and 4, copyright obligations with respect to existing works shall be solely determined under Article 18 of the Berne Convention (1971), and obligations

with respect to the rights of producers of phonograms and performers in existing phonograms shall be determined solely under Article 18 of the Berne Convention (1971) as made applicable under paragraph 6 of Article 14 of this Agreement.

3. There shall be no obligation to restore protection to subject matter which on the date of application of this Agreement for the Member in question has fallen into the public domain.

4. In respect of any acts in respect of specific objects embodying protected subject matter which become infringing under the terms of legislation in conformity with this Agreement, and which were commenced, or in respect of which a significant investment was made, before the date of acceptance of the WTO Agreement by that Member, any Member may provide for a limitation of the remedies available to the right holder as to the continued performance of such acts after the date of application of this Agreement for that Member. In such cases the Member shall, however, at least provide for the payment of equitable remuneration.

5. A Member is not obliged to apply the provisions of Article 11 and of paragraph 4 of Article 14 with respect to originals or copies purchased prior to the date of application of this Agreement for that Member.

6. Members shall not be required to apply Article 31, or the requirement in paragraph 1 of Article 27 that patent rights shall be enjoyable without discrimination as to the field of technology, to use without the authorization of the right holder where authorization for such use was granted by the government before the date this Agreement became known.

7. In the case of intellectual property rights for which protection is conditional upon registration, applications for protection which are pending on the date of application of this Agreement for the Member in question shall be permitted to be amended to claim any enhanced protection provided under the provisions of this Agreement. Such amendments shall not include new matter.

8. Where a Member does not make available as of the date of entry into force of the WTO Agreement patent protection for pharmaceutical and agricultural chemical products commensurate with its obligations under Article 27, that Member shall:

(a) notwithstanding the provisions of Part VI, provide as from the date of entry into force of the WTO Agreement a means by which applications for patents for such inventions can be filed;

(b) apply to these applications, as of the date of application of this Agreement, the criteria for patentability as laid down in this Agreement as if those criteria were being applied on the date of filing in that Member or, where priority is available and claimed, the priority date of the application; and

(c) provide patent protection in accordance with this Agreement as from the grant of the patent and for the remainder of the patent term, counted from the filing date in accordance with Article 33 of this Agreement, for those of these applications that meet the criteria for protection referred to in subparagraph (b) .

9. Where a product is the subject of a patent application in a Member in accordance with paragraph 8(a) , exclusive marketing rights shall be granted, notwithstanding the provisions of Part VI, for a period of five years after obtaining marketing approval in that Member or until a product patent is granted or rejected in that Member, whichever period is shorter, provided that, subsequent to the entry into force of the WTO Agreement, a patent application has been filed and a patent granted for that product in another Member and marketing approval obtained in such other Member.

Article 71
Review and Amendment

1. The Council for TRIPS shall review the implementation of this Agreement after the expiration of the transitional period referred to in paragraph 2 of Article 65. The Council shall, having regard to the experience gained in its implementation, review it two years after that date, and at identical intervals thereafter. The Council may also undertake reviews in the light of any relevant new developments which might warrant modification or amendment of this Agreement.

2. Amendments merely serving the purpose of adjusting to higher levels of protection of intellectual property rights achieved, and in force, in other multilateral agreements and accepted under those agreements by all Members of the WTO may be referred to the Ministerial Conference for action in accordance with paragraph 6 of Article X of the WTO Agreement on the basis of a consensus proposal from the Council for TRIPS.

Article 72
Reservations

Reservations may not be entered in respect of any of the provisions of this Agreement without the consent of the other Members.

Article 73
Security Exceptions

Nothing in this Agreement shall be construed:

(a) to require a Member to furnish any information the disclosure of which it considers contrary to its essential security interests; or

(b) to prevent a Member from taking any action which it considers necessary for the protection of its essential security interests;

(i) relating to fissionable materials or the materials from which they are derived;

(ii) relating to the traffic in arms, ammunition and implements of war and to such traffic in other goods and materials as is carried on directly or indirectly for the purpose of supplying a military establishment;

(iii) taken in time of war or other emergency in international relations; or

(c) to prevent a Member from taking any action in pursuance of its obligations under the United Nations Charter for the maintenance of international peace and security.

WIPO Copyright Treaty (WCT) (1996) *,**

TABLE OF CONTENTS

---

* This treaty was adopted by the WIPO Diplomatic Conference on Certain Copyright and Neighboring Rights Questions in Geneva, on December 20, 1996.

** The agreed statements of the Diplomatic Conference (that adopted the treaty) concerning certain provisions of the WCT are reproduced in footnotes under the provisions concerned.

Preamble

The Contracting Parties,

Desiring to develop and maintain the protection of the rights of authors in their literary and artistic works in a manner as effective and uniform as possible,

Recognizing the need to introduce new international rules and clarify the interpretation of certain existing rules in order to provide adequate solutions to the questions raised by new economic, social, cultural and technological developments,

Recognizing the profound impact of the development and convergence of information and communication technologies on the creation and use of literary and artistic works,

Emphasizing the outstanding significance of copyright protection as an incentive for literary and artistic creation,

Recognizing the need to maintain a balance between the rights of authors and the larger public interest, particularly education, research and access to information, as reflected in the Berne Convention,

Have agreed as follows:

Article 1
Relation to the Berne Convention

(1) This Treaty is a special agreement within the meaning of Article 20 of the Berne Convention for the Protection of Literary and Artistic Works, as regards Contracting Parties that are countries of the Union established by that Convention. This Treaty shall not have any connection with treaties other than the Berne Convention, nor shall it prejudice any rights and obligations under any other treaties.

(2) Nothing in this Treaty shall derogate from existing obligations that Contracting Parties have to each other under the Berne Convention for the Protection of Literary and Artistic Works.

(3) Hereinafter, "Berne Convention" shall refer to the Paris Act of July 24, 1971, of the Berne Convention for the Protection of Literary and Artistic Works.

(4) Contracting Parties shall comply with Articles 1 to 21 and the Appendix of

the Berne Convention. ①

Article 2

Scope of Copyright Protection

Copyright protection extends to expressions and not to ideas, procedures, methods of operation or mathematical concepts as such.

Article 3

Application of Articles 2 to 6 of the Berne Convention

Contracting Parties shall apply *mutatis mutandis* the provisions of Articles 2 to6 of the Berne Convention in respect of the protection provided for in this Treaty. ②

Article 4

Computer Programs

Computer programs are protected as literary works within the meaning of Article 2 of the Berne Convention. Such protection applies to computer programs, whatever may be the mode or form of their expression. ③

Article 5

Compilations of Data (Databases)

Compilations of data or other material, in any form, which by reason of the selection or arrangement of their contents constitute intellectual creations, are protected as such. This protection does not extend to the data or the material itself and

---

① Agreed statement concerning Article 1(4): The reproduction right, as set out in Article 9 of the Berne Convention, and the exceptions permitted thereunder, fully apply in the digital environment, in particular to the use of works in digital form. It is understood that the storage of a protected work in digital form in an electronic medium constitutes a reproduction within the meaning of Article 9 of the Berne Convention.

② Agreed statement concerning Article 3: It is understood that, in applying Article 3 of this Treaty, the expression "country of the Union" in Articles 2 to 6 of the Berne Convention will be read as if it were a reference to a Contracting Party to this Treaty, in the application of those Berne Articles in respect of protection provided for in this Treaty. It is also understood that the expression "country outside the Union" in those Articles in the Berne Convention will, in the same circumstances, be read as if it were a reference to a country that is not a Contracting Party to this Treaty, and that "this Convention" in Articles 2(8) , 2bis(2) , 3, 4 and 5 of the Berne Convention will be read as if it were a reference to the Berne Convention and this Treaty. Finally, it is understood that a reference in Articles 3 to 6 of the Berne Convention to a "national of one of the countries of the Union" will, when these Articles are applied to this Treaty, mean, in regard to an intergovernmental organization that is a Contracting Party to this Treaty, a national of one of the countries that is member of that organization.

③ Agreed statement concerning Article 4: The scope of protection for computer programs under Article 4 of this Treaty, read with Article 2, is consistent with Article 2 of the Berne Convention and on a par with the relevant provisions of the TRIPS Agreement.

is without prejudice to any copyright subsisting in the data or material contained in the compilation. ④

Article 6
Right of Distribution

(1) Authors of literary and artistic works shall enjoy the exclusive right of authorizing the making available to the public of the original and copies of their works through sale or other transfer of ownership.

(2) Nothing in this Treaty shall affect the freedom of Contracting Parties to determine the conditions, if any, under which the exhaustion of the right in paragraph (1) applies after the first sale or other transfer of ownership of the original or a copy of the work with the authorization of the author. ⑤

Article 7
Right of Rental

(1) Authors of

(i) computer programs;

(ii) cinematographic works;and

(iii) works embodied in phonograms, as determined in the national law of Contracting Parties,

shall enjoy the exclusive right of authorizing commercial rental to the public of the originals or copies of their works.

(2) Paragraph (1) shall not apply

(i) in the case of computer programs, where the program itself is not the essential object of the rental; and

(ii) in the case of cinematographic works, unless such commercial rental has led to widespread copying of such works materially impairing the exclusive right of reproduction.

(3) Notwithstanding the provisions of paragraph (1) , a Contracting Party that, on April 15, 1994, had and continues to have in force a system of equitable remuneration of authors for the rental of copies of their works embodied in phonograms may maintain that system provided that the commercial rental of works embodied in phonograms is not giving rise to the material impairment of the exclusive right of

---

④ Agreed statement concerning Article 5: The scope of protection for compilations of data (databases) under Article 5 of this Treaty, read with Article 2, is consistent with Article 2 of the Berne Convention and on a par with the relevant provisions of the TRIPS Agreement.

⑤ Agreed statement concerning Articles 6 and 7: As used in these Articles, the expressions "copies" and "original and copies," being subject to the right of distribution and the right of rental under the said Articles, refer exclusively to fixed copies that can be put into circulation as tangible objects.

reproduction of authors. ⑥ ⑦

Article 8
Right of Communication to the Public

Without prejudice to the provisions of Articles 11(1) (ii) , 11*bis*(1) (i) and (ii) , 11*ter*(1) (ii) , 14(1) (ii) and 14*bis*(1) of the Berne Convention, authors of literary and artistic works shall enjoy the exclusive right of authorizing any communication to the public of their works, by wire or wireless means, including the making available to the public of their works in such a way that members of the public may access these works from a place and at a time individually chosen by them. ⑧

Article 9
Duration of the Protection of Photographic Works

In respect of photographic works, the Contracting Parties shall not apply the provisions of Article 7(4) of the Berne Convention.

Article 10
Limitations and Exceptions

(1) Contracting Parties may, in their national legislation, provide for limitations of or exceptions to the rights granted to authors of literary and artistic works under this Treaty in certain special cases that do not conflict with a normal exploitation of the work and do not unreasonably prejudice the legitimate interests of the author.

(2) Contracting Parties shall, when applying the Berne Convention, confine any limitations of or exceptions to rights provided for therein to certain special cases that do not conflict with a normal exploitation of the work and do not unreasonably

⑥ Agreed statement concerning Articles 6 and 7: As used in these Articles, the expressions "copies" and "original and copies," being subject to the right of distribution and the right of rental under the said Articles, refer exclusively to fixed copies that can be put into circulation as tangible objects.

⑦ Agreed statement concerning Article 7: It is understood that the obligation under Article 7(1) does not require a Contracting Party to provide an exclusive right of commercial rental to authors who, under that Contracting Party' s law, are not granted rights in respect of phonograms. It is understood that this obligation is consistent with Article 14(4) of the TRIPS Agreement.

⑧ Agreed statement concerning Article 8: It is understood that the mere provision of physical facilities for enabling or making a communication does not in itself amount to communication within the meaning of this Treaty or the Berne Convention. It is further understood that nothing in Article 8 precludes a Contracting Party from applying Article 11bis(2) .

prejudice the legitimate interests of the author.⑨

Article 11
Obligations concerning Technological Measures

Contracting Parties shall provide adequate legal protection and effective legal remedies against the circumvention of effective technological measures that are used by authors in connection with the exercise of their rights under this Treaty or the Berne Convention and that restrict acts, in respect of their works, which are not authorized by the authors concerned or permitted by law.

Article 12
Obligations concerning Rights Management Information

(1) Contracting Parties shall provide adequate and effective legal remedies against any person knowingly performing any of the following acts knowing, or with respect to civil remedies having reasonable grounds to know, that it will induce, enable, facilitate or conceal an infringement of any right covered by this Treaty or the Berne Convention:

(i) to remove or alter any electronic rights management information without authority;

(ii) to distribute, import for distribution, broadcast or communicate to the public, without authority, works or copies of works knowing that electronic rights management information has been removed or altered without authority.

(2) As used in this Article, "rights management information" means information which identifies the work, the author of the work, the owner of any right in the work, or information about the terms and conditions of use of the work, and any numbers or codes that represent such information, when any of these items of information is attached to a copy of a work or appears in connection with the communication of a work to the public.⑩

⑨ Agreed statement concerning Article 10: It is understood that the provisions of Article 10 permit Contracting Parties to carry forward and appropriately extend into the digital environment limitations and exceptions in their national laws which have been considered acceptable under the Berne Convention. Similarly, these provisions should be understood to permit Contracting Parties to devise new exceptions and limitations that are appropriate in the digital network environment.

It is also understood that Article 10(2) neither reduces nor extends the scope of applicability of the limitations and exceptions permitted by the Berne Convention.

⑩ Agreed statement concerning Article 12: It is understood that the reference to "infringement of any right covered by this Treaty or the Berne Convention" includes both exclusive rights and rights of remuneration.

It is further understood that Contracting Parties will not rely on this Article to devise or implement rights management systems that would have the effect of imposing formalities which are not permitted under the Berne Convention or this Treaty, prohibiting the free movement of goods or impeding the enjoyment of rights under this Treaty.

Article 13

Application in Time

Contracting Parties shall apply the provisions of Article 18 of the Berne Convention to all protection provided for in this Treaty.

Article 14

Provisions on Enforcement of Rights

(1) Contracting Parties undertake to adopt, in accordance with their legal systems, the measures necessary to ensure the application of this Treaty.

(2) Contracting Parties shall ensure that enforcement procedures are available under their law so as to permit effective action against any act of infringement of rights covered by this Treaty, including expeditious remedies to prevent infringements and remedies which constitute a deterrent to further infringements.

Article 15

Assembly

(1) (a) The Contracting Parties shall have an Assembly.

(b) Each Contracting Party shall be represented by one delegate who may be assisted by alternate delegates, advisors and experts.

(c) The expenses of each delegation shall be borne by the Contracting Party that has appointed the delegation. The Assembly may ask the World Intellectual Property Organization (hereinafter referred to as "WIPO") to grant financial assistance to facilitate the participation of delegations of Contracting Parties that are regarded as developing countries in conformity with the established practice of the General Assembly of the United Nations or that are countries in transition to a market economy.

(2) (a) The Assembly shall deal with matters concerning the maintenance and development of this Treaty and the application and operation of this Treaty.

(b) The Assembly shall perform the function allocated to it under Article 17(2) in respect of the admission of certain intergovernmental organizations to become party to this Treaty.

(c) The Assembly shall decide the convocation of any diplomatic conference for the revision of this Treaty and give the necessary instructions to the Director General of WIPO for the preparation of such diplomatic conference.

(3) (a) Each Contracting Party that is a State shall have one vote and shall vote only in its own name.

(b) Any Contracting Party that is an intergovernmental organization may participate in the vote, in place of its Member States, with a number of votes equal to the number of its Member States which are party to this Treaty. No such intergovernmental organization shall participate in the vote if any one of its Member States exercises its right to vote and *vice versa*.

(4) The Assembly shall meet in ordinary session once every two years upon convocation by the Director General of WIPO.

(5) The Assembly shall establish its own rules of procedure, including the convocation of extraordinary sessions, the requirements of a quorum and, subject to the provisions of this Treaty, the required majority for various kinds of decisions.

Article 16
International Bureau

The International Bureau of WIPO shall perform the administrative tasks concerning the Treaty.

Article 17
Eligibility for Becoming Party to the Treaty

(1) Any Member State of WIPO may become party to this Treaty.

(2) The Assembly may decide to admit any intergovernmental organization to become party to this Treaty which declares that it is competent in respect of, and has its own legislation binding on all its Member States on, matters covered by this Treaty and that it has been duly authorized, in accordance with its internal procedures, to become party to this Treaty.

(3) The European Community, having made the declaration referred to in the preceding paragraph in the Diplomatic Conference that has adopted this Treaty, may become party to this Treaty.

Article 18
Rights and Obligations under the Treaty

Subject to any specific provisions to the contrary in this Treaty, each Contracting Party shall enjoy all of the rights and assume all of the obligations under this Treaty.

Article 19
Signature of the Treaty

This Treaty shall be open for signature until December 31, 1997, by any Member State of WIPO and by the European Community.

Article 20
Entry into Force of the Treaty

This Treaty shall enter into force three months after 30 instruments of ratification or accession by States have been deposited with the Director General of WIPO.

Article 21

Effective Date of Becoming Party to the Treaty

This Treaty shall bind:

(i) the 30 States referred to in Article 20, from the date on which this Treaty has entered into force;

(ii) each other State, from the expiration of three months from the date on which the State has deposited its instrument with the Director General of WIPO;

(iii) the European Community, from the expiration of three months after the deposit of its instrument of ratification or accession if such instrument has been deposited after the entry into force of this Treaty according to Article 20, or, three months after the entry into force of this Treaty if such instrument has been deposited before the entry into force of this Treaty;

(iv) any other intergovernmental organization that is admitted to become party to this Treaty, from the expiration of three months after the deposit of its instrument of accession.

Article 22

No Reservations to the Treaty

No reservation to this Treaty shall be admitted.

Article 23

Denunciation of the Treaty

This Treaty may be denounced by any Contracting Party by notification addressed to the Director General of WIPO. Any denunciation shall take effect one year from the date on which the Director General of WIPO received the notification.

Article 24

Languages of the Treaty

(1) This Treaty is signed in a single original in English, Arabic, Chinese, French, Russian and Spanish languages, the versions in all these languages being equally authentic.

(2) An official text in any language other than those referred to in paragraph (1) shall be established by the Director General of WIPO on the request of an interested party, after consultation with all the interested parties. For the purposes of this paragraph, “interested party” means any Member State of WIPO whose official language, or one of whose official languages, is involved and the European Community, and any other intergovernmental organization that may become party to this Treaty, if one of its official languages is involved.

Article 25

Depositary

The Director General of WIPO is the depositary of this Treaty.

WIPO Performances and Phonograms Treaty (WPPT)[*,**]

(1996)

TABLE OF CONTENTS

* This treaty was adopted by the WIPO Diplomatic Conference on Certain Copyright and Neighboring Rights Questions in Geneva, on December 20, 1996.

** The agreed statements of the Diplomatic Conference (that adopted the Treaty) concerning certain provisions of the WPPT are reproduced in footnotes under the provisions concerned.

Preamble

The Contracting Parties,

Desiring to develop and maintain the protection of the rights of performers and producers of phonograms in a manner as effective and uniform as possible,

Recognizing the need to introduce new international rules in order to provide adequate solutions to the questions raised by economic, social, cultural and technological developments,

Recognizing the profound impact of the development and convergence of information and communication technologies on the production and use of performances and phonograms,

Recognizing the need to maintain a balance between the rights of performers and producers of phonograms and the larger public interest, particularly education, research and access to information,

Have agreed as follows:

Chapter I

General Provisions

Article 1

Relation to Other Conventions

(1) Nothing in this Treaty shall derogate from existing obligations that Contracting Parties have to each other under the International Convention for the Protection of Performers, Producers of Phonograms and Broadcasting Organizations done in Rome, October 26, 1961 (hereinafter the "Rome Convention") .

(2) Protection granted under this Treaty shall leave intact and shall in no way affect the protection of copyright in literary and artistic works. Consequently, no provision of this Treaty may be interpreted as prejudicing such protection. ①

(3) This Treaty shall not have any connection with, nor shall it prejudice any rights and obligations under, any other treaties.

Article 2

Definitions

For the purposes of this Treaty:

(a) "performers" are actors, singers, musicians, dancers, and other persons who act, sing, deliver, declaim, play in, interpret, or otherwise perform literary or artistic works or expressions of folklore;

(b) "phonogram" means the fixation of the sounds of a performance or of other sounds, or of a representation of sounds, other than in the form of a fixation

① Agreed statement concerning Article 1(2): It is understood that Article 1(2) clarifies the relationship between rights in phonograms under this Treaty and copyright in works embodied in the phonograms. In cases where authorization is needed from both the author of a work embodied in the phonogram and a performer or producer owning rights in the phonogram, the need for the authorization of the author does not cease to exist because the authorization of the performer or producer is also required, and vice versa.

It is further understood that nothing in Article 1(2) precludes a Contracting Party from providing exclusive rights to a performer or producer of phonograms beyond those required to be provided under this Treaty.

incorporated in a cinematographic or other audiovisual work; ②

(c) "fixation" means the embodiment of sounds, or of the representations thereof, from which they can be perceived, reproduced or communicated through a device;

(d) "producer of a phonogram" means the person, or the legal entity, who or which takes the initiative and has the responsibility for the first fixation of the sounds of a performance or other sounds, or the representations of sounds;

(e) "publication" of a fixed performance or a phonogram means the offering of copies of the fixed performance or the phonogram to the public, with the consent of the rightholder, and provided that copies are offered to the public in reasonable quantity; ③

(f) "broadcasting" means the transmission by wireless means for public reception of sounds or of images and sounds or of the representations thereof; such transmission by satellite is also "broadcasting"; transmission of encrypted signals is "broadcasting" where the means for decrypting are provided to the public by the broadcasting organization or with its consent;

(g) "communication to the public" of a performance or a phonogram means the transmission to the public by any medium, otherwise than by broadcasting, of sounds of a performance or the sounds or the representations of sounds fixed in a phonogram. For the purposes of Article 15, "communication to the public" includes making the sounds or representations of sounds fixed in a phonogram audible to the public.

Article 3
Beneficiaries of Protection under this Treaty

(1) Contracting Parties shall accord the protection provided under this Treaty to the performers and producers of phonograms who are nationals of other Contracting Parties.

(2) The nationals of other Contracting Parties shall be understood to be those performers or producers of phonograms who would meet the criteria for eligibility for protection provided under the Rome Convention, were all the Contracting Parties to this Treaty Contracting States of that Convention. In respect of these criteria of eligibility, Contracting Parties shall apply the relevant definitions in Article 2 of

② Agreed statement concerning Article 2(b): It is understood that the definition of phonogram provided in Article 2(b) does not suggest that rights in the phonogram are in any way affected through their incorporation into a cinematographic or other audiovisual work.

③ Agreed statement concerning Articles 2(e) , 8, 9, 12, and 13: As used in these Articles, the expressions "copies" and "original and copies," being subject to the right of distribution and the right of rental under the said Articles, refer exclusively to fixed copies that can be put into circulation as tangible objects.

this Treaty.[④]

(3) Any Contracting Party availing itself of the possibilities provided in Article 5(3) of the Rome Convention or, for the purposes of Article 5 of the same Convention, Article 17 thereof shall make a notification as foreseen in those provisions to the Director General of the World Intellectual Property Organization (WIPO) .[⑤]

Article 4
National Treatment

(1) Each Contracting Party shall accord to nationals of other Contracting Parties, as defined in Article 3(2) , the treatment it accords to its own nationals with regard to the exclusive rights specifically granted in this Treaty, and to the right to equitable remuneration provided for in Article 15 of this Treaty.

(2) The obligation provided for in paragraph (1) does not apply to the extent that another Contracting Party makes use of the reservations permitted by Article 15(3) of this Treaty.

Chapter II

Rights of Performers

Article 5
Moral Rights of Performers

(1) Independently of a performer's economic rights, and even after the transfer of those rights, the performer shall, as regards his live aural performances or performances fixed in phonograms, have the right to claim to be identified as the performer of his performances, except where omission is dictated by the manner of the use of the performance, and to object to any distortion, mutilation or other modification of his performances that would be prejudicial to his reputation.

(2) The rights granted to a performer in accordance with paragraph (1) shall, after his death, be maintained, at least until the expiry of the economic rights, and shall be exercisable by the persons or institutions authorized by the legislation of the Contracting Party where protection is claimed. However, those Contracting Parties whose legislation, at the moment of their ratification of or accession to this Treaty, does not provide for protection after the death of the performer of all rights

④ Agreed statement concerning Article 3(2): For the application of Article 3(2) , it is understood that fixation means the finalization of the master tape ("bande-mère") .

⑤ Agreed statement concerning Article 3: It is understood that the reference in Articles 5(a) and 16(a)(iv) of the Rome Convention to "national of another Contracting State" will, when applied to this Treaty, mean, in regard to an intergovernmental organization that is a Contracting Party to this Treaty, a national of one of the countries that is a member of that organization.

set out in the preceding paragraph may provide that some of these rights will, after his death, cease to be maintained.

(3) The means of redress for safeguarding the rights granted under this Article shall be governed by the legislation of the Contracting Party where protection is claimed.

Article 6

Economic Rights of Performers in their Unfixed Performances

Performers shall enjoy the exclusive right of authorizing, as regards their performances:

(i) the broadcasting and communication to the public of their unfixed performances except where the performance is already a broadcast performance; and

(ii) the fixation of their unfixed performances.

Article 7

Right of Reproduction

Performers shall enjoy the exclusive right of authorizing the direct or indirect reproduction of their performances fixed in phonograms, in any manner or form. ⑥

Article 8

Right of Distribution

(1) Performers shall enjoy the exclusive right of authorizing the making available to the public of the original and copies of their performances fixed in phonograms through sale or other transfer of ownership.

(2) Nothing in this Treaty shall affect the freedom of Contracting Parties to determine the conditions, if any, under which the exhaustion of the right in paragraph (1) applies after the first sale or other transfer of ownership of the original or a copy of the fixed performance with the authorization of the performer. ⑦

Article 9

Right of Rental

(1) Performers shall enjoy the exclusive right of authorizing the commercial rental to the public of the original and copies of their performances fixed in

---

⑥ Agreed statement concerning Articles 7, 11 and 16: The reproduction right, as set out in Articles 7 and 11, and the exceptions permitted thereunder through Article 16, fully apply in the digital environment, in particular to the use of performances and phonograms in digital form. It is understood that the storage of a protected performance or phonogram in digital form in an electronic medium constitutes a reproduction within the meaning of these Articles.

⑦ Agreed statement concerning Articles 2(e) , 8, 9, 12, and 13: As used in these Articles, the expressions "copies" and "original and copies," being subject to the right of distribution and the right of rental under the said Articles, refer exclusively to fixed copies that can be put into circulation as tangible objects.

phonograms as determined in the national law of Contracting Parties, even after distribution of them by, or pursuant to, authorization by the performer.

(2) Notwithstanding the provisions of paragraph (1) , a Contracting Party that, on April 15, 1994, had and continues to have in force a system of equitable remuneration of performers for the rental of copies of their performances fixed in phonograms, may maintain that system provided that the commercial rental of phonograms is not giving rise to the material impairment of the exclusive right of reproduction of performers. ⑧

Article 10

Right of Making Available of Fixed Performances

Performers shall enjoy the exclusive right of authorizing the making available to the public of their performances fixed in phonograms, by wire or wireless means, in such a way that members of the public may access them from a place and at a time individually chosen by them.

Chapter III

Rights of Producers of Phonograms

Article 11

Right of Reproduction

Producers of phonograms shall enjoy the exclusive right of authorizing the direct or indirect reproduction of their phonograms, in any manner or form. ⑨

Article 12

Right of Distribution

(1) Producers of phonograms shall enjoy the exclusive right of authorizing the making available to the public of the original and copies of their phonograms through sale or other transfer of ownership.

(2) Nothing in this Treaty shall affect the freedom of Contracting Parties to determine the conditions, if any, under which the exhaustion of the right in paragraph

---

⑧ Agreed statement concerning Articles 2(e) , 8, 9, 12, and 13: As used in these Articles, the expressions "copies" and "original and copies," being subject to the right of distribution and the right of rental under the said Articles, refer exclusively to fixed copies that can be put into circulation as tangible objects.

⑨ Agreed statement concerning Articles 7, 11 and 16: The reproduction right, as set out in Articles 7 and 11, and the exceptions permitted thereunder through Article 16, fully apply in the digital environment, in particular to the use of performances and phonograms in digital form. It is understood that the storage of a protected performance or phonogram in digital form in an electronic medium constitutes a reproduction within the meaning of these Articles.

(1) applies after the first sale or other transfer of ownership of the original or a copy of the phonogram with the authorization of the producer of the phonogram. ⑩

Article 13
Right of Rental

(1) Producers of phonograms shall enjoy the exclusive right of authorizing the commercial rental to the public of the original and copies of their phonograms, even after distribution of them, by or pursuant to, authorization by the producer.

(2) Notwithstanding the provisions of paragraph (1) , a Contracting Party that, on April 15, 1994, had and continues to have in force a system of equitable remuneration of producers of phonograms for the rental of copies of their phonograms, may maintain that system provided that the commercial rental of phonograms is not giving rise to the material impairment of the exclusive rights of reproduction of producers of phonograms. ⑪

Article 14
Right of Making Available of Phonograms

Producers of phonograms shall enjoy the exclusive right of authorizing the making available to the public of their phonograms, by wire or wireless means, in such a way that members of the public may access them from a place and at a time individually chosen by them.

Chapter IV

Common Provisions

Article 15
Right to Remuneration for Broadcasting and Communication to the Public

(1) Performers and producers of phonograms shall enjoy the right to a single equitable remuneration for the direct or indirect use of phonograms published for commercial purposes for broadcasting or for any communication to the public.

(2) Contracting Parties may establish in their national legislation that the single equitable remuneration shall be claimed from the user by the performer or by the producer of a phonogram or by both. Contracting Parties may enact national

⑩ Agreed statement concerning Articles 2(e) , 8, 9, 12, and 13: As used in these Articles, the expressions "copies" and "original and copies," being subject to the right of distribution and the right of rental under the said Articles, refer exclusively to fixed copies that can be put into circulation as tangible objects.

⑪ Agreed statement concerning Articles 2(e) , 8, 9, 12, and 13: As used in these Articles, the expressions "copies" and "original and copies," being subject to the right of distribution and the right of rental under the said Articles, refer exclusively to fixed copies that can be put into circulation as tangible objects.

legislation that, in the absence of an agreement between the performer and the producer of a phonogram, sets the terms according to which performers and producers of phonograms shall share the single equitable remuneration.

(3) Any Contracting Party may, in a notification deposited with the Director General of WIPO, declare that it will apply the provisions of paragraph (1) only in respect of certain uses, or that it will limit their application in some other way, or that it will not apply these provisions at all.

(4) For the purposes of this Article, phonograms made available to the public by wire or wireless means in such a way that members of the public may access them from a place and at a time individually chosen by them shall be considered as if they had been published for commercial purposes. [⑫][⑬]

Article 16
Limitations and Exceptions

(1) Contracting Parties may, in their national legislation, provide for the same kinds of limitations or exceptions with regard to the protection of performers and producers of phonograms as they provide for, in their national legislation, in connection with the protection of copyright in literary and artistic works.

(2) Contracting Parties shall confine any limitations of or exceptions to rights provided for in this Treaty to certain special cases which do not conflict with a normal exploitation of the performance or phonogram and do not unreasonably prejudice the legitimate interests of the performer or of the producer of the

⑫ Agreed statement concerning Article 15: It is understood that Article 15 does not represent a complete resolution of the level of rights of broadcasting and communication to the public that should be enjoyed by performers and phonogram producers in the digital age. Delegations were unable to achieve consensus on differing proposals for aspects of exclusivity to be provided in certain circumstances or for rights to be provided without the possibility of reservations, and have therefore left the issue to future resolution.

⑬ Agreed statement concerning Article 15: It is understood that Article 15 does not prevent the granting of the right conferred by this Article to performers of folklore and producers of phonograms recording folklore where such phonograms have not been published for commercial gain.

phonogram.⑭⑮

Article 17
Term of Protection

(1) The term of protection to be granted to performers under this Treaty shall last, at least, until the end of a period of 50 years computed from the end of the year in which the performance was fixed in a phonogram.

(2) The term of protection to be granted to producers of phonograms under this Treaty shall last, at least, until the end of a period of 50 years computed from the end of the year in which the phonogram was published, or failing such publication within 50 years from fixation of the phonogram, 50 years from the end of the year in which the fixation was made.

Article 18
Obligations concerning Technological Measures

Contracting Parties shall provide adequate legal protection and effective legal remedies against the circumvention of effective technological measures that are used by performers or producers of phonograms in connection with the exercise of their rights under this Treaty and that restrict acts, in respect of their performances or phonograms, which are not authorized by the performers or the producers of phonograms concerned or permitted by law.

Article 19
Obligations concerning Rights Management Information

(1) Contracting Parties shall provide adequate and effective legal remedies against any person knowingly performing any of the following acts knowing, or with respect to civil remedies having reasonable grounds to know, that it will

---

⑭ Agreed statement concerning Articles 7, 11 and 16: The reproduction right, as set out in Articles 7 and 11, and the exceptions permitted thereunder through Article 16, fully apply in the digital environment, in particular to the use of performances and phonograms in digital form. It is understood that the storage of a protected performance or phonogram in digital form in an electronic medium constitutes a reproduction within the meaning of these Articles.

⑮ Agreed statement concerning Article 16: The agreed statement concerning Article 10 (on Limitations and Exceptions) of the WIPO Copyright Treaty is applicable mutatis mutandis also to Article 16 (on Limitations and Exceptions) of the WIPO Performances and Phonograms Treaty. [The text of the agreed statement concerning Article 10 of the WCT reads as follows: "It is understood that the provisions of Article 10 permit Contracting Parties to carry forward and appropriately extend into the digital environment limitations and exceptions in their national laws which have been considered acceptable under the Berne Convention. Similarly, these provisions should be understood to permit Contracting Parties to devise new exceptions and limitations that are appropriate in the digital network environment.

It is also understood that Article 10(2) neither reduces nor extends the scope of applicability of the limitations and exceptions permitted by the Berne Convention."]

induce, enable, facilitate or conceal an infringement of any right covered by this Treaty:

(i) to remove or alter any electronic rights management information without authority;

(ii) to distribute, import for distribution, broadcast, communicate or make available to the public, without authority, performances, copies of fixed performances or phonograms knowing that electronic rights management information has been removed or altered without authority.

(2) As used in this Article, "rights management information" means information which identifies the performer, the performance of the performer, the producer of the phonogram, the phonogram, the owner of any right in the performance or phonogram, or information about the terms and conditions of use of the performance or phonogram, and any numbers or codes that represent such information, when any of these items of information is attached to a copy of a fixed performance or a phonogram or appears in connection with the communication or making available of a fixed performance or a phonogram to the public. ⑯

Article 20
Formalities

The enjoyment and exercise of the rights provided for in this Treaty shall not be subject to any formality.

Article 21
Reservations

Subject to the provisions of Article 15(3) , no reservations to this Treaty shall be permitted.

Article 22
Application in Time

(1) Contracting Parties shall apply the provisions of Article 18 of the Berne Convention, *mutatis mutandis*, to the rights of performers and producers of phonograms provided for in this Treaty.

⑯ Agreed statement concerning Article 19: The agreed statement concerning Article 12 (on Obligations concerning Rights Management Information) of the WIPO Copyright Treaty is applicable mutatis mutandis also to Article 19 (on Obligations concerning Rights Management Information) of the WIPO Performances and Phonograms Treaty. [The text of the agreed statement concerning Article 12 of the WCT reads as follows: "It is understood that the reference to 'infringement of any right covered by this Treaty or the Berne Convention' includes both exclusive rights and rights of remuneration.

It is further understood that Contracting Parties will not rely on this Article to devise or implement rights management systems that would have the effect of imposing formalities which are not permitted under the Berne Convention or this Treaty, prohibiting the free movement of goods or impeding the enjoyment of rights under this Treaty."]

(2) Notwithstanding paragraph (1) , a Contracting Party may limit the application of Article 5 of this Treaty to performances which occurred after the entry into force of this Treaty for that Party.

Article 23
Provisions on Enforcement of Rights

(1) Contracting Parties undertake to adopt, in accordance with their legal systems, the measures necessary to ensure the application of this Treaty.

(2) Contracting Parties shall ensure that enforcement procedures are available under their law so as to permit effective action against any act of infringement of rights covered by this Treaty, including expeditious remedies to prevent infringements and remedies which constitute a deterrent to further infringements.

Chapter V

Administrative and Final Clauses

Article 24
Assembly

(1) (a) The Contracting Parties shall have an Assembly.

(b) Each Contracting Party shall be represented by one delegate who may be assisted by alternate delegates, advisors and experts.

(c) The expenses of each delegation shall be borne by the Contracting Party that has appointed the delegation. The Assembly may ask WIPO to grant financial assistance to facilitate the participation of delegations of Contracting Parties that are regarded as developing countries in conformity with the established practice of the General Assembly of the United Nations or that are countries in transition to a market economy.

(2) (a) The Assembly shall deal with matters concerning the maintenance and development of this Treaty and the application and operation of this Treaty.

(b) The Assembly shall perform the function allocated to it under Article 26(2) in respect of the admission of certain intergovernmental organizations to become party to this Treaty.

(c) The Assembly shall decide the convocation of any diplomatic conference for the revision of this Treaty and give the necessary instructions to the Director General of WIPO for the preparation of such diplomatic conference.

(3) (a) Each Contracting Party that is a State shall have one vote and shall vote only in its own name.

(b) Any Contracting Party that is an intergovernmental organization may participate in the vote, in place of its Member States, with a number of votes equal to the number of its

Member States which are party to this Treaty. No such intergovernmental organization shall participate in the vote if any one of its Member States exercises its right to vote and vice versa.

(4) The Assembly shall meet in ordinary session once every two years upon convocation by the Director General of WIPO.

(5) The Assembly shall establish its own rules of procedure, including the convocation of extraordinary sessions, the requirements of a quorum and, subject to the provisions of this Treaty, the required majority for various kinds of decisions.

Article 25

International Bureau

The International Bureau of WIPO shall perform the administrative tasks concerning the Treaty.

Article 26

Eligibility for Becoming Party to the Treaty

(1) Any Member State of WIPO may become party to this Treaty.

(2) The Assembly may decide to admit any intergovernmental organization to become party to this Treaty which declares that it is competent in respect of, and has its own legislation binding on all its Member States on, matters covered by this Treaty and that it has been duly authorized, in accordance with its internal procedures, to become party to this Treaty.

(3) The European Community, having made the declaration referred to in the preceding paragraph in the Diplomatic Conference that has adopted this Treaty, may become party to this Treaty.

Article 27

Rights and Obligations under the Treaty

Subject to any specific provisions to the contrary in this Treaty, each Contracting Party shall enjoy all of the rights and assume all of the obligations under this Treaty.

Article 28

Signature of the Treaty

This Treaty shall be open for signature until December 31, 1997, by any Member State of WIPO and by the European Community.

Article 29

Entry into Force of the Treaty

This Treaty shall enter into force three months after 30 instruments of ratification or accession by States have been deposited with the Director General of WIPO.

Article 30
Effective Date of Becoming Party to the Treaty

This Treaty shall bind

(i) the 30 States referred to in Article 29, from the date on which this Treaty has entered into force;

(ii) each other State from the expiration of three months from the date on which the State has deposited its instrument with the Director General of WIPO;

(iii) the European Community, from the expiration of three months after the deposit of its instrument of ratification or accession if such instrument has been deposited after the entry into force of this Treaty according to Article 29, or, three months after the entry into force of this Treaty if such instrument has been deposited before the entry into force of this Treaty;

(iv) any other intergovernmental organization that is admitted to become party to this Treaty, from the expiration of three months after the deposit of its instrument of accession.

Article 31
Denunciation of the Treaty

This Treaty may be denounced by any Contracting Party by notification addressed to the Director General of WIPO. Any denunciation shall take effect one year from the date on which the Director General of WIPO received the notification.

Article 32
Languages of the Treaty

(1) This Treaty is signed in a single original in English, Arabic, Chinese, French, Russian and Spanish languages, the versions in all these languages being equally authentic.

(2) An official text in any language other than those referred to in paragraph (1) shall be established by the Director General of WIPO on the request of an interested party, after consultation with all the interested parties. For the purposes of this paragraph, "interested party" means any Member State of WIPO whose official language, or one of whose official languages, is involved and the European Community, and any other intergovernmental organization that may become party to this Treaty, if one of its official languages is involved.

Article 33
Depositary

The Director General of WIPO is the depositary of this Treaty.

Beijing Treaty on Audiovisual Performances*

TABLE OF CONTENTS

* This Treaty was adopted by the Diplomatic Conference on the Protection of Audiovisual Performances in Beijing, on June 24, 2012.

Preamble

The Contracting Parties,

Desiring to develop and maintain the protection of the rights of performers in their audiovisual performances in a manner as effective and uniform as possible,

Recalling the importance of the Development Agenda recommendations, adopted in 2007 by the General Assembly of the Convention Establishing the World Intellectual Property Organization (WIPO), which aim to ensure that development considerations form an integral part of the Organization's work,

Recognizing the need to introduce new international rules in order to provide adequate solutions to the questions raised by economic, social, cultural and technological developments,

Recognizing the profound impact of the development and convergence of information and communication technologies on the production and use of audiovisual performances,

Recognizing the need to maintain a balance between the rights of performers in their audiovisual performances and the larger public interest, particularly education, research and access to information,

Recognizing that the WIPO Performances and Phonograms Treaty (WPPT) done in Geneva on December 20, 1996, does not extend protection to performers in respect of their performances fixed in audiovisual fixations,

Referring to the Resolution concerning Audiovisual Performances adopted by the Diplomatic Conference on Certain Copyright and Neighboring Rights Questions on December 20, 1996,

Have agreed as follows:

Article 1
Relation to Other Conventions and Treaties

(1) Nothing in this Treaty shall derogate from existing obligations that Contracting Parties have to each other under the WPPT or the International Convention

for the Protection of Performers, Producers of Phonograms and Broadcasting Organizations done in Rome on October 26, 1961.

(2) Protection granted under this Treaty shall leave intact and shall in no way affect the protection of copyright in literary and artistic works. Consequently, no provision of this Treaty may be interpreted as prejudicing such protection.

(3) This Treaty shall not have any connection with treaties other than the WPPT, nor shall it prejudice any rights and obligations under any other treaties[①②].

Article 2
Definitions

For the purposes of this Treaty:

(a) "performers" are actors, singers, musicians, dancers, and other persons who act, sing, deliver, declaim, play in, interpret, or otherwise perform literary or artistic works or expressions of folklore[③];

(b) "audiovisual fixation" means the embodiment of moving images, whether or not accompanied by sounds or by the representations thereof, from which they can be perceived, reproduced or communicated through a device[④];

(c) "broadcasting" means the transmission by wireless means for public reception of sounds or of images or of images and sounds or of the representations thereof; such transmission by satellite is also "broadcasting"; transmission of encrypted signals is "broadcasting" where the means for decrypting are provided to the public by the broadcasting organization or with its consent;

(d) "communication to the public" of a performance means the transmission to the public by any medium, otherwise than by broadcasting, of an unfixed performance, or of a performance fixed in an audiovisual fixation. For the purposes of Article 11, "communication to the public" includes making a performance fixed in an audiovisual fixation audible or visible or audible and visible to the public.

Article 3

① Agreed statement concerning Article 1: It is understood that nothing in this Treaty affects any rights or obligations under the WIPO Performances and Phonograms Treaty (WPPT) or their interpretation and it is further understood that paragraph 3 does not create any obligations for a Contracting Party to this Treaty to ratify or accede to the WPPT or to comply with any of its provisions.

② Agreed statement concerning Article 1(3): It is understood that Contracting Parties who are members of the World Trade Organization (WTO) acknowledge all the principles and objectives of the Agreement on Trade-Related Aspects of Intellectual Property Rights (TRIPS Agreement) and understand that nothing in this Treaty affects the provisions of the TRIPS Agreement, including, but not limited to, the provisions relating to anti-competitive practices.

③ Agreed statement concerning Article 2(a): It is understood that the definition of "performers" includes those who perform a literary or artistic work that is created or first fixed in the course of a performance.

④ Agreed statement concerning Article 2(b): It is hereby confirmed that the definition of "audiovisual fixation" contained in Article 2(b) is without prejudice to Article 2(c) of the WPPT.

Beneficiaries of Protection

(1) Contracting Parties shall accord the protection granted under this Treaty to performers who are nationals of other Contracting Parties.

(2) Performers who are not nationals of one of the Contracting Parties but who have their habitual residence in one of them shall, for the purposes of this Treaty, be assimilated to nationals of that Contracting Party.

Article 4
National Treatment

(1) Each Contracting Party shall accord to nationals of other Contracting Parties the treatment it accords to its own nationals with regard to the exclusive rights specifically granted in this Treaty and the right to equitable remuneration provided for in Article 11 of this Treaty.

(2) A Contracting Party shall be entitled to limit the extent and term of the protection accorded to nationals of another Contracting Party under paragraph (1), with respect to the rights granted in Article 11(1) and 11(2) of this Treaty, to those rights that its own nationals enjoy in that other Contracting Party.

(3) The obligation provided for in paragraph (1) does not apply to a Contracting Party to the extent that another Contracting Party makes use of the reservations permitted by Article 11(3) of this Treaty, nor does it apply to a Contracting Party, to the extent that it has made such reservation.

Article 5
Moral Rights

(1) Independently of a performer's economic rights, and even after the transfer of those rights, the performer shall, as regards his live performances or performances fixed in audiovisual fixations, have the right:

(i) to claim to be identified as the performer of his performances, except where omission is dictated by the manner of the use of the performance; and

(ii) to object to any distortion, mutilation or other modification of his performances that would be prejudicial to his reputation, taking due account of the nature of audiovisual fixations.

(2) The rights granted to a performer in accordance with paragraph (1) shall, after his death, be maintained, at least until the expiry of the economic rights, and shall be exercisable by the persons or institutions authorized by the legislation of the Contracting Party where protection is claimed. However, those Contracting Parties whose legislation, at the moment of their ratification of or accession to this Treaty, does not provide for protection after the death of the performer of all rights set out in the preceding paragraph may provide that some of these rights will, after his death, cease to be maintained.

(3) The means of redress for safeguarding the rights granted under this Article shall be governed by the legislation of the Contracting Party where protection is claimed ⑤.

Article 6

Economic Rights of Performers in their Unfixed Performances

Performers shall enjoy the exclusive right of authorizing, as regards their performances:

(i) the broadcasting and communication to the public of their unfixed performances except where the performance is already a broadcast performance; and

(ii) the fixation of their unfixed performances.

Article 7

Right of Reproduction

Performers shall enjoy the exclusive right of authorizing the direct or indirect reproduction of their performances fixed in audiovisual fixations, in any manner or form ⑥.

Article 8

Right of Distribution

(1) Performers shall enjoy the exclusive right of authorizing the making available to the public of the original and copies of their performances fixed in audiovisual fixations through sale or other transfer of ownership.

(2) Nothing in this Treaty shall affect the freedom of Contracting Parties to determine the conditions, if any, under which the exhaustion of the right in paragraph (1) applies after the first sale or other transfer of ownership of the original or a copy

---

⑤ Agreed statement concerning Article 5: For the purposes of this Treaty and without prejudice to any other treaty, it is understood that, considering the nature of audiovisual fixations and their production and distribution, modifications of a performance that are made in the normal course of exploitation of the performance, such as editing, compression, dubbing, or formatting, in existing or new media or formats, and that are made in the course of a use authorized by the performer, would not in themselves amount to modifications within the meaning of Article 5(1)(ii). Rights under Article 5(1)(ii) are concerned only with changes that are objectively prejudicial to the performer's reputation in a substantial way. It is also understood that the mere use of new or changed technology or media, as such, does not amount to modification within the meaning of Article 5(1)(ii).

⑥ Agreed statement concerning Article 7: The reproduction right, as set out in Article 7, and the exceptions permitted thereunder through Article 13, fully apply in the digital environment, in particular to the use of performances in digital form. It is understood that the storage of a protected performance in digital form in an electronic medium constitutes a reproduction within the meaning of this Article.

of the fixed performance with the authorization of the performer ⑦.

Article 9
Right of Rental

(1) Performers shall enjoy the exclusive right of authorizing the commercial rental to the public of the original and copies of their performances fixed in audiovisual fixations as determined in the national law of Contracting Parties, even after distribution of them by, or pursuant to, authorization by the performer.

(2) Contracting Parties are exempt from the obligation of paragraph (1) unless the commercial rental has led to widespread copying of such fixations materially impairing the exclusive right of reproduction of performers ⑧.

Article 10
Right of Making Available of Fixed Performances

Performers shall enjoy the exclusive right of authorizing the making available to the public of their performances fixed in audiovisual fixations, by wire or wireless means, in such a way that members of the public may access them from a place and at a time individually chosen by them.

Article 11
Right of Broadcasting and Communication to the Public

(1) Performers shall enjoy the exclusive right of authorizing the broadcasting and communication to the public of their performances fixed in audiovisual fixations.

(2) Contracting Parties may in a notification deposited with the Director General of WIPO declare that, instead of the right of authorization provided for in paragraph (1), they will establish a right to equitable remuneration for the direct or indirect use of performances fixed in audiovisual fixations for broadcasting or for communication to the public. Contracting Parties may also declare that they will set conditions in their legislation for the exercise of the right to equitable remuneration.

(3) Any Contracting Party may declare that it will apply the provisions of paragraphs (1) or (2) only in respect of certain uses, or that it will limit their application in some other way, or that it will not apply the provisions of paragraphs (1) and (2) at all.

---

⑦ Agreed statement concerning Articles 8 and 9: As used in these Articles, the expression "original and copies," being subject to the right of distribution and the right of rental under the said Articles, refers exclusively to fixed copies that can be put into circulation as tangible objects.

⑧ Agreed statement concerning Articles 8 and 9: As used in these Articles, the expression "original and copies," being subject to the right of distribution and the right of rental under the said Articles, refers exclusively to fixed copies that can be put into circulation as tangible objects.

Article 12
Transfer of Rights

(1) A Contracting Party may provide in its national law that once a performer has consented to fixation of his or her performance in an audiovisual fixation, the exclusive rights of authorization provided for in Articles 7 to 11 of this Treaty shall be owned or exercised by or transferred to the producer of such audiovisual fixation subject to any contract to the contrary between the performer and the producer of the audiovisual fixation as determined by the national law.

(2) A Contracting Party may require with respect to audiovisual fixations produced under its national law that such consent or contract be in writing and signed by both parties to the contract or by their duly authorized representatives.

(3) Independent of the transfer of exclusive rights described above, national laws or individual, collective or other agreements may provide the performer with the right to receive royalties or equitable remuneration for any use of the performance, as provided for under this Treaty including as regards Articles 10 and 11.

Article 13
Limitations and Exceptions

(1) Contracting Parties may, in their national legislation, provide for the same kinds of limitations or exceptions with regard to the protection of performers as they provide for, in their national legislation, in connection with the protection of copyright in literary and artistic works.

(2) Contracting Parties shall confine any limitations of or exceptions to rights provided for in this Treaty to certain special cases which do not conflict with a normal exploitation of the performance and do not unreasonably prejudice the legitimate interests of the performer[9].

Article 14
Term of Protection

The term of protection to be granted to performers under this Treaty shall last, at least, until the end of a period of 50 years computed from the end of the year in which the performance was fixed.

Article 15
Obligations concerning Technological Measures

Contracting Parties shall provide adequate legal protection and effective legal remedies against the circumvention of effective technological measures that are

⑨ Agreed statement concerning Article 13: The Agreed statement concerning Article 10 (on Limitations and Exceptions) of the WIPO Copyright Treaty (WCT) is applicable *mutatis mutandis* also to Article 13 (on Limitations and Exceptions) of the Treaty.

used by performers in connection with the exercise of their rights under this Treaty and that restrict acts, in respect of their performances, which are not authorized by the performers concerned or permitted by law [10][11].

Article 16
Obligations concerning Rights Management Information

(1) Contracting Parties shall provide adequate and effective legal remedies against any person knowingly performing any of the following acts knowing, or with respect to civil remedies having reasonable grounds to know, that it will induce, enable, facilitate, or conceal an infringement of any right covered by this Treaty:

(i) to remove or alter any electronic rights management information without authority;

(ii) to distribute, import for distribution, broadcast, communicate or make available to the public, without authority, performances or copies of performances fixed in audiovisual fixations knowing that electronic rights management information has been removed or altered without authority.

(2) As used in this Article, "rights management information" means information which identifies the performer, the performance of the performer, or the owner of any right in the performance, or information about the terms and conditions of use of the performance, and any numbers or codes that represent such information, when any of these items of information is attached to a performance fixed in an audiovisual fixation [12].

---

⑩ Agreed statement concerning Article 15 as it relates to Article 13: It is understood that nothing in this Article prevents a Contracting Party from adopting effective and necessary measures to ensure that a beneficiary may enjoy limitations and exceptions provided in that Contracting Party' s national law, in accordance with Article 13, where technological measures have been applied to an audiovisual performance and the beneficiary has legal access to that performance, in circumstances such as where appropriate and effective measures have not been taken by rights holders in relation to that performance to enable the beneficiary to enjoy the limitations and exceptions under that Contracting Party' s national law. Without prejudice to the legal protection of an audiovisual work in which a performance is fixed, it is further understood that the obligations under Article 15 are not applicable to performances unprotected or no longer protected under the national law giving effect to this Treaty.

⑪ Agreed statement concerning Article 15: The expression "technological measures used by performers" should, as this is the case regarding the WPPT, be construed broadly, referring also to those acting on behalf of performers, including their representatives, licensees or assignees, including producers, service providers, and persons engaged in communication or broadcasting using performances on the basis of due authorization.

⑫ Agreed statement concerning Article 16: The Agreed statement concerning Article 12 (on Obligations concerning Rights Management Information) of the WCT is applicable *mutatis mutandis* also to Article 16 (on Obligations concerning Rights Management Information) of the Treaty.

Article 17
Formalities

The enjoyment and exercise of the rights provided for in this Treaty shall not be subject to any formality.

Article 18
Reservations and Notifications

(1) Subject to provisions of Article 11(3), no reservations to this Treaty shall be permitted.

(2) Any notification under Article 11(2) or 19(2) may be made in instruments of ratification or accession, and the effective date of the notification shall be the same as the date of entry into force of this Treaty with respect to the Contracting Party having made the notification. Any such notification may also be made later, in which case the notification shall have effect three months after its receipt by the Director General of WIPO or at any later date indicated in the notification.

Article 19
Application in Time

(1) Contracting Parties shall accord the protection granted under this Treaty to fixed performances that exist at the moment of the entry into force of this Treaty and to all performances that occur after the entry into force of this Treaty for each Contracting Party.

(2) Notwithstanding the provisions of paragraph (1), a Contracting Party may declare in a notification deposited with the Director General of WIPO that it will not apply the provisions of Articles 7 to 11 of this Treaty, or any one or more of those, to fixed performances that existed at the moment of the entry into force of this Treaty for each Contracting Party. In respect of such Contracting Party, other Contracting Parties may limit the application of the said Articles to performances that occurred after the entry into force of this Treaty for that Contracting Party.

(3) The protection provided for in this Treaty shall be without prejudice to any acts committed, agreements concluded or rights acquired before the entry into force of this Treaty for each Contracting Party.

(4) Contracting Parties may in their legislation establish transitional provisions under which any person who, prior to the entry into force of this Treaty, engaged in lawful acts with respect to a performance, may undertake with respect to the same performance acts within the scope of the rights provided for in Articles 5 and 7 to 11 after the entry into force of this Treaty for the respective Contracting Parties.

Article 20
Provisions on Enforcement of Rights

(1) Contracting Parties undertake to adopt, in accordance with their legal systems, the measures necessary to ensure the application of this Treaty.

(2) Contracting Parties shall ensure that enforcement procedures are available under their law so as to permit effective action against any act of infringement of rights covered by this Treaty, including expeditious remedies to prevent infringements and remedies which constitute a deterrent to further infringements.

Article 21
Assembly

(1) (a) The Contracting Parties shall have an Assembly.

(b) Each Contracting Party shall be represented in the Assembly by one delegate who may be assisted by alternate delegates, advisors and experts.

(c) The expenses of each delegation shall be borne by the Contracting Party that has appointed the delegation. The Assembly may ask WIPO to grant financial assistance to facilitate the participation of delegations of Contracting Parties that are regarded as developing countries in conformity with the established practice of the General Assembly of the United Nations or that are countries in transition to a market economy.

(2) (a) The Assembly shall deal with matters concerning the maintenance and development of this Treaty and the application and operation of this Treaty.

(b) The Assembly shall perform the function allocated to it under Article 23(2) in respect of the admission of certain intergovernmental organizations to become party to this Treaty.

(c) The Assembly shall decide the convocation of any diplomatic conference for the revision of this Treaty and give the necessary instructions to the Director General of WIPO for the preparation of such diplomatic conference.

(3) (a) Each Contracting Party that is a State shall have one vote and shall vote only in its own name.

(b) Any Contracting Party that is an intergovernmental organization may participate in the vote, in place of its Member States, with a number of votes equal to the number of its Member States which are party to this Treaty. No such intergovernmental organization shall participate in the vote if any one of its Member States exercises its right to vote and vice versa.

(4) The Assembly shall meet upon convocation by the Director General and, in the absence of exceptional circumstances, during the same period and at the same place as the General Assembly of WIPO.

(5) The Assembly shall endeavor to take its decisions by consensus and shall establish its own rules of procedure, including the convocation of extraordinary

sessions, the requirements of a quorum and, subject to the provisions of this Treaty, the required majority for various kinds of decisions.

Article 22
International Bureau

The International Bureau of WIPO shall perform the administrative tasks concerning the Treaty.

Article 23
Eligibility for Becoming Party to the Treaty

(1) Any Member State of WIPO may become party to this Treaty.

(2) The Assembly may decide to admit any intergovernmental organization to become party to this Treaty which declares that it is competent in respect of, and has its own legislation binding on all its Member States on, matters covered by this Treaty and that it has been duly authorized, in accordance with its internal procedures, to become party to this Treaty.

(3) The European Union, having made the declaration referred to in the preceding paragraph in the Diplomatic Conference that has adopted this Treaty, may become party to this Treaty.

Article 24
Rights and Obligations under the Treaty

Subject to any specific provisions to the contrary in this Treaty, each Contracting Party shall enjoy all of the rights and assume all of the obligations under this Treaty.

Article 25
Signature of the Treaty

This Treaty shall be open for signature at the headquarters of WIPO by any eligible party for one year after its adoption.

Article 26
Entry into Force of the Treaty

This Treaty shall enter into force three months after 30 eligible parties referred to in Article 23 have deposited their instruments of ratification or accession.

Article 27
Effective Date of Becoming Party to the Treaty

This Treaty shall bind:

(i) the 30 eligible parties referred to in Article 26, from the date on which this Treaty has entered into force;

(ii) each other eligible party referred to in Article 23, from the expiration of three months from the date on which it has deposited its instrument of ratification or accession with the Director General of WIPO.

Article 28
Denunciation of the Treaty

This Treaty may be denounced by any Contracting Party by notification addressed to the Director General of WIPO. Any denunciation shall take effect one year from the date on which the Director General of WIPO received the notification.

Article 29
Languages of the Treaty

(1) This Treaty is signed in a single original in English, Arabic, Chinese, French, Russian and Spanish languages, the versions in all these languages being equally authentic.

(2) An official text in any language other than those referred to in paragraph (1) shall be established by the Director General of WIPO on the request of an interested party, after consultation with all the interested parties. For the purposes of this paragraph, "interested party" means any Member State of WIPO whose official language, or one of whose official languages, is involved and the European Union, and any other intergovernmental organization that may become party to this Treaty, if one of its official languages is involved.

Article 30
Depositary

The Director General of WIPO is the depositary of this Treaty.

Marrakesh Treaty to Facilitate Access to Published Works for Persons Who Are Blind, Visually Impaired, or Otherwise Print Disabled*

CONTENTS

* This Treaty was adopted by the Diplomatic Conference to Conclude a Treaty to Facilitate Access to Published Works by Visually Impaired Persons and Persons with Print Disabilities on June 27, 2013.

Preamble

The Contracting Parties,

Recalling the principles of non-discrimination, equal opportunity, accessibility and full and effective participation and inclusion in society, proclaimed in the Universal Declaration of Human Rights and the United Nations Convention on the Rights of Persons with Disabilities,

Mindful of the challenges that are prejudicial to the complete development of persons with visual impairments or with other print disabilities, which limit their freedom of expression, including the freedom to seek, receive and impart information and ideas of all kinds on an equal basis with others, including through all forms of communication of their choice, their enjoyment of the right to education, and the opportunity to conduct research,

Emphasizing the importance of copyright protection as an incentive and reward for literary and artistic creations and of enhancing opportunities for everyone, including persons with visual impairments or with other print disabilities, to participate in the cultural life of the community, to enjoy the arts and to share scientific progress and its benefits,

Aware of the barriers of persons with visual impairments or with other print disabilities to access published works in achieving equal opportunities in society, and the need to both expand the number of works in accessible formats and to improve the circulation of such works,

Taking into account that the majority of persons with visual impairments or with other print disabilities live in developing and least-developed countries,

Recognizing that, despite the differences in national copyright laws, the positive impact of new information and communication technologies on the lives of persons with visual impairments or with other print disabilities may be reinforced by an enhanced legal framework at the international level,

Recognizing that many Member States have established limitations and exceptions in their national copyright laws for persons with visual impairments or with other print disabilities, yet there is a continuing shortage of available works in accessible format copies for such persons, and that considerable resources are required for their effort of making works accessible to these persons, and that the lack of possibilities of cross-border exchange of accessible format copies has necessitated duplication of these efforts,

Recognizing both the importance of rightholders' role in making their works accessible to persons with visual impairments or with other print disabilities and the importance of appropriate limitations and exceptions to make works accessible to these persons, particularly when the market is unable to provide such access,

Recognizing the need to maintain a balance between the effective protection of the rights of authors and the larger public interest, particularly education, research and access to information, and that such a balance must facilitate effective and timely access to works for the benefit of persons with visual impairments or with other print disabilities,

Reaffirming the obligations of Contracting Parties under the existing international treaties on the protection of copyright and the importance and flexibility of the three-step test for limitations and exceptions established in Article 9(2) of the Berne Convention for the Protection of Literary and Artistic Works and other international instruments,

Recalling the importance of the Development Agenda recommendations, adopted in 2007 by the General Assembly of the World Intellectual Property Organization (WIPO), which aim to ensure that development considerations form an integral part of the Organization's work,

Recognizing the importance of the international copyright system and desiring to harmonize limitations and exceptions with a view to facilitating access to and use of works by persons with visual impairments or with other print disabilities,

Have agreed as follows:

Article 1
Relation to Other Conventions and Treaties

Nothing in this Treaty shall derogate from any obligations that Contracting Parties have to each other under any other treaties, nor shall it prejudice any rights that a Contracting Party has under any other treaties.

Article 2
Definitions

For the purposes of this Treaty:

(a) "works" means literary and artistic works within the meaning of Article 2(1) of the Berne Convention for the Protection of Literary and Artistic Works, in the form of text, notation andfor related illustrations, whether published or otherwise made publicly available in any media ①;

(b) "accessible format copy" means a copy of a work in an alternative manner or form which gives a beneficiary person access to the work, including to permit the person to have access as feasibly and comfortably as a person without visual impairment or other print disability. The accessible format copy is used exclusively by beneficiary persons and it must respect the integrity of the original work, taking due consideration of the changes needed to make the work accessible in the alternative format and of the accessibility needs of the beneficiary persons;

(c) "authorized entity" means an entity that is authorized or recognized by the government to provide education, instructional training, adaptive reading or information access to beneficiary persons on a non-profit basis. It also includes a government institution or non-profit organization that provides the same services to beneficiary persons as one of its primary activities or institutional obligations ②.

An authorized entity establishes and follows its own practices:

(i) to establish that the persons it serves are beneficiary persons;

(ii) to limit to beneficiary persons andfor authorized entities its distribution and making available of accessible format copies;

(iii) to discourage the reproduction, distribution and making available of unauthorized copies; and

(iv) to maintain due care in, and records of, its handling of copies of works, while respecting the privacy of beneficiary persons in accordance with Article 8.

Article 3
Beneficiary Persons

A beneficiary person is a person who:

(a) is blind;

(b) has a visual impairment or a perceptual or reading disability which cannot be improved to give visual function substantially equivalent to that of a person who has no such impairment or disability and so is unable to read printed works to

① Agreed statement concerning Article 2(a): For the purposes of this Treaty, it is understood that this definition includes such works in audio form, such as audiobooks.

② Agreed statement concerning Article 2(c): For the purposes of this Treaty, it is understood that "entities recognized by the government" may include entities receiving financial support from the government to provide education, instructional training, adaptive reading or information access to beneficiary persons on a non—profit basis.

substantially the same degree as a person without an impairment or disability ③; or

(c) is otherwise unable, through physical disability, to hold or manipulate a book or to focus or move the eyes to the extent that would be normally acceptable for reading;

regardless of any other disabilities.

Article 4

National Law Limitations and Exceptions Regarding Accessible Format Copies

1. (a) Contracting Parties shall provide in their national copyright laws for a limitation or exception to the right of reproduction, the right of distribution, and the right of making available to the public as provided by the WIPO Copyright Treaty (WCT), to facilitate the availability of works in accessible format copies for beneficiary persons. The limitation or exception provided in national law should permit changes needed to make the work accessible in the alternative format.

(b) Contracting Parties may also provide a limitation or exception to the right of public performance to facilitate access to works for beneficiary persons.

2. A Contracting Party may fulfill Article 4(1) for all rights identified therein by providing a limitation or exception in its national copyright law such that:

(a) Authorized entities shall be permitted, without the authorization of the copyright rightholder, to make an accessible format copy of a work, obtain from another authorized entity an accessible format copy, and supply those copies to beneficiary persons by any means, including by non-commercial lending or by electronic communication by wire or wireless means, and undertake any intermediate steps to achieve those objectives, when all of the following conditions are met:

(i) the authorized entity wishing to undertake said activity has lawful access to that work or a copy of that work;

(ii) the work is converted to an accessible format copy, which may include any means needed to navigate information in the accessible format, but does not introduce changes other than those needed to make the work accessible to the beneficiary person;

(iii) such accessible format copies are supplied exclusively to be used by beneficiary persons; and

(iv) the activity is undertaken on a non-profit basis;

and

(b) A beneficiary person, or someone acting on his or her behalf including a primary caretaker or caregiver, may make an accessible format copy of a work for the personal use of the beneficiary person or otherwise may assist the beneficiary person to make and use accessible format copies where the beneficiary person has

---

③ Agreed statement concerning Article 3(b): Nothing in this language implies that "cannot be improved" requires the use of all possible medical diagnostic procedures and treatments.

lawful access to that work or a copy of that work.

3. A Contracting Party may fulfill Article 4(1) by providing other limitations or exceptions in its national copyright law pursuant to Articles 10 and 11 ④.

4. A Contracting Party may confine limitations or exceptions under this Article to works which, in the particular accessible format, cannot be obtained commercially under reasonable terms for beneficiary persons in that market. Any Contracting Party availing itself of this possibility shall so declare in a notification deposited with the Director General of WIPO at the time of ratification of, acceptance of or accession to this Treaty or at any time thereafter ⑤.

5. It shall be a matter for national law to determine whether limitations or exceptions under this Article are subject to remuneration.

Article 5
Cross-Border Exchange of Accessible Format Copies

1. Contracting Parties shall provide that if an accessible format copy is made under a limitation or exception or pursuant to operation of law, that accessible format copy may be distributed or made available by an authorized entity to a beneficiary person or an authorized entity in another Contracting Party ⑥.

2. A Contracting Party may fulfill Article 5(1) by providing a limitation or exception in its national copyright law such that:

(a) authorized entities shall be permitted, without the authorization of the rightholder, to distribute or make available for the exclusive use of beneficiary persons accessible format copies to an authorized entity in another Contracting Party; and

(b) authorized entities shall be permitted, without the authorization of the rightholder and pursuant to Article 2(c) , to distribute or make available accessible format copies to a beneficiary person in another Contracting Party;

provided that prior to the distribution or making available the originating authorized entity did not know or have reasonable grounds to know that the accessible format

④ Agreed statement concerning Article 4(3): It is understood that this paragraph neither reduces nor extends the scope of applicability of limitations and exceptions permitted under the Berne Convention, as regards the right of translation, with respect to persons with visual impairments or with other print disabilities.

⑤ Agreed statement concerning Article 4(4): It is understood that a commercial availability requirement does not prejudge whether or not a limitation or exception under this Article is consistent with the three-step test.

⑥ Agreed statement concerning Article 5(1): It is further understood that nothing in this Treaty reduces or extends the scope of exclusive rights under any other treaty.

copy would be used for other than beneficiary persons ⑦.

3. A Contracting Party may fulfill Article 5(1) by providing other limitations or exceptions in its national copyright law pursuant to Articles 5(4), 10 and 11.

4. (a) When an authorized entity in a Contracting Party receives accessible format copies pursuant to Article 5(1) and that Contracting Party does not have obligations under Article 9 of the Berne Convention, it will ensure, consistent with its own legal system and practices, that the accessible format copies are only reproduced, distributed or made available for the benefit of beneficiary persons in that Contracting Party's jurisdiction.

(b) The distribution and making available of accessible format copies by an authorized entity pursuant to Article 5(1) shall be limited to that jurisdiction unless the Contracting Party is a Party to the WIPO Copyright Treaty or otherwise limits limitations and exceptions implementing this Treaty to the right of distribution and the right of making available to the public to certain special cases which do not conflict with a normal exploitation of the work and do not unreasonably prejudice the legitimate interests of the rightholder ⑧ ⑨.

(c) Nothing in this Article affects the determination of what constitutes an act of distribution or an act of making available to the public.

5. Nothing in this Treaty shall be used to address the issue of exhaustion of rights.

Article 6

Importation of Accessible Format Copies

To the extent that the national law of a Contracting Party would permit a beneficiary person, someone acting on his or her behalf, or an authorized entity, to make an accessible format copy of a work, the national law of that Contracting Party shall also permit them to import an accessible format copy for the benefit of beneficiary persons, without the authorization of the rightholder ⑩.

---

⑦ Agreed statement concerning Article 5(2): It is understood that, to distribute or make available accessible format copies directly to a beneficiary person in another Contracting Party, it may be appropriate for an authorized entity to apply further measures to confirm that the person it is serving is a beneficiary person and to follow its own practices as described in Article 2(c) .

⑧ Agreed statement concerning Article 5(4)(b): It is understood that nothing in this Treaty requires or implies that a Contracting Party adopt or apply the three-step test beyond its obligations under this instrument or under other international treaties.

⑨ Agreed statement concerning Article 5(4)(b): It is understood that nothing in this Treaty creates any obligations for a Contracting Party to ratify or accede to the WCT or to comply with any of its provisions and nothing in this Treaty prejudices any rights, limitations and exceptions contained in the WCT.

⑩ Agreed statement concerning Article 6: It is understood that the Contracting Parties have the same flexibilities set out in Article 4 when implementing their obligations under Article 6.

Article 7

Obligations Concerning Technological Measures

Contracting Parties shall take appropriate measures, as necessary, to ensure that when they provide adequate legal protection and effective legal remedies against the circumvention of effective technological measures, this legal protection does not prevent beneficiary persons from enjoying the limitations and exceptions provided for in this Treaty[11].

Article 8

Respect for Privacy

In the implementation of the limitations and exceptions provided for in this Treaty, Contracting Parties shall endeavor to protect the privacy of beneficiary persons on an equal basis with others.

Article 9

Cooperation to Facilitate Cross-Border Exchange

1. Contracting Parties shall endeavor to foster the cross-border exchange of accessible format copies by encouraging the voluntary sharing of information to assist authorized entities in identifying one another. The International Bureau of WIPO shall establish an information access point for this purpose.

2. Contracting Parties undertake to assist their authorized entities engaged in activities under Article 5 to make information available regarding their practices pursuant to Article 2(c) , both through the sharing of information among authorized entities, and through making available information on their policies and practices, including related to cross-border exchange of accessible format copies, to interested parties and members of the public as appropriate.

3. The International Bureau of WIPO is invited to share information, where available, about the functioning of this Treaty.

4. Contracting Parties recognize the importance of international cooperation and its promotion, in support of national efforts for realization of the purpose and objectives of this Treaty[12].

---

⑪ Agreed statement concerning Article 7: It is understood that authorized entities, in various circumstances, choose to apply technological measures in the making, distribution and making available of accessible format copies and nothing herein disturbs such practices when in accordance with national law.

⑫ Agreed statement concerning Article 9: It is understood that Article 9 does not imply mandatory registration for authorized entities nor does it constitute a precondition for authorized entities to engage in activities recognized under this Treaty; but it provides for a possibility for sharing information to facilitate the cross-border exchange of accessible format copies.

Article 10

General Principles on Implementation

1. Contracting Parties undertake to adopt the measures necessary to ensure the application of this Treaty.

2. Nothing shall prevent Contracting Parties from determining the appropriate method of implementing the provisions of this Treaty within their own legal system and practice [13].

3. Contracting Parties may fulfill their rights and obligations under this Treaty through limitations or exceptions specifically for the benefit of beneficiary persons, other limitations or exceptions, or a combination thereof, within their national legal system and practice. These may include judicial, administrative or regulatory determinations for the benefit of beneficiary persons as to fair practices, dealings or uses to meet their needs consistent with the Contracting Parties' rights and obligations under the Berne Convention, other international treaties, and Article 11.

Article 11

General Obligations on Limitations and Exceptions

In adopting measures necessary to ensure the application of this Treaty, a Contracting Party may exercise the rights and shall comply with the obligations that that Contracting Party has under the Berne Convention, the Agreement on Trade-Related Aspects of Intellectual Property Rights and the WIPO Copyright Treaty, including their interpretative agreements so that:

(a) in accordance with Article 9(2) of the Berne Convention, a Contracting Party may permit the reproduction of works in certain special cases provided that such reproduction does not conflict with a normal exploitation of the work and does not unreasonably prejudice the legitimate interests of the author;

(b) in accordance with Article 13 of the Agreement on Trade-Related Aspects of Intellectual Property Rights, a Contracting Party shall confine limitations or exceptions to exclusive rights to certain special cases which do not conflict with a normal exploitation of the work and do not unreasonably prejudice the legitimate interests of the rightholder;

(c) in accordance with Article 10(1) of the WIPO Copyright Treaty, a Contracting Party may provide for limitations of or exceptions to the rights granted to authors under the WCT in certain special cases, that do not conflict with a normal exploitation of the work and do not unreasonably prejudice the legitimate interests of the author;

---

⑬ Agreed statement concerning Article 10(2): It is understood that when a work qualifies as a work under Article 2(a) , including such works in audio form, the limitations and exceptions provided for by this Treaty apply *mutatis mutandis* to related rights as necessary to make the accessible format copy, to distribute it and to make it available to beneficiary persons.

(d) in accordance with Article 10(2) of the WIPO Copyright Treaty, a Contracting Party shall confine, when applying the Berne Convention, any limitations of or exceptions to rights to certain special cases that do not conflict with a normal exploitation of the work and do not unreasonably prejudice the legitimate interests of the author.

Article 12
Other Limitations and Exceptions

1. Contracting Parties recognize that a Contracting Party may implement in its national law other copyright limitations and exceptions for the benefit of beneficiary persons than are provided by this Treaty having regard to that Contracting Party's economic situation, and its social and cultural needs, in conformity with that Contracting Party's international rights and obligations, and in the case of a least-developed country taking into account its special needs and its particular international rights and obligations and flexibilities thereof.

2. This Treaty is without prejudice to other limitations and exceptions for persons with disabilities provided by national law.

Article 13
Assembly

1. (a) The Contracting Parties shall have an Assembly.

(b) Each Contracting Party shall be represented in the Assembly by one delegate who may be assisted by alternate delegates, advisors and experts.

(c) The expenses of each delegation shall be borne by the Contracting Party that has appointed the delegation. The Assembly may ask WIPO to grant financial assistance to facilitate the participation of delegations of Contracting Parties that are regarded as developing countries in conformity with the established practice of the General Assembly of the United Nations or that are countries in transition to a market economy.

2. (a) The Assembly shall deal with matters concerning the maintenance and development of this Treaty and the application and operation of this Treaty.

(b) The Assembly shall perform the function allocated to it under Article 15 in respect of the admission of certain intergovernmental organizations to become party to this Treaty.

(c) The Assembly shall decide the convocation of any diplomatic conference for the revision of this Treaty and give the necessary instructions to the Director General of WIPO for the preparation of such diplomatic conference.

3. (a) Each Contracting Party that is a State shall have one vote and shall vote only in its own name.

(b) Any Contracting Party that is an intergovernmental organization may participate in the vote, in place of its Member States, with a number of votes equal to the number of its Member States which are party to this Treaty. No such intergovernmental organization shall participate in the vote if any one of its Member States exercises its right to vote and vice versa.

4. The Assembly shall meet upon convocation by the Director General and, in the absence of exceptional circumstances, during the same period and at the same place as the General Assembly of WIPO.

5. The Assembly shall endeavor to take its decisions by consensus and shall establish its own rules of procedure, including the convocation of extraordinary sessions, the requirements of a quorum and, subject to the provisions of this Treaty, the required majority for various kinds of decisions.

Article 14
International Bureau

The International Bureau of WIPO shall perform the administrative tasks concerning this Treaty.

Article 15
Eligibility for Becoming Party to the Treaty

1. Any Member State of WIPO may become party to this Treaty.

2. The Assembly may decide to admit any intergovernmental organization to become party to this Treaty which declares that it is competent in respect of, and has its own legislation binding on all its Member States on, matters covered by this Treaty and that it has been duly authorized, in accordance with its internal procedures, to become party to this Treaty.

3. The European Union, having made the declaration referred to in the preceding paragraph at the Diplomatic Conference that has adopted this Treaty, may become party to this Treaty.

Article 16
Rights and Obligations Under the Treaty

Subject to any specific provisions to the contrary in this Treaty, each Contracting Party shall enjoy all of the rights and assume all of the obligations under this Treaty.

Article 17
Signature of the Treaty

This Treaty shall be open for signature at the Diplomatic Conference in Marrakesh, and thereafter at the headquarters of WIPO by any eligible party for one year after its adoption.

Article 18

Entry into Force of the Treaty

This Treaty shall enter into force three months after 20 eligible parties referred to in Article 15 have deposited their instruments of ratification or accession.

Article 19

Effective Date of Becoming Party to the Treaty

This Treaty shall bind:

(a) the 20 eligible parties referred to in Article 18, from the date on which this Treaty has entered into force;

(b) each other eligible party referred to in Article 15, from the expiration of three months from the date on which it has deposited its instrument of ratification or accession with the Director General of WIPO.

Article 20

Denunciation of the Treaty

This Treaty may be denounced by any Contracting Party by notification addressed to the Director General of WIPO. Any denunciation shall take effect one year from the date on which the Director General of WIPO received the notification.

Article 21

Languages of the Treaty

1. This Treaty is signed in a single original in English, Arabic, Chinese, French, Russian and Spanish languages, the versions in all these languages being equally authentic.

2. An official text in any language other than those referred to in Article 21(1) shall be established by the Director General of WIPO on the request of an interested party, after consultation with all the interested parties. For the purposes of this paragraph, "interested party" means any Member State of WIPO whose official language, or one of whose official languages, is involved and the European Union, and any other intergovernmental organization that may become party to this Treaty, if one of its official languages is involved.

Article 22

Depositary

The Director General of WIPO is the depositary of this Treaty.

Done in Marrakesh on the 27th day of June, 2013.

译者说明

这部文件集包含了从 1886 年《伯尔尼公约》到 2013 年《马拉喀什条约》跨度 120 余年间与版权和相关权有关的国际法律文件。自然，其中绝大多数是 20 世纪中期以后的。这些文件，有的已有较正式的中译本，有的只有非正式或工作用的中译本，有的似乎还没有中译本。译本当中，有的放在一起出版过，有的分别出版过，有的似乎还没有出版过。这次全部汇辑在一起，不仅便于查阅，更有利于通过比较分析对知识产权这一领域国际上的发展变化和现状进行总体的把握。

此次结集出版，少数文件是新译，大部分是重译。之所以要重译，是因为经过几十年的改革开放，我国在知识产权领域有了长足发展，法律制度更成熟，实践经验更丰富，学术研究更系统。同时，与国际上的交流和对外部事务的了解也更加广泛和深入。所有这些，都有利于我们对国际法律文件的背景、相互关系、内容、话语有更切近和准确的理解。在此基础上，再翻译成中文时，也许可以做得更好。换句话说，如果这次重译能够做得比过去更好，相当程度上是更加适宜的大环境提供了更为有利的条件。

就这部文件集的出版，有以下一些总的情况需要说明：

1. 关于“重译”。“重译”是指此次翻译完全根据原文并独立于已有的译文。而“独立于”已有译文，是指在内容和意思的理解上和行文的结构组织上。尽管是重译，新译仍然在整体上与原有译文保持了一致。这主要有两个原因。首先，原有译文无论如何有一定的基础，而国际法律文件内容本身在理解和翻译表达上也没有太大的灵活空间，许多情况下甚至很难有另外的译法。另外，也是更重要的，这些法律文件原有的译文已经在中国使用多年，被广泛作为学习研究的对象和引用的来源，有的甚至作为我国加入这些文件（公约、条约、协定）的依据。因此，对于已经进入我国法律文件的原有译法，新译中也需要作最大限度的照顾。

2. 关于可读性。国际版权条约是专业性很强的法律文件，不像大众读物那样通俗易懂。而外文的叙事方法也跟中文不同。因此，翻译得跟中文叙事一样，不仅不易，有时甚至不宜，因为会因词害义。但无论如何，既然是给中文读者看的，新译仍然力求在忠实于原文和照顾中文读者之间保持一种平衡。而由于内容的性质和特定的说法，在两者之间又不得不偏向一点前者。所以，尽管对原文的特有语序和复杂长句作了调整或拆分，仍然会有不少句子需要反复看才能读懂。由于译者尽量采取办法保证句法结构的清晰，对于有一些语言基础和背景知识的人，读通这些句子大概是没有问题的。

3. 关于与国内法律用语的协调。新译中，凡原文词在我国法律文件中有对应词的，都按我国的对应词翻译。但是，带有公法性质的国际法律文件在用语上有自己的一套要求和习惯，经常会有与国内法接近而意思或措词不大一样的说法。翻译时要尊重和照顾这种情况，不能强行使用我们自己的而与之有出入的“熟悉”词。在用语的协调上，新译更重视的是这些公约、条约和协定的译文之间在用语上的一致。也就是说，无论哪个文件，凡原文表述一样的地方，译文也完全一样。在这一点上，由于所有文件由一个人翻译，再加上可以全部放在一起进行通读统看，新译较之过去的译文有很大改进。

4. 关于体例。这些文件，签署的时间和背景不同，原文的体例不尽统一。例如，有的有主管国际组织增加的目录和条款标题，有的则没有；有的每个条款原来有标题，有的则原来就没有。此次重译，没有目录的，编制增加了目录；没有标题的，编制增加了标题（目录与标题是一致的）。这样，不仅使所有文件的体例统一，也便于读者阅读查找。

5. 关于条款编号系统。这些文件的条款编号系统，也不尽统一。例如，有的用阿拉伯数字，有的用罗马数字。条款之下的项、分项、目的编号，也不尽统一。个别文件内部，同一层次的条文，编号也不统一。这些都维持原貌不变。问题在于，使用罗马数字的编号，中文读者可能不熟悉，要不要改成中文的数字？甚至说，条款的编号，原文使用阿拉伯数字，要不要改成中文法律文件中习惯用的中文数字（似乎用阿拉伯数字不够正式）？改换成中文数字，如果是单纯的中文本，无需参照原文，也许可以。但这部文件集，是中英对照的，两种文本放在一起互相对照。如果编号系统不一样，便增加了对照的困难。另外，条款一层变了，下面几层也要相应地变；编号系统变了，内部条文中所有引述的地方也要变。更何况，一部文件变了，所有其他文件也要相应地变，因为经常有不同文件之间互相引述条款的情况。这样一来牵动便太大。所以，中译在条款编号系统上基本维持了原文的样子。

下面，就若干具体的翻译问题作一些说明。

1. 关于文件的标题。此次重译，对若干文件标题的译法作了稍许调整。

《伯尔尼公约》，标题英文全文是 Bern Convention for the Protection of Literary and Artistic Works。之前译作《保护文学艺术作品伯尔尼公约》。此次在“文学艺术”中间加上一个“和”字，以按照原文区分出两种不同大类的作品。

《与贸易有关知识产权协定》，之前译作“与贸易有关的知识产权协议”或“与贸易有关知识产权的协议”。由于实际涉及的是“知识产权的与贸易有关方面”，前译意思虽确定但有游离。此次去掉“的”字，增加意思上的灵活性，使理解可以往正确方向上靠。另外，将前译的“协议”改为“协定”。因为“协议”涵义比较宽泛，可以包括一般和简单的协商约定。作为正式的国际法律文件，还是应当译作“协定”。这也与世界贸易组织前身的《关税和贸易总协定》表述一致。

《马拉喀什条约》，标题英文全文是 Marrakesh Treaty to Facilitate Access to Published Works for Persons Who Are Blind, Visually Impaired, or Otherwise Print Disabled。比较忠实的中译应是“便利失明、视力障碍或另因对印本失能者利用已出版作品的马拉喀什条约”。考虑到中文语言习惯，将其中的“另因对印本失能者”改为“另外阅读失能者”。其实，这些人并非于阅读本身有障碍（不是“reading disabled”），而是在使用印刷出版物进行阅读上有困难，包括视力不能集中或无法用手持握和翻动书页。虽然也是一种阅读能力限制，但终归与原文的 print disabled 有出入，故应向读者做出说明。

另外，《马拉喀什条约》中多处提到 accessible format copy，指供失能者使用的经过特殊处理的无障碍格式本。“无障碍格式本”是原有的译法，或许是参照了“无障碍通道”的说法。“格式”现在多指数据处理、存储和显示的某种特定组织结构。而从条约的内容看，所要解决的，似乎不完全是“格式”问题，还涉及读物的样式安排。尽管如此，翻译时，仍保留了“格式”一说，但将“无障碍格式本”改作“便利格式本”，既简化语词使行文更通畅，也照应条约标题中提到的“便利”。

2. 关于 IP 和 IPR。《与贸易有关知识产权协定》中，不仅有 intellectual property（IP）的说法，还有 intellectual property rights（IPR）的说法。不同的说法，自然有不同的意思。如果要区分，就要将后者中的 rights 翻译出来。曾有学者对将 intellectual property 译作“知识产权”提出质疑，认为应当译作“知识财产”。如果这样，IPR 便可以译作“知识财产权”。但是，已经译作“知识产权”，就不能再来一个“知识产权权利”；译作“知识产权诸权利”也会在行文上引起极大不便（例如遇到“IPR 理事会”这样的机构名称)。改变 IP 目前已经固定的译法，不是本次重译能做的。因此，只好对 IPR 采取了与 IP 不加区分的译法。这是对原文的一定减损，虽然无关要害实质，但是需要向读者说明。

3. 关于《伯尔尼公约》中的 dramatico-musical work。前译作“戏剧音乐作品”。原文中两者是并列的，应该是“戏剧 - 音乐作品”。由于它与戏剧作品属于同一类，实际意思更侧重戏剧，所以按中文习惯说法译作“音乐剧作品”。

4. 关于 phonogram。《罗马公约》中的 phonogram 一直译作“唱片”。该公约签署于 1961 年，当时录音手段主要是唱片。后来尽管出现录音磁带和光盘，phonogram 的说法仍然没有变。随着国外逐渐有 sound recording 的说法，国内也有人将 phonogram 译作“录音制品”。此次重译，仍维持了“唱片”的译法，这既是尊重历史也是尊重原文(phonogram 作唱片解已经是后起义，原始义是记音符号系统)。《与贸易有关知识产权协定》中采用了phonograms (sound recordings) 的办法，显示了意思的扩容演进。更近来，出现了 fixation 的说法，意在将数字录制技术也包括进去。之前，有人将 fixation 译作“录音制品”，显然也不合时宜。重译时译作更为中性的“固定物”。

5. 关于 copy。版权法律文件中大量出现 copy 一词。过去将其译作“复制品”或“复制件”。这种译法无论正面或负面意思都比较重。而 copy 其实是个比较中性的词，多用在一般叙述上，强调物件的多重份数，不像 reproduction 比较强调作为复制行为的产物。重译时，除用作量词时译成“份”以外，用作名词时均译作“复本”。过去有将 copy 译作“副本”的，至少可能有风险，因为 copy 经常不具有区别正本和副本的作用。

6. 关于 original work。这个语词怎样译，取决于具体所指。如果是相对于派生作品而言，应译作“原作”：在翻译的情况下指被翻译的作品，在改编的情况下指被改编的作品。“原作”自成一词，不是“原始作品”的简称：前者完全为相对义，后者可有绝对义。何况，“原作”前面还可能有“原作”。如果是就可保护性而言，应译作“原创作品”，即不是抄袭而来的东西。汇编作品应该不是“原作”，但也可以作为“原创作品”保护，因为在内容的选取和编排上可能体现原创性。

7. 关于 subject matter。在知识产权法律文件中，这个语词在不同的情况下出现。它的基本义是“主题”。具体怎样翻译，应该根据它在不同情况下的具体所指。如果是合同中的，可译作“标的”(同 object)。如果作为保护或权利所指向的物，可译作“客体”或“对象”(同 object)。如果就一项专利申请而言，可译作“主题”或者“内容”(同 subject)。如果就法律一个章节所涉及的事项而言，可译作“主题”（同 theme）。

8. 关于 unreasonably。法律文件中经常出现这个词，一般译作“无故”、“无理”或“不合理地”。涉及对权利的限制或例外时，会有这样的句子：does not unreasonably prejudice the legitimate interests of the author。这里的 unreasonably 译成“无故”或“无理”似乎不太合适。在限制和例外之下使用作品，会对作者的利益有一定损害。这种“损害”只是法律允许的，并非使用的目的，因此不存在“无故”或“无理”损害的问题。这里，应该取 unreasonable 的 beyond the limit of acceptability（超出可接受的限度）的意思，译作“过度”。

9. 关于 denunciation。这个词过去都译作“退约”，即退出公约或条约。但其本义是“指斥其为错”，并没有“退出”的意思。此次均译作“声明无效”。因为这是与本义最近的译法。另外，有时 denounce 并不针对整个条约，而只是其中一部分，不承认这部分并不是“退约”。再者，如果不是条约或公约，而是其他文件，用“退约”也不合适。可以参照的是，参加公约或条约，只是开头，还要经过签署、承认、加入获批准，然后它才在某一时间对有关国家生效。所以是生效和不复有效的程序。如果条款标题只是 denunciation，便无须增加成分，译作“声明无效”即可。《字体保护及其国际交存维也纳协定》第 28 条第（7）款中出现的 denunciation，对象是一项义务，似乎只有译作“声明义务无效”一途。

10. 关于 subject to。这个词组可以有各种译法，此次重译中一律取其 conditional upon 的意思，译作“以……为条件”。只在后面接 conditions 的时候译作“取决于……条件”。这样做，一方面是为了使句子简短，避免诸如“在遵守……的情况下”这样较啰嗦的译法。

11. 关于 geographical indications。目前国内正式文件中使用的对译是“地理标志”（与“地理标识”同义）。地理标志是用以表示地表特征的符号，是就地理本身而言。而 geographical indications 显示的是某一产品的特点与某一地域的特点之间联系，其内涵仅就产品的来源地而言（因而有另一种说法是“原产地名称”）。此次重译，改作“产地标示”。这不妨碍已有译法的使用，只是提供一个更准确或更符合本意的译法。

12. 关于 legal entity。在涉及权利主体时，国际法律文件中除了人（person）、自然人（natural person）、法人（legal person）和法人团体（corporate body），还提到 legal entity。legal entity 实际上是指不构成法人的组织，所以不能译作“法人单位”，也不能译作与字面义不符的“非法人团体”。因与“法人”无关，所以译作“法律实体”，符合比较中性的原意。这个概念或可用于替代我国著作权法中的“其他组织”。

13. 关于 typeface。出现在《字体保护及其国际交存维也纳协定》中。“字体”，是 typeface 的原有译法。“字体”在中文中常指书法的派别，如柳体、颜体、欧体和赵体等，以及手书的形体，如楷、行和草等。而 typeface 则指印刷字模顶部的字形设计，因而引起些质疑，并有译作“字形”或“字型”的建议。其实，印刷行业中不但有“字体”的说法，还有“字体设计”，指“用于活字排版、照相排版、计算机输出、屏幕显示的文字字体的设计”；还特别提到“西文字母字体品种更远比汉字为多”（均见于上海辞书出版社版《出版词典》)。需要指出的是，typeface 不仅仅指字体，而是泛指凡印刷排版用金属模顶部表面凸出的部分，包括各种符号和图纹花饰。维也纳协定乃是保护所有这些东西的。

14. 关于“修改”的不同提法。关于“修改”，国际法律文件的原文中有 revise，amendment，modify, change 和 alter 几种提法，译文中分别作“修订”、“更改”、“修改”、“更动”或“变动”。revise 多针对主文件（尤其涉及实体规定)，amendment 多针对细则条例，且常放在一起，分别作“修订”和“更改”，以用文字区别开。其余则完全是以不同的词分别定下一个统一的译法。

15. 关于加入国际条约的提法。加入国际条约，国际法律文件的原文中有 adherence，becoming party to，accession，acceptance，ratification 和 approval。译文中分别作“恪守”、“参加”、“加入”、“承认”、“批准”和“同意”。其中的 ratification 和 approval 意思都是批准，但前者是立法机构的正式批准，后者是政府的一般性批准，为了不增加缀语，将后者译作“同意”。

16. 关于 copyright 的译法。译作“著作权”还是“版权”，似乎不是翻译的问题，而是恰当选择使用法律用语的问题。我国著作权法规定“著作权即版权”，使得无论怎样选择都是正确的。因此产生无结果的争论和不必要的混乱。此次重译无意触及这个问题。本文件集中一律沿用旧译“版权”。原因只有一个，省事方便。

17. 在几份文件中，就某些条款，有脚注形式的 agreed statement。前有译作“议定声明”的。其内容，是通过文件时大家就某些条款的理解达成的一致意见。Statement 不全是声明，经常只是较正式的陈述，例如这里的情况。因多处出现，译作“声明”便到处都是，但为简约，也只好这样，只是将“议定”改为“一致”：“议定”意思太重，且结果多是文件（如议定书)。或可译作“商定”，但和“议定”一样，与“声明”搭配，突出了本来并没有强调的之前过程。既然 agreed 就是大家同意的，便直译作“一致”。有些一致声明的内容，以 it is understood 开头。这个表述，意思是对不言而喻或字面上可以延伸理解出的意思有一致意见。为了行文简便，就译作“兹同意”。因为结合接下来的句子，被“同意”的，就是对某种意思的“一致理解”。

18. making available to the public。国际版权和相关权法律文件中，即使是号称的“互联网条约”中，都没有出现“互联网传播”的说法。凡涉及互联网传播时，都以 making available to the public 表述，本文件集中译作“向公众提供”。之所以不会引起歧义，是因为还有限定，即须以公众可以选择时间和地点的方式提供。这是互联网传播与传统传播的关键区别。另外，由于是在互联网上，显然不是指提供物件，而是在文字作品的情况下使之可以被读到，在音乐作品或视听作品的情况下使之可以被听到或被听到和看到。

以上只是择要说明。也许译文中还有一些其他译法需要有所交待或解释的，这里不能一一列举，否则变成译文分析了。即使译者认为无需交待或解释的地方，由于这本文件集是中英对照的，读者也会通过比较提出质疑或不同意见。所以，最好的办法是，译者保持开放和负责任的态度，愿意对读者提出的任何问题做出认真回应。

本文件集的翻译过程中，曾向多方面的人和多种信息来源咨询求证。尤其应当提到的是，国家版权局的高思女士通读过大部分译文的初稿，提出了很多具体意见和修改建议。译稿基本齐备后，国家版权局还将其装订成册，由王自强先生、高思女士和许炜先生出面，组织了统稿会，对主要文件的译稿作了逐字审读。他们就译文中各种表述的准确性、可读性和统一性提出的意见，对提高重译本的质量有极大的帮助。国际法律文件的格式较为复杂，加之除中译外还附有原文，核对、编辑和排版殊不容易，中国书籍出版社的责任编辑牛超先生和宋然女士付出了巨大努力。另外，国家版权局副局长阎晓宏先生为这本文集撰写了序言，对其编译出版作为一项基础性工作的意义做了高位的阐述，为学习研究其中的内容提供了纵观的视角。对所有这些，译者在此表示深切的谢意。

裘安曼

2016 年元月